REVELATION EXPLAINED

Terry Swift

Copyright © 2022 Terry Swift.

All rights reserved. No part of this book may be used or reproduced by any means, graphic, electronic, or mechanical, including photocopying, recording, taping or by any information storage retrieval system without the written permission of the author except in the case of brief quotations embodied in critical articles and reviews.

LifeRich Publishing is a registered trademark of The Reader's Digest Association, Inc.

LifeRich Publishing books may be ordered through booksellers or by contacting:

LifeRich Publishing
1663 Liberty Drive
Bloomington, IN 47403
www.liferichpublishing.com
844-686-9607

Because of the dynamic nature of the Internet, any web addresses or links contained in this book may have changed since publication and may no longer be valid. The views expressed in this work are solely those of the author and do not necessarily reflect the views of the publisher, and the publisher hereby disclaims any responsibility for them.

Any people depicted in stock imagery provided by Getty Images are models, and such images are being used for illustrative purposes only. Certain stock imagery © Getty Images.

Scripture quotations marked NIV are taken from the Holy Bible, NEW INTERNATIONAL VERSION®, NIV® Copyright © 1973, 1978, 1984, 2011 by Biblica, Inc.® Used by permission. All rights reserved worldwide.

Scripture quotations marked KJV are from the Holy Bible, King James Version (Authorized Version). First published in 1611. Quoted from the KJV Classic Reference Bible, Copyright © 1983 by The Zondervan Corporation

ISBN: 978-1-4897-4141-7 (sc)
ISBN: 978-1-4897-4140-0 (hc)
ISBN: 978-1-4897-4142-4 (e)

Library of Congress Control Number: 2022908182

Print information available on the last page.

LifeRich Publishing rev. date: 05/18/2022

CONTENTS

Introduction xix
    Seven Keys To Understanding The Book Of Revelation xxii
    Key 1. The Indwelling of the Spirit xxii
    Key 2. The Date Of The Book xxv
    Key 3. "Things That Must Soon Take Place" xxviii
    Key 4. These Things Were Signified, Figurative Language xxx
    Key 5. Sacred and Secular History xxx
    Key 6. The Writings Of The Prophets And Their Prophecies xxxii
    Key 7. Israel, the Spiritual Promise of God xxxv

Chapter One 1
    Verse 1. The Revelation of Jesus Christ 1
    Verse 2. Who Testifies To Everything He Saw 6
    Verse 3. Blessed Is The One Who Reads 6
    Verse 4. ToThe Seven Churches 6
    Verse 5. From The Firstborn From The Dead 9
    Verse 6. He Made Us A Kingdom and Priests 10
    Verse 7. Look, He Is Coming 12
    Verse 8. I Am The Alpha And Omega 15
    Verse 9. I John, On The Island Of Patmos 16
    Verse 10. In The Spirit On The Day Of The Lord 20
    Verse 11. Send It To The Seven Churches 21
    Verse 12. The Voice Speaking To Me 22
    Verse 13. One Like The Son Of Man 22
    Verse 14. His Eyes Like Blazing Fire 23
    Verse 15. His Voice Like Rushing Waters 24
    Verse 16. Out Of His Mouth A Sharp Two-edged Sword 25

Verse 17. I Fell At His Feet As Though Dead 26
Verse 18. I Was Dead, Behold I Am Alive For Ever And Ever 26
Verse 19. Write What You Have Seen, Now, And What
   Is About To Take Place 29
Verse 20. The Mystery Is.. 29

Chapter Two 30
Verse 1. To Ephesus 30
Verse 2. I Know Your Hard Work 31
Verse 3. You Have Persevered 31
Verse 4. You Have Forsaken Your First Love 31
Verse 5. You Have Fallen.. 32
Verse 6. The Nicolaitans I Also hate 34
Verse 7. The Right To Eat Of The Tree Of Life 35
Verse 8. To Smyrna 36
Verse 9. I Know Your Afflictions And Poverty 37
Verse 10. You Are About To Suffer... 37
Verse 11. Will Not Be Hurt By The Second Death 38
Verse 12. To Pergamum 38
Verse 13. Where Satan Has His Throne... 39
Verse 14. Things against You 40
Verse 15. Those Who Hold To The Teaching Of The Nicolaitans ... 41
Verse 16. Repent 41
Verse 17. The Hidden Manna And The White Stone 42
Verse 18. To Thyatira.. 44
Verse 19. Now Doing More.. 44
Verse 20. You Tolerate That Woman Jezebel 45
Verse 21. I Have Giver Her Time To Repent.................................. 47
Verse 22. A Bed Of Suffering... 48
Verse 23. Repay You According To Your Deeds 48
Verse 24. Satan's So-called Deep Secrets 49
Verse 25. Hold On To What You Have 50
Verse 26. Authority Over the Nations 50
Verse 27. Dash Them To Pieces Like Pottery 50
Verse 28. Give Him The Morning Star 51
Verse 29. Let Him Hear.. 52

Chapter Three... 53
  Verse 1. To Sardis, You Are Dead.................................... 53
  Verse 2. Not Found Your Deeds Complete 56
  Verse 3. Repent! Wake Up 57
  Verse 4. Walk With Me Dressed In White..................... 58
  Verse 5. I Will Acknowledge His Name 59
  Verse 6. Let Him Hear. Listen Up!.................................. 59
  Verse 7. To Philadelphia 59
  Verse 8. An Open Door 60
  Verse 9. Those Of The Synagogue Of Satan 60
  Verse 10. Keep You From The Hour Of Trial 60
  Verse 11. I Am Coming Soon... 62
  Verse 12. A New Name... 62
  Verse 13. Let Him Hear! Listen Up................................. 64
  Verse 14. To Laodicea 65
  Verse 15. I Wish You Were Either Cold Or Hot 65
  Verse 16. I Will Vomit You Out 66
  Verse 17. You say, 'I Do Not Need Anything' 66
  Verse 18. Put Salve On Your Eyes So You Can See..... 67
  Verse 19. Those I Love I Rebuke And Discipline......... 67
  Verse 20. I Stand At The Door And Knock 68
  Verse 21. Sit With Me On My Throne 68
  Verse 22. Let Him Hear... 68

Chapter Four.. 69
  Verse 1. Come Up Here 69
  Verse 2. A Throne In Heaven... 70
  Verse 3. A Rainbow Encircled The Throne 70
  Verse 4. 24 Thrones and 24 Elders.................................. 72
  Verse 5. Seven Lamps Were Blazing 72
  Verse 6. The Sea Of Glass And Four Living Creatures... 73
  Verse 7. The Four Living Creatures................................. 75
  Verse 8. Holy, Holy, Holy 76
  Verse 9. Give Glory To Him On The Throne 76
  Verse 10. Worship Him Who Lives For Ever And Ever ... 76
  Verse 11. You Are Worthy... 77

Chapter Five 78
   Verse 1. The Scroll With Seven Seals 78
   Verse 2. Who Is Worthy To Open The Scroll 78
   Verse 3. No One Could Open It 78
   Verse 4. I Wept 79
   Verse 5. The Lion Of The Tribe Of Judah, The Root Of David ... 81
   Verse 6. The Lamb That Was Slain 82
   Verse 7. He Took The Scroll 82
   Verse 8. The Four Living Creatures And 24 Elders 82
   Verse 9. They Sang A New Song 83
   Verse 10. A Kingdom And Priests 84
   Verse 11. The Voice of Many Angels 87
   Verse 12. Worthy Is The Lamb That Was Slain 88
   Verse 13. Every Creature In Heaven And On Earth Praised Him 88
   Verse 14. Fell Down And Worshiped 88

Chapter Six 89
   Verse 1. The Lamb Opened The First Seal 94
   Verse 2. A Conqueror Bent On Conquest 95
   Verse 3. The Lamb Opened The Second Seal 97
   Verse 4. A Fiery Red Horse 97
   Verse 5. The Lamb Opened The Third Seal 98
   Verse 6. Do Not Damage The Oil Or The Wine 101
   Verse 7. The Lamb Opened The Fourth Seal 101
   Verse 8. A Pale Horse 101
   Verse 9. He Opened the Fifth Seal 102
   Verse 10. How Long To Avenge Our Blood 104
   Verse 11. A Little Longer 104
   Verse 12. He Opened The Sixth Seal 105
   Verse 13. Stars In The Sky Fell 109
   Verse 14. The Sky Rolled Up 110
   Verse 15. They Hid In Caves 112
   Verse 16. Hide Us From The Face Of Him 113
   Verse 17. The Great Day Of Wrath Has Come 116

Chapter Seven 118
    Verse 1. Four Angels At The Four Corners Of The Earth 119
    Verse 2. Angel From The East 120
    Verse 3. Do Not Harm Land, Sea, Or Trees 120
    Verse 4. The 144,000 120
    Verse 5. Judah, Reuben, Gad 121
    Verse 6. Asher, Naphtali, Manasseh 121
    Verse 7. Simeon, Levi, Issachar 121
    Verse 8. Zebulin, Joseph, Benjamin 121
    Verse 9. The Great Multitude 123
    Verse 10. Salvation Belongs To God And The Lamb 124
    Verse 11. All The Angels Worshiped 124
    Verse 12. Praise, Glory, Wisdom, Honor, Power, Strength Be 124
    Verse 13. Who Are They 124
    Verse 14. The Great Tribulation 125
    Verse 15. Will Spread His Tent Over Them 125
    Verse 16. The Sun Will Not Beat Upon Them 126
    Verse 17. Their Shepherd 126

Chapter Eight 131
    Verse 1. He Opened The Seventh Seal 131
    Verse 2. Seven Angels Were Given Seven Trumpets 131
    Verse 3. The Prayers Of All The Saints 132
    Verse 4. Incense With The Prayers Rose 132
    Verse 5. Fire From The Altar Hurled To The earth 132
    Verse 6. Trumpets Prepared To Sound 133
    Verse 7. A Third Burned Up 134
    Verse 8. A Huge Mountain Was Thrown Into The Sea 136
    Verse 9. A Third Of Living Creatures Died 138
    Verse 10. A Great Star Blazing Fell 138
    Verse 11. The Name Of The Star Is Wormwood 139
    Verse 12. A Third Of The Sun, Moon, And Stars Were Struck ... 140
    Verse 13. An Eagle Flying In Midair 142

Chapter Nine 143
- Verse 1. The Star Was Given The Key To 148
- Verse 2. He Opened The Abyss..149
- Verse 3. Locusts Given Power Like Scorpions...........................149
- Verse 4. Harm Only Those Who Do Not Have The Seal 150
- Verse 5. They Were Not To Kill Them 152
- Verse 6. Death Will Elude Them 153
- Verse 7. Their Faces Resembled Human Faces 154
- Verse 8. Hair Like Women, Teeth Like Lions............................155
- Verse 9. Breastplates Of Iron 155
- Verse 10. Torment For Five Months 156
- Verse 11. King Abaddon/Apollyon 157
- Verse 12. Two Woes To Come 158
- Verse 13. A Voice From The Golden Altar 158
- Verse 14. Four Angels At The Great River Euphrates...............159
- Verse 15. The Four Angels Were Released 160
- Verse 16. 200 Million Mounted Troops 161
- Verse 17. Horses And Riders 161
- Verse 18. Three Plagues Of Fire 163
- Verse 19. Power In Mouth And Tail 163
- Verse 20. Still Did Not repent..163
- Verse 21 Nor Did They Repent Of 164

Chapter Ten 165
- Verse 1. A Mighty angel - His Face Like The Sun 165
- Verse 2. A Little Scroll 168
- Verse 3. Voices Of Seven Thunders.. 168
- Verse 4. Seal up The Seven Thunders 169
- Verse 5. The Angel On The Sea And Land 170
- Verse 6. He Swore by Him 170
- Verse 7. No More Delay 170
- Verse 8. Take The Scroll 170
- Verse 9. Take It And It Eat...171
- Verse 10. It Tasted Sweet, but My Stomach Turned Sour 172
- Verse 11. Prophesy Again 172

Chapter Eleven 175
   Verse 1. Go And Measure The Temple...175
   Verse 2. Exclude The Outer Court.. 177
   Verse 3. Two Witnesses 179
   Verse 4. Two Olive Trees And Two Lampstands 184
   Verse 5. Fire Comes From Their Mouths 184
   Verse 6. The Power To Shut Up The Sky 185
   Verse 7. The Beast Would Kill Them. 185
   Verse 8. Their Bodies Will Lie In The Street.............................. 187
   Verse 9. For 3 ½ Day They Refuse Them Burial........................ 187
   Verse 10. They Will Gloat Over Them 188
   Verse 11 The Breath Of Life Entered Them 189
   Verse 12. Come Up Here 198
   Verse 13. A Severe Earthquake..198
   Verse 14. The Third Woe...199
   Verse 15. The Seventh Trumpet Sounded..................................199
   Verse 16. They Fell On Their Faces 200
   Verse 17. You Did Reign.. 200
   Verse 18. The Time Has Come For Judging............................... 201
   Verse 19. God's Temple In Heaven Was Opened....................... 202

Chapter Twelve 205
   Verse 1. A Woman Clothed With The Sun 205
   Verse 2. She Was About To Give Birth....................................... 206
   Verse 3. An Enormous Red Dragon 208
   Verse 4. His Tail Swept A Third Of the Stars..............................210
   Verse 5. A Son, A Male Child 212
   Verse 6. The Woman Fled Into The Desert................................213
   Verse 7. War In Heaven..214
   Verse 8. They Lost Their Place In Heaven 215
   Verse 9. The Great Dragon Was Hurled Down 215
   Verse 10. The Accuser Has Been Hurled Down 215
   Verse 11. They Did Not Love Their Lives So Much 216
   Verse 12. Woe To The Earth..217
   Verse 13. The Dragon Pursued The Woman..............................218
   Verse 14. The Woman Was Given Two Wings Of A Great Eagle....219

Verse 15. The Serpent Spewed Water 220
Verse 16. The Earth Helped The Woman 220
Verse 17. The Dragon Was Enraged 220

Chapter Thirteen 221
Verse 1. The Beast Out Of The Sea 221
Verse 2. The Beast I Saw 226
Verse 3. The Beast Had A Fatal Wound - Healed 227
Verse 4. Men Worshiped The Dragon 228
Verse 5. Exercise His Authority 42 Months 230
Verse 6. He Opened His Mouth To Blaspheme 230
Verse 7. War Against The Saints 230
Verse 8. All Worship The Beast Whose Names Are Not Written ... 235
Verse 9. Let Him Hear 236
Verse 10. If Anyone Is - Will Be 237
Verse 11. The Earth Beast 237
Verse 12. Made The Earth's Inhabitants Worship The
    First Beast 237
Verse 13. Causing Fire to Come Down 239
Verse 14. He Deceived The Inhabitants Of The Earth 240
Verse 15. He Gave Breath To The Image Of The First Beast 240
Verse 16. Forced Everyone To Receive A Mark On His Forehead ... 241
Verse 17. No One Could Buy Or Sell 241
Verse 18 His Number Is 666 242

Chapter Fourteen 244
Verse 1. The 144,000 248
Verse 2. The Harpist Playing Their Harps 249
Verse 3. They Sang A New Song 249
Verse 4. Those Who Do Not Defile Themselves 250
Verse 5. They Are Blameless 250
Verse 6. Another Angel Flying In Mid-Air 256
Verse 7. The Hour Of Judgment Has Come 256
Verse 8. Fallen! Fallen! Is Babylon The Great 256
Verse 9. If Anyone Worship The Beast 257
Verse 10. The Wine Of God's Fury 257

- Verse 11. Their torment rises forever 259
- Verse 12. Remain Faithful To Jesus.. 260
- Verse 13. Blessed Are The Dead Who Died In The Lord 260
- Verse 14. Seated On The Cloud Was One Like The Son Of Man ... 261
- Verse 15. Take Your Sickle And Reap 262
- Verse 16. The Earth was Harvested.. 262
- Verse 17. Another Angel To Reap 263
- Verse 18. Earth's Grape Vine Is Harvested 263
- Verse 19. Grapes Thrown Into The Winepress Of God's Wrath..... 264
- Verse 20 They Were Trampled 264

Chapter Fifteen 265
- Verse 1. The Last Seven Plagues.. 265
- Verse 2. Those Who Had Been Victorious 266
- Verse 3. The Song Of Moses And The Lamb 266
- Verse 4. You Alone Are Holy 266
- Verse 5. The Tabernacle Of The Testimony Was Opened 267
- Verse 6. Seven Angels With Seven Plagues............................... 267
- Verse 7. Seven Golden Bowls Filled With The Wrath Of God 267
- Verse 8. No One Could Enter The Temple 268

Chapter Sixteen... 269
- Verse 1. Go Pour Out The Bowls Of God's Wrath..................... 271
- Verse 2. The First Angel Poured Out His Bowl......................... 271
- Verse 3. The Second Angel Poured Out His Bowl..................... 272
- Verse 4. The Third Angel Poured Out His Bowl........................ 272
- Verse 5. You Are Just... 272
- Verse 6. Blood To Drink As They Deserve................................. 273
- Verse 7. True And Just Are Your Judgments 273
- Verse 8. The Fourth Angel Poured Out His Bowl...................... 273
- Verse 9. They Were Seared By The Intense Heat....................... 274
- Verse 10. The Fifth Angel Poured Out His Bowl 275
- Verse 11. They Refused To Repent.. 275
- Verse 12. The Sixth Angel Poured Out His Bowl...................... 277
- Verse 13. Three Evil Spirits That Looked Like Frogs.................. 278
- Verse 14 The Kings Of The Earth To Gather For Battle............. 280

Verse 15. I Come Like A Thief 280
Verse 16. Armageddon 281
Verse 17. The Seventh Angel Poured Out His Bowl 284
Verse 18. No Earthquake Like It Has Ever Occurred 284
Verse 19. The Great City Split Into Three Parts 285
Verse 20. Every Island Fled 286
Verse 21. Huge Hailstones Of About A Hundred Pounds Fell 286

Chapter Seventeen 288
Verse 1. The Punishment Of The Great Prostitute 288
Verse 2. Intoxicated With The Wine Of Her Adulteries 289
Verse 3. A Woman Sitting On A Scarlet Beast 289
Verse 4. A Golden Cup Filled With Abominable Things 290
Verse 5. Mystery Babylon The Great Mother Of Prostitutes 291
Verse 6. Drunk With The Blood Of The Saints 292
Verse 7. The Mystery Of The Woman And THe Beast 292
Verse 8. The Beast That Once Was, Now Is Not, And
    Will Come 293
Verse 9. Seven Heads Are Seven Hills 293
Verse 10. The Seven Heads Are Also Seven Kings 293
Verse 11 The Beast Is An Eighth King 295
Verse 12. Ten Horns Are Ten Kings 297
Verse 13. They Have One Purpose 303
Verse 14. War Against The Lamb 303
Verse 15. The Waters You Saw 304
Verse 16. The Beast And Ten Horns Hate The Prostitute 304
Verse 17. God Has Put It In Their Hearts 304
Verse 18. The Great City That Rules Over The Kings
    Of The Earth 305

Chapter Eighteen 306
Verse 1. The Earth Was Illuminated 306
Verse 2. Fallen! Fallen is Babylon The Great 306
Verse 3. The Maddening Wine Of Her Adulteries 307
Verse 4. Come Out Of Her My People 308
Verse 5. Her Sins Are Piled Up To Heaven 308

 Verse 6. Pay Her Back Double 309
 Verse 7. Give Her As Much Torture 311
 Verse 8. In One Day Her Plagues Will Overtake Her 312
 Verse 9. The Kings Of The Earth - See The Smoke Of
  Her Burning..315
 Verse 10. In One Hour Your Doom Has Come............................316
 Verse 11. No One Buys Their Cargoes 316
 Verse 12. Cargoes Of 316
 Verse 13. Cargoes Of 316
 Verse 14. The Fruit Is Gone From You 317
 Verse 15. Terrified At Her Torment..317
 Verse 16. Woe! Woe! Oh Great City...318
 Verse 17. Such Great Wealth Has Been Brought To Ruin.............318
 Verse 18. The Smoke Of Her Burning 319
 Verse 19. All The Ships Had Become Rich...................................319
 Verse 20. Rejoice Saints, Apostles, and Prophets 319
 Verse 21. A Boulder The Size Of A Large Millstone.....................319
 Verse 22. Never Be Heard In You Again 320
 Verse 23. By Your Magic Spell - Led Astray 321
 Verse 24. In Her - The Blood Of Prophets And Saints.................321

Chapter Nineteen.. 323
 Verse 1. The Roar Of A Great Multitude 323
 Verse 2. True And Just Are His Judgments 324
 Verse 3. The Smoke Of Her Goes Up For Ever And Ever............ 324
 Verse 4. The Twenty-four Elders And Four Living Creatures 324
 Verse 5. Praise Our God All You His Servants 325
 Verse 6. Our Lord God Almighty Reigns.................................... 325
 Verse 7. The Wedding Of The Lamb Has Come......................... 325
 Verse 8. Fine Linen, Bright And Clean... 326
 Verse 9. Blessed Are Those Who Are Invited............................... 327
 Verse 10. I Am A Fellow Servant 327
 Verse 11. Heaven Standing Open 328
 Verse 12. A Name No One Knows.. 329
 Verse 13. A Robe Dipped In Blood 330
 Verse 14. The Armies Of Heaven Were Following 330

- Verse 15. A Sharp Sword Out Of His Mouth 331
- Verse 16. Name - King Of Kings And Lord Of Lords 333
- Verse 17. An Angel Standing In The Sun 333
- Verse 18. Eat The Flesh Of 333
- Verse 19. The Beast And The Kings Of The Earth Gathered 334
- Verse 20. Thrown Alive Into The Fiery Lake 335
- Verse 21. The Rest Of Them Were Killed With The Sword 336

Chapter Twenty 338
- Verse 1. The Key To The Abyss 338
- Verse 2. He Bound Him For A Thousand Years 339
- Verse 3. He threw Him Into The Abyss, Locked and Sealed It 342
- Verse 4. The Souls of Those Beheaded Came To Life 343
- Verse 5. The Rest Of The Dead Did Not Come To Life Until 345
- Verse 6. The First Resurrection 346
- Verse 7. The Thousand Years Are Over 352
- Verse 8. Gog And Magog 352
- Verse 9. Surrounded The Camp Of God's People 353
- Verse 10. The Devil Was Thrown Into The Lake Of Burning Sulfur 354
- Verse 11. A Great White Throne 358
- Verse 12. The Dead Standing Before The Throne 358
- Verse 13. The Sea, Death And Hades Gave Up Their Dead 359
- Verse 14. The Lake Of Fire Is The Second Death 360
- Verse 15. Thrown Into The Lake Of Fire 364

Chapter Twenty-One 365
- Verse 1. A New Heaven And A New Earth 365
- Verse 2. The Holy City The New Jerusalem 367
- Verse 3. Now The Dwelling Of God Is With Men 368
- Verse 4. The Old Order Of Things Has Passed 368
- Verse 5. I Am Making Everything New 369
- Verse 6. It Is Done 371
- Verse 7. Overcome - Inherit All Of This 371
- Verse 8. Their Place Will Be 372
- Verse 9. Come, I Will Show you The Bride 372

Verse 10. He Showed Me The Holy City 372
Verse 11. It Shone With The Glory Of God 374
Verse 12. On The Gates Were Written The Names Of
    THe Twelve Tribes 375
Verse 13. Three Gates On The 376
Verse 14. Twelve Foundations 376
Verse 15. A Measuring Rod Of Gold 377
Verse 16. The City Was Laid Out Like A Square 377
Verse 17. A 144 Cubits Thick 380
Verse 18. The Wall Was Made Of 380
Verse 19. The Foundations Were
    Decorated With Every Precious 381
Verse 20. The Stones 382
Verse 21. Each Gate A Single Pearl 382
Verse 22. The Lord And Lamb Are Its Temple 383
Verse 23. The City Did Not Need The Sun 384
Verse 24. The Kings Of The Earth Will Bring Their Splendor ... 385
Verse 25. There Will Be No Night There 385
Verse 26. Glory Will Be Brought Into It 385
Verse 27. Nothing impure will enter it 386

Chapter Twenty-Two 387
  Verse 1. The River Of The Water Of Life 387
  Verse 2. The Tree Of Life 388
  Verse 3. No Longer Any Curse 390
  Verse 4. They Will See His Face 391
  Verse 5. They Will Not Need The Light Of 392
  Verse 6. Things That Must Soon take Place 393
  Verse 7. Behold, I Am Coming Soon 395
  Verse 8. I Fell Down To Worship 396
  Verse 9. Do Not Do It 398
  Verse 10. Do Not Seal Up The Words Of The Prophecy 398
  Verse 11. Let Him Who Does Wrong Continue To 399
  Verse 12. Behold, I Am Coming Soon 399
  Verse 13. I Am THe Beginning And The End 399
  Verse 14. Blessed are Those Who Wash Their Robes 399

Verse 15. Outside Are The Dogs... 400
Verse 16. I Am The Bright Morning Star..................................... 402
Verse 17. The Spirit And The Bride Say Come............................ 403
Verse 18. A Warning... 403
Verse 19. If Anyone Takes Words Away....................................... 404
Verse 20. I Am Coming Soon 405
Verse 21. Grace Be With God's People 405

INTRODUCTION

The subject of the Book of Revelation is fascinating to the public as well as to Christendom. Why? Because it appeals to the imagination. It has a dragon with seven heads and ten horns. It has a beast that rises out of the sea and one that rises out of the earth. There are 144,000 who were sealed. There is the Lamb who was slain. There are the souls under the altar who cry out "How long?". There is the throne room scene. There is an amazing figure walking around among the seven golden candlesticks. There are dozens of figures, symbols, cataclysmic events and scenes that can leave you thoroughly puzzled or breathless.

Revelation can profit everyone wonderfully in various ways. It instructs. It inspires. It strikes one with wonder. It can chastise. It can be fulfilled. It does something for everyone. It is challenging on every level of our understanding. Parts we may not be ready for. Parts we have to really humble ourselves to perceive. All of it requires study, research, and pondering. Most of all, for the one who would understand it accurately, it requires a close walk with the Spirit for He is the true teacher who knows the mind of God. The book is spiritually understood. We all walk closer to God sometimes, than at other times. Pride, arrogance, bitterness, resentment, anger, jealousy – many things can get in the way of the Spirit working with us. When we draw near to God and humble ourselves, the Spirit draws near to us and opens up our understanding. If we resist him and lean on our own understanding, the Spirit resists us. Leaning on our own understanding, no matter how scholarly we feel we are, God resists us. That is where the many interpretations of Revelation come from. They come from a man who is full of himself. Man is full of pride and arrogance and leans on his ideas and the scholarly credentials of others in books and seminaries. God is not subject to man. The book of Revelation is not subject to private interpretation. It is God's revelation to Jesus Christ, given through John, to us. God revealed it. God knows it. We must get our understanding of it from him.

There have been countless explanations of the book of Revelation over many centuries. Every generation since Revelation was written has predicted that Jesus would come in their generation and that the book of Revelation would be fulfilled. Even in my own time, that was a very popular thing to predict - the coming of Jesus before the year 2000 (Y2K, as it was referred to). I have 22 commentaries written before 2000 in my library on the book of Revelation. They predicted the end of the world by the year 2000. They were all proven false prophets and false teachers as the year 2000 came and went. Now as I write this, it is the year 2022. Even Pope Sylvester II predicted the Lord would return in the year 1000. I read on the internet that Bruce Metzger (a prominent Greek and Bible Manuscript scholar) of Princeton seminary offered a class which taught that the end time predictions have been a recurring theme throughout church history. Such predictions go on and on and those in religious circles who speak continually of it say it is obvious we are in the "end times"; as did the many generations before them. I do not listen to these predictors. The Bible makes it clear what the book of Revelation is really about. That is what I want to share with you, the reader.

When I decided to write a verse-by-verse commentary on the book of revelation, I decided to approach the endeavor with scripture only, and let the scripture teach me. I did use tools like a Greek concordance and a Greek Interlinear. I checked various translations and used some Greek word studies and dictionaries. I also used the first century historians: Josephus, Tacitus, and Suetonius. However, I did not rely on commentaries or other written opinions on the book. I did not want the various and conflicting ideas of others to bog me down, deter, or confuse me from a focused contemplation of the scripture. I resisted going to others' opinions for two reasons. I wanted my thoughts to be led by the Holy Spirit, comparing spiritual things with spiritual words of scripture. The second reason is in 1 Corinthians

2, where that passage warns us that God's word does not rest on human wisdom, but on God's power, verse 5. The spiritual man is not subject to mere human judgment. The things of God are "spiritually discerned," or learned "through the Spirit".

To understand the Revelation and get enlightenment, you need its author, the Holy Spirit. You need the indwelling Spirit of God as a child of God. John wrote – "you need not anyone teach you but as his Spirit teaches you and is true," 1 Jn.2:20,27 (NIV). When I approached the book of Revelation to understand it, I had already been through some classes on it and through sermons on it. I had heard many ideas of many and conflicting approaches to the book. I had ideas of my own. However, I approached the book with the idea that, even though I had heard many things and had ideas of my own, I did not know what I should believe about the book. I asked the Spirit to help me see his message and teach me what to believe. I knew, without the Spirit's help I could not unlock the understanding He wanted me to see. I am human, not a prophet, not a sage, not a wise man. But I believe that all Christians are given the Holy Spirit to indwell them and guide them. We have to be conscious of his presence and rely on him. It is a spiritual process to learn. It is not a miraculous audible voice that tells me what to believe. It is a walk of faith, trusting in the Spirit's Word and trying to pay close attention to details that come from his Revelation. The Spirit teaches here a little and there a little in scripture. Trust him, and the journey to understanding will be yours also. It is delightful and exciting. The discoveries and connections in scripture are amazing. Have fun.

Understanding overall the Book of Revelation is not for the unregenerate man. The common man cannot understand the things of God. Nor, is it for the unspiritual man who does not walk with the Spirit. He will never understand it no matter how many interpretations he dreams up of the meaning of its contents. Understanding the book is for the spiritual man, the man who has been born again and has the indwelling Spirit of God. It is for the Christian who knows how to follow the lead of the Spirit and depend on him for his understanding. It is for the man who is keeping in step with the Spirit. We, as Christians, can get out of step with the Spirit and not even realize it. When we do, hopefully we will realize we are out of step and will get in step again. Another thing to be aware of is – the Spirit reveals to us understanding when He thinks we are ready for it. It is at His discretion, at his timing. There are some things we will not understand until He thinks we are ready. Wait upon the Spirit. Depend on His details, his timing. Let him teach you as he wants you to see it. Be a blank piece of paper he writes on. Learn to recognize how he works with you.

I have included seven keys to understanding the book of Revelation. Hopefully those keys are derived from following the lead of the Spirit. There could be ten keys or twelve or whatever. But it is the Spirit who gives us the clues to understanding what he has revealed. These seven keys are addressed below:

Seven Keys To Understanding The Book Of Revelation

1. Indwelling of the Spirit of God.
2. The date of the Book.
3. Things that must soon take place.
4. These things were signified, figurative language.
5. Sacred history and secular history.
6. The writings of the Prophets and their prophecies.
7. Israel – the spiritual promise of God.

Key 1. The Indwelling of the Spirit

"The man without the Spirit does not receive the things that come from the Spirit of God, for they are foolishness to him, and <u>he cannot understand them</u>, because <u>they are spiritually discerned</u>." 1 Cor.2:14, (NIV). The man who has not become a Christian, who has not been "born again, born from above" cannot understand the Bible. Why? Because he does not have the Spirit of God within him. When you become a Christian, you receive the "gift of the Holy Spirit" to indwell you and help you. Acts 2:38. When Jesus explained in Jn.3:3,5, to Nicodemus that he must be born again, born from above, Nicodemus did not understand. Why? He had not been born again yet. Jesus said, "You are Israel's teacher, and you do not understand these things?" Jn.3:10, (NIV). Nope! He did not have the Spirit.

The Bible reveals the mind of God. No one knows the thoughts of a man but the spirit of a man within him. So too, no one knows the thoughts of God, but the Spirit of God, 1 Cor.2:11, (in own words). We need the indwelling Spirit to learn the things God has revealed. Wait. If God has revealed his mind in his word, doesn't that mean He has made it known. Yes. It is no longer secret or hidden. But even when he tells us, it does not mean we will understand. God wants us to seek him in his word and not to depend on our own knowledge and thoughts to understand it. He wants us to learn to depend on him to understand it. So, Paul goes on to say: "We have not received the spirit of the world but the Spirit who is from God that <u>we may understand</u> what God has freely given to us, 1 Cor.2:12, (NIV). What God has freely given to us is his word. His word has been revealed by His holy apostles and prophets. Even though he has revealed it, you still cannot understand it without his Spirit. It is "<u>spiritually discerned</u>."

What does "<u>spiritually discerned</u>" mean? Well, it does not mean that God in an audible voice tells me what it means. That would be a miraculous event like when Saul was struck blind and God talked to him from heaven, Acts 9. The miraculous (Greek - charismati) is not spiritual (Greek – pneumatikos). The Corinthians did not lack any (Greek -charismati, miraculous gift), 1 Cor.1:7. (The translations there that say "spiritual" do not convey the difference between "miraculous"- "charismati" and "spiritual" – pneumatikos"). The Corinthians were Christians. They did not lack any miraculous gift. But that did not make them "spiritual". They still did not know how to be led by the Spirit of God. Paul tells them in 3:1 "Brothers, I could not address you as <u>spiritual</u> but as <u>worldly</u> (Greek – sarkinois, meaning fleshly, worldly) – mere infants in Christ," (NIV). In other words, they were depending upon the flesh, their state of existence in this world, earthy. They were depending upon their own abilities being in the flesh. They were sarx - the flesh. Verse 3, they "<u>walked as mere men</u>." Therefore, as men in the flesh, they did what the flesh directed and had envy and strife (divisions like the denominations. Denomination is a word which means division). They did not walk depending on the Holy Spirit that had been given to them at spiritual rebirth. They did not know how to walk with the

Spirit. That was a doctrine, but not a reality for them, nor an experience they had. As Christians, we are to walk as spiritual, not as fleshly, as mere men.

When you are born physically, you are given many gifts. However, you are not even aware of them yet. You have to learn about what you were born with. You discover your fingers and toes; how to walk; how to run. It is all a process of growth and development. In parallel, the same is true when you are born spiritually from above. You are given wonderful gifts from God, but you are not even aware of their presence yet. The Spirit dwells with your spirit as a Christian as a gift to you. You have to discover his presence, his voice, how to walk with him and how to please him.

You also have to learn how to be led by the Spirit to "understand the things of God" that have been freely given to us. Continuing in 1 Cor. 2: 13, we learn that we are to compare spiritual truths with spiritual words (what is written). We must study the word, and pray for the Spirit to give us "enlightenment" (understanding), Eph.1:17. It is a process that is spiritual. Will you know when you finally understand something from the Spirit? Yes. It does not however always happen that you are in line with the Spirit. We can have "good intentions" and yet be very wrong because we are really following the flesh, following human reasoning and reaction. Observing a human reaction is when Peter was with Jesus and responded to what Jesus had said - that he must go to Jerusalem, suffer many things, and be killed. Peter rebuked Jesus and told him, "Never Lord, this shall never happen to you." Jesus then turned to Peter and said to him, "Get behind me Satan! You are a stumbling block to me; you do not have in mind the things of God." Mt.16:23, (NIV). Was Peter a follower of Jesus? Yes. But, at that moment he was relying on his own understanding and human effort. He was not "minding the things of God." Sure, Peter had good intentions, to defend his Lord; but he was wrong. He must follow the Spirit.

Even if you are a Christian, you must let the Spirit lead you in your understanding of Revelation in every detail – phrase by phrase, word by word. If you are following what he is teaching you and then stray and follow your own knowledge and understanding; your understanding may veer way off. You get derailed when the flesh creeps in. If you pay attention to commentators, you can tell if they are following the Spirit in their understanding or not; and if they stray, you can tell when they do that too. Being led by his Spirit requires discipline of heart and mind, staying on course with him. God bless you in your reading and study of Revelation.

[Note: all scripture quotations are from the NIV unless otherwise specifically indicated]

Key 2. The Date Of The Book

There is no external evidence for the date of the book that we can trust like internal evidence from the book. The Bible is all inspired by God. Dealing with external evidence, I have written briefly about it in my comments in chapter 1, verse 9.

Internal evidence of the book.

1. Rev.17:10 – Five kings had fallen, one is… The 5th king was Nero, emperor of Rome. He died June 9, 68 A.D. That puts you just after that date in A.D. 68.

2. Rev.11:1 – John was to go measure the Temple. That means the Temple was still standing. The time then was before the destruction of the Temple in Jerusalem in A.D.70.

3. Rev.3:10 – Jesus was going to keep the church of Philadelphia from the "<u>hour of trial</u>" (NIV) that was going to (Greek – about to) come upon the whole world. (Cf, Lk:35). That "<u>hour of trial</u>" was a figurative expression for the final judgment on earth that the Jews would suffer in Jerusalem when it was finally destroyed in A.D. 70.

4. Matt. 24:30 – Jesus predicted that He would return to earth in power and great glory with his angels "<u>immediately after the distress</u> (verse 20) <u>of those days</u>" (verse 29) and "<u>at that time</u>" (verse 30) "the sign of the son of man would appear." (NIV). Jesus predicted his second coming to be in the lifetime of his generation (Mt. 16:27-28 and in multiple passages in the New Testament.) (See Appendix A: "Coming of Jesus"). Jesus predicted his coming would be right after the destruction of Jerusalem, Mt.24:30; Mk13:24- 26). If Jesus did not come at the time Jerusalem was destroyed – THEN HE IS A FALSE PROPHET, Deut. 18:22.

5. Lk. 21:22 - Many Prophecies were to be fulfilled connected to the time of the destruction of Jerusalem and all prophecies were to be fulfilled by the time of the destruction of Jerusalem. (See Appendix E: "The Judgment"; Appendix F: "The Resurrection"; Appendix I: "The Restoration of All Things"; and so forth) This was the "<u>time of punishment in fulfillment of all that had been written.</u>" Lk.21:22.(NIV).

The late date of A.D. 94-96 of modern scholars misses the fulfillment of multiple prophecies by at least 24-26 years. What the book of Revelation is talking about had already occurred or been fulfilled before A.D. 94-96. The book of Revelation had already been fulfilled before modern scholars even get started looking for fulfillment. They are left groping for answers in the years following A.D. 96. Their time completely ignores (as we shall see) the clues and keys the Spirit gives us for understanding the book.

6. Relevance – the book was written to real churches in Asia Minor of the first century. Even though there are lessons we can learn today from the letters to these churches; what was said was first specific to them and relevant to them. Several things that are mentioned are highly specific to their day. For example, the letters to Ephesus and Pergamum, mention the Nicolaitans. They do not exist now, nor have they for almost 1900 years. In the letter to Thyatira it mentions a Jezebel who was a prophetess in their midst. These letters were specific to them. The book is first specific to the first century and the fulfillment of all prophecies – fulfilled in their generation.

7. There is NO evidence in the book or in the Bible for all the things that are wildly claimed today about the book. To claim that Jesus has <u>not come yet</u> is highly destructive to the teachings of the New Testament. The church is very immature in their understanding and willing to claim all kinds of things they imagine and interpret "without using the Spirit." I share this because Jesus did. Jesus taught in Matt.13:14-15:

"In them is fulfilled the prophecy of Isaiah: 'You will be ever hearing but never understanding; you will be ever seeing but never perceiving. For this people's heart has become calloused; they hardly hear with their ears, and they have closed their eyes.

Otherwise, they might see with their eyes, hear with their ears, understand with their hearts and turn, and I would heal them." (NIV).

How can Jesus say that? How can Jesus condemn people for not understanding? He says it is because their hearts are hard.

Yikes. How can we explain this? Paul had the same type of problem with Christians. In Gal.3:2-3 he writes:

"I would like to learn just one thing from you: Did you receive the Spirit by observing the law, or by believing what you heard? Are you so foolish? After beginning with the Spirit, are you now trying to attain your goal by human effort?" (NIV). The Galatians received the Spirit by faith when they were born again, born from above. But Paul indicates they were trying to be "perfected" (grow) by their own human effort. That includes understanding. They were trying to understand the scripture by their own human effort, by their ideas, by their human knowledge. They were not depending on God, nor on His Spirit. They never learned how to recognize the lead of the Spirit, the mind of the Spirit, in studying the things of God. They were depending on themselves.

Are there such followers of God throughout all history, who study diligently the scriptures and still do not yet understand? The Jews had experts in the Law and rejected Jesus and the fulfillment of the prophecies about him. Yet, they were very knowledgeable in the scripture. The Sadducees and the Pharisees argued all the time about what was right about 'issues' and rejected the righteousness that comes from God, and went about to establish their own righteousness, Rom. 10:2-3. (My paraphrase). They did not follow the Spirit who makes the Word "alive and active". It is a "spiritual book". It is not like any book on earth. It is the only book from God. It is spiritual.

The Church is no different. There are some 300+ denominations that all protect their flock with their brand of truth. They all contradict each other as if God' word is of private interpretation and that God is pleased with that. No, he is not! Jesus prayed for our unity in John. 17. Denominations are not united! Can two walk together unless they agree? No. They at best tolerate each other and lie about "loving each other."

They are full of strife and division. They are friends with the world. What is wrong? We are not being led by the Spirit! This shows up a lot in the way the churches interpret Revelation. Churches are all over the place in interpretations. Most Christians are convinced nobody really understands the book and their advice is - to just not study it to avoid arguments. That's easier than getting in step with the Spirit. We can still live our life marching to our own spirit. Does this sound harsh? Yes. I know it does. Please God, help us wake up to the "spiritual life within us." Jesus' gift of the Holy Spirit dwelling within us was given to help us understand the mind of God (1 Cor. 2) and be transformed (2 Cor.3:18), to make ourselves ready to be his bride, without any spot or wrinkle. The desire for, and love of Christ for his bride is beautiful. Follow His Spirit! Adorn yourself (by his Spirit) for Jesus.

Key 3. "Things That Must Soon Take Place"

I have discussed this in chapter 1, verse 1, a lot. It is so important that we get what the Spirit is telling us; that I repeat it here. "Must" is from the Greek word - dei. It means- it behoves to; it is necessary; it is obligated to; it has to; it MUST. "Soon" – is from the Greek word – tachi. It is translated and means - soon, with haste, speedily, shortly. Soon means soon.

It is important that we do not make up things or apply them incorrectly. God uses words like we do. He is not trying to trick us or use some "religious mysterious code" to communicate to us. It is true, in prophecy, he uses figurative language and expression to represent ideas. We do too, in our use of language. We have to study to understand how he uses those ideas. Soon means soon! Don't arbitrarily say, "well with God – "soon" may mean – "in a thousand years." because a day is like a thousand years with God." That is first a misinterpretation of what Peter is talking about in that passage and conjecture. If God communicated like that it would make his Word nonsensical. God's Word is spiritual, not illogical and illusive.

"Take place" is from the Greek – genesthai. It simply means – to occur; to happen. Now that sounds simple, but again we add guesses and comments to what it says such as – "It could mean it "begins to take place." People want it to fit "their theories". One theory is that Revelation is about the apostasy of the Roman catholic (universal) church down through the centuries. So, conveniently such interpreters say – "Revelation began to soon take place or soon be fulfilled and continues to be fulfilled down through the ages." That sounds like a reasonable interpretation but it is not following the Spirit. It is adding words to the understanding of the text to fit what we believe or what our theory is. Don't do that. Part of following the Spirit is being very careful to follow "His words", His phrases". We must let the Spirit teach us what to believe. We must not use human ideas and reasoning.

Concerning the phrase in verse 1 of chapter 1 – "of things that must soon take place", it is in reference to the "revelation of Jesus Christ'. The revelation "was soon to take place", all of it. It is not "part of it" that was soon to take place. No, the Revelation was soon to take place. John says it here at the beginning of Revelation and at the end of revelation in 22:6. This is key to understanding the book. All of it was "soon to take place."

Why was it all soon to take place? Because the appointed time for the fulfillment of many prophecies was about to take place. They "must" be fulfilled as God appointed. (cf. Mt.26:52-54). The prophecies were connected to the destruction of Jerusalem that was "about to" (Greek -mellei), take place. Even though the Greek word for "about to" is not used here in Rev.1:1, the phrase "soon to take place" is. The phrase "must soon take place" matches the idea of many prophecies that use the word "about to" –as prophecies concerning the "about to be" resurrection, Acts 24:15 ("to be about to be", Greek – mellein esesthai); and the "about to be" judgment, James 2:12 ("being about to be judged", Greek – mellontes krinesthai); and Rev.3:10 "the hour of trial being 'about to come' (Greek- mellouses erxesthai) on the inhabited earth." What was "soon to take place" was "about to be" in regard to the fulfillment of many prophecies and would complete all prophecies.

It is important to note something else here. Rev.1:19 says "Write thou therefore the things which thou sawest, the things which are, and the things which are about to occur," (Marshalls' Interlinear Translation). The visions in the Revelation are of things in the past, the present, and the near future. So, you will need to keep this verse in mind in interpreting the various visions.

Key 4. These Things Were Signified, Figurative Language

"Signified" comes from a Greek word for "sign", "to express something with signs." There are many "signs" in Revelation. There are stars, candlesticks, locusts, beasts, the sea, the earth, trumpets, vials, a dragon, numbers, and 100's more. Why is Revelation so hard to understand? Well God filled it with all kinds of "signs" that represent ideas. The book captures the visual imagination. It's like watching a movie as God unfolds the story to us. We see what he has revealed, like a movie; but we do not understand it. We have to let the Spirit teach us what all these signs are. Some signs are interpreted in the text. Some are interpreted in other prophecies in the Old Testament. Some we have to try to understand by the way they are being used in different scriptures. The Psalms help us to understand many of them. So do the prophetic books of the Old Testament. Some things we have to understand from the stories that are told in the Old Testament and the New. The book of Revelation is not for the unlearned. The Spirit needs to teach you a lot over the years to be ready to understand the Revelation. It takes a lot of study, diligence and most importantly – following the lead of the Spirit in every detail. I have tried to help you with the commentary. I go verse by verse and try to explain these signs by comparing "spiritual ideas to spiritual words"; comparing passages, here a little and there a little, line upon line - like Isaiah says.

Key 5. Sacred and Secular History

Sacred history is real history. It is God - breathed, word by word, in the pages of the scripture. It is sacred because the history follows the stream of God's activity in bringing about the fulfillment of his purposes throughout time. Sacred history is about what God has done to bring about man's salvation and fellowship with him. It only follows what is important to God in revealing himself to us. It does not talk about China, or Russia, or Australia, or South America or much of our global world. It talks about the Bible lands and what God did with a nation

(Israel) in the middle of the Bible lands to work his plan.

In the book of Revelation, many of the stories of sacred history (the Bible) are alluded to and symbols borrowed from it. To understand Revelation, you must familiarize yourself with the stories, the names, the events, the interpretations of both the Old and New Testament. Revelation is the pulling together of everything in the Bible into one grand finale. We will never understand the "last act" of God's redemption and the "fulfilling of everything", if we do not understand the events that led up to the "last act." We must study sacred history. Without the other books of the Bible you would never understand Revelation.

Secular history is of course the histories that man has written. God wants us to know that the Bible is not mythological. It is not "made up". It is not a novel, nor a fairy tale. It is real history woven into and through the histories of men as God acted. God wants us to know the reality of the events that he has written in the sacred pages. We can compare the Bible to secular history and find verification of the reality of the bible events over and over. We do need to be aware that secular history does not always agree. Secular history is written by man. He is not always honest nor objective. Man has tried to rewrite the history of his own time to suit him many times. Even in the first century a Jewish historian mentions man doing this. Listen to what Josephus, the first century Jewish historian, says:

"However, I may justly blame the men among the Greeks, who, when such great actions have been done in their own times, which, upon the comparison, quite eclipse the old wars, do yet sit as judges of those affairs, and pass bitter censures upon the labors of the best writers of antiquity." (Josephus, "The Jewish Wars", Preface, sect.5.)

In other words, later writers censure earlier writers and re-write history as it suits them. The problem existed 2000 years ago, in the first century, when Josephus wrote; and it has always been a problem. It is a problem now, in our day, in the rewriting of American history. Liberals are trying to divert the populace's opinions to socialism. Does that invalidate history? No. Usually, it is not the facts and events that are altered, but rather the vantage point – the interpretation of the facts. [Though sometimes the facts are lied about and twisted also]

Now why bring all this up about history? There are many things we could not understand in the Old Testament nor the New Testament unless we study secular history alongside our bibles. Bible writers wrote within the context of their times. For example, you cannot understand what Daniel 8:1-14 or chapter 11 is even talking about without studying the secular history that parallels that time. The book of Revelation is certainly the same. You would not be able to figure out who the seven kings of Rev.17:10 were, or which "five had fallen" or the eighth king - if you did not study it alongside secular history. The Bible is an historical book. Much of Revelation cannot be understood without secular history.

You will especially need a copy of the history written by Josephus, the first century Jewish historian, – "The Jewish War," to understand Revelation. The Histories of Tacitus, a Roman historian and Suetonius, historians of the time are also helpful. Some of what is talked about in the letters to the churches you cannot understand without some of the writers of the Apostolic Fathers, who wrote from about 80-160 A.D.

Key 6. The Writings Of The Prophets And Their Prophecies

Particularly, the writing of the prophets helps us to understand the prophecy of John, in the book of Revelation. For example, Rev.13 speaks of the "beast who rises out of the sea." (NIV). Who is he? Daniel answers that for us in Dan.7:17 "The four great beasts are four kingdoms" (NIV). By the time of the fourth beast, we are at the time of the Roman empire. "The fourth beast is a fourth kingdom" (NIV), he says in Daniel 7:23ff. Daniel continues to describe the fourth kingdom that helps us interpret and understand Rev.13 and 17.

You especially need to study Isaiah, Jeremiah, Ezekiel, Daniel, and Zechariah to help you interpret Revelation. Psalms and Isaiah are great for the interpretation of prophetic symbols. Exodus is a great history to figure out the symbols related to the plagues that come down in Revelation. The book of Revelation is a very Jewish book. Every 3 out of 4 verses in Revelation directly allude to the Old

Testament, especially the prophets. The old saying among us is – "You cannot understand the New without the Old". "The Old Testament is the New concealed and the New Testament is the Old revealed." May the Spirit guide you! Have fun! God is exciting and amazing!

You also need to pay attention to the New Testament prophets. Jesus predicted his second coming (his return to the earth) many times. Yet, people today have never had their attention drawn to those prophecies to set them in their minds. They have been told by false teachers (men of the flesh who follow men of the flesh) that Jesus has not come yet. What a failure on the part of church leaders to teach the Truth. They are the blind leading the blind. They deny the very thing Jesus prophesied – that he would come back within the lifetime of those he taught. (See Appendix – "Coming of Jesus"). If we knew what Jesus actually taught, and his apostles, we would know that many things were prophesied to occur by the time of the destruction of Jerusalem. Our people, Christian brothers and sisters, "do not know the scripture." They do not know how to nor do they follow the Spirit in their understanding of scripture. God help us!

It is very important to know of the prophecies that were to be fulfilled within the time of the generation of Jesus. A generation would be the average lifetime of a person. The Bible tells us that the average is threescore and ten years, or 70 years, Psalms 90:10, Matt.1. Those who lived in the generation of Jesus were to see "all things come together" and be fulfilled. Jesus predicts four of those major prophecies. I think it is very important to refer to those prophecies here. They were to be fulfilled in the Revelation.

1. The first prophecy <u>– the destruction of Jerusalem</u>. Jesus predicted the destruction of Jerusalem in Matt.24; mk.13; and Lk.21. The destruction was to be fulfilled before his generation would pass away, Mt.24:34.

2. The second prophecy – <u>Jesus' second coming</u>. Tied to the time of the destruction of Jerusalem, at the end of that destruction Jesus was to come back. <u>Mt. 24:29-30</u>, NIV speaks of the signs in the heavens and says, "<u>Immediately after the distress of those days</u> (NIV) (the destruction of Jerusalem) the sun will be darkened… and so forth. Then in verse 30 he says,

"At that time" the sign of the Son of Man will appear in the sky...." Jesus was to come "at that time," - while there were signs in the heavens following the distress of the destruction of Jerusalem. Jesus had predicted several times he was coming back in their lifetime. There are about 35 scriptures in which Jesus tells us he would return in his generation.

Mt.10:23 "I tell you the truth, you will not finish going through the cities of Israel before the Son of Man comes." (NIV)

Mt.16:27-28 "For the Son of Man is going to come in his Father's glory with his angels, and then he will reward each person according to what he has done. (NIV) (Notice verse 31- the judgment). I tell you the truth, some of you who are standing here will not taste death before they see the Son of Man coming in his kingdom." (NIV) [Some claim this is a coming that was in judgment but not seen – an invisible coming. That interpretation does not work here in Matt. 16 or Matt.24. Jesus comes: 1. In his Father's glory, 2. With his angels, 3. And rewards each person according to either good or bad.]

Mt.26:64 "But I say to all of you, In the future you will see the Son of Man sitting at the right hand of the mighty one, and coming on the clouds of the heaven." (NIV)

Jn.21:22-23 "If I want him (John) to remain alive until I return, what is that to you." (NIV). Jesus was saying John would still be alive when he (Jesus) returned. [There are only two comings – the first to die for sin, the second to bring salvation and judgment, Heb.9:28]

1 Thess.4:15-16 "According to the Lord's own word, we tell you that we who are still alive; who are left to the coming of the Lord, will certainly not precede those who have fallen asleep." (NIV) (Why? Each would be raised in his own turn, 1 Cor.15:23. Paul verified Jesus 'teaching – some of them would still be alive when Jesus returned. (see Appendix: Coming of Jesus).

3. The third prophecy – <u>Judgment in Jesus' generation</u>.

   Jn. 5:28-29 speaks of "A time is coming and <u>has now come</u>" in which the dead would be raised." (NIV). In the appointed time period (the generation) had arrived in which the resurrection was to take place and "<u>those had have done evil wouldl rise to be condemned</u>." Jesus spoke many parables to tell us of the judgment that was to take place in his generation.

   <u>Acts 24:15</u> speaks of - there was "about to be" (Greek – Mellein) "the resurrection of both the righteous and the wicked."

   <u>2 Tim.4:1</u> "who is 'about to' (Greek - mellontos) judge the living and the dead."

4. The fourth prophecy – <u>the resurrection</u>.'

   Jn.5:25-29 we have looked at. Jesus said the "<u>time is coming and has now come</u>" They were in that generation in which the resurrection would occur.

   Many prophecies in the Old and New Testament; and the completion of all prophecies were fulfilled in the time of the book of Revelation.

Key 7. Israel, the Spiritual Promise of God

Israel, in the Old Testament, was God's instrument, his object lesson, to teach us what would come to pass and be fulfilled in the New Testament. God's dealings with Israel and the Mosaic system were a "shadow and a type" to teach us about what we have in the heavens as Christians. The things of the Old Testament on earth were a shadow and type of the "reality" in the heavens. What do we mean? God was using earthly things, things we can see and experience, to tell us what is in the unseen, the spiritual world. For example, in the Old Testament they had the physical, earthly "promised land", Gen.15:18. But that was not the home of believers, Heb.11:14-15. Believers are looking for a far better country – "a heavenly one". It is called "Beulah land" (meaning "married") in prophecy and it is in heaven. Beulah land represents those who are "married to Christ". They are his bride. We could go through many parallels in detail in scripture between the "shadow" on earth and the "reality" in heaven. There was an earthly promised land – there is a heavenly promised land. There was an earthly temple. There is a heavenly temple. There was an earthly priesthood; there is a heavenly priesthood. There was an earthly Jerusalem (Gal.4:21ff) and there is a heavenly Jerusalem. There was an earthly kingdom (Israel) and there is a heavenly kingdom. (Spiritual Israel). Can you see it yet? The things that were on earth in the O.T. was a mirror of what is in the heavens in the New.

If we interpret prophecies in the O.T. with an earthly fulfillment – we miss the Truth. If you do that, you are making the same mistakes that the Jews of the first century made who rejected Christ. They were looking for the fulfillment of an earthly kingdom by Christ. Jesus told them – "my kingdom is not of this world," Jn18:36. (NIV). And it will not be of this world. Christ's kingdom has already been built and it's in the heavens. It is the "mountain of the Lord's house" in the heavens. It is the "heavenly Jerusalem" in the heavens. All of this doctrine of men that is being taught - that Christ will come back to earth someday to his people Israel (meaning over in the middle East) to Jerusalem on earth and set up his kingdom is false and a lie. Yes, - a lie. The Bible and the prophecies in it do not ever, anywhere teach such a lie. It's made up by human reasoning and is a big misinterpretation. The coming of Jesus some day, and setting up his kingdom on earth is NOT what the book of Revelation is even talking about.

Many get off track in the very beginning of scripture with the promises to the patriarchs.

There are many promises to the patriarchs in Genesis 12:1-3; 22:18. 1. <u>The great nation promise</u> – "I will make you into a great nation." 2. <u>The bless all nations promise</u> - "All people of the earth will be blessed through you." 3. <u>The land promise</u> (or promised land). Many today interpret these promises as not fulfilled yet. They say that God has not fulfilled his promises to Israel yet. They are still waiting, like the Jews of the first century, for an earthly fulfillment.

There is an inspired interpretation of the promises to the patriarchs in Gal 3:16:

"The promises were spoken to Abraham and to his seed. The

scripture does not say 'and to seeds,' meaning many people, but 'and to your seed,' meaning one person, who is Christ." (NIV)

The promises to Abraham were not to all his seed or all his descendants. Even translators have translated the Hebrew word – zera, for "seed" (meaning one seed -Gal.3:16) as "descendants" (meaning many). The translators did not understand the prophecies. We would by human understanding have the same problem in English. Our English word seed can be understood as both singular and plural. It is the inspired interpretation of the passages in Genesis that corrects our understanding. The promises made to Abraham were never for his descendants, but for One seed, who is Christ. Christ, the one seed, would create a new spiritual nation through his death. He is the second Adam, the beginning of a new creation, Rom.5. That spiritual nation would be as numerous as the stars of the sky and the sand on the seashore. Through Jesus, the one seed, all nations would be blessed -by faith in Him and by faith all nations could flow into him. The promised land? Through Jesus, the One seed, we can reach the promised land in the heavens. Of course, we see a type of physical application and fulfillment to Israel in history. After all, the promises applied to the shadow - as a shadow of what was to come. The shadow must in some way represent the Reality to be fulfilled. Israel was an earthly type, a pattern of what was in the heavens – just as was the tabernacle, Heb.8:5. (See further the topics in the Appendix K: "Israel"; and Appendix P: "Jerusalem").

[Note: all scripture quotations are from the NIV unless otherwise specified.]

CHAPTER ONE

Verse 1. The Revelation of Jesus Christ

"The revelation of Jesus Christ, which God gave him, to show his servants what must soon take place. He made it known by sending his Angel to his servant John," (NIV).

This is a <u>revelation</u> (greek – "apokalupto", to uncover, to unveil, from Greek –"apo" –from, and "kalupto" to cover. It is in contrast to the Greek- "sunkalupto"- to cover up). The book of Revelation is a revealing, a making known, a disclosing, an uncovering. It is meant to be understood. It can be understood. "<u>The things that are revealed belong unto us</u>," scripture tells us in Deut.29:29, NIV. Understanding it does require that we follow what the Spirit teaches us throughout the scriptures. We must compare spiritual words with scripture. In other words, many things are interpreted for us in other scriptures. So, we compare line upon line, precept upon precept, search here a little and there a little in the scripture.

This is "<u>the revelation of Jesus Christ which God gave to him</u>." (NIV). That is a very significant statement. God gave the Revelation to Jesus. God the Father made it known to Jesus. Why? And what revelation could be revealed to Jesus, who is God, something that he did not know? Is he not the son of God? Perhaps Matthew 24:36 can give us the answer - "<u>no man knows the day or hour</u> of his coming neither the angels in heaven <u>nor even the Son</u>, but only the father." (NIV). With this scripture in mind, Matt.24:36, gives us the correct answer. <u>This revelation is about Jesus' coming back to earth the second time</u>. It is about the day and hour of Jesus' coming. God the Father gave

Jesus the revelation. It is about the fulfillment of his coming in the prophecies. We find statements in the revelation that help us confirm what we have observed. In this chapter, verse 7 says, "Look he is coming (present tense in the Greek) with the clouds". (NIV). To the letters of the churches he says, "I will soon come to you," (NIV), as he does in 2:16, and nearly in every letter to the seven churches. At the end of the book, in chapter 22, he repeats that he is coming soon several times. Finally, he says, in Rev.22:20, "Yes! I am coming soon! Amen. Come Lord Jesus." (NIV). The Father had given his Son the Revelation - it was the time for Jesus' return to the earth, his second coming. The time for the consummation of all things had arrived.

"What must soon take place." NIV). The phrase of this verse is highly significant. It is -" what must soon take place." The Spirit of God gives us a major key here in understanding the book. The things in the book must soon take place. When he says - they must soon take place, the emphasis is on the words - *must soon*. The word must, Greek -"dei", means "it behoves", "it is necessary" to take place. It is used in Matthew 16:21.

"From that time on Jesus began to explain to his disciples that he must go to Jerusalem and suffer many things at the hands of the elders, chief priests, and teachers of the law, and that he must be killed and on the third day be raised to life." NIV

We could not deny the necessity that Jesus must be killed and rise on the third day. That was God's plan. He died for our sins. Without his death we could not be forgiven. He must rise from the dead. Paul said in 1 Cor.15 if Jesus was not raised then we cannot be raised and our faith is vain. These things must have happened and they did.

We go on to learn more of why things *must* take place in other passages. When Jesus and three disciples were in the garden in Matthew 26, large crowds with swords and clubs came to arrest Jesus. At one point, Peter drew his sword and cut off Malchus' ear, the servant of the high priest. Jesus tells Peter to put up his sword and then heals the servant. Then in verse 53-54, Jesus says, "Do you think I cannot call my Father, and he will at once put at my disposal more than twelve legions of angels, but how then would the scriptures be fulfilled that say it must happen in this way." (NIV). "Peter," Jesus explains, "Things <u>must</u> happen this way <u>in order to fulfil scripture</u>."

In the Book of Revelation, "things <u>must soon</u> take place". Why? Because those prophecies are being fulfilled at their appointed time, as they are predicted in Scripture. God's appointed time for things to be fulfilled had arrived in this book. They must take place soon, at their appointed time.

What things were soon to be fulfilled? One thing is the prophecies about Jesus coming back. He had said he would come back before some of them he taught would die, Matt.16:27-28. Jesus taught that the twelve would not finish going through the cities of Israel before he came back, Matt. 10:22-23. Jesus told the high priests, council, elders, scribes, those who held his trial that they would "see him at the right hand of the Mighty One and coming in the clouds," Matt.26:64. (NIV). Jesus taught in many places that his return would be in their lifetime. He did not reveal to his followers the <u>day</u> nor the <u>hour</u>. Only the Father knew that. He was to come as a thief in the night. Yet, his followers were to be ready and be watchful so they would not be caught unawares and not be ready. (cf. 1 Thess.5:1-11) Now, in the Revelation, his coming was imminent. It was soon.

The word "<u>soon</u>," greek - "taxei", is translated "with speed, haste, shortly, quickly." It is used consistently throughout the New Testament. <u>Soon means soon</u>. So, here in verse 1, the <u>Spirit give us a huge key</u> by which we can interpret what he says. The things in the book- of necessity "<u>must soon</u> take place." This book is the fulfillment of the things that are prophesied in the Old Testament, and by Jesus and his apostles. It completes the Bible. It puts the ending to the sacred story. It brings everything together to completion in this book.

"<u>He made it known</u>", (NIV) or "he <u>signified</u>," (Greek -esemanen) sending through the angel" [Marshall's Greek interlinear]. "He sent and <u>signified</u> it by his angel", (KJV). The Greek word for signified comes from the root "<u>sema</u>," a sign. To signify, give a sign, to indicate. These things were signified to his servant John. That means that even though these things are revealed in the revelation, they are not easily understood. Perhaps there are two reasons for these things being signified.

The first reason was for the benefit of John's readers in the first century. This revelation was given during a time of persecution, as indicated in verse 9. John was exiled to the island of Patmos. He was a companion with his readers in suffering. An easily obtainable interpretation of the revelation could put his readers in more danger. The Roman empire may seek to destroy its message. The message was for believers, who knowing the Old Testament prophets for many years, would understand it.

The second reason may be for the benefit of its many readers in the many centuries following its writing. The Spirit of God wants us to seek, to meditate, to ponder his message. An understanding of the message is not easily obtained. The understanding is given to those who consistently seek and ponder to know and understand. The understanding is given here a little and there a little, line upon line. We must have the attitude of Jacob who wrestled with the angel. As he said, 'I will not let you go unless you bless me;' NIV (Gen.32:26). So too, we must wrestle with different verses until we get an understanding and a blessing. God 's word is amazing, full of life, and many, many blessings. It reveals itself and gives understanding to those, who having the Spirit, seek continually after its blessings.

"His angel." Jesus made the Revelation "known by sending his angel" (NIV) to his servant John. Revelation 22:6 says, "the Lord the God who inspires the prophets sent his angel to show his servants the things that must soon take place". (NIV). In 22:16 it says, "I, Jesus, have sent my angel to give you this testimony for the churches." (NIV).

"To his servant John". (NIV). This testimony was given to John. That is important. John was still alive. He had lived until this time and had not been killed through persecution. In John 21, Jesus had told Peter how he would die. But concerning John he said in verse 22, 'if I want him to remain alive until I return, what is that to you'? (NIV). Jesus repeats his words in verse 23, 'if I want him to remain alive until I return, what is that to you?' (NIV). John was to be the writer of the Revelation. He was to be alive when it was time for Jesus to return. 'Behold, I am coming soon, Jesus said, in Revelation 22:7,12. 'Do not seal up the book. The time is at hand,' 22:10. (NIV).

Just hear someone may object. They may say, "yes, Revelation begins to be fulfilled soon, but continues to be fulfilled over many centuries, and it is showing the apostasies of the church down through the Ages. So, with their explanation, they are claiming that the revelation only begins to be fulfilled in John's time, but is also about many centuries in the future. In answer to that objection, let us compare the book of Daniel and make some observations there. In the Book of Daniel, in chapter 2, Daniel has a dream. The dream is of a figure that represents four kingdoms that will exist in the future, one following after the other. God is willing, in the chapter, of giving Daniel the interpretation of the dream. In Daniel chapter 7, Daniel has a dream about four beasts. Again, the dream is about those four kingdoms. Again, God is willing to give him an interpretation of the dream.

However, even though God was willing to give Daniel previous interpretations of the dreams; in chapter 12 he tells Daniel verse 4, "but you Daniel, <u>close up and seal the words of the scroll</u> until the time of the end. Many will go here and there to increase knowledge." (NIV). In Daniel 12:9, God tells Daniel "Go your way Daniel because the words are <u>closed up and sealed</u> until the time of the end." (NIV). Then again in verse 13, "as for you, go your way till the end. You will rest and then at the end of the days you will rise to receive your allotted inheritance." (NIV).

If much of the revelation is about the distant future, God could have given John an interpretation for the part that was about to be fulfilled in his time. Then he could have told John that the rest of it he should seal up, go his way because it concerned the distant future. (According to the interpretation of many – a future that still has not happened after 2000 years). He could have told John that, but he did not. It did not fit the things in the book. In no place in the revelation does God say to seal up anything. Throughout the book, the things of the book are imminent. The readers are told to take the revelation to heart because the time is at hand. There are no parts of the revelation that would let us know that that part is about a distant time. All speculation to such an interpretation would put us outside of the guidance of the Holy Spirit. It would have to be an interpretation that we guessed from our own imaginations. The Bible is not arbitrary, nor is it subject to our own imaginations for interpretation. This is a spiritual book, and requires respect and adherence to the things of the Spirit to understand it. We must compare spiritual truths with spiritual words. We seek our understanding from the things that the Spirit has revealed in his Word.

Verse 2. Who Testifies To Everything He Saw

"Who testifies to everything he saw- that is, the word of God and the testimony of Jesus Christ." (NIV).

Verse 3. Blessed Is The One Who Reads

"Blessed is the one who reads aloud the words of this prophecy and blessed are those who hear it and take to heart what is written in it, because the time is near". (NIV)

There is a blessing pronounced up on the one who reads aloud the book. In John's time the words of Prophecy were read aloud to the churches. The blessing was to come also upon the ones who heard it and took it to heart. Again, it is emphasized "the time is near"- meaning the time of the fulfillment of what was read was near.

Verse 4. ToThe Seven Churches

"John, to the seven churches in the province of Asia, Grace and peace to you from him who is, and who was, and who is to come, and from the seven spirits before his throne." (NIV)

"Seven." John addresses the revelation to the seven churches in the province of Asia. The number 7 is used throughout the Book of Revelation. There are seven churches, 1:4; seven spirits; seven lampstands,1:12; seven stars 1:16; seven seals, 5:11; seven angels, 3:2; seven trumpets, 8:6; seven lamps, 4:5; seven thunders, 10:3; seven bowls, 16:1; seven angels, 15:1; seven last plagues; seven heads, seven hills, and seven Kings in 17:9. The number 7 is prominent throughout the book. It means "complete, all." The number 7 begins in Genesis. God created a seven - day week. Seven days is all the days of a week. It is a complete week. There are many other examples in scripture showing this meaning. Also, the number 7 is associated with something that is of God or from God. There are the seven Spirits of God, Isa.11:1-2. Or, there are the seven eyes (of Jehovah) upon the stone (Jesus), Zech. 3:9. Jesus had seven eyes in Rev.5:6. Seven is what is "complete, all" and is associated with God.

John writes to the "seven churches" in the province of Asia. He is writing to all the churches if we take seven to mean "complete or all." They were from or of God, associated with God. There were more churches in Asia. However, some no longer existed. Colossae and Hierapolis had been destroyed by an earthquake in 61 A.D. Laodicea was also destroyed by the earthquake but it had been rebuilt by the time Revelation was written. (The earthquake was one of the signs of the" beginning of birth pains" that Jesus mentions in Matt. 24:10, which would occur before Jerusalem was destroyed.)

These seven Roman cities, where the churches were located, had a large concentration of Jews. Much of Revelation is about the Judgment of God upon the Jews for their wickedness, for killing the Son of God, and for their rejection of the gospel. These churches would also be affected by these judgments and Jesus warns these churches so that they might not be included in the judgments but may remain faithful through the judgments. The Revelation does not address other churches by name here or in chapters 2 and 3. The mother church in Jerusalem is not mentioned here, even though much of the Revelation is about Jerusalem, the center of all things Jewish. The large church at Antioch is not mentioned, nor the churches of Galatia, Corinth, Philippi, Thessalonica and others. Many churches are not mentioned. Seven churches are addressed here to represent the whole. It seems these churches would be most affected by the judgment of the Jews that was soon to take place.

"Grace" (God's free gift) and "peace" (the result of that gift) is given by him "who is" – "the being one", and "who was"- in the past, and "who is to come." "Who is to come" can leave us with the idea that he was coming sometime in the future, even a far- away future. That would not be correct. The right idea is "the coming one" meaning progressive coming, nearness, imminent return. Remember our key in verse one - "soon take place". That is what the Greek means here too.

"Seven spirits before his throne" (NIV) is footnoted - the "sevenfold Spirit."

Chapter 3:1 says,

"To the angel of the church in Sardis write: these are the words of him who holds the seven Spirits of God and the seven stars." (NIV).

Jesus has the "seven spirits of God." Chapter 4:5 mentions them-

"Before the throne, seven lamps were blazing. These are the seven spirits of God." (NIV)

In speaking of the Lamb in 5:6, scripture says,

"He had seven horns and seven eyes, which are the seven spirits of God sent out into the earth." (NIV).

In that verse, Jesus has "all power or authority (seven horns) and he sees and understands all (seven eyes).

I believe the number seven is again used for completeness, the completeness of God's Spirit, - the all-seeing eyes, spirits, of God are aware of all the earth, and see all things. Nothing is hid from him, Heb.4:13. They are seven lamps blazing – they give complete light, make the vision clear, cause you to understand, they enlighten you, Eph.1:17-18.

Some name the seven spirits from the prophecy about Christ in Isaiah 11:1-2:

"A shoot will come up from the stump of Jesse, from his roots a branch will bear fruit. the spirit of the Lord will rest on him- the spirit of wisdom and of understanding, the spirit of counsel and of power, the spirit of knowledge and of the fear of the Lord." NIV

The Septuagint translation, with a translation into English, says:

"And there shall come forth a rod out of the root of Jesse, and a blossom shall come up from its root: and the spirit of God shall rest upon him, the spirit of wisdom and understanding, the spirit of counsel and strength, the spirit of knowledge and godliness shall fill him; the spirit of the fear of God." (Septuagint English Translation).

The Septuagint includes the phrase - "godliness shall fill him." According to this passage, the seven spirits of the Lord include: the spirit of wisdom, the spirit of understanding, the spirit of counsel, the spirit of power (strength), the spirit of knowledge, the spirit of godliness, and the fear of the Lord." In this passage, the seven spirits exemplify the all-knowing, all-understanding and all-powerful character of God.

The Revelation is from the fullness of God the Father, who gave it to the Son, and the sevenfold Spirit of God. God the Father, verse 4, "who is, who was, and who is to come", and the sevenfold Spirit of God, and verse 5 - from Jesus Christ, who is the faithful witness." (NIV). The whole nature and fullness of God acts in agreement as one. The flesh does not dominate the Spirit, nor is the spirit and flesh contrary to one another, Gal.5:17, as in fallen, unregenerate man. God's nature is not divided. God's whole nature moves and acts as one.

Verse 5. From The Firstborn From The Dead

"And from Jesus Christ who is the faithful Witness, the firstborn from the dead and the ruler of the kings of the Earth. To him who loves us and has freed us from our sins by his blood." (NIV)

"The faithful Witness" is used in chapter 3 verse 14, and in 19:11. In 19:11, "the faithful witness" helps us to identify the rider on the White Horse as Jesus. Isaiah 55:3-4 says,

"I will make an Everlasting Covenant with you, my faithful love promised to David. See, I have made him a witness to the people, a leader and commander of the peoples. NIV

"The firstborn from the dead" (NIV) certainly speaks of Jesus being the first one resurrected in the new spiritual creation in the Kingdom of God. The contrast between the first creation (being the physical creation) with Adam, the first man, and then the new spiritual creation, with Jesus being the first born from the dead, is made in Rom. 5. Because Jesus was raised, then all those in Him can also be raised. (cf. 1 Cor.15:12-22).

Col.1:18 "And he is the head of the body, the church; he is the beginning, and the firstborn from among the Dead, so that in everything he might have the supremacy." (NIV)

Not only was Jesus the first to be raised from the dead in the new spiritual creation, but as the Firstborn, He is to have all the supremacy.

Heb. 1:5,6 - "For to which of the Angels did God ever say, 'you are my son today I have become your father' or again, "I will be his father and he will be my son." (NIV)

That passage is quoting Ps. 2. There in the passage, God says in verse 6, "I have installed my king on Zion, my holy hill." (Jesus had been resurrected, ascended and sat down at the right hand of God to reign.) In verse 7 God says "You are my Son. Today I have become your Father." I believe Jesus became the Son of God incarnate as a man when he was born of Mary. He was "Immanuel", God with us. His life as a man ended with his death on the cross. His life in the spiritual world began again when he was "born from the dead to die no more". When he was born into the spiritual world (raised from the dead) God raised him up. God said, "You are my Son, today I have become your Father." God had become his Father in the sense that he was God who gave him birth from the dead. Of course, God the Father has always been with the Son from eternity. Actually, it can be understood that the Spirit raised him up, Rom. 1:1, and that Jesus lay down his life and he took it up again, John 10:17.

"The ruler of the kings of the Earth" (NIV). Jesus is here called the ruler of the kings of the Earth. In his Ascension, Jesus was raised and seated far above all rule and authority and power and dominion and every title that can be given, Eph. 1:21. He set down at the right hand of God and began to reign. He was to reign until he put all of his enemies down, then return the kingdom back to the Father, 1 Cor.15: 25-28. Jesus was ruling and accomplishing the purpose which God had ordained for him to do. Jesus was in the midst of accomplishing his purpose until he had brought all things under his control, and accomplished all things that had been written. The Book of Revelation is the fulfilling of that purpose.

Verse 6. He Made Us A Kingdom and Priests

"And has made us to be a kingdom and Priests to serve his God and Father- to him be glory and power forever and ever! Amen" (NIV).

"The Kingdom."

Jesus had preached that the kingdom of God was near (that is – "close") in his ministry. He had appointed his apostles to lay the foundation of his kingdom. He was the Chief Cornerstone. Jesus came to build his kingdom.

He sent his Spirit back to the earth and the Spirit was poured out on the day of Pentecost. The revelation of the mystery of God began to be disclosed and for the first time through faith in Christ, believers were added to the kingdom, Acts 2:41. He gave miraculous gifts of different offices and functions of people in Ephesians 4 to build his kingdom. These offices and functions were to exist until they came into full knowledge of the Son of God, unto the fullness of Christ, Eph.4:13. The Old World Order under the Mosaic system, (1 Cor. 7:31; Heb.9:10; Rev.21:4) and the New Kingdom of God that was being built existed side by side. The Old World Order was getting old, outdated, and passing away, 1 Cor.7:31. It would be rolled up like a scroll and be changed, Heb.1:11-12. The New World Order - the Kingdom of God was being built by Jesus, not by human hands, but a place built by God, Heb.11:15-16. The Revelation tells us - "the old order of things passed away." God said, "I am making everything new." NIV, Rev.21:4-5. God has given to us today and to all his saints from A.D. 70 forward "everything that pertains to life and godliness", 2 Pet.1:3. There is nothing he has not done yet or not accomplished to provide for his people.

Jesus had ascended it into the heavens to prepare a place for his people. The heavens had to be cleansed from the Fallen Angels and Satan and all the dominion's, powers, and authorities that stood against him in the spiritual realm, Eph.6:12. Jesus entered the true Tabernacle of God in the heavens to offer himself for us, Heb.9:23-24. The New Order of Things - the kingdom of God, would come into its fullness. Then the old Order of Things that was centered in Old Testament worship and the Temple in Jerusalem would be destroyed completely in AD. 70. The temple in the heavens, in the new Kingdom, would open up, Rev. 11:19; 15:8. The mystery of God would be fully revealed. The renewal of all things would have been accomplished. The kingdom in its fullness would have arrived and opened up in the heavens. All Nations from then on could flow into it by faith. John was part of that Kingdom and the saints that he wrote to. They were <u>Kings</u>

and Priests unto God to offer up spiritual sacrifices to our Lord and his Christ. The Book of Revelation is about all of this in fulfillment of everything that had been written.

Verse 7. Look, He Is Coming

"Look he is coming with the clouds and every eye will see him, even those who pierced him; and all the peoples of the earth will mourn because of him. So shall it be, amen!" (NIV).

"He is coming" is a translation of - "erxetai". It is in the present indicative tense. It is not in the future tense. When John is writing the coming of Jesus was in the present. John was in the time of the second coming. When Jesus ascended into the clouds to heaven in Acts chapter 1, the apostles stood there gazing. Then the scripture says, verse11, "men of Galilee, why do you stand here looking into the sky? This same Jesus, who has been taken from you into heaven, we'll come back in the same way you have seen him go into heaven." NIV.

At this point, many readers may be in doubt and have questions. They might object and say - "but there is no historical reference to the second coming having come. There is no evidence. It could not have already come." To this I reply the following quotations from Josephus, a first-century Jewish historian, and from Tacitus, a 1st century Roman historian

(Josephus, The Jewish War, Book 6, Chap.5, Sect.3):

"A few days after the feast, on the 21st of Artemisios, a supernatural apparition was seen, too amazing to be believed. What I have to relate would, I suppose, have been dismissed as an invention, had it not been vouched for by eyewitnesses and followed by disasters that bore out the signs. Before sunset there were seen in the sky, over the whole country, chariots and regiments in arms speeding through the clouds and encircling the towns. again, at the Feast of Pentecost, when the priest had gone into the inner court of the Temple at night to perform the usual ceremonies, they declared that they were aware, first of a violent movement and a loud crash, the end of a concerted cry: 'let us go hence'."

(Tacitus, Annals Histories Agricola Germania, book v, pp. 618-619):

"Prodigies had occurred, which this nation, prone to superstition, but hating all religious rites, did not deem it lawful to expiate by offering and sacrifice. there had been seen hosts joining battle in the skies, the fire a gleam of arms, the temple illuminated by a sudden Radiance from the clouds the doors of the inner Shrine were suddenly thrown open, and a voice of more than a mortal phone was heard to cry that the gods were departing. at the same instant there was a Mighty stir as of departure. some few put a fearful meaning on these events, but in most there was a firm persuasion, that the ancient records other priests which contained a prediction of how at this very time the East was to grow powerful, and rulers coming from Judea where to acquire Universal Empire these mysterious prophecies had pointed to Vespasian and Titus, with the common people, with the usual blindness of ambition add interpreted these Mighty Destinies of themselves and could not be brought even by disasters to believe the truth. I have heard the total number of besieged of every age and both sexes amounted to 600000."

These two passages from history are speaking of what was seen by many at the close of the destruction of Jerusalem. They saw chariots and battles in the sky. According to Matthew 24:29, immediately following the great distress of Jerusalem there were to be signs in the heavens and the heavens would be shaken. The shaking speaks of God's judgment in the heavens. What the historians recorded and saw was also the leaving of the" gods" (as the pagans believed) in the temple. During that same time that these things occurred, following upon it, Jesus was to be seen in the skies in the clouds, coming back, Matt.24:30, by those waiting for him, Heb.9:28. We cannot say there is no history that records Jesus' coming in the first century. Matthew and Luke say Jesus coming was to be immediately after the distress of those days in Jerusalem. Jerusalem fell in A.D. 70. when Jesus came back. This would be in keeping with what Jesus predicted in Matt. 16:27-28. He would come back within the lifetime of those who stood before him during his earthly ministry. (See Appendix A: 'Coming of Jesus") Here in verse 7 Jesus "is coming" - present tense.

Again, an objection may be "Jesus could not have come back because we are still here. The world is still here. The end of the world and the end of time has not come." In reply, that is a 21st century understanding of what was to occur in Revelation; but it is not biblical. Nowhere does the Bible teach it. It is based on perhaps sincere but what becomes wild misinterpretation of passages and speculation. There is no place in the Bible that mentions the "end of time." That would be the Greek – "telos chronos" or "telos kainos." The scripture does not refer to that anywhere. There is no end of time in scripture. Consider these scriptures: Psalms 148; Jer.33:17-25 and Eccl.1:4.

Eccl.1:4 "Generations come and generations go, but the earth remains forever." (NIV). That passage does not use prophetic language or figurative speech. It plainly says "the earth remains forever." It is true, 2 Peter 3:10 says, "the heavens will disappear with a roar, the elements will be destroyed by fire, and the earth and everything in it will be laid bare". Peter is using prophetic language, figurative speech. He is not talking about a literal destruction of the physical heavens and earth. (See Appendix U: 2 Peter 3). We must interpret what he says with an understanding of what was meant in the first century by the figurative speech.

Heb.1:11-12 says heaven and earth would wear out like a garment, they would be rolled up like a robe, they would be changed. Again, that is figurative language and we must understand it from the first century understanding, and from the teaching of scripture. Is the world going to be burned up or wear out like a garment at the same time? How do we explain these figurative passages and the clear passage that "the earth remains forever"? That is what we are here in this book to do - seek understanding, responsibly and spiritually – handling right the word of God. Let us be patient. Let the Holy Spirit teach us with his word. It all makes sense. It all fits together. We will get there.

"Every eye will see him, even those who pierced him." This is in keeping with what Jesus had said in Matthew 26:64: "I say to all of you: in the future you will see the son of man sitting at the right hand of the mighty one and coming on the clouds of heaven." (NIV). He was talking to the high priest, the Sanhedrin, the council, and the teachers of the law. They were responsible for his death and his being pierced. Many of them would live long enough to see him coming back.

"And all the peoples of the Earth will mourn because of him". (NIV). This is in fulfillment of Zech.12:10 -11. There Zechariah says,

> "And I will pour out on the House of David and the inhabitants of Jerusalem a spirit of Grace and supplication. They will look on me, the one they have pierced and they will mourn for him as one mourns for an only child, and grieves bitterly for him is one grieves for a firstborn son. (NIV).

Verse 8. I Am The Alpha And Omega

"I am the Alpha and the Omega says the Lord God, who is, and who was, and who is to come the Almighty." (NIV).

"The Alpha and Omega"

In Rev.22:13 Jesus identifies himself as,

"I am the Alpha and the Omega, the First and the Last, the Beginning and the End." (NIV)

Saying the same thing three different ways emphasizes what he says. He is the Beginning. He "The late date - A.D.96, does not fit the time of things fulfilled in the Revelation".

Very significant [world changing] events occurred before and up to 70 A. D. If Revelation was written between A.D. 94-96, it would have no relevance to those events which had already happened 26 years earlier. That would place The Revelation outside of the time of fulfillment for the events predicted by Daniel, Zechariah, Jesus, the apostles and other prophets. If those events, such as the destruction of Jerusalem, Jesus' second coming, the resurrection, the judgment, the consummation of all things and the renewal of all things (all predicted for that time); if they did not occur; it would make Jesus and the prophets false prophets. The fulfillment of these prophecies were tied to the destruction of Jerusalem. Luke 21, in speaking of the destruction of Jerusalem says,

"For this is the time of punishment in fulfillment of all that has been written." (NIV)

What had been written (connected to the same time as the destruction of Jerusalem- was the coming of Christ, Matt.24:30, and the judgment, Matt. 24:31). Then a summary statement in verse 34:

"I tell you the truth, this generation will certainly not pass away until all these things have happened." (NIV).

is the end.

John 1:3 "through him all things were made; without him nothing was made that has been made." (NIV).

Col. 1:16 "For in Him all things were created in heaven and on earth, visible and invisible, whether they be thrones, or dominions or principalities, or powers. All things were created <u>through him</u> and <u>for him</u>. (NIV).

All things, from beginning to end, were created by him and for him. The creation is about him and for Him. The entire Bible is about Him, from beginning to end. If you see Him, you have seen the Father for it is the Son who reveals the Father. The Son glorifies the Father and the Father glorifies the Son. He is the beginning and the end.

"<u>Who is, and who was, and who is to come the Almighty.</u>" (NIV). "<u>ho on</u>" (Greek) - the one being; "<u>ho en</u>" (Greek) the one who was; "<u>ho erxomenos</u>" (Greek) the one coming.

Verse 9. I John, On The Island Of Patmos

"I John, your brother and companion in the suffering and Kingdom and patient endurance that are ours in Jesus, was on the island of Patmos because of the word of God and the testimony of Jesus." (NIV).

"<u>John...exiled to the island of Patmos.</u>"

There were 4 different islands that prisoners of Rome were exiled to: Kampos, Patmos, Etroggulo, and Leipsoi. These were islands in the Aegean Sea, south of Asia Minor, on the northern part of the Mediterranean Sea.

The question of the date of the book of Revelation, when it was written, comes up here. For modern scholars, the date of the book is tied to the question of when John was exiled to the island of Patmos. They point to statements by Tertullian and Irenaeus. Though we address what they say here, what they say cannot carry much weight. It is their evidence that is external evidence, outside the Bible. It is the internal evidence of the book, evidence from the book of Revelation itself which is inspired by God that must carry the deciding evidence for the date of the book. [see, "the date of the book" under keys to understanding the Revelation]

"Tertullian and Irenaeus statements about the exile of John".

"The claim of modern scholars". Modern scholars claim that John was exiled to Patmos during the reign of the eleventh emperor Domitian, and wrote the Revelation between 94-96 A.D. Their claim is largely based upon a statement made by Tertullian, born in 160 A. D., who was in Africa. Many church writers after Tertullian used Tertullian's writings and misunderstood what he wrote. Irenaeus, born in 130 A.D., also agrees with Tertullian. They are misunderstood. Tertullian actually said John was exiled during the reign of *Domitianou*, or *Domitius Nero* (the 5th emperor of Rome who reigned from 54-68 A.D.). Later writers inaccurately took *Domitianou* for *Domitianikos* or Domitian (the 11th emperor of Rome who reigned from 81-96 A.D.). Robert Young, the writer of an English Concordance – "Young's Analytical Concordance", wrote a commentary on the book of Revelation in 1885. In it; Young points out the error of those who misinterpret what Tertullian and Irenaeus said - that is: taking his words to mean Domitian rather than Domitius Nero. **(That Nero was called Domitius, see Tacitus, "Annals' ', Book XII, 41)**. Modern scholars continue to follow and insist upon this misinterpretation of Irenaeus. No matter, there is plenty of internal evidence in the book of Revelation that would put the writing of the book before A.D. 70.

The fulfillment of all the prophecies of what had been written are tied to the destruction of Jerusalem. It is a historical fact that Jerusalem was destroyed by Titus and his armies in A.D. 70. The A.D. 96 date for the book would place the book outside of those events that the Revelation is about. Interpreters would be thrown outside of the context of Biblical predictions and their fulfillment if they use the late date. They would be left to speculate and search for clues in history since the first century without any biblical evidence for their guesses and human reasonings. It is such speculation that has produced the many wild and irresponsible interpretations that we have today. What a disrespect for, and reckless handling of the word of God. We must follow the words of the Holy

Spirit and rightly handle his word, comparing scripture with scripture, to understand the Revelation.

"The relevance of the Revelation to whom it was written"

There is something else also significant to be considered. What relevance would the Revelation have to the ones to whom it was written in A.D. 96?

What about <u>Jews</u>? The first Jewish-Roman war or Judean war was from A.D. 66-70. When Titus, the Roman general, destroyed Jerusalem and utterly leveled the temple (Josephus, book 7, first paragraph) and destroyed the city, the Jews were defeated. Everything in the Jewish world, culture and religion was tied to the temple and its worship in Jerusalem. Everything Jewish centered there. With the destruction of Jerusalem, everything Jewish, and the world order under the Mosaic covenant was destroyed – <u>IN A.D. 70</u>. The date, A.D. 96 misses it all! It already happened!

Then there were <u>Christians</u>. Christians were first persecuted under Saul in Acts 8:1, Christians were scattered everywhere from the mother church in Jerusalem. Because of the edict of Claudius (4th emperor of Rome, who reigned from A.D. 41-54) and the expulsion of the Jews from Rome, Acts 18:2, Christian enjoyed some protection from persecution. The church grew by thousands. Then, persecution of Christians occurred under Nero (the 5th emperor of Rome who reigned from A.D 54-68. After Rome burned in A.D. 64 Nero blamed the fire on Christians and there was great persecution of Christians from A.D. 64-68. Thousands of Christians suffered and died as martyrs for Christ. Even under Domitian, the persecution that many believe he committed against Christians would have been committed before 96 A.D. Domitian was the 11th emperor, who reigned from Sept. A.D. 81 to A.D. 96. His reign was over before what scholars say (A.D. 94-96) was the date of Revelation. Everything relevant to the churches John wrote about would have been over.

What about <u>Romans</u>? The Roman empire experienced civil war 68-70 A.D. after the death of Nero in 68 A.D. The 4 generals of Nero fought each other to be emperor. In two years, the position was occupied by Galba, then Otho, then by Vitellius, and finally by Vespasian in late A.D.

69. Vespasian stabilized his power and reigned from A.D. 69-79. The Roman empire had uprisings and rebellions by different factions all over the empire. Rome was certainly not at peace. But Rome put down the Jewish rebellions and destroyed Jerusalem by A.D. 70.

The whole Roman world: the Romans, the Jews, and the Christians were experiencing terrible horrible things before A.D. 70. The whole world - Jews, Christians, Romans were all experiencing war, death, persecutions. Jesus himself said in Matt.24:21 that there would be "<u>great distress, unequaled from the beginning of the world until now - and never to be equaled again.</u>" (NIV) The time and events that occurred before and up to the destruction of Jerusalem would not be like anything before or after. With all that was happening before A.D. 70, what things could ever compare to the events before A.D. 70 that came after 96 A.D.? What could John have written after 96 A.D. that would matter to the ones who had come through the events 26 years earlier?

You miss the whole fulfillment of what the Bible predicted. The late date of 96 A.D. makes everything irrelevant to those who lived in the first century.

<u>Everything was to come upon "that generation"</u> of Jesus' time. 1 Cor.10:11 says, "These things happened to them (in the O.T.) as examples and were written down as warnings for <u>us</u> (the generation to whom Paul wrote) <u>on whom the fulfillment of the ages has come</u>." (NIV). All the blood of the prophets was to come upon that generation, Matt. 23:35-36. The Great tribulation, the destruction of Jerusalem, the second coming of Jesus, Matt.24:29-30, were to come upon that generation, Matt.24:34. The generation was the time of Jesus. (Jesus was born 4-3 B.C. and died in 30 A.D.) Those of <u>His generation</u>, who heard him in his ministry, would almost all have died by 96A.D. The very few left would have been very old. What could John have written to Jesus' generation that would even matter at such a late date in their life? Even if they were still alive at all? The year A. D. 96 is certainly outside the scope of the fulfillment of the things the Bible talks about. The earlier date certainly fits for the Revelation. John was exiled to Patmos during Nero's reign, 54-68 A.D., specifically during the time of

the persecution of Christians, 64-68 A.D. after the burning of Rome.

It is my belief that God used the next "40 years" after Jesus' death, 30 A.D to 70 A.D., as a time of testing. Just as the children of Israel were tested for 40 years in the wilderness when they came out of Egypt; and just as Jesus was tested by Satan for 40 days and nights; so also, the Jews, who had crucified Jesus, were tested by the Gospel for 40 years, from 30-70 A.D. Matt.24:14 says the gospel was to be taken to the whole world, and then the end would come. (My paraphrase). The end was the destruction of Jerusalem and the end of the Jewish system and Christ's coming back and final judgment on the Jews. God held off the end and judgment, until the gospel was preached to the known biblical world of that time, Col.1:23:

"This is the gospel that you heard and that has been proclaimed to every creature under heaven, and of which I, Paul, have become a servant." (NIV). [See the Appendix D: Gospel to the World].

God is not willing that any perish, but that all come to repentance, 2 Pet.3:9. (My paraphrase). So, God patiently waited for the gospel to be taken to the world before he was willing to bring judgment. What a patient, loving God we have.

Verse 10. In The Spirit On The Day Of The Lord

"On the Lord's Day I was in the Spirit, and I heard behind me a loud voice like a trumpet." (NIV).

"The Lord's Day" is not Sunday in the scripture. It has always referred to the Day of God's reckoning. It is the day of salvation for the righteous believers. It is a day of condemnation for the wicked, Jn.5.:29. Isaiah describes the Lord's Day in many passages. Here are some.

Isaiah 2:12 "the Lord Almighty has a day in store for all the proud and lofty ...17 the arrogance of man will be brought low and the pride of men humbled... 19 men will flee to caves in the rocks and two holes in the ground from the dread of the Lord and the splendor of his majesty when he rises to shake the Earth." (NIV)

Isaiah 13:9-11 "See the day of the Lord is coming, a cruel day with wrath and fierce anger....10 The stars of heaven and their constellations will not show their light. The rising sun will be darkened. The moon will not give its light. 11 I will punish the world for its evil, the wicked for their sins." (NIV)

Many churches point to the passage in Hebrews 10: 25 to say that we should attend church on Sunday "<u>as you see the day</u> approaching". (NIV) Perhaps church attendance should be encouraged, or better fellowship should be encouraged, but that is not the context of the passage nor the intention of the writer. The next two verses speak of judgment and raging fire. The day of the Lord was to be soon upon them, and they were to be vigilant knowing that judgment was coming soon. At the end of the same chapter, he says in verse 37-

In Revelation, John was saying that when he was "in spirit" (caught up in a vision), that the time of the vision, the time he was caught up into was on the <u>Lord's Day</u>, the day of judgment, the Day of the Lord's reckoning.

<u>In the spirit</u> - meaning he was receiving revelation.

When he was in the Spirit, he was seeing the things concerning the judgment. That is what the Lord's Day is about. If he was saying he was in the Spirit on Sunday, that would make no difference to us or to the message of the Revelation. It does not matter what day of the week he received the revelation. It certainly matters when we realize what the revelation was about - The Lord's Day - judgment.

"<u>I heard behind me a loud voice, like a trumpet</u>." (NIV). What should that remind John of? 1`Thess. 4:16 says,

"For the Lord himself will come down from heaven with a <u>loud command</u> with the voice of the archangel, and with the <u>trumpet call</u> of God". (NIV).

John heard a loud voice like a trumpet. Many passages speak of God's voice as being very loud and his voice like a trumpet. "In Spirit"- it was on the "day of the Lord". This is Jesus's revelation, and John is his scribe. John writes it down as Jesus speaks to him. We shall see that the figure walking among the churches is Jesus. John sees and talks to Jesus while he is in the Spirit.

Verse 11. Send It To The Seven Churches

"Which said, write on a scroll what you see and send it to the seven churches: to Ephesus, Smyrna, Pergamum,

Thyatira, Sardis, Philadelphia, and Laodicea." (NIV).

"Write on a scroll". Usually when a prophet wrote on a scroll, we would think of it being a record of his time and pointing to time in the future. Yet, what John is to write down is "soon to take place." Blessings are pronounced on those who read it and take it to heart, for the time was near. What was it that John was to urgently give to the churches? It was a warning of what would soon take place. Believers would understand it, but the world would not. The Book of Revelation serves to let them know that the prophecies of the destruction of Jerusalem, the coming of Jesus, the judgment, and the resurrection and more were soon to come true. The time was upon them. What he was about to write would bring together the completion of the ages, the fulfillment of prophecy, the completion of the mystery, the restoration of all things. It would bring in the Kingdom of God in its fullness and close out the "Old World Order" (the Mosaic system and all related to it).

The Churches had to be warned. Their salvation hung in the balance. They could know that the fulfillment of all things was near. However, the day or the hour of his coming and judgment they could not know. He was to come as a thief. They had to stay ready, be on their guard, and be watchful.

Verse 12. The Voice Speaking To Me

"I turned around to see The Voice that was speaking to me. And when I turned, I saw seven golden lamp stands." (NIV).

"The seven golden lampstands" - are seven separate lampstands. This is not the Jewish Menorah, like in the tabernacle. Each Church was a lampstand. We do not have to interpret here. The scripture plainly tells us in verse 20. "And the Seven lamp stands are the seven churches." Each Church was giving out their light in their city.

Verse 13. One Like The Son Of Man

"and among the lampstands was someone "like a son of man", dressed in a robe reaching down to his feet and with a golden sash around his chest." (NIV).

"Like a son of man" is a phrase that can be found elsewhere in scripture. We compare those scriptures with its usage here.

Dan.3:25 "He said, 'Look, I see four men walking around in the fire, unbound and unharmed, and the fourth looks like a son of the gods (NIV, 1988).

"Like the Son of God" (KJV)

> Dan, 7:13 "In my vision at night I looked, and there before me was one like a son of man, coming with the clouds of Heaven. He approached the Ancient of Days and was led into his presence. He was given authority, glory and Sovereign power. All peoples, nations and men of every language worshiped him. His Dominion is an everlasting Dominion that will not pass away, and his kingdom is one that will never be destroyed. (NIV).

> Matt.24:30 "And then shall appear the sign of the son of man in heaven. and then shall all the tribes of the earth mourn. And they shall see the son of man coming in the clouds Of Heaven with power and great Glory." (NIV).

Jesus is called "the son of man" in multiple scriptures throughout the gospels, for example -

Mk. 2:10-11; Mk.8:31; Acts 7:56; Mk 14:62. This and the rest of the descriptions here let us know this is Jesus.

"Dressed in a robe down to his feet." He was in kingly and priestly attire.

"A golden sash around his chest." The sash symbolizes two things. It symbolizes purity because it is gold. Gold is refined in the fire until all impurities are removed. Though Jesus had no sin, yet he was still refined by trial. Hebrews 2:16-17 says,

"For surely it is not Angels he helps, but Abraham's descendants. For this reason, he had to be made like his brothers in every way in order that he might become a merciful and faithful high priest in service to God, and that he might make atonement for the sins of the people." (NIV).

Verse 14. His Eyes Like Blazing Fire

"His head and hair were white like wool, as white as snow, and his eyes were like blazing fire." (NIV).

"His head and hair were white like wool." (NIV).

In the Bible, gray hair symbolizes the following:

> Prov.16:31 "Gray hair is a crown of splendor. It is attained by a righteous life." (NIV).

Another passage to compare:

> Dan.7:9 "As I looked, thrones were set in place, and the Ancient of Days took his seat. His clothing was white as snow; the hair of his head was white like wool." (NIV).

"His eyes were like blazing fire," (NIV).

Earlier, we said that the faithful witness - who is Christ, 1:5, helped us identify the rider on the white horse in 19:11. Here too, the eyes of blazing fire, 1:14, is also the description of the rider on the white horse, 19:12. Here in chapter one, and there in chapter 19, it is a description of Jesus.

Verse 15. His Voice Like Rushing Waters

"Feet were like bronze glowing in a furnace, and his voice was like the sound of rushing waters." (NIV).

"Feet were like bronze glowing in a furnace." (NIV).

In a description, in Ezekiel chapter one, of what I call "God's war chariot", God rides through the heavens above on an expanse carried by four living awesome creatures. God is described this way:

"Above the expanse over their heads was what looked like a throne of sapphire and high above the throne was a figure like that of a man. I saw that from what appeared to be his waist up he looked like glowing metal, as if full of fire, and that from there down he looked like fire; and brilliant light surrounded him." (NIV). Does it remind you of the passage that says God is a consuming fire, Heb.12:29? He is a figure full of fire.

Here, Jesus' "feet are like bronze glowing in a furnace." (NIV). He may be covered with a white robe reaching down to his feet, but he is a figure of fire, with blazing eyes of fire. How can he be a figure of fire and be covered with a robe down to his feet? Why doesn't the robe burn up? Remember Moses and the burning bush? The bush was burning with fire but the bush was not burned up. In our physical laws on earth, the bush would burn up. But the laws of the spiritual world are not the same. Remember the three friends of Daniel who were thrown into the burning furnace. They walked around in the flames and when they came out not even the smell of smoke was on them. Jesus' body is all aflame, but his robe is still there. The flames are subject to his will. The flames are under his command. Even the angels are flames of fire, Heb.1. Can you imagine being in Jesus' presence? I would fall down like a dead man too. I would not be able to move or breathe. No wonder prophets had to be strengthened.

"His voice was like the sound of rushing waters." (NIV). God's voice is like "rushing waters", Ezek.1:24; 43:2; Jer.10:13; (cf. Ps.29:3-9)

Verse 16. Out Of His Mouth A Sharp Two-edged Sword

"In his right hand he held Seven Stars, and out of his mouth came a sharp double-edged sword. His face was like the sun shining in all its brilliance. (NIV).

"In his right hand he held seven stars." (NIV). The stars are interpreted for us, verse 20: "The seven stars are the angels of the seven churches.", (NIV). Stars are often symbolic of angels. The Dragon's tail swept a third of the stars out of the sky,12:4. A star that had fallen from the sky to the earth was given the key to the shaft of the abyss, 9:1.

Dan.12:3 speaks of stars this way: "Those who are wise will shine like the brightness of the heavens, and those who lead many to righteousness, like the stars for ever and ever." (NIV). Does not Jesus teach that there will not be marrying or giving of marriage in heaven, but that we will be like the angels? Then, we as Christians, will shine like the brightness of the heavens.

"Out of his mouth came a sharp double-edged sword." (NIV). This is a definite reference to Jesus. Heb.4:12 "the word (Jn.1:1) of God is sharper than any two-edged sword". Jesus is the Word, Jn1:1. The Word can pierce the conscience and reveal to us the innermost thoughts of the heart. It is good when used by those who seek God. But it also cuts both ways. To the evil doer it brings consequences and judgment. It either brings righteousness or judgment. It is a double - edged sword. The Word can either save us or condemn us. We cannot refuse to decide- or try to be neutral. We cannot stand in the middle. Jesus is either our choice fully, or we reject him. He is a double-edged sword.

"His face was like the sun." (NIV).

Lk.1:78 speaks of Jesus – "the rising sun will come to us from heaven." (NIV). Prophetically Jesus is the rising sun."

Ps. 84:11 says, "For the Lord God is a sun and a shield," (NIV).

Jesus is the morning star, the sun. "The bright morning star", (NIV). Rev.22:16.

In speaking of the heavenly Jerusalem, Rev.21:23 says, "The city does not need the sun or the moon to shine on it, for the glory of God gives it light, and the Lamb is its lamp." (NIV).

"His face was like the sun." (NIV). Heaven does not need a sun. How brilliant is the light of the sun! We cannot in this life look into its light without blinding ourselves.

1 Tim.6:16 says God lives in "unapproachable light whom no one has seen or can see". Jn.1:18 says, "No one has ever seen God (the Father)". (NIV). Yet, in heaven, with transformed bodies, "we will see his face", Rev.22:4. (NIV). Hooray! Someday we will see him. Praise him who is worthy of all praise and glory. Hooray!

Verse 17. I Fell At His Feet As Though Dead

"When I saw him, I fell at his feet as though dead. Then he placed his right hand on me and said: "Do not be afraid, I am the first and the last." (NIV)

"When I saw him, I fell at his feet as though dead." (NIV). Do we need an explanation for that response? Absolutely not.

To see a burning fiery figure brighter than the sun in front of us whose voice is like rushing waters and a trumpet - help us not to die!

"I am the first and the last" (NIV). (See verse 8)

Verse 18. I Was Dead, Behold I Am Alive For Ever And Ever

I am the living one, I was dead, and behold I am alive forever and ever and I hold the keys of death and Hades. (NIV).

"I am the living one, I was dead, and behold I am alive for ever and ever." (NIV).

Jesus died on the cross. He gave up his Spirit, Matt.27:50. "I lay down my life and I take it up again, No one takes it from me, but I lay it down of my own accord," Jn.10:17-18. (NIV). Death had no hold on Him. He was sinless. Instead, he died in our place. And he is the firstborn from the dead, the first and prototype of all who will die no more. He lives forever and is the first of the new spiritual creation, a new spiritual nation. He created that "new creation" in Himself.

"And I hold the keys to death and Hades" (NIV).

Jesus robbed the strong man (Satan) of his spoils. Satan had power over man by reason of sin to hold man in Hades (the place of disembodied spirits both for the righteous - Abraham's bosom; and the unrighteous - in burning fire.) He could hold men in the state of death, separated from a body. The righteous were spoken of as "in sleep". When Jesus died on the cross for our sins, he took away the power of sin that brought death and held us in death. He took away Satan's power.

At the appointed time, death and Hades were thrown into the lake of fire, Rev.20:14. Before that, the place of the righteous dead (that was in the earthly lower regions) was moved to the heavens when Jesus died. Jesus told the thief on the cross, "this day you shall be with me in paradise," Lk.23:43. (NIV). In 2 Cor.12:2,4 Paul speaks of knowing a man who was caught up into the "third heaven", verse 2, which was "paradise", verse 4. Paradise was moved to heaven. When? Eph. 4:8-10 tells us - Jesus descended into the lower earthly regions and when he ascended, he led captives (those held in the grave by reason of sin) in his train. He rescued the righteous from the grave and took them to heaven.

They (the righteous dead) did not receive their spiritual bodies at that time. They would receive them when he returned to earth (second coming in A.D.70). The already dead in Christ, Christ would bring with him, 1 Thess.4:14. The ones who were still alive when he came in A.D. 70 would not precede those who had "fallen asleep". (NIV). The already dead would be transformed with new spiritual bodies, then those who remained alive would be transformed, in the twinkling of an eye. And so, they would ever be with the Lord. Heb.11:40 says,

"Since God had planned something better for us (Those to whom Hebrews is written, Christians of the generation of Jesus) so that only together with us would they be made perfect." (NIV). The Old Testament saints had not yet inherited perfection (their resurrected spiritual bodies). Only together with the Christians (on Resurrection Day) of the first century, at the appointed time of the resurrection in A.D. 70, when Jesus came would they inherit. Jesus came to those who were also still alive at that time who were "waiting for him," Heb.9:28.

Not all those who were alive were taken. Some would be taken (those who lived under the Mosaic covenant, the "Old World Order"), and some would be left, Matt.24:40. (The ones <u>left</u> were born <u>after</u> Jesus' death and officially under the New Covenant time.) No longer would man be held by Satan in the grave because of sin. Rather, "Blessed are they who die in the Lord from now on," Rev. 14:13. (NIV). Christians die and immediately go to be with the Lord. They are not held in the grave as they were before Jesus'

second coming. The Old Testament describes how the righteous were waiting in the grave. Psalms 49:10-15 describes it very well. The Christian can now cry out, "Where, O death is your victory? Where O death is your sting?" "Death has been swallowed up in victory." 1 Cor.15:54-55. (NIV). After his death, Jesus obtained and held the keys to death and Hades. At judgment, Jesus threw them (death and hades) into the Lake of fire, Rev.20:14. The righteous do not suffer the second death (spiritual death in the lake of fire, Rev.20:14). All men suffer physical death, the first death.

Death was "loosed" under Christ, and death is under his power; but death was not "destroyed" by him (as some translations have inaccurately translated – "destroyed"). Death still serves the purpose of God. All men still experience physical death. (The wicked have no hope of life after death. The righteous who trust in Christ are victorious over physical death and are raised with spiritual bodies. The wicked are thrown into the lake of fire, which is the second death. The righteous are not harmed by the second death). Men do not wait in hades (the place of disembodied spirits, the place which used to be for the dead) anymore. Man is not held in death anymore. He either goes to heaven to be eternally with God or he is judged and thrown into the lake of fire. [See Appendix R: Death].

Verse 19. Write What You Have Seen, Now, And What Is About To Take Place

"Write therefore, what you have seen, what is now and what will take place later." (NIV).

The things John wrote about in Revelation were both "what is now" (what was present in John's time, when he wrote) and "what will take place later", (what would "soon take place", Rev.1:1). The Greek actually says – "mellei genesthai" - the things that "are about to occur.". (See Marshalls' Interlinear Translation).

Verse 20. The Mystery Is

"The mystery of the Seven Stars that you saw in my right hand and of the seven golden candlesticks is this: the Seven Stars are the Angels of the seven churches, and the seven lamp stands are the seven churches. (NIV).

It is interesting that there is an angel with each church. We traditionally also believe from Heb.1:14 that there is an angel to minister to each of us who will inherit salvation. It is a huge thought to realize that God may use myriads of angels to carry out his commands for this world that we never see nor are aware of. The spiritual world is a mystery not revealed to us. We do not have spiritual senses to perceive that world; yet it is all around us.

CHAPTER TWO

Verse 1. To Ephesus

"To the angel of the church in Ephesus write: these are the words of him who holds the Seven Stars in his right hand and walks among the seven golden lamp stands:" (NIV).

"<u>The church in Ephesus</u>" – was established by Paul on his second missionary journey, (52 A.D.), after leaving Corinth, Acts 18:19. Paul left Priscila and Aquila there. It was at Ephesus that Paul found some disciples who had not received the Holy Spirit when they believed, Acts 19:1-2. On Paul's third missionary journey, Paul spent 2-3 years there at Ephesus teaching, Acts 19:8-10. Paul taught at a rented school of Tyrannus. He was so successful there that there was a burning of magic books and repentance, Acts 19:18-20. Silversmiths that made idols of Artemis (the "great mother goddess", many breasted, extremely popular in the ancient world) in the city started an uproar in the city because Paul was putting them out of business, Acts 19:26-41. In 57 A.D., Paul met with the Ephesian elders on the island of Miletus. In 62 A.D., Paul wrote the Ephesian letter commending their faith and love, Eph.1:15. There were many things in the letter that required some more mature understanding of the mystery of God and its coming fulfillment. By the mid 60's A.D., Paul mentions to Timothy, whom he had left at Ephesus, "to command certain men not to teach false doctrines any longer, nor to devote themselves to myths and endless genealogies", 1 Tim.1:3-4. The church had begun to drift doctrinally. Ephesus was one of the churches of the seven in Revelation written to in Asia Minor. Ephesus was one of the greatest seaports, situated at the mouth of the Cayster river on the Aegean Sea.

Verse 2. I Know Your Hard Work

"I know your Deeds, your hard work and your perseverance. I know that you cannot tolerate wicked men, that you have tested those who claim to be apostles, but are not, and have found them false." (NIV).

These are great things to say of the church. And there is more.

Verse 3. You Have Persevered

"You have persevered and have endured hardships for my name, and have not grown weary." (NIV).

Wow! Now that is great! What a great church. Yeah! I want to attend there.

Verse 4. You Have Forsaken Your First Love

"Yet I hold this against you: you have forsaken your first love." (NIV).

I don't understand. How could a church be all these things of verses 2 and 3 and yet had "forsaken their first love"? Read it again of all the great things he had commended them for. How? How? How could he say they had left their first love? Could it mean- "Love for Jesus MUST be first above everything?" Jesus says something in Matt.10:34-39 that is very difficult and challenging:

"Do not suppose that I have come to bring peace to the earth. I did not come to bring peace, but a sword. For I have come to turn a man against his father, a daughter against her mother, a daughter-in-law against her mother-in-law - a man's enemies will be the members of his own household. Anyone who loves his father or mother more than me is not worthy of me; anyone who loves his son or daughter more than me is not worthy of me; and anyone who does not take his cross and follow me is not worthy of me. Whoever finds his life will lose it, and whoever loses his life for my sake will find it." (NIV). (cf. Luke 14:25-27).

There is no other way. We must love the Lord with all of our heart, soul, mind, and strength, more than our own life, more than anything. Activity, doctrinal purity and defense, expelling the wicked, cannot necessarily reveal a true love, an all - encompassing love, that we have for Jesus. We can practice religion and our convictions, but

God searches our heart to find our surrendering, adoring, rejoicing love of HIM. We must treasure our time with him, rejoice to have his presence in our life. He is always in our thoughts, our spiritual talk, our thanksgiving, our goals and our aspirations. We MUST be wholly "in love with Him." Nothing can be more profound, more life-shaking than what we find in these verses - "<u>You have forsaken your first love.</u>" Dear heart, let us all pray to discover how to love Him with that much passion, with that all-inclusive love. I need to read no further to realize I have much re-commitment and deeper commitment to make. I need to repent and reconsider what dying to the old man requires. This is very demanding and an "all in" demand upon my heart. God help us. I am not capable of such commitment without his help.

Verse 5. You Have Fallen

"Remember the height from which you have fallen! repent and do the things you did at first. if you do not repent, I will come to you and remove your lampstand from its place." (NIV).

"<u>Remember the height from which you have fallen</u>" (NIV).

Jesus tells them they had fallen. They had fallen from a great height. Their fervor, their rejoicing, their excitement, their delight in the Lord; they had it, but they fell! Could it be that it started with their savior as an exciting, trusting, rejoicing, thankful relationship; but then it became an obligation, a living out a course of belief and doctrine and moral purity only? God wants a relationship with us, not a duty. The hotter our relationship is with Him, the better. Our hearts should burn within us! Our rejoicing with him should be our way of life. God is exciting. He is amazing. We want to know him better, the riches of Him, the power of Him, Eph.1:17-19. We should want to adore Him and contemplate Him like the Psalmist. He is our delight!

"<u>Remember</u>". How did we start? Did we fill like a big weight had been removed? Was there an unexplainable comfort and peace that came over us. Did we feel so happy? Optimistic? Did we feel renewed and invigorated? Did I feel Jesus was my best friend? Did I feel He would be there for me? Did He make my future seem certain and bright because I had Him? I was so happy to be with Him! I could come to him feeling a fullness of release, coming to him unconditionally. "<u>REMEMBER</u>?" Yet, time can cause those things to fade. Those feelings fade. Christ and his message become commonplace, not special and lifting. My walk with him can become compartmentalized. I can still "serve him"; yet begin to reserve parts of my life for the pleasures of the flesh, and pride. I can hide behind "doing good", seeing myself as a good person, and yet refusing to fully "put to death" the flesh and its desires. I may not even know how to do that by the Spirit. I must be renewed. I must come to him again, fresh and unconditional., humbled and with a surrendered heart.

"<u>Do the things you did at first</u>!" (NIV). Couples "fall out of love". What does the counselor advise? Do what you did at the first. Open the door for her again. Go on dates again. Bring some little special gift home again, just because you like her and wanted too. Gaze into her eyes like a puppy again. Delight in her presence. Laugh again. Hold her hand again. Kiss her. Dress up for her again. Find the special restaurant. "<u>Do the things you did at first</u>". Can you do that for Jesus? Talk about him again. Talk to Him again. Praise him. Adore Him. Worship Him. Discover his Word again. Rejoice with His people again. Share him happily again. Keep GROWING!

2 Pet.1:5-8 "…make every effort to add to your faith goodness; and to goodness, knowledge; and to knowledge, self-control; and to self-control, perseverance; and to perseverance, godliness; and to godliness, brotherly kindness; and to brotherly kindness, love … and if these things are in you, they shall make you so that you shall never fall." (NIV).

Remember! Remember! Remember! Fall in love with Him again!

Some folks may ask me, some folks may say, who is this Jesus, you talk about every day?

He is my savior. He set me free. Now listen while I tell you, what He means to me –

He is my everything. He is my all. He is my everything, both great and small.

He gave his life for me. - made everything new. He is my everything, now how about you? (He is my Everything! By Elvis Presley).

Remember?

Verse 6. The Nicolaitans I Also hate

"But you have this in your favor; you hate the practices of the Nicolaitans, which also I hate." (NIV).

To find who the Nicolatains were, we have to explore the writings of the Apostolic Fathers (typically dated around 80-180- A.D.) We cannot find anything about them elsewhere in the New Testament. At the time of the Apostolic Fathers, as Polycarp, a disciple of John; and Clement, an early bishop of Rome; Hermas, and others, we find the heresies plaguing the church, of them, a main heresy was Gnosticism (Many N.T. Letters address Gnostic issues), and Docetism; and here, what the Nicolatains taught.

This heresy is mentioned here (Ephesus hated the practices of the Nicolatains, 2:6; and to the letters written to Pergamum (which held to the teaching of the Nicolatains, 2:15); and to Thyatira (the so-called prophetess Jezebel was considered part of the Nicolatains). In the letter to Thyatira it mentions those who "…do not hold to her teaching (the prophetess) and have not learned Satan's so called deep secrets." (NIV). Gnostics taught that there was a deeper knowledge (Greek – "gnosis") one must learn, which was necessary in order to know and understand the real nature of God. With this deeper knowledge, in regard to the flesh and spirit, one would realize the true relationship of flesh and spirit. One group of Gnostics became severe ascetics, denying the practice of any fleshly appetite. They were severe in their "buffeting of the flesh", denying one many things that God never forbid. The other group of Gnostics went to the opposite extreme in viewing flesh and spirit. They were what is now called "antinomian" (meaning – "against law"). Basically, they taught the indulgence of the flesh did not matter. Flesh was separate from the spirit. That seems to be what was practiced in Thyatira. Jezebel (the name used figuratively of a wicked woman) had taught and misled Jesus' servants into practicing sexual immorality and eating food sacrificed to idols. (Both were forbidden in the decree of the apostles in Acts 15:28f.) We are not to use our freedom in Christ as a license for sin, Gal. 5:13.

The Nicolatains had their "apostles and prophets". The so-called prophetess of Thyatira was one such prophet. John threatens to cast her on a bed of suffering, 2:22; and to strike her children dead, 12:23. Irenaeus of Asia Minor called them a "branch of the false movement called Gnosis" (iii. ii. i). Tertullian compares them to the satanic sect of the Cainites of which the "false teachers" of the book of Jude are compared and are said to be very disrespectful, slanderous, polluted, and "had taken the way of Cain". Hippolytus describes the Nicolatains as having a gnostic way of teaching. According to him the Nicolatains taught there was no resurrection of the body. Clement of Alexandria tells us of the person of Nicolaus. Some scholars think that the Nicolatains were started by the deacon Nicolaus from Antioch chosen in Acts 6:5. There is no clear proof of that. The heresy did exist through the 2nd century.

Verse 7. The Right To Eat Of The Tree Of Life

"He who has an ear, let him hear what the Spirit says to the churches. To him who overcomes I will give the right to eat from the Tree of Life which is in the paradise of God." (NIV).

"The right to eat from the Tree of Life" (NIV).

Gen.3:22-23 "And the Lord said, the man has become like one of us, knowing good and evil. He must not be allowed to reach out his hand and take also from the tree of life and eat, and live forever. So, the Lord God banished him from the Garden of Eden." (NIV). If man had been healed from the tree of life, he would have lived forever in a lost state. First, God provided the redemption of man and after saving him, in heaven he may eat of the tree of life with healing in its leaves and there will be no more curse – no more death, Rev. 22:2-3.

What a promise! "To eat of the tree of Life". We will die no more. There will be no more sickness. We will be full of life and vigor. Real life. No aches, no pains, no allergies, no tiredness, no hearing problems, no seeing problems, no glasses, no weight problems, no digestion problems, no cancer, no dementia, no shaking, no falling, no frailty, no cripples, no one full of sores, no emaciated – but full, totally filled up and healthy LIFE!

"He that has the Son, has the Life. He that does not have the Son does not have life." 1 Jn.5:12. (NIV).

TO THE CHURCH IN SMYRNA

The church in Smyrna is not mentioned in the book of Acts. It was probably established while Paul was staying in Ephesus, Acts 19. The city of Smyrna is about 35 miles north of Ephesus. It is one of the three of the seven cities of Revelation that were seaports on the Aegean Sea. The modern-day Smyrna is Izmir, Turkey. The name Smyrna means myrrh in Hebrew. That is one of the spices used in the burning of incense, Ex.30:7-8; 2 Chron.13:11. It was used in making the anointing oil in the tabernacle. Myrrh was combined with olive oil to make the sacred anointing oil, Ex.30: 22-25. It was one of the three gifts: gold (a symbol of kingship), frankincense (an incense), and myrrh (an embalming oil- as a symbol of death), given at Jesus' birth, Matt.2:1-12. The church of Smyrna, meaning myrrh, was a church that was crushed by suffering and persecution, thus releasing the sweet smell of the aroma of Christ, 2 Cor.2:14-15. Jesus does not say anything to the church of Smyrna that is criticism. He has nothing "against them." He does not tell them of anything to correct. Jesus writes his letter with only a warning of coming days of persecution. This was the church of "perfection in suffering".

As a note, worthy to mention here – Polycarp (A.D. 69-155), a disciple of John the apostle, was a bishop of Smyrna and lived in Smyrna until bound and burned at the stake for his faith in Christ. His name meant "much fruit" in Greek. Irenaeus, Tertullian, and even Jerome talked about Polycarp. Polycarp was considered as one of three of the main Apostolic Fathers (A.D.80-180). The other two were Clement of Rome and Ignatius of Antioch.

Verse 8. To Smyrna

"To the angel of the church in Smyrna write: these are the words of him who is the first and the last, who died and came to life again." (NIV).

To each of the churches Jesus identifies himself with two of the descriptions of Himself that are made earlier in chapter one. It is almost as if with two or three witnesses something is established. Yes, this is Jesus talking. This is "the first and the last"; "He who died and came to life again."

Verse 9. I Know Your Afflictions And Poverty

"I know your afflictions and your poverty - yet you are rich! I know the slander of those who say they are Jews and are not, but are a synagogue of Satan. (NIV).

"I know your afflictions and your poverty..." (NIV).

Economically they were poor and afflicted. Spiritually they were rich!

"I know the slander of those who say they are Jews..." (NIV).

Jews had become major persecutors of Christians. They rejected Christ and his followers. They slandered them, falsely accused them, twisted their teachings, persecuted them even unto death. The Jews would enlist the help of the Roman rulers to destroy them. The Jews were a "synagogue of Satan." Like in Jn 8:44, They were "of their father the devil."

Verse 10. You Are About To Suffer

"Do not be afraid of what you are about to suffer. I tell you - the devil will put some of you in prison to test you, and you will suffer persecution for 10 days. Be faithful, even to the point of death, and I will give you the Crown of Life." (NIV).

"Do not be afraid of what you are about to suffer". (NIV).

Jesus warns the church they were about to suffer. "Do not be afraid," he says. How Lord? How can I not be afraid? Because, "Greater is he that is in you than he that is in the world," 1 Jn.4:4. "You are from God, and you have overcome them." NIV, I Jn. 4:4, Jn.16:33. You will suffer, some would even die; but the final outcome has already been decided in your favor. You will overcome it. You will be victorious, even over death, 1 Cor.15:55. You will receive "the crown of life," eternal life with the Son. We should know, as Christians, we will suffer in this world. "In me you may have peace. In this world you will have trouble," NIV, Jn.16:33.

"Suffer persecution for 10 days".

The Most Holy Place was 10 x10x10 cubits. It represented holiness and perfection. The ten commandments represented a law of holiness and perfection. "Ten days" may be a symbolic number of days of "suffering for the perfection of their holiness." God made the author

Verse 11. Will Not Be Hurt By The Second Death

"He who has an ear, let him hear what the Spirit says to the churches. He who overcomes will not be hurt at all by the second death." (NIV).

"Overcomes will not be hurt at all by the second death". (NIV).

The one who overcomes is the one who is faithful until death. He cannot be hurt by the second death. The first death is physical death. We all experience that death. "It is appointed for man once to die and then the judgment," Heb.9:27. (NIV). The second death is spiritual death, the final judgment of the wicked, which is to be thrown into the lake of fire, Rev.20:14-15.

TO THE CHURCH IN PERGAMUM

Pergamum was the most Northern city of the seven churches in Revelation. It was on a high mesa, over 1000 ft high, overlooking the Aegean Sea. Three of the seven cities were seaports. Most northern was Pergamum, then Smyrna, and then Ephesus. The four that lay inland from them were first Thyatira, the 2nd most northern of the seven, then Sardis, Philadelphia, and last Laodicea. Pergamon had an outdoor theater below the mesa in which almost 10,000 attended each night. Pergamum came to prominence during the time of the Greek empire after the death of Alexander the Great in 323 B.C. Its greatness rivaled Alexandria in Egypt. It had the 2nd largest library in the world, next to Alexandria. It was a great trade route. During the Roman rule, it was the major political city in the area.

The church at Pergamum and its founding is not mentioned in the book of Acts. Acts only mentions that Paul passed through the region of Mysia, where Pergamum is located, on his second missionary journey. The most we can learn of the church there is here in Revelation.

Verse 12. To Pergamum

"To the angel of the church in Pergamum write: these are the words of him who has the sharp double-edged sword." (NIV).

Him who has the sharp double-edged sword." (NIV).

Jesus is well known to be the one with the sharp two-edged sword that proceeds out of his mouth: Rev.1:16; 19:15. The sword is double-edged. It cuts both ways. (See Rev. 1:16 comments).

Verse 13. Where Satan Has His Throne

"I know where you live- where Satan has his throne; yet you remain true to my name. You did not renounce your faith in me, even in the days of Antipas, my faithful witness, who was put to death in your city - where Satan lives." (NIV).

"Where Satan has his throne ...where Satan lives." (NIV). Could these statements be literal? I don't really know. But there is much reason to believe they could be. Why? In Daniel 10:21 Gabriel mentions to Daniel- "Michael, your prince". Daniel 12:1 mentions "Michael, the great prince, who protects your people." Evidently, Michael, the great prince, the archangel watched over Daniel's people Israel. Perhaps Michael's main location was in Jerusalem. Different angels had different assignments over cities and kingdoms, peoples and kings.

Satan was a fallen angel, a created being. He was not God. He could not be everywhere. But I believe he tried to locate himself in the world where he could do the most damage. In the beginning, he was in the Garden of Eden and tempted the first man. One hundred years after the flood, he may have been in Shinar (later called Babylon), Gen.11:2; and encouraged the idolatrous Tower of Babel and all the idolatrous worship from there. During that time idolatry spread by the building of ziggurats, (other pyramid type towers) all over the world. Each ziggurat had idolatrous temples of worship at their tops, the worship of the gods of the stars. These ziggurats (or step pyramids) were by the dozens in Mesopotamia, hundreds in China, the pyramids of the Incas in Peru, the Mayan Pyramids in Mexico, dozens in North America, all worshiped the gods in the stars at the tops of their pyramids. Later, I believe Satan may have moved his main place of residence and influence to Tyre, "a marketplace of the nations", Isa.23:3, which spread idolatry everywhere, Isa. 23:17.

Here, in Revelation, within the Roman empire, Satan had his throne at Pergamum. Why? It was strategic for his purposes. It was the political center of the whole region for the Roman Empire. The city had three idolatrous temples: one dedicated to the worship of the Roman emperor (Pergamum was the capital of Caesar worship), another for the goddess Athena, and the Great Altar of Zeus, the king of the Greek gods. It was the center for the worship of Dionysus and many Greek gods. Rick Renner wrote a book about Pergamum called "A Light in the Darkness". In it he tells of a healing center called Asklepion, built in honor of Asklepios, the Greek serpent god. In the first century, it was like a cross between a hospital and a health spa. People came there to be healed, even emperors. The center had priests of the god. Patients that entered drank a sedative and stayed in dormitories while non-poisonous snakes crawled over them. It was a dark place indeed. People believed the snakes carried the healing power of Asklepios.

Whether it was literally the base of operation for Satan, or so dark a city that Jesus called it the "place of Satan's throne" or maybe was even both, I don't know. But I do know, because Jesus called it "Satan's throne", it was a very tough place to be.

"The days of Antipas, my faithful martyr" (NIV) –

Again, in Renner's book, he tells us that Antipas was a bishop of Pergamum, ordained by the apostle John. In the book he says, "He (Antipas) had cast out so many demons that the demons had been complaining to the pagans, saying, you've got to do something about this Antipas". The pagan priests went to the Roman governor and complained. The governor ordered that Antipas offer a sacrifice to the statue of the Roman emperor and declare that the emperor was "lord and god". Of course, Antipas refused. Antipas was sentenced to death on the Altar of Zeus.

Verse 14. Things against You

"Nevertheless, I have a few things against you: you have people there who hold to the teaching of Balaam, who taught Balak to entice the Israelites to sin by eating food sacrificed to idols and by committing sexual immorality." (NIV).

Balaam was a prophet of God in Numbers 22. Balak, the king of Moab, summoned Balaam and asked him to curse Israel. Balaam knew as God's prophet that he could not just curse Israel. He knew he could only say what God had commanded, Num.22:18. Balaam informed Balak that he could only "speak what God had put in his mouth", Num.22:38; 23:12,26; 24:13. However, Balaam's path was a reckless one, Num.22:32. In Numbers 25:1-3, the men of Israel indulged in sexual immorality with the Moabite women. The Moabite women invited the men to sacrifice to their gods. So, Israel joined in the worship of the Baal of Peor. According to Rev.2:14, Balaam taught Balak to entice the Israelites to commit sexual immorality. Balaam could not speak any words, as a prophet, that God had not given him to speak, but he went around it and taught Balak how to seduce Israel to compromise their commitment to God. The church of Pergamum had those within it who encouraged and taught others to compromise their walk with God: to commit sexual immorality and eat food sacrificed to idols. Both actions were probably connected with the idolatrous temples and idol worship that were very much a part of the culture and people in Pergamum. Christians in Pergamum, were living in a city that was full of opportunity and influence that would entice them to first dabble in such behavior and then to be fully drawn into such corruption. Prov.4:14-15 says,

Do not set foot on the path of the wicked or walk in the way of evil men. Avoid it. Do not travel on it. Turn from it and go on your way." "Can a man scoop fire into his lap without his clothes being burned?" Prov.6:27-28. (NIV). The Christians were living in a city of filth and evil opportunity everywhere.

Verse 15. Those Who Hold To The Teaching Of The Nicolaitans

"Likewise you have those who hold to the teaching of the Nicolaitans." (NIV).

(See under Nicolaitans, 2:6).

Verse 16. Repent

"Repent therefore! otherwise, I will soon come to you and we'll fight against them with the sword of my mouth." (NIV).

"Repent". They had a lot to repent of, a lot of the flesh to set aside. That is the ONLY choice. Repent! Turn from it. Completely turn from it and don't look back. Make an absolute decision and determination. You must make up your mind totally – with your whole heart, emotions, affections, will, allegiances. Leave no room for the flesh. Delightfully in God who is our life, our hope and our rejoicing!

"I will *soon come* to you". (NIV). All through the Revelation – we see the imminence, closeness of Jesus' coming for the second time. This was not an invisible coming in judgment -see Chapter 1:7.

"Fight against them with the sword of my mouth" (NIV). We really, really don't want that! "With the sword of His mouth he strikes down the nations, and his robe is dripping with blood, Rev.19:13,15. He is the King of kings and Lord of lords. He never loses. For those who choose to follow sin, he has no mercy. Sober up. Wake up sinner. If you are rejecting Him; choose Him and live.

Verse 17. The Hidden Manna And The White Stone

"He who has an ear let him hear what the spirit says to the churches. To him who overcomes I will give some of the Hidden manna, I will also give him a white stone with a new name written on it, known only to him who receives it." (NIV).

"Him who overcomes" (NIV) – is he who is faithful until death.

"Hidden manna" (NIV) – why hidden? Perhaps hidden to us because it is in the world of the unseen, in the spirit world. The manna was not the bread that could be seen that physically came down in the time of Moses. The true bread was Christ, a spiritual bread, the bread of life, that we partake of by faith. Jn.6:32-33 says:

"I tell you the truth, it is not Moses who has given you the bread from heaven, but it is my Father who gives you the true bread from heaven. For the bread of God is he who comes down from heaven and gives life to the world." NIV.

"a white stone", known only to him who receives it." (NIV).

"white"- a color that stands for many good things -purity, innocence, victory.

Historically, in ancient Greece, jury members would cast a white stone for acquittal and a black stone to condemn.

"With a new name written on it", (NIV). On the breastplate of the high priest – there were 12 stones, each stone had the name of the tribe, Ex.39:10-14. The high priest carried the names of God's people into the presence of God. Perhaps, the stone represents our being justified, declared innocent before God, and therefore we can be carried into his presence.

"Known only to him who receives it." (NIV). The heavenly Jerusalem got a new name -Hephzibah, "my delight is in her" of Isaiah 62:4. But there, it is talking about the name for the new Jerusalem. Here, it is a new name given to each who "overcomes". It is known only to him who receives it. We are given a new name, a special individual name by God himself. I will not carry the name I had on earth. This will be God's name for me. Think of it. "The Lion of the tribe of Judah". "The Comforter". The "Son of Consolation". "The Great Encourager." – No. Those names belong to someone else. But it will be a special name because as God's redeemed son, you and I will be special to him and he will honor you and me with our own special name. It will only be known to us – meaning only we will have that name. It will belong to no one else. It will belong only to the individual to whom it is given.

It is interesting that the rider on the white horse has a name written on him "that no one knows but he himself," Rev.19:12. (NIV). It is also interesting that he tells us his name in verse 13. "His name is the Word of God" (NIV). Then, how is it that he could have a name no one knew but he himself; and then he tells everyone that his name is the "Word of God"? It must be that no one knew that name or HAD that name but him. No one else will be known by that name. It will be known only to him. It was only FOR him. It is a special name that only he has. So also, it will be for us – We will have our own special name known only to us. No one else will have that name. Why? Because each name is very significant. It has meaning. It always did in the Old Testament. The name they got at birth meant something special about who they were or what they would become. There will not be thousands of Terrys, or Loras, or Karens, or Bobs, etc. Only you will carry that special name, a name given by God. And, it will mean something special about you.

TO THE CHURCH IN THYATIRA

The city of Thyatira is now the modern city of Akhisar (white castle) in Turkey. It is about 50 miles from the Aegean Sea.

Thyatira was the home of Lydia, a dealer of purple cloth, Acts16:14. She opened her heart to Paul's message and she and her household were baptized. Paul and his companions stayed in her house. Inscriptions and coins from brief explorations of the archaeological site of Thyatira reveal that gods as Zeus, Artemis, Apollo, Demeter and Athena were worshiped there. Several trade guilds for wool, linen, baking, leather, bronze, pottery and dyes existed there. The purple dye used there was made from the madder root. The low cost and high volume of the dyed garments made it very profitable.

The church of Thyatira of Revelation was the working, loving, faithful church that TOLERATED that woman Jezebel to mislead God's servants into sexual immorality.

Verse 18. To Thyatira

"To the angel of the church in Thyatira write: these are the words of the son of God, whose eyes are like blazing fire and whose feet are like burnished bronze." (NIV).

These are the words of the Son of God" (NIV) – good! We don't have to guess who he is. The Spirit tells you who he is whose eyes are blazing like fire and whose feet are like burnished bronze. These descriptions found in chapter one, are identified here as of - the Son of God. He is the rider on the white horse in 19:12. His identity in both chapter 1 and 19 is clear. Isn't the Spirit great how he lets you know who Jesus is in those two chapters? He helps us, doesn't he? He lets you know. He helps you understand- here a little and there a little, comparing spiritual words with spiritual things. The Spirit does work with our Spirit to help us understand his word. (See Keys to understanding Revelation- the indwelling Spirit).

Verse 19. Now Doing More

"I know your Deeds. Your Love, and faith, your service and perseverance, and that you are now doing more than you did at first." (NIV).

That is a whole lot – "your deeds, faith, love, service, perseverance."

"You are doing more than you did at first." (NIV). This relationship is getting better and better. It is growing. How rich, how promising and fulfilling!

Verse 20. You Tolerate That Woman Jezebel

"Nevertheless, I have this against you: you tolerate that woman Jezebel who calls herself a prophetess. By her teaching she misleads my servants into sexual immorality and the eating of food sacrificed to idols." (NIV)

We can be doing many "good things" and yet "tolerate evil", and look past it, overlook it, avoid dealing with it. We avoid what is unpleasant to us. God is not pleased with that. We must be able to "hate evil" and expose it as well as "love what is good." The flesh must be dealt with, even in the church as a group.

"You tolerate that woman Jezebel who misleads my servants into sexual immorality." (NIV). (See about Jezebel under Nicolaitans in 2:6).

"Jezebel" – was the daughter of Ethbaal, king of the Sidonians. Ahab, king of Israel, married Jezebel, and began to serve Baal and worship him, 1 Ki.16:31. The influence of the Sidonians and Tyre is seen in Isa. 23. There, the cities are called the marketplace of the nations, 23:3. Her trade was seen as a prostitute for hire (idolatry) that she did it with all kingdoms on the face of the earth, 23:17. Jezebel was from there. She was a very wicked queen that led Ahab into idolatrous worship. Ahab thought it trivial to commit the sins of Jeroboam (who led Israel into idolatry 1 Ki.14: 9,16); but he also married the evil Jezebel and made her queen and followed her. To be called "a Jezebel" is awful. That means you are really, really evil.

Isn't there a connection here between verse 14 and verse 20? Balaam taught people to compromise and to commit sexual immorality and eat food sacrificed to idols. This Jezebel does too. What was happening in Pergamum was also happening in Thyatira.

Is there a lesson here for us? At first, we may feel distant from their situation. We don't eat food sacrificed to idols. We are not tempted by temple prostitutes. That was a different world. But, was it? Don't we have Jezebels who are bringing sin into the church today?

Let's see. Our application of this verse could be very real and compelling. Ask - "How can a church like Thyatira tolerate sexual immorality? Or even more, the church of Corinth (1 Cor. 5) tolerate sexual immorality and be "<u>proud of it</u>",1 Cor. 5:2? 1 Cor.5:1-2 says –

"It is actually reported that there is sexual immorality among you, and of a kind that does not occur even among pagans: A man has his father's wife. <u>And you are proud!</u> Shouldn't you be rather filled with grief and have <u>put out of your fellowship</u> the man who did this?" (NIV).

Now compare it to what we are doing in churches today. We are proud that we invite homosexuals into our fellowships. We think that we can win them over by our niceness. We do not criticize what they do. We do not call it sin. We just invite them to "come to Jesus." "Jesus loves everyone just as they are." "He is loving and accepting." "He is not judgmental." Really? This is SHAMEFUL! What a milk toast adulterated invite that is to come to Christ. Where is repentance? Where is the dying to the old man? We offer them fellowship in Jesus without repentance of sin. We are so proud of being loving and gentle, not condemning – that we insult the blood of Christ that was shed for our sins. We make sin of no offense, no issue at all. Everyone is welcome to join - just as they are- without repentance and recognition of their sin. If we can be saved without Christ who died for our <u>SIN</u> and without repentance, then Christ died for nothing. Is everyone saved in their sin?" Absolutely NOT! Sin brings death. If we do not teach that we <u>too</u> must die to sin, die to the old man and be raised with Christ we are wrong! Wrong! Wrong! The gospel we peddle is no gospel at all today. We are just like Thyatira – LOST! We invite the world to be a part of our midst without repenting of sin and we are proud of it. We invite the homosexuals in as they are. We ignore the many men and women in college who are just living together in sin and yet are an active part of our church youth. We ignore the many sins rampant in our churches because we don't want to offend anyone or cause them to leave our midst. We are proud of our numbers, our popularity, our charisma as a church – but not proud of Jesus and being his holy people.

We try to understand why the churches were like they were; how they got there; and apply what we learn to our own experience. Suffice it to say

We have not condemned sin in its many forms in our day. The churches have hushed. They have bought into peddling a very soft "gospel" that claims to be more loving and non-judgmental. We do not speak out against sin but proclaim love, love, love. Such a gospel is not love at all, except love of self. We agree with those in the world who redefine words to deceive. We call what is good – evil, and what is evil as good. We have new ways of talking so we are not "offensive" to anyone. We are Biblically illiterate and call everything according to our own worldly standards and judgments. We are not trained in righteousness and it shows. We are not lights in the world. We are dark blemishes.

Fellowship is for believers. We are not supposed to be friends of the world, neither love the things in the world. We do not persuade men to repent and be converted but rather are loving and accepting them in their sin. We should preach the gospel – the good news that they can be delivered FROM sin, not IN their sin. If they can be accepted IN their sin, then there is no consequence for our sin and Christ died for nothing. We are brought into the fellowship of BELIEVERS – those who have died to sin and surrendered to Christ. Why and how can churches get so mixed up and get it all backwards? Is it because we have fellowships with those who have never repented? Are we a religious social club? Do we make it up for ourselves as we go? Who is leading these so-called churches?

Verse 21. I Have Giver Her Time To Repent

"I have given her time to repent of her immorality, but she is unwilling." (NIV).

"I have given her time to repent"

God is long suffering. "He is patient with you; not wanting anyone to perish, but everyone to come to repentance," 2 Pet3:9. (NIV). He was long suffering in the days of Noah, even when "every inclination of the hearts of men were only evil all the time, Gen.6:5. (NIV). Yet, God still waited for almost 100 years, (Gen.5:32; 7:6) to bring judgment.

Verse 22. A Bed Of Suffering

"So I will cast her on a bed of suffering, and I will make those who commit adultery with her suffer intensely, <u>unless they repent</u> of her ways." (NIV).

"<u>I will make those who commit adultery with her suffer intensely</u>." (NIV).

What? Jesus is talking and says, "I will make those who commit adultery with her <u>suffer intensely – unless they repent</u> of her ways. Can that be true?

Would a loving, merciful God cause people to <u>suffer intensely</u>? For their sin? Surely, we cannot believe God would do that. Or should we? Weren't they warned? Weren't they given time to repent? Didn't they know what they were doing was evil? If they rejected here what Jesus said, if they rejected the Son – if they would not repent – there remains no more sacrifice for sin. Heb. 10:26-27 says,

"If we deliberately keep on sinning after we have received a knowledge of the truth, no sacrifice for sin is left, but only a fearful expectation of judgment and of raging fire that will consume the enemies of God." (NIV).

1 Thess.4:3-8 is very revealing to us here. We are to control our own body in honor and holiness, not in passionate lust. And anyone who rejects that warning rejects the command of God who gives us his Holy Spirit. The Spirit lives in Christians. We should not defile his temple.

"If we <u>deliberately keep on sinning</u> after we have received the knowledge of the truth, <u>no sacrifice for sin is left</u>, but only a fearful expectation of judgment and of raging fire that will consume the enemies of God." (NIV). Dear Heart - without the sacrifice of Jesus, there will be no mercy in judgment. We do not want to face God who is a consuming fire in that way. God help us! – we must repent. Turn back to God.

Verse 23. Repay You According To Your Deeds

"I will strike her children dead. Then all the churches will know that I am he who searches hearts and minds, and I will repay each of you according to your deeds." (NIV).

"Then all the churches will know that I am he who searches hearts and minds" (NIV).

God will not be ignored. He will make himself known as He did in the 10 lessons (plagues) he sent Egypt. He makes himself known regardless of whether we have acknowledged him or not. In the Gog and Magog battle, Rev.20:7, God in that battle, Ezekial 38-39, says three different times in the text – "I will show my greatness and my holiness, and I will make myself known in the sight of many nations," Ezek.38:23. Someday at the name of Jesus "Every knee would bow, in heaven and on earth and under the earth, and every tongue confess that Jesus is Lord," Phil.2:10. (NIV).

Here, Jesus would "strike her children dead". Did God strike the children dead that came from such sinful adultery with her. Would it be like the child that was born and who died when David committed adultery with Bathsheba? God refused to let the child live. Would the churches experience the same fate because of their unholy sexual unions? They would certainly know then that Jesus searches hearts and minds, wouldn't they?

Verse 24. Satan's So-called Deep Secrets

"Now I say to the rest of you in Thyatira, to you who do not hold to her teaching and have not learned Satan's so-called deep secrets (I will not impose any other burden on you):" (NIV).

"Satan's so-called deep secrets." (NIV).

I believe this is an allusion to the teachings of the Gnostics (of which the Nicolaitans and this Jezebel were a sect). They believed that one must have a special, deeper knowledge of the spiritual world and God. The "deep things of God" are the secret counsels of his mind, God's secret wisdom, some of which (in regard to the mystery of his will) he made known at the proper time revealing it by his Spirit, 1 Cor.2:6-10. Satan's so-called deep secrets are, for the teaching of the Gnostic, supposed to reveal deeper truths about God's working. That so called deeper knowledge was a corruption of what was true - a deception, a lie. Somehow, it was connected to the practice of sexual immorality and food sacrificed to idols. What a perversion. (Understanding more about such a perversion, one might study about

Gnosticism and its influence in the first and second century).

Verse 25. Hold On To What You Have

"Only hold on to what you have until I come." (NIV).

Again, in this verse, we are reminded that Jesus was <u>coming soon</u>. "Only hold on to what you have (that is good) <u>until I come</u>."

Jesus coming was to visually come again within his "that generation" Mt.23:36; 24:34. (see Appendix – "the Coming of Jesus").

Verse 26. Authority Over the Nations

"To him who overcomes and does my will to the end, I will give authority over the nations," (NIV).

<u>"Does my will to the end"</u> (NIV).

We must be faithful "to the end." We must finish the race of life set before us. We cannot quit, or God will not be pleased with us.

<u>"Authority (power) over the nations"</u> (NIV). We reign with Christ in this life through righteousness, Rom.5:17,21. That reign crosses all national boundaries and cannot be halted. Jesus can become the savior and Lord of anyone anywhere. His kingdom was to break in pieces and consume (overrun) all other kingdoms. His kingdom cannot be stopped from generation to generation and of his kingdom there is no end, Dan.2:44.

Verse 27. Dash Them To Pieces Like Pottery

"He will rule them with an iron scepter; he will dash them to pieces like pottery; just as I have received Authority from my father." (NIV).

<u>"He will rule them with an iron scepter; he will dash them to pieces like pottery."</u>(NIV).

The scepter of Christ is first prophesied in Jacob's prophecy in Gen.49:10.

Again, it is in the prophecy of Ps.2:9. Verse 6 tells us "I have installed my king on Zion, my holy hill." When he "rules the nations with an iron scepter" (NIV), of course - it is when Jesus was installed as king at the right hand of God in the heavens. Then, in the Psalms, the writer says in verse 10, "Therefore, you kings, be wise; be warned, you rulers of the earth. Serve the Lord with fear and rejoice with trembling. Kiss the Son; lest he be angry." (NIV). God put Jesus on the throne.

Just as Jesus received power over the nations from his Father in heaven, so Jesus promised here – he would give those who were faithful unto the end "power over the nations."

Verse 28. Give Him The Morning Star

"I will also give him the Morning Star." (NIV).

Jesus says he is the bright Morning star, Rev.22:16. The morning star brings the dawn and the day. Jesus has brought the Eternal day. That is in contrast to those in darkness and hell where there was deep darkness and NO light. In the New Jerusalem, in heaven, there is no more night, Rev.22:5. There is no sun, for God is its light, and the Son its lamp, Rev. 22:5. The day speaks of the resurrection that occurred in 70 A.D. In the Old Testament, in Ps. 49:10-11, the foolish and senseless – their tombs would be their homes for ever. Why? They have no life after death. "He that has the Son has life. He that does not have the Son does not have life," 1 Jn. 5:12 (NIV). There is no live spiritual seed, no rebirth for the wicked. They die with no hope. But, in Ps. 49:14-15, of the righteous \it says – "The upright will rule over them in the morning. Their forms (the wicked, T.S.) will decay in the grave. But God will redeem my life from the grave." (NIV). See the thought – in the morning (when the day comes) the writer would come out of the grave, his resurrection. Jesus said – "I am the resurrection and the life: he that believeth in me, though he were dead, yet shall he live." Jn.11:25 (NIV). Jesus was saying to the ones faithful unto the end – I will raise you up from the grave and give you Eternal day, everlasting life.

Peter says something very beautiful in regard to this. Let's read him:

"And we have the words of the prophets made more certain, and you will do well to pay attention to it, as to a light shining in a dark place, until the day dawns and the morning star rises in your hearts." (NIV).

The words of the prophets is like a light shining in a dark place (this world lives in darkness, Jn1:4) and we should pay attention to the prophets, hold their teachings close to our hearts until "the day dawns (the resurrection) and the morning star (Jesus) rises in our hearts (gives us life again, starts life beating again).

Verse 29. Let Him Hear

"He who has an ear, let him hear what the Spirit says to the churches." (NIV).

Are you listening? Do you hear what the Spirit is saying?

CHAPTER THREE

The church of Sardis was 32 miles from Pergamos and 27 miles from Philadelphia. It was one of the seven churches that was inland from the Aegean coast. It had the Pactolus River that was water for the area. Gold was found near its banks. The city was noted for its fruits, wool and a temple dedicated to the goddess Cybele. An earthquake had destroyed the city in 17 A.D. but the city was rebuilt. The first silver and gold coins were made in Sardis. They were first made in about 610-560B.C. by king Alyattes, the father of Croesus, their most notable king. Sardis was the ancient capital of the Kingdom of Lydia (about 1200 – 546B.C.) It was a city that sat on a hill, about 1500 feet above the valley floor, surrounded by steep cliffs with only one narrow way of approach from the south. The worship of Cybele dated back to the time of kings Alyattes and Croesus in the 7th and 6th century B.C. She was a mother goddess, often accompanied by lions. The idol Artemis also had a sanctuary at Sardis.

The history of the establishment of the church is not known in scripture. It is assumed that it may have been established during Paul's stay in Ephesus in Acts 19. We know little of the church but what is mentioned here.

Verse 1. To Sardis, You Are Dead

"To the angel of the church in Sardis write: these are the words of him who holds the seven Spirits of God and the seven Stars. I know your Deeds; you have a reputation of being alive, but you are dead." (NIV)

"Who holds the seven spirits of God and the seven stars." (NIV).

Of course, this description is referring to Jesus in 1:12-20.

The <u>seven spirits of God</u> are mentioned in 1:4; and 5:6 which says, "Then I saw a Lamb, looking as if it had been slain, standing in the center of the throne...He had seven horns and seven eyes, which are the seven spirits of God sent out into all the earth."

Rev.1:20 tells us - "the <u>seven stars</u> are the angels of the seven churches." NIV.

"<u>You have a reputation of being alive, but you are dead</u>" (NIV).

I do not know what was historically happening in this church. However, I can think of some things that seem to fit this description very well. Paul, in Gal. 3:2-5 says:

"I would like to learn just one thing from you: Did you receive the Spirit by observing law, or by believing what you heard? Are you so foolish? After beginning with the Spirit, are you now trying to attain your goal by human effort? Have you suffered so much for nothing- if it really was for nothing? Does God give you his Spirit and work miracles among you because you observe the law, or because you believe what you heard?" (NIV)

The application of Paul's words here are very real. Many church members start out believing they are saved by God's grace and faith in Jesus. But how they start out, they soon change. They set up rules taught by men. They change the grace of God for salvation into law keeping - "you must observe the Sabbath." "You can't eat flesh." "We must meet every first day of the week." "We must take the Lord's supper every first day of the week." "You must sing and give on the first day of the week." "We must go to confession." There is no end to the requirements we insist on that we must keep in order to be "right with God." "You must be a member of the right church, the only church, the New Testament church." That means their denomination. According to the denominations, "their brand is the right church, the true church." "They all believe they are the right church, the closest church, and many believe the "only true church".

The churches have their lists and practices of the "requirements" of God. The denominations are all practicing division, demanding that their members conform to their church rules and often that they must sign their list of doctrinal beliefs in order to participate in a meaningful way in their church. They are following the flesh (pride and arrogance) in demanding conformity to them instead of encouraging everyone's allegiance to following the Spirit. They divide believers so conveniently after discovering differences in belief over myriads of different things that don't really matter. They are not open to disagreement and discussion. The flesh and pride take over. People get embarrassed, offended, and angry, even bitter and part ways. They silence and censure those who disagree with them. They are followers of men. They are like the Corinthians who followed after Cephas, Apollos, or others, 1 Cor. 1:10-12. The denominations were created following John Huss, John Wesley, John Calvin, Alexander Campbell, Martin Luther, and many others. The churches have been divided into Lutherans, Baptists, Presbyterians, Methodist, Pentecostals, and a host more, well over 300 denominations. Each of those have divided again multiple times. For example, there are First, Second, and Third Baptists, Northern Baptists and Southern Baptists, Missionary Baptists and so forth. Of the Churches of Christ, they have divided into Disciples of Christ and the Christian Church; and each of those have divided over instrumental music, "one cup and one loafers, over church kitchens, and at least 30 different things. Denominations are divided and continue to divide. We as Christians are still following the flesh and God is not pleased with us. We keep the body divided. We do not understand what unity of the Spirit is nor do we know how to practice it.

What goes along with this is "legal requirements of law-keeping", "church law", and a dependence on self to feel right before God. There are churches that teach that the Holy Spirit only works representatively through his word. They search the scriptures to understand them, but only by their own human effort. They have piles of commentaries, appeal to scholars, and attempt to become authorities in the Word, "experts of the Law". They deny what the Indwelling Holy Spirit was given for - to work in them and teach them. They may have begun with the Spirit but now depend upon the flesh to advance in the things of God.

True learning is a spiritual process of the Spirit working with our spirit, teaching us line upon line, comparing spiritual truths with spiritual words. We pray for understanding. We seek the

Spirit's guidance in understanding the Word. The indwelling Spirit makes the Word a living word. It is understood only with His spiritual help. It cannot be understood only by human effort. "The person without the Spirit does not accept the things that come from the Spirit, ... they are discerned only through the Spirit, 1 Cor. 2:14. (NIV).

Legalists are people who start out trusting God, but they turn to rules of men and New Testament instructions are turned into law keeping and a "law of commandments". They make Christ's law of faith no different than the Old Testament "law of commandments contained in ordinances". They are using their own human effort to grow and be acceptable to God. They offer up their own "human righteousness" which is as filthy rags. They have not learned how to "walk with the Spirit," and depend on the Spirit. Once, they were alive, but now spiritually they are dead. Their works give the impression they are alive, but they are spiritually dead. We cannot leave the Spirit of God out of our life or there is no spiritual life. The Spirit is not a book. He makes the book alive and active. We must pray for enlightenment to understand him better, Eph.1.

Verse 2. Not Found Your Deeds Complete

"Wake up, strengthen what remains and is about to die, for I have not found your deeds complete in the sight of my God." (NIV),

"Wake up, strengthen what remains and is about to die." (NIV)

What was left? What remained? I do not know. Not much when you abandon the Spirit and go on your own.

"I have not found your deeds complete" (NIV).

Oh the grace- of finishing grace, completing what you started. Many start the Christian life and never finish. They fall away. They lose interest. Life changes. They move on to something new, something different. Paul wrote in 1 Cor.9:24-27,

"Do you not know that in a race all the runners run, but only one gets the prize? Run in such a way as to get the prize. Everyone who competes in the games goes into strict training. They do it to get a crown that will not last; but we do it to get a crown that will last forever. Therefore, I do not run like a man running aimlessly; I do not fight like a man beating the air. No, I beat my body and make it my slave so that after I have preached to others, I myself will not be disqualified for the prize." (NIV).

I knew some churches in California in years past who were fully stirred by controversy. Many congregations met together in a meeting to warn the local churches of what they believed to be a heresy spreading in the brotherhood from the East coast. Hundreds of people showed up. At the same time, another congregation in the area had advertised a seminar on how to equip yourself in teaching people to become new Christians. Only a handful showed up at that church. The churches demonstrated they could get excited about controversy but not about spreading the gospel. Their excitement about becoming a new Christian had died down. Their activity had slowed to a slow drudgery. It took controversy, conflict, finding the villains to get them off their benches. How sad.

Verse 3. Repent! Wake Up

"Remember therefore, what you have received and heard; obey it and repent. But if you do not wake up, I will come like a thief, and you will not know at what time I will come to you." (NIV).

"Remember therefore" - God's words are unchanging – remember and repent.

Have you ever realized that we often repeat a sin that we thought we had defeated? I used to think that you overcome a sin, that you learn how to beat it, get it out of your life and then move on to a better man. I have done that with having a temper. I would get angry quickly. I read the scriptures on anger (especially in Proverbs), thought it through, applied boundaries to myself, laid out a new way of thinking and acting – and thought I had defeated the problem. Yeah, I beat it. Lo and behold, a year later- I would catch myself repeating the anger I thought I had defeated. I finally had to learn – you don't just defeat sin and move on. As long as we are in the flesh, the temptation to repeat the sin is there. The flesh never gives up. That is when you realize, you have to walk with the Lord every day and stay close to the Lord to keep sin at bay. Don't let the flesh get a foothold.

Faithfulness is not about something accomplished. It is about staying close to the Lord; walking with the Spirit every day. It is about not relying on self but trusting and dependence on God all the time.

"<u>What you have received and heard; obey it and repent.</u>" (NIV).

I can't help but think here – If we could only live up to what we already know. We fall short of even that; yet, there is still more growing and learning to do. Well, we cannot do it "as we should" without the Spirit living in us and enabling us.

"<u>I will come like a thief, and you will not know at what time I will come to you.</u>" (NIV).

Jesus had taught his generation at many times and in many ways that He would come back in their lifetime. (See Appendix A: "The Coming of Jesus"). Even though they knew he was coming back within the lifetime of that generation, they did not know the day nor the hour. Neither did the Son of man while on earth, Matt.24:36. They were told to keep watch, verse 42, be ready, verse 44.

Concerning Jesus coming like a thief, Paul said the day of his coming would come upon them suddenly, 1 Thess.5:3. But then in verses 4-6 Paul says, "But you brothers, are not in darkness, so that this day should surprise you like a thief. We do not belong to the night or to the darkness. So then, let us not be like others, who are asleep, but let us be alert and self-controlled."

Here, in Revelation, Jesus says to them, "<u>wake up</u>".

Verse 4. Walk With Me Dressed In White

"Yet you have a few people in Sardis who have not soiled their clothes. They will walk with me dressed in white for they are worthy." (NIV).

"<u>Who have not soiled their clothes</u>" (NIV) – in other words, "sinned and become filthy".

Zech.3:3-4: "Now Joshua was dressed in filthy clothes as he stood before the angel. The angel said to those who were standing before him, 'Take off his filthy clothes.' Then he said to Joshua, "See I have taken away your sin, and I will put rich garments on you."(NIV).

"They will walk with me, dressed in white"(NIV),

White stands for purity or innocence. We are purified by the blood of the Lamb. We are declared innocent in his court. We are clothed with the "righteousness of Christ", Rom.13:14.

Verse 5. I Will Acknowledge His Name

"He who overcomes will like them - be dressed in white. I will never blot out his name from The Book of Life, but will acknowledge his name before my father and his angels. (NIV)

Verse 6. Let Him Hear. Listen Up!

"He who has an ear, let him hear what the Spirit says to the churches. (NIV)

Are you listening? Do you hear?

TO THE CHURCH IN PHILADELPHIA

The city of Philadelphia was just north of three cities that had been clustered together: Colossae, Hieropolis, and Laodicea. There had been an earthquake in 61 A.D. that destroyed all three cities. Only Laodicea was rebuilt and existed of the three at the time of this letter. The city of Philadelphia was destroyed by an earthquake (17A.D.) but it was quickly rebuilt. Philadelphia was inland from the Aegean Sea and was on the Cogamus River. It stood on a terrace 650 feet above the sea. The name is Greek and means "city of brotherly love". Many Jews lived there and had a synagogue.

The church is not mentioned elsewhere in the Bible.

Verse 7. To Philadelphia

"To the angel of the church in Philadelphia write: these are the words of him who is holy and true, who holds the key of David. What he opens no one can shut and what he shuts no one can open." (NIV).

"Who holds the key of David." (NIV).

This is in fulfillment to Isa.22:22, "I will place on his shoulder the key to the house of David: what he opens no one can shut, and what he shuts no one can open. I will drive him like a peg into a firm place; he will be a seat of honor for the house of his father. All the glory of his family will hang on him: its offspring and offshoots – all its lesser vessels, from the bowls to all the jars." NIV. Peter says of David, who was a prophet, that "God had promised him on oath that he would place one of his descendants on his throne," Acts 2:30, NIV. Jesus was set on David's throne. He is King of kings forever after the power of an endless life.

"What he opens no one can shut and what he shuts no one can open." (NIV).

Jesus has all authority in heaven and on earth, Mt.28:18. What he does, no one can change.

Verse 8. An Open Door

"I know your Deeds. see I have placed before you an Open Door that no one can shut. I know that you have little strength, yet you have kept my word and have not denied my name. (NIV).

Placed before you an open door that no one can shut. (NIV).

Jesus has all authority in heaven and on earth, Mt.28:18. What he opens, no one can shut. What he bound in the heavens, was then bound on earth. What he loosed in the heavens, was then loosed on the earth, Mt 16:19. He is over all things both in heaven and on earth. It is his New Covenant. He is our king.

You have kept my word. (NIV).

In obedience there is blessing. In following Jesus, there is protection and opportunity.

Verse 9. Those Of The Synagogue Of Satan

"I will make those who are of the synagogue of Satan, who claimed to be Jews though they are not, but are liars- I will make them come and fall down at your feet and acknowledge that I have loved you." (NIV).

"Synagogue of Satan." (NIV).

They were a Jewish synagogue. They claimed to serve God. But they really served Satan and did his work, Jn.8:44.

Verse 10. Keep You From The Hour Of Trial

"Since you have kept my command to endure patiently, I will also keep you from the hour of trial that is going to come upon the whole world to test those who live on the Earth." (NIV)

Since you have kept my command, also verse 8 – You have kept my word.

"I will also keep you from the hour of trial that is going to come upon the whole world to test those who live on the earth." (NIV).

("being about to come" -Marshall's Interlinear translation of the Greek- mellouses erxesthai). In other words, the time of its coming was just about there. Lk.21:36 says, "pray that you may escape what is about to happen."

"Whole world" (NIV) - (Greek – oikoumenes -inhabited earth or land)

This same wording of Rev.3:10, is found in Luke 21:34-35 where it says:

"Be careful, or your hearts will be weighed down with dissipation, drunkenness and the anxieties of life, and that day will close on you like a trap. For it will come upon all those who live upon the face of the whole earth. Be always on the watch, and pray that you may be able to escape all that is about to happen." (NIV)

What is the context of the Luke passage? He is speaking of the days when "they would see Jerusalem surrounded by armies", verse 20, right before the destruction of the temple and the city by those armies in 70 A.D. Verse 22 says, "For this is the time of punishment in fulfillment of all that has been written." (NIV). The Roman armies of Titus laid siege ("that day will close on you like a trap", Lk. 21:34, NIV) to the city of Jerusalem for 5 months, between April14 and September 8, 70 A.D. Because it was the time of the Passover, the Romans allowed pilgrims to enter the city but refused to let them leave – thus depleting food and water supplies within Jerusalem. Even though the Romans besieged and conquered Jerusalem and destroyed it; there had been 3 rebel Jewish factions that had controlled it since 66 A.D. They had done much fighting and destruction within Jerusalem even before the Romans arrived. The suffering was intolerable and inescapable. Matthew 24 says the "great distress" of those days, verse 20, were "unequaled from the beginning of the world until now" (NIV) (when the armies arrived). It is all in the same context in Matt 24 and Luke 21.

Jesus promises the church of Philadelphia that he would keep them from that "hour of trial." Wow oh wow! What a blessing! What a promise! I absolutely would want to be at that church. What did Jesus do? How did he do it? I can't tell here. What I do know is He always keeps his promises. He is faithful. He delivered his promise. (For the answer to "How did he do it?", see the comments on Chap.11:11) It was wonderful!

The deliverance of Philadelphia reminds me of the story about the Assyrian king, Sennacherib, who surrounded Jerusalem and boasted against God. Hezekiah prayed for deliverance. Isaiah prophesied Jerusalem would be delivered. That night the angel of the Lord went out and killed 185,000 men of Sennacherib's army. The next morning, Sennacherib woke up, saw all the dead bodies of his army; and he broke camp and left, 2 Ki.19. God's people were delivered! How beautiful for those who trust God. He delivers us. When the situation looks impossible, God can do the impossible.

In Jeremiah 37:5, the Babylonians were besieging Jerusalem. They heard that Pharaoh's army had marched out of Egypt. The Babylonians withdrew from Jerusalem. God can deliver us with a simple report to our enemies. He can do it with a quiet whisper. Our part, like the church of Philadelphia – "keep his commands, endure patiently". Wait upon the Lord and He will lift you up. (my paraphrase).

Verse 11. I Am Coming Soon

"I am coming soon. Hold on to what you have, so that no one will take your crown. (NIV)

"I am coming soon". (NIV). Jesus says that over and over in the book of Revelation. He was "coming soon." The time was at hand.

"soon" – quickly, Greek- taxu.

"Hold on to what you have." (NIV). If you have a good thing – hold on to it, cling to it. Be steadfast, immoveable, 1 Cor.15:58, and you will receive the crown of life.

Verse 12. A New Name

"Him who overcomes I will make a pillar in the temple of my God. Never again will he leave it. I will write on him the name of my God and the name of the city of my God, the New Jerusalem, which is coming down out of Heaven from my God; and I will also right on him my new name." (NIV).

"Make a pillar in the temple of my God." (NIV).

"Write on him the name of my God." (NIV).

In Rev.7:3, the 144,000 are sealed with the seal of God in their foreheads. In 14:1 we learn they had the Lamb's name and the Father's name written on their foreheads. (When you put your name on something, it is a sign of ownership. This belongs to me. "This one belongs to Jehovah.") How wonderful. "If God is for us, who can be against us?" Rom.8:31 (NIV). NO ONE!

"The New Jerusalem, which is coming down out of Heaven". (NIV).

The impression we get is that Jerusalem is coming out of heaven to the earth, and that God (according to modern theorists) will establish Jerusalem on earth. I think the thought is rather – The New Jerusalem which Christ built in the heavens, and reigns from there – extends down also to the earth. While Christians live on the earth, their citizenship is in heavens, Phil.3:20-21. On earth we participate in the heavenly Jerusalem by faith. "The Jerusalem that is above, she is our mother," Gal.4:26. The Jerusalem that was below, she was in bondage or in slavery with her children. Gal.4:25. God destroyed the earthly Jerusalem and the covenant that was centered there in 70 A.D. He will not bring it back. Why would he? We have the heavenly kingdom now that Christ built. Col.1:5 speaks of the "hope that is stored up for you in the heavens."

"I will write on him my new name." (NIV).

Rev.19:12 speaks of the rider on the white horse. "He has a name written on him that no one knows but He himself." Then, verse13 says, "His name is the Word of God." (NIV).

Isaiah 56:5 "To them I will give in My house and with My walls a memorial, and a name better than of sons and daughters; I will give them an everlasting name which will not be cut off." (NIV).

Isaiah 62:1-4 "For Zion's sake I will not keep silent, for Jerusalem's sake I will not remain quiet, till her righteousness shines out like the dawn, her salvation like a blazing torch. The nations will see your righteousness, and all kings your glory; you will be called by a <u>new name</u> that the mouth of the Lord will bestow. You will be a crown of splendor in the Lord's hand. A royal diadem in the hand of your God. No longer will they call you Deserted, or name your land Desolate. But you will be called <u>Hephzibah</u> (my delight is in her) and your land <u>Beulah</u> (Married)." (NIV).

Verse 13. Let Him Hear! Listen Up

"He who has an ear let him hear what the Spirit says to the churches." (NIV)

Are you listening? Do you hear?

TO THE CHURCH IN LAODICEA

The city of Laodicea was just south of Philadelphia, an inland city in Asia Minor. It had been destroyed by an earthquake in 61A.D. along with the cities of Colossae and Hierapolis. Only Laodicea was rebuilt. The city was first founded in 260 B.C. by Antiochus II Theos, king of Syria, and was named in honor of his wife Laodice. The city passed into Roman hands in 133 B.C.

Laodicea was a center of the textile industry and of banking. When the city was destroyed by the earthquake in 61A.D., they refused the aid of the Roman empire and rebuilt the city from their own wealth. (Tacitus, Annals, 14:27). Their wealth is indicated in the letter to the church. In 3:17 it says, "You say, 'I am rich; I have acquired wealth and do not need a thing." The riches of the city must have corrupted members in the church also.

Knowing that the cities of Colossae, Hierapolis and Laodicea were physically in the same close area, we read in Colossians 4:12-13 "Epaphras who is one of you and a servant of Christ Jesus sends greetings. He is always wrestling in prayer for you, that you may stand firm in the will of God, mature and fully assured. I vouch for him that he is working hard for you <u>and for those at Laodicea</u> and Hierapolis." Verse 16 says, "After this letter has been read to you see that it is also read in the church of the <u>Laodiceans</u> and that you in turn read the letter from Laodicea. The three churches seemed to have had a close connection. After the earthquake, Laodicea's riches could have easily made them feel that their riches had rescued them and given them their security and status.

There does exist a letter to the Laodiceans, very similar to other of Paul's letters. I do not know why it was not included in the canon of the New Testament. From what I remember when reading it, it did not contain anything new or different from what we already have in the New Testament.

Nearly all of what we have in the New Testament of the church of Laodicea is here in the book of Revelation.

Verse 14. To Laodicea

"To the angel of the church in Laodicea write: these are the words of the amen, the faithful and true Witness, the ruler of God's creation." (NIV)

"The faithful and true witness" (NIV).

In Rev.19:11 Jesus is called "the Faithful and True." In Rev. 1:5 Jesus is called the "faithful witness."

"The ruler of God's creation" (NIV).

In Rev.1:5 Jesus is called the ruler of the kings of the earth. In Eph.1:20-21 it says Jesus was seated at God's right hand in the heavenly realms "far above all rule, authority, power and dominion, and every name that can be given."

Verse 15. I Wish You Were Either Cold Or Hot

"I know your deeds that you are neither cold nor hot. I wish you were either one or the other!" (NIV).

How interesting. Jesus tells them they were "lukewarm". He wishes they were rather "cold" or "hot". Is being cold better than lukewarm? Why? It may be because the lukewarm were rich, self-sufficient and hard to reach. They did not need a thing. They did not need God. (Maybe - they liked to throw a little money to the poor. They liked to support humanitarian causes and get recognized for it. Maybe they could discuss religious puzzles and the deeper themes. Who knows? But Jesus says in verse 17 they were wretched, pitiful, poor, blind and naked." That's a lot of negative description.

Verse 16. I Will Vomit You Out

"So, because you are lukewarm- neither hot nor cold- I am about to spit you out of my mouth. (NIV).

"about to spit you out of my mouth." The word and thought is much stronger in Greek. Marshall's Interlinear Greek says – "I am about to vomit (Greek – emesai, where we get our word emesis, vomit) you out of my mouth."

Verse 17. You say, 'I Do Not Need Anything'

"You say, I am rich; I have acquired wealth and do not need a thing. But you do not realize that you are wretched, pitiful, poor, blind, and naked." (NIV).

This verse reveals the cause of their lukewarm attitude – "you say, 'I am rich; I have acquired wealth and don't need a thing." NIV. They trusted in their riches rather than in God. Did they believe in God? Yes. But where was their trust? Their treasure? Their focus in life? Prov.30:8-9 says,

"Give me neither poverty nor riches, but give me only my daily bread. Otherwise, I may have too much and disown you, and say, 'who is the Lord?' Or I may become poor and steal." (NIV).

Why do riches divert its owner away from God? Eccl 7:12 helps us see the answer: "Wisdom is a shelter, as money is a shelter, but the advantage of knowledge is this; that wisdom preserves the life of its possessor." (NIV).

You know the effect of having money, plenty of money. The car needs brakes. I don't have to wait to get money to buy parts and fix it myself. The rich just drop it off and have it fixed that day. Or, they just buy a new car. My refrigerator quits. My wife and I have to wait weeks before we can afford to buy a new one. The rich just call on the phone and have a new one delivered and installed. Maybe their servants take care of all that and they are not even bothered with it. Whatever the need, the rich don't experience the problem, they just use their money and problem solved. It is easy for them to "depend" on their money. But money brings "pleasure". The rich can go on fantastic vacations, buy fancy cars, yachts, and houses. They can pamper themselves because they are rich, really rich. Do you see the point? Money is a shelter. They can depend on it. They get many pleasures from it. God is sort of irrelevant for them. They trust in their riches.

"They are wretched, pitiful, poor, blind, and naked." (NIV).

Riches can rob you of the real spiritual treasures that cannot be taken away. Look in the mirror. Do you see a rich man in an expensive suit? Or, a man pitiful, poor and naked? Wake up!

Verse 18. Put Salve On Your Eyes So You Can See

"I counsel you to buy from me gold refined in the fire, so you can become rich; and white clothes to wear, so you can cover your shameful nakedness; and salve to put on your eyes, so you can see." (NIV).

Of course, Jesus counsels them to buy the true riches, put on clothes of true righteousness, Let the salve of God's word open their eyes.

Verse 19. Those I Love I Rebuke And Discipline

"Those whom I love I rebuke and discipline. So be earnest and repent." (NIV)

God's discipline is not limited to the so-called "harsh God of the Old Testament." Even in the New Testament, Heb.12:5-11 teaches us his discipline can be harsh. Verse 11 says, "No discipline seems pleasant at the time, but painful." Verse 6 says, "the Lord disciplines those he loves, and he punishes (Mastigoi) everyone he accepts as a son." (NIV) ("scourges" KJV – Greek – mastigoi. People were scourged with a mastix, a small whip.) (Another Greek word -phragellion, a whip, from Latin flagellum. It is used for the scourge of small cords which the Lord made himself and employed in cleansing the temple. God can discipline harshly, and for our own good. Maybe we should rethink the so-called "harsh discipline" of putting a kid in "time out", or "go to your room." Maybe God's instruction to us on discipline might reveal some important insights and changes. Do you think? Do you trust what God tells you or not? Our culture calls what God does in Heb 12 – "abuse." Jesus was "abusive" in the temple according to our modern - day views.

Verse 20. I Stand At The Door And Knock

"Here I am! I stand at the door and knock. If anyone hears my voice and opens the door, I will come in and eat with him and he with me." (NIV).

Jesus is inviting them to let him in. He has the true treasures. They can have fellowship, have a meal together and reunite.

Verse 21. Sit With Me On My Throne

"To him who overcomes, I will give the right to sit with me on my throne just as I overcame and sat down with my father on his throne." (NIV)

That is quite a promise. Overcome, and you can sit on the king's throne. Wow. He is not just the king of some place you have never heard of. He is the King of Kings and Lord of Lords in heaven and on earth. He is the Eternal King who lives for ever and ever. He can give to you - life forever. You can sit on his throne with Him.

Verse 22. Let Him Hear

"He who has an ear, let him hear what the Spirit says to the churches." (NIV)

Are you listening?

CHAPTER FOUR

THE THRONE IN HEAVEN

Verse 1. Come Up Here

"After this I looked, and there before me was a door standing open. in heaven. And the voice I had first heard speaking to me like a trumpet said, 'come up here and I will show you what must take place after this.'" (NIV)

"After this" – introduces a new vision. In the revelation, we need to pay attention to when it's a new vision. The scene often changes. The subject can change. The time can change. In each change we have to reorient to where he is, when he is, and to the new subject matter.

"A door standing open in heaven" (NIV) – Oh! Now I know he is looking into heaven and what is going on there. Maybe these words are not hard to understand, but it sets the scene.

"The voice I had first heard speaking to me like a trumpet." (NIV) That was the voice of Jesus, Rev.1:10,12. The trumpet voice was also the voice that was heard when Jesus returned, 1 Thess.4:16. Specifically, when He returned, it was at the sounding of the 7th trumpet, Rev.11:15; I Cor.15:52.

Jesus says, "come up here (into heaven in a vision) and I will show you what must take place after this." (NIV). It "must take place" here; like in 1:1 it says it "must soon take place"- because it is appointed in God's plan to happen. It must be fulfilled. Isaiah 46: 9-10 says,

"I am God, and there is no other; I am God, and there is none like me. I have made known the end from the beginning, from ancient times, what is still to come. I say: My purpose will stand; I will do all that I please." In verse 11 he says "What I have said, that will I bring about. What I have planned, that will I do." (NIV).

Verse 2. A Throne In Heaven

"At once I was in the Spirit, and there before me was a throne in heaven with someone sitting on it." (NIV)

"At once I was in the Spirit" (NIV) – meaning he was caught up into a vision. This is like 1:9 when he was "in the Spirit on the Lord's Day". His vision there was about the Lord's Day or day of judgment. Here in 4:2, he is "in the Spirit" viewing the throne room scene in the heavens.

Verse 3. A Rainbow Encircled The Throne

"And the one who sat there had the appearance of jasper and carnelian. A rainbow resembling an emerald encircled the throne." (NIV)

"jasper and carnelian" (NIV)

Jasper – is commonly red. It is believed by some scholars that jasper was an emerald green gem on the breastplate of the high priest. Jasper comes from the Hebrew yashpheh. The root word means "to polish". In Rev.21:18-19, the wall of the city, the New Jerusalem, is of jasper. The first foundation stone of the city walls is jasper. Carnelian is the color of red, deep blood red.

If both jasper and carnelian are a shade of red in the text, it would fit with the appearance of God, a figure full of fire from the waist up and from the waist down, Ezek.1:27. God is a consuming fire. His angels are also "flames of fire", Heb.1:7. (NIV)

In Mark 12:25 Jesus says, "When the dead rise...they will be like the angels in heaven." (NIV) Will we be like "flames of fire? John says in 1 Jn. 3:2-3: "...what we will be has not yet been made known, but we know that when he appears, we shall be like him." (NIV). Phil. 3:21 says "...will transform our lowly bodies so that they will be like his glorious body." (NIV) What a thought to contemplate. What will a "spiritual body" be like? "What glories will be given to us?" What perfection? What powers? The spiritual world – we can only wonder in amazement.

"A rainbow resembling an emerald encircled the throne." (NIV)

Of course, we think of the rainbow when we read this. The rainbow was the sign God gave of his covenant with man for all generations to come – "never again would the waters become a flood to destroy all of life," Gen.9:12-15. (NIV) The rainbow represented the overarching rule of heaven in which God's character and love would predominate over man. The symbol of the rainbow tells us God is a merciful God. Ps. 103:13-14 says,

"The Lord has compassion on those who fear him; for he knows how we are formed; he remembers that we are dust." (NIV)

Here, the rainbow that encircled the throne I believe represents God's glory, his "shekinah" glory.

Glory is the Greek – doxa; Hebrew -kabod. God's "shekinah glory" – is not found in our Bibles, but it is understood by many to be that God's glory is linked to the Hebrew "shekinah" of the Holy Spirit. It is the radiance of his glory as it is manifested to us in all its fullness through the Holy Spirit. It is the relation of God toward the world. In Jewish thinking, the shekinah glory, which means "the indwelling glory" either "rested upon" or "dwelled in" those whom God favored. The thought was, in Deut. 23:14, that the "shekinah of the Lord" walked among them. There it says, "the Lord your God moves about in your camp to protect you. Your camp must be holy, so that he will not see among you anything indecent and turn away from you." (NIV)

"A rainbow resembling an emerald". (NIV) Ezek.1:28 says, "Like the appearance of a rainbow in the clouds on a rainy day, so the radiance around him. This was the appearance of the likeness of the glory of the Lord." (NIV) Emerald green may generally signify abundance, prosperity, growth within all aspects of life. This may be the association in Ezek 27:16, "Aram was your customer because of the abundance of your goods; they paid for your wares with emeralds, purple, embroidered works, fine linen, coral and rubies." (NIV). Now, this may be a stretch for the symbolic meaning. I do not really know. Green however, is the abundant and predominant color of all things on earth that grow in the plant world. Maybe we are close to its meaning. God's radiance is an intense light of Green around him, perhaps revealing the abundance of life he produces in the world. He gives us life and he sustains us in abundance.

Verse 4. 24 Thrones and 24 Elders

"Surrounding the throne were twenty-four other thrones, and seated on them were 24 elders. They were dressed in white and had crowns of gold on their heads." (NIV)

"Twenty four other thrones – seated on them were twenty four elders" (NIV)

Who are these? I believe they may represent the courses of the priests listed in 1 Chron.24, the divisions of the sons of Aaron. There were Eleazar, which had 16 heads of families, and Ithamar, which had 8 heads of families. This number 24 represents the priests of Israel, but the "sanctified", the remnant that was saved. Why the remnant, the saved? Because they have received the crown of the "overcomer", the "stephanoi". They are dressed in white garments which are the righteous deeds of the overcoming saints in 3:4-5; 19:8. Why are there 24 elders that surround his throne? They represent the leaders of the Old Testament saints that have come out of spiritual Israel. They are now before the throne of God. Perhaps it represents Old and New Testament saints. Why? The 12 tribes represent Old Testament Jewish saints and the 12 apostles represent the New Testament saints. Saints, represented in the Old and New Testaments would be 24.

Verse 5. Seven Lamps Were Blazing

"From the throne came flashes of lightning, Rumblings and peels of thunder. Before the Throne seven lamps were blazing. These are the seven spirits of God." (NIV)

"Flashes of lightning, rumblings, peels of thunder" (NIV) -come from the throne.

This comes from the throne every time a judgment is completed and when something in the heavens is announced. It is God who confirms and agrees with what has taken place. It is God that has initiated it and announced it through his servants.

"Seven lamps were blazing" (NIV) – from Zech.4:2,10 where the lampstand, (which stood opposite the table of shewbread) has seven lamps blazing or seven branches. "These seven are the eyes of the Lord, which range throughout the earth," verse 10.

"Before the throne seven lamps were blazing – these are the seven spirits of God."(NIV)

God is a consuming fire, Heb.12:29. God is light, and in him is no darkness at all, 1 Jn.1:5. So it is with his Spirit. The Son is also described that way. In Rev. 21:23 it says that in New Jerusalem there will not be a need for the sun or moon, "for the glory of God gives it light, and the Lamb is its lamp." 1 Thess.1:7 says, "This will happen when the Lord Jesus is revealed from heaven in blazing fire with his powerful angels." The eyes of Jesus are a "flame of fire," Rev.19:12. Jesus said, "I am come to cast fire upon the earth; and how I wish it were already kindled." Lk.12:49. Rev. 5:6 tells us the Lamb had "seven horns and seven eyes, which are the seven Spirits."

God the Father, the Son, the Holy Spirit – they are one. They are described in the same way. They act as one. The Father glorifies the Son. The Son glorifies the Father. The Spirit gives glory to the Son and the Father. The same Spirit belongs to the Father as the Son, Rom.8:9; Isa.11:2. He is the Spirit that dwells in Christians. God raised Jesus from the dead, 1 Cor.6:14. Jesus laid down his life and he took it up again, Jn 10:17. The Spirit raised Jesus up, Rom.8:11. They are one. They act as one. They are not three persons in one. They are one person with three united integrated working existence. We are one person -body, soul, and Spirit; made in God's image and likeness. God exists as three existences in one. He is not three persons. A person has body, soul, and spirit. Three persons would have three bodies, three souls, and three spirits. No, God cannot be described as three persons. He is One. He is one person as we are with three "parts" integrated into one. He acts as One in everything. We worship only One God. There is only One creator. The Father, the Son and the Holy Spirit represent only one Person – God.

Verse 6. The Sea Of Glass And Four Living Creatures

"Also Before the Throne there was what looked like a sea of glass, clear as Crystal. In the center around the *throne, we're four living creatures, and they were covered with eyes, in front and in back." (NIV)*

"Before the throne… a sea of glass, clear as crystal." (NIV)

Here, what is before the throne is a sea of glass, as clear as crystal. It is pure water and healing water. In Daniel, what Daniel sees is a river of fire flowing, coming out from before him, Dan.7:10. In Ezekiel - Ezekiel sees water coming out from under the threshold of the temple in heaven. The water gets deeper and deeper and flows down into the Arabah, the desert regions, and everything the water touches turns green and is given life. (What a beautiful picture in that chapter is revealed to us!) Then, in Revelation, when the heavens are opened and the mystery of God is completed, we see a view of the heavenly Jerusalem. In chapter 22 we see the river of life, clear as crystal flowing from the throne of God, Rev.22:1.

When this passage mentions a sea of glass, I think of being out at the lake. In waking up early in the morning at the lake, I would see it was a beautiful day, with no wind. The lake was calm and peaceful and looked like a sea of glass. The sun was reflecting down on the surface of the lake. We would take the ski boat out on the lake while still early to capture the beauty and peace of being out there. Skiing outside the wake of the boat was like gliding on a sea of glass. The sea of glass made you feel calm, peaceful, filled with wonder and happiness. Then I think of the song – "When peace like a river attendeth my way". The focus of the song says – "it is well with my soul" (by Horatio Spafford). The sea of glass, the river from the temple, the river of the water of life from before his throne – turns everything green and gives us life. It is beautiful, and it is abundant, it is filling and refreshing. It continually renews us, sustains us with perfect life in his presence.

But there can be what flows from his throne a river of fire, a fire burning hot, a consuming fire, like a molten flowing burning rock that flows down like the fiery river from a volcano, Dan.7:10. It cannot be escaped, and it has no mercy. That is reserved for the enemies of God. Rev.14:9-11 says,

"If anyone worships the beast and his image and receives his mark on their forehead or their hand, he too will drink the wine of God's fury, which has been poured full strength into the cup of his wrath. <u>He will be tormented with burning sulfur in the presence of the holy angels and of the Lamb.</u> And the smoke of their torment rises forever and ever." (NIV)

Could this torment be in the river of fire before the throne in the presence of the holy angels and the Lamb?

<u>"Four living creatures… covered with eyes, in front and back.</u>" (NIV)

The four living creatures are described in detail in Ezekiel chapters 1 and 10. The description there is astounding, overwhelming creatures of such great power and appearance it strikes us with motionless fear and terror. You simply must read about them there. Being covered with eyes all over in front and back, that is, with eyes all over their bodies, under their wings and on them, on legs and torsos, on their backs, everywhere. You cannot at any time escape their gaze. They are cherubim, Ezek.10:1,2,5.

Verse 7. The Four Living Creatures

"The first living creature was like a lion, the second was like an ox, the third had a face like a man, and the fourth was like a flying eagle." (NIV)

The four living creatures in Ezekiel 1and 10 are cherubim, and they each had 4 faces: the face of man, a lion, an ox, and an eagle. They had four wings. Here, in verse 7, each creature had one face; one with the face of a man, another with the face of a lion, another with the face of an ox, and finally one with the face of an eagle. In verse 8, we find they had six wings, like in Isa.6:1-4. In Isaiah 6 they are seraphs, not cherubim. The name seraphim means "burning ones, flying serpents". Only in Isaiah are seraphs mentioned. They seem to be busy praising God, and from the meaning of their name, it reminds us of Heb.1:7:

"In speaking of the angels he says, 'He makes his angels- winds, his servants -flames of fire." (NIV). They seem to be zealous for the holiness of God. They cry out ``Holy, Holy, Holy is the Lord God almighty." (NIV)

In the case of the two cherubs that overlooked the mercy seat that was on the top of the ark of the covenant, Heb.9:5, the message seems to be that the angels are again zealous for the holiness, righteousness, and justice of God. In looking at the mercy seat, the angels are held back from harsh judgment for the sake of holiness only as they look upon the mercy seat. The curtains of the tabernacle were woven with angels all through the tapestry. It was indeed a holy, holy place. No unrighteous can dwell with God, Psalm 15.

Verse 8. Holy, Holy, Holy

"Each of the four living creatures had six wings and was covered with eyes all around, even under his wings. Day and night they never stop saying: 'holy, holy, holy is the Lord God Almighty - who was, and is, and is to come.'" (NIV)

Again, the emphasis of the scene is the holiness of God. He is Holy, wholly and completely holy and worthy of all praise. Even the heaven of heavens cannot praise him enough. Heb. 12:14 says, "Without holiness no one will see the Lord". (NIV). We MUST be holy to dwell with God. There is no righteousness of our own. We must put on the Lord Jesus Christ, Rom.13:14. "He is our righteousness, holiness, and redemption", 1 Cor. 1:30. (NIV) We are totally dependent on Jesus. It is interesting that in Ezekiel 40-46 there is a description of the temple. I do not understand all that is talked about in those chapters, but one passage stands out to me in chapter 46:9-10. It speaks of the people of the land coming before the Lord. "The prince is to be among them, going in when they go in and going out when they go out." (NIV). The people could not enter without the prince. He was their "passport", so to speak. Yet, according to 44:3 the prince himself was the only one who could eat in the presence of the Lord. How can we be in the presence of the Lord? Only when we come with Jesus Christ, our righteousness.

Verse 9. Give Glory To Him On The Throne

"Whenever the living creatures give glory, honor and thanks to him who sits on the throne and who lives forever and ever," (NIV)

Verse 10. Worship Him Who Lives For Ever And Ever

"The 24 Elders fall down before him who sits on the throne and worship him who lives forever and ever. They lay their crowns before the Throne and say," (NIV)

Verse 11. You Are Worthy

"You are worthy our Lord and God to receive glory and honor and power for you created all things and by your will they were created and have their being." (NIV).

Col.1:16-17 "For by him all things were created: things in heaven and things on the earth, visible and invisible, whether thrones or powers or rulers or authorities: all things were <u>created by him and for him</u>. He is before all things, and in him all things hold together. (NIV)

("All things consist," KJV). (or "have their being", T.S.).

Col. 1:19 "For God was pleased to have <u>all his fulness dwell in Him</u>, and through him to reconcile to himself all things, whether things on earth or things in heaven, by making peace through his blood, shed on the cross." (NIV)

All things were created by Christ. By Him all things continue to have their existence. All things were reconciled to the Father by Christ. All things were restored by Him. Yet, it is because He gave his human life for us, suffered our death, suffered our pain - that we say he is worthy. He is worthy because he has accomplished all things for us.

CHAPTER FIVE

THE SCROLL AND THE LAMB

Verse 1. The Scroll With Seven Seals

"Then I saw in the right hand of him who sat on the throne a scroll with writing on both sides and sealed with seven seals." (NIV)

A "scroll with writing on both sides" (NIV) – this scroll was full, there was not more to add. There was writing on both sides.

"And sealed with seven seals." (NIV) – the scroll was sealed (closed, concealed, shut). It had seven seals, that is it had been sealed by the activity of God until its appointed time to be fulfilled. Seven seals indicated the activity of God or the Spirit. God sealed it. Things associated with God or the activity of God are symbolized by the number seven. There are "seven lamps blazing before the throne which are the seven spirits of God," Rev. 4:5. There are seven eyes of the Lamb, Rev.5:6. The book of Revelation is from God, Jesus, and "the seven Spirits before God's throne," Rev.1:4.

Verse 2. Who Is Worthy To Open The Scroll

"And I saw a mighty angel proclaiming in a loud voice,' Who is worthy to break the seals and open the scroll?" (NIV)

The song – "Worthy is the Lamb" is a beautiful song. It expresses in song what we see here and in the words of verse 12.

Verse 3. No One Could Open It

"But no one in heaven or on earth or under the earth could open the scroll or even look inside it." (NIV)

Who could step forward and claim the power, the honor, the worthiness? Who in heaven and earth and under the earth? Who? Step forward. All the creation and created stood silent.

"<u>or under the earth</u>" – this speaks of the realm of the dead, the realm of spirits that have laid aside their bodies in the grave and were being kept in HADES (the place of disembodied spirits). (See Ezek.26:19-21). Jesus, after his death on the cross, descended into the "lower earthly regions" to get the righteous dead (that were captive there, Satan held them in the grave by the power of sin). Jesus freed them and took them to Paradise, the third heaven, 2 Cor. 12:2,4. When Jesus descended and brought them out of Hades, this could be understood as the first fruits unto God, Rev.14:4; 1 Cor.15:23. However, the context concerning the first fruits is in regard to the resurrected body on the day of resurrection. Those he had taken out of captivity to the third heaven, would come back with Jesus on resurrection day to receive their resurrection bodies 1 Thess. 4:16 (their inheritance together with us, Heb.11:39). Here, in this verse 3, no one in the spirit world of all the dead of all generations could step forward. No one for all time was worthy.

Verse 4. I Wept

"I wept and wept because no one was found who was worthy to open the scroll or look inside." (NIV)

"<u>No one was found who was worthy.</u>" (NIV)

No one was worthy – except God himself. Isa.63:5 says, "I looked, but there was no one to help, I was appalled that no one gave support; so, <u>my own arm</u> worked salvation for me." (NIV). Isa.59:15-16 says, "The Lord looked and was displeased that there was no justice, He saw that there was no one, he was appalled that there was no one to intervene; so, <u>his own arm</u> worked salvation for him." (NIV). Isaiah 59 starts out – "Surely <u>the arm of the Lord</u> is not too short to save…but your iniquities have separated you from God." (NIV). Jesus is prophetically the right arm of God. Isaiah 53 starts out saying "Who has believed our message and to whom has <u>the arm of the Lord</u> been revealed? (NIV). The rest of the chapter prophecies in detail about Jesus. How wonderful. Jesus, the Lamb that was slain,

Jesus the arm of the Lord, HE IS WORTHY.

Ps. 49:7 says, "No man can redeem the life of another or give to God a ransom for him. The ransom for a life is too costly, no payment is ever enough- that he should live on forever and not see decay." (NIV) (See Eccl. 9:5) Why couldn't he die for him? Physical death passed upon all men because of the sin of Adam. God told Adam – "In the day that you eat thereof, (Hebrew meaning - "dying you shall die.") (My paraphrase, T.S.)

Adam's sin brought in the "aging process" whereby dying, we shall die. Rom.5:12 says, "Therefore, just as sin entered the world through one man, and death through sin, and in this way, death came to all men." (NIV). All men are already under the sentence of physical death because of the sin of Adam. Man is born already "a dead man" so to speak. He is already under the condemnation of physical death. How can a dead man die for another dead man? How can a condemned man rescue another condemned man? He can't.

Then how could Jesus die for us? He was a man. How is it that He could give his life, not just for one other man, but for all men who come to Him? The answer is in the virgin birth. It was a necessity that he <u>not</u> be born of the seed of Man. Why? It was through the man that death passed. Adam is the federal head of the human race. He represented the whole human race. Because Jesus was not born of the seed of man, death had no power in him or over him. Satan had no hold on him, Jn.14:30. "It was impossible for death to keep its hold on him," Acts 2:24. (NIV) The prophecy that he would be of the seed of woman, Gen. 3:15; born of a virgin, Isa.7:14; was a NECESSITY. ONLY Jesus qualified to save us from death and destruction. ONLY he can give us life. 1 Jn.5:12 says, "He who has the son has life; he who does not have the son does not have life." (NIV) Period. There is no Life after death except through the son.

Well, how did Jesus die for <u>everyone</u> who comes to him, and not just one other man? Jesus is the federal head of the new spiritual creation. He is the very first one born from the dead. Because he is, he is able to also save us to the utmost. He can give us life. This is explained in Rom.5. Read it. How much more, the chapter explains, have we been given in Christ, than what we lost through Adam. It's beautiful. He has blessed us with unspeakable, wonderful blessings. He is WORTHY.

The Lamb who was slain – he is worthy!

Verse 5. The Lion Of The Tribe Of Judah, The Root Of David

"Then one of the elders said to me' do not weep! See the lion of the tribe of Judah, the root of David, has triumphed. He is able to open the scroll and it's Seven Seals. (NIV)

The "lion of the tribe of Judah". This is a title for Jesus. Jesus was of the tribe of Judah. He is prophesied about in Gen 49:9-10. There he is a lion, and the ruler's staff would not depart from Judah until he came to whom it belonged. Judah, had the banner of a lion that it carried to represent them among Israel. Jesus fulfilled the prophecy of Gen 49. Heb.7:14 says, "It is clear the Lord descended from Judah." (NIV). His lineage is clear in Matt. 1 and Luke 3. To show the lineage of Jesus and that he is the fulfillment of many prophecies, those chapters trace his lineage all the way back to the beginning.

"The root of David" (NIV) - this is Jesus too. Isaiah prophesies of this is in 11:2: "A shoot will come up from the stump of Jesse (the father of David, 1Sam. 16:1,13); from his roots a Branch will bear fruit." (NIV). Jesus is the branch prophetically, Zech. 3:8; 6:12-13.

It is interesting that the lion (the lion of the tribe of Judah) in the Zodiac has his foot on the head of the snake. It symbolizes the prophecy in Gen 3:15 that "the lion of the tribe of Judah"- Jesus, would crush the serpent, Satan's head, Rom. 16:20.

Not only that, but the Virgin in the zodiac is holding the "branch" – who is prophetically Jesus. You can read the book, "The Gospel in the Stars", by Joseph Seiss, and realize all the constellations point to Jesus. It is so sad that man uses the zodiac in such a corrupted way now.

Jesus only was worthy to open the scroll. Why would he open it? Because the appointed time for it to happen had arrived. "Open the book – the time is now for all to be fulfilled" - was the message to the churches in Revelation.

Verse 6. The Lamb That Was Slain

"Then I saw a lamb, looking as if it had been slain, standing in the center of the throne, encircled by the four living creatures and the elders. He had seven horns and seven eyes, which are the seven spirits of God sent out into all the Earth." (NIV)

"The lamb that was slain" (NIV) – this figure was symbolized beginning in the first sacrifices made, with Cain and Abel. Only Abel's sacrifice of his flocks was acceptable to God, but not the fruit of the soil, Gen. 4:3-5. Later, God made the symbol of the lamb even more detailed. In Exodus 12, He instituted the first Passover. God's death angel, the destroyer, passed over those houses that were marked by the blood of the Lamb. The families had eaten the Lamb. Not a bone was broken of the lambs. Jesus gave the Passover new meaning – when he applied it to himself, Matt. 26:18-29. 1 Cor. 5:7 says, "For Christ, our Passover lamb, has been sacrificed." (NIV).

"The four living creatures (seraphs) and twenty-four elders" (NIV) (O.T. leaders that were saints in Israel or Old and New Testament saints - 12 tribes plus 12 apostles)

"He had seven horns" (NIV) – He has complete, and Godly power. He is God.

"He had seven eyes" (NIV) – As God, he is all seeing and all knowing. "Everything is uncovered and laid bare before his eyes." Heb.4:13. His knowledge is perfect.

Verse 7. He Took The Scroll

"He came and took the scroll from the right hand of him who sat on the throne." (NIV)

Verse 8. The Four Living Creatures And 24 Elders

"And when he had taken it, the four living creatures and the 24 Elders fell down before the lamb. Each one had a harp and they were holding golden bowls full of incense, which are the prayers of the Saints." (NIV)

"harp" – the word is used about fifty times in the Old and New Testaments. It was used in worship of God. In 1 Sam. 16:14:19, David played the harp for king Saul whenever an evil spirit sent from God tormented him. The harp playing helped him to feel better, 16:16. We are not to play instruments in worship to be entertained, but they do help us to feel better. We are to worship God with all of what we are. We are to worship him in spirit and in truth. To worship God in spirit includes emotions. We cannot deny we are emotional. We are to worship Him with everything we are, to give everything to Him. Some say they do not need an instrument to worship him. Fine. If you make it a law that you cannot use musical instruments in worship, you are binding what God has not bound and perverting God's pure grace by mixing walking by faith with a law-keeping system, Rom, 11:6. Christ is the "end of law for those that believe," Rom.10:4. NIV. You are causing people to fall by binding on others what God has not bound. The arguments against musical instruments can be easily refuted. The arguments twist the context of the passages they use. It is shameful to bind law-keeping on others. Let them use their harps. Let them rejoice in God.

"Incense, which are the prayers of the saints." (NIV) Our prayers go up continually before God as a sweet-smelling savor. Ps. 141:2 says,

"May my prayer be set before you like incense; may the lifting up of my hands be like the evening sacrifice." (NIV).

It is especially important that we pray as Jesus prayed, "My Father, if it is possible, may this cup be taken from me, Yet not as I will, but as you will", Mt 26:39 (NIV). We should try to pray to the greatest advantage spiritually. Pray for strength to become what God wants in your life, to fulfill HIS purpose for you.

Pray for the fruits of the Spirit in your life. Pray for guidance. Pray for God to search your heart and if there is anything false, may he reveal it to you, so you can change. Prayer should release what I want, give it up to him, and help me focus on what He wants in me. We are bought with a price. We are not our own.

The wrong way to pray is described in James 4:3, "When you ask, you do not receive, because you ask with wrong motives, that you may spend it upon your pleasures." (NIV).

Verse 9. They Sang A New Song

"And they sang a new song: 'you are worthy to take the scroll and to open its seals, because you were slain, and with your blood you purchased men from

God from every tribe and language and people and Nation." (NIV)

AMEN! They sang a new song in Rev.14:3 also. Only the 144,000 redeemed from the earth could learn it. Here in Rev.5:9, we sing what has been made today, a beautiful song - "Worthy is the Lamb".

Verse 10. A Kingdom And Priests

"You have made them to be a kingdom and priests to serve our God, and they will reign on the Earth." (NIV)

"a kingdom" – Some say – "we are in the Kingdom but the kingdom is not yet", that it actually has not come yet. This is double talk, confusing and not true. The Kingdom was being built by Christ in the first century - laying the foundation through the apostles, adding living stones (Christians) by spreading the gospel, etc. until it came to its completion in heaven in 70 A.D. It was opened up then, and all nations ever since flow into it by faith. Christ's kingdom is "not of this world" Jesus said. "The kingdom is within you." NIV. Christ rules in our hearts by faith. He is sitting on the throne of His kingdom and he has been ever since he ascended into the Heavens and sat down at the right hand of God. He completed the building of his Kingdom and "restored everything" to under his control by A.D. 70. He rules over heaven and earth. He accomplished this when he ascended into heaven to do just that – "restore everything". After the kingdom was nearly finished or built in the heavens, he returned to earth to get those who belonged to Him (those waiting for him, Heb.9:28) in 70 A.D. He closed out the O.T. system by destroying the Temple and Jerusalem. He raised up his people and they were transformed to ever be with him. The judgment took place, the last plagues were completed, and then the completed kingdom opened up. It has been completed and open ever since 70 A.D. (or at least soon after). Perhaps judgment of the Jews was not completed until Masada was destroyed in 73 A.D.

The belief that Christ has not returned, but some day will return to the earth and again establish his kingdom on earth is false. People who teach it interpret the prophecies just like the world of the first century. "Will you at this time restore the kingdom unto Israel," they asked? Acts 1:6. (NIV). People are still looking for an earthly, physical kingdom on earth, just like they did then, but they have totally missed it.

Those who teach the kingdom still need to be accomplished on earth, forget Eph.4:10 – Jesus "is the very one who ascended higher than all the heavens, in order to fill the whole universe." (NIV) Has Jesus been trying to do that for over 2000 years and still hasn't been able to fulfill those words? Of course not! What an impotent, weak, and unworthy savior that would be! Is that what you claim about Jesus? Is that what you actually believe? No! Emphatically NO! My Lord is King of kings and Lord of lords of the whole universe. He is worthy of ALL praise and Glory.

The kingdom is spiritual in the heavens. The prophecies have a spiritual fulfillment in Christ. This world, the heavens and earth will continue for ever and ever, Eccl.1:4; Ps.148.

And "priests"- Rom.12:1 says, we "offer our bodies as living sacrifices, holy and pleasing to God" (NIV)

Heb.13:15 says, "Through Jesus therefore, let us continually offer to God a sacrifice of praise – the fruit of lips that confess his name." (NIV)

There is no doubt in the New Testament we (as Christians) are all priests unto God, 1 Pet.2:5. We are like living stones, being built into a spiritual house to be a holy priesthood, offering spiritual sacrifices acceptable to God through Jesus Christ. But our priest hood is not like Jesus. Jesus is the High Priest, after the order of Melchizedek, a priest hood of ONE, with the power of an endless life. We are not and cannot be of the order of Melchizedek. We are the fulfillment of the type, the shadow, of the Aaronic priesthood, of what would be the reality above in the heavens, in the Kingdom of God. Jeremiah 33:17-22 says,

"For this is what the Lord says: David will never fail to have a man to sit on the throne of the house of Israel, nor will the priests who are Levites, ever fail to have a man to stand before me continually to offer burnt offerings, to burn grain offerings, and to present sacrifices. The word of the Lord came to Jeremiah: This is what the lord says: If you can break my covenant with the day and my covenant with the night, so that day and night no longer come at their appointed time, then my covenant with David my servant- and my covenant with the Levites who are priests ministering before me – can be broken and David will no longer have a descendant to reign on his throne. I will make the descendants of David my servant and the Levites who minister before me as countless as the stars of the sky and as measureless as the sand on the seashore." (NIV)

This is in connection to the promises to Abraham, Gen. 22:17. God would make his descendants as numerous as the stars. That promise was not about physical Israel. Paul explains that the promises to the patriarchs were of ONE seed, Christ, Gal.3:16. Christians are of Christ seed, and are as numerous as the stars of the sky. We are priests, in fulfillment of the Aaronic priesthood, the shadow or type, of the Old Testament. We offer up spiritual sacrifices continually.

"They will reign (Greek - basileusousin, future, indicative, active) on (Greek – epi- "on or "over") the earth (Greek – gys- land)" from Marshall's Interlinear. This agrees with Tischendorf's Greek N.T. In this Greek text – it is future. In the ASV it says – "and they reign upon the earth". This follows the Greek text of the Textus Receptus of 1894 and 1550, which uses the word "basileusomen"- they reign.

The saints were reigning even then with Christ, Eph.2:6, through his word and the preaching of the Gospel. Jesus was then at the right hand of God and reigning; yet in Heb. 2:8, "not all things were yet subject to Him" (NIV). How does Christ reign through his saints? Rom. 5:21 answers: "Just as sin reigned in death, so grace might reign through righteousness to bring eternal life through Jesus Christ our Lord." (NIV). Not all things were yet subject to Jesus before 70 A.D. They would be in fact when the kingdom came to its completion in 70A.D. (or soon after that) and Jesus would hand the kingdom over to the Father, 1 Cor. 15: 27-28. However, reigning with Christ was still the future in the sense that it would continue. Their relationship with Christ would not end by death or persecution. They will reign over the earth.

It is interesting to read Lk 19:11-27. There was a man of noble birth (Jesus) who went to a distant country (earth) to have himself appointed king (king of the Jews), and then return. The Jews refused for him to be king over them. Some however did become his servants and brought forth fruit in different amounts. The nobleman (Jesus) returned and judged those upon the earth. Verse 27 says that those who did not want him to be king over them were his enemies, and he ordered that they be killed in front of Him. The return of the nobleman, Jesus, was the time the servants received their full inheritance (their redemption of the body and the resurrection). For his servants, that relationship began when they became sons, and God sent the Spirit of his son into their hearts. We also start reigning with Christ when we become his sons. That process is completed and we reign with Christ forever when we receive the full inheritance at our death.

Some say that can't be true. They argue that if Jesus was now reigning over the earth, we would not see all the wickedness and corruption that we see now. The same argument could be made based on appearances by those that deny there is a God. They say, if there really is a God, then how do you explain all the wickedness in the world. Appearances do not reveal the truth of God's kingdom. Jesus reigns in the hearts of believers all over the world. All nations can flow into the kingdom by faith and have been ever since the first century. His Kingdom is very much alive and well.

Verse 11. The Voice of Many Angels

"Then I looked and heard the voice of many angels, numbering thousands upon thousands, and ten thousand times ten thousand. they encircled the throne and the living creatures and the elders." (NIV)

Here, we see the emphasis of the innumerable company of angels that encircle the throne. They are as countless as the stars. They are all servants of God at his command. (When Rev. 9:16 speaks of 200 million mounted troops, I immediately think of this passage. That passage would answer to an angelic army, ready and commanded by the Lord of hosts. No armies on earth were ever even a significant fraction of 200 million.) The heavens are full of the Hosts of heaven, all praising and serving God. Wow. Awesome. Praise Him.

Verse 12. Worthy Is The Lamb That Was Slain

"In a loud voice they sang: 'Worthy is the Lamb who was slain, to receive power and wealth and wisdom and strength and honor and glory and praise!'" (NIV)

I love this verse. I love the modern song (by Hillsong Worship or Gateway Worship) that goes with it. Join with me – "Worthy is the Lamb who was slain, to receive power, and glory, and wealth, and wisdom, and strength and honor and glory and praise." HE IS WORTHY! PRAISE HIM!

Verse 13. Every Creature In Heaven And On Earth Praised Him

"Then I heard every creature in heaven and on Earth and under the Earth and on the sea and all that is in them singing: 'to him who sits on the throne and to the lamb be praise and honor and glory and power forever and ever!'" (NIV)

WOW! What must that be like? Can you imagine being there, hearing such an enormous host of heavenly beings all joining together in praise – far beyond anything we could ever know on earth. Every creature in heaven joined in singing. Heaven is a place full of praise and rejoicing.

Verse 14. Fell Down And Worshiped

"The four living creatures said amen and the elders fell down and worshiped. (NIV)

True singing, adoration, and praise – naturally results in a true heart full of worship. We are filled by Him, lifted up by Him, exalted by Him – so we effortlessly fall down and worship Him.

CHAPTER SIX

I am aware of two interpretations of the seals. The first, would follow scriptural thinking but seems it would lack clarity in the details. I will present it because some of the interpretation has some merit. However, I favor the second interpretation as being more relevant to John's time and the focus of the revelation.

The two approaches involve - 1. Seeing the seals as an unfolding of judgments sent upon the Jews since the time they were sent into captivity until John's time. 2. The seals are an unfolding of the events Jesus predicted in Matt. 24 leading up to the destruction of Jerusalem.

1.View – seeing the seals as an unfolding of judgments sent upon the Jews since the time they were sent into captivity.

To see the big picture for this view, let us first explore some concepts that lead up to an understanding of the view. John has said in Rev.1:19 "Write therefore, what you have seen, what is now, and what will take place later." (NIV). Marshall's Interlinear Translation translates it more accurately – "Write therefore the things which thou sawest and the things which are and the things which are about to occur." In other words, John was having visions of the past, the present, and the near future. With that understanding, we would understand that the <u>time</u> of the visions we would have to determine in each vision. A vision could start with the past and bring us through time up to the present and then even into the near future.

Now let us set the stage for understanding this view. God had warned Israel that if they insisted in not obeying him, he would scatter them among the nations and punish them. This warning is detailed in the covenant of blessing and cursing that God made with them in Deut. 27-30. If they disobeyed, God would bring them into judgment. Ezekiel 20:33-38 expresses well what happened to Israel – "As surely as I live, declares the sovereign Lord, I will rule over you with a mighty hand and an outstretched arm and with outpoured wrath. I will bring you from the nations and gather you from the countries where you have been scattered – with a mighty hand and an outstretched arm and with outpoured wrath. I will bring you into the desert of the nations and there, face to face, I will execute judgment upon you. As I judged your fathers in the desert of the land of Egypt, so I will judge you, declares the sovereign Lord. I will take note of you as you pass under my rod, and I will bring you under the bond of the covenant. I will purge you of those who revolt and rebel against me. Although I will bring them out of the land where they are living, yet they will not enter the land of Israel. Then you will know that I am the Lord." (NIV)

Israel was scattered into the nations as a judgment for their unfaithfulness. He would also destroy those who rebelled against him. They would never enter his rest (as their fathers who came out of Egypt, Heb. 3.)

God would bring them into the "desert of the nations". (Remember the great prostitute that John sees in the desert, Rev.17:3? She is about to be punished, Rev.17:1)

God punished the Israelites for their sin from the time they were sent into captivity. Daniel prophesies that there would be four world kingdoms that would rule over them until with the fourth, they would be gathered and punished and destroyed. This view of the opening of the seven seals starts with those judgments when Israel is sent into captivity.

6:2. The First Seal that is opened reveals the first world kingdom, Babylon. Israel was first sent to them for judgment. In the first seal we have a rider on a <u>white horse</u>. <u>Horses are associated with war in scripture</u>. Prov.21:31 says "The horse is made ready for the day of battle, but victory rests with the Lord." (NIV) (see Zech.9:10; 10:3) The rider has a <u>bow</u> in his hand. At least in two scriptures, the bow is associated with Babylon. In speaking of Babylon, Jeremiah 6:22-23 says, "Look, an army is coming from the land of the north; a great nation is being stirred up from the ends of the earth. They are armed with bow and spear; they are cruel and show no mercy. They sound like the roaring sea as they ride on their horses; they come like men in battle formation to attack you, o daughter of Zion." (NIV). (See also Jer.50:13-14).

The rider was <u>given a crown</u>. This tells us he was a king. That kingship was given to him. By whom? By God in order to carry out God's purpose.

Nebuchadnezzar is called "king of kings", Dan.2:37; Ezek.26:7. He was a world ruler.

The rider <u>went out to conquer</u>. Nebuchadnezzar was a king who went out to conquer other nations. He did not just go out to fight a battle to defend his kingdom. He was a world ruler. This description fits him well.

<u>6:3,4 The Second Seal</u>. This seal seems to be associated with the rider in Zechariah 1.

<u>The fiery red horse.</u> This was during the time of Darius, the Mede. The Medo - Persian empire was the second world empire. Zech. 1:7-15 records the rider on the red horse with other horses behind him. The rider reports to the angel of the Lord that they found the <u>whole world at rest and in peace</u>. Verse 12 says – "Then the angel of the Lord said, Lord Almighty, how long will you withhold mercy from Jerusalem and from the towns of Judah, which you have been angry with these seventy years?" …14 "This is what the Lord almighty says, I am very jealous for Jerusalem and Zion, and I am very angry with the nations that feel secure. I was only a little angry, but they went too far with the punishment." (NIV) In Revelation, it is a rider on a red horse that is given power to take peace from the earth. The idea is that in Zechariah, the whole world is found at peace, but the angels say God is very angry with the nations. Here the rider is given power to take peace from the earth. In Darius' time, war followed, peace was taken from the earth. The red horse symbolizes bloodshed as seen in battle.

<u>6:5-6, The Third Seal</u>. This seal has a black horse with a rider holding a pair of scales. The scales weigh out wheat and barley. Because they are rationed out, it symbolizes scarcity. Ezek.4:9-17 tells us. In verses 16-17 it says, "The people will eat rationed food in anxiety and drink rationed water in despair, for food and water will be scarce." NIV. In Revelation 6:6 it says, "A quart of wheat for a day's wages, and three quarts of barley for a day's wages and do not

damage the oil and wine." (NIV). The KJV says – "and they shall eat bread by weight, and with care; and they shall drink water by measure, and with astonishment." Weights were measured by grains of wheat and an obol (obolos) was 12 grains in ancient Greece. Here in the Greek text, it says "choinix" of wheat for a "denarius".

There is some evidence of great famine in Greece in the second and third quarters of the 4th century B.C. Athens was especially affected. One writer quotes Encyclopedia Britannica, C1994-2003, saying – "The economy of mainland Greece declined during the Hellenistic age, though standards rose briefly about 260 B.C, and there were pockets of prosperity. – The general picture is one of poverty, unemployment, falling wages, depopulation, and emigration. The forests were stripped, the land neglected, and small holdings swallowed upon large estates, which were, however, under - developed. The Athenian silver mines at Larium were depleted, though they reopened briefly at the end of the third century B.C. Demand for painted pottery ceased. Athenian wine was of poor quality. Olive oil, however, continued to command a market."

The third seal by this view would be during the 3rd world empire, the Grecian. It would be characterized by a judgment of famine and scarcity.

By the time of the interpretation of the second and third seals, the details do not necessarily fit what the Revelation is talking about. It seems we could be straining to make the details fit. Let's look at the second interpretation – the unfolding of the judgments upon Israel that Jesus outlined in Matt. 24.

Chapter 6 begins with the opening of the 7 seals and the judgments that ensue as each is opened. It is helpful to our understanding of the Revelation to discover the times in which visions occur and the events to which they refer. If we follow the outline Jesus gave us in Matt. 24, by comparing that to Revelation it helps us to sort things out. Matt, 24 works for us as an outline and guide to those times and events in Revelation. (Parallel passages to Matt.24, containing the same subject matter, are in Mk 13, and Lk.21. These are the Olivet discourses of the synoptic gospels. The Gospel of John does not include the Olivet discourse. However, The Revelation of John does contain

The Olivet discourse in prophetic language -in panoramic view and detail.)

In Matt. 24, Jesus has just alluded to the destruction of Jerusalem and that not one brick of the temple would be left upon another. The disciples ask him three questions about it:

1. "When will these things happen?"
2. "What will be the sign of your coming?"
3. "When will be the end of the age?"

Jesus gives them signs: 1. <u>Many will claim to be the Christ</u>. 2. You will hear of <u>wars and rumors of wars</u>. Then, he says the end is not yet. 3. <u>Nation will rise against nation</u>. 4. There will be <u>famines</u> and <u>earthquakes</u>. (There was a great famine that came over the Roman world in Acts 11:28-29 in the time of emperor Claudius reign, around 46 A.D. There were several earthquakes in different places. One earthquake happened in 61 A.D. and destroyed 3 cities of Asia Minor: Colossae, Hierapolis, and Laodicea. Colossae and Hierapolis were not rebuilt. Laodicea was rebuilt.) In verse 8, Jesus says, "<u>These are the beginning of birth pains.</u>" The world would have many birth pains and distress before a new spiritual nation, the heavenly Jerusalem, was born, (cf. Isaiah 66:7-11). 5. <u>Many will turn away from the faith</u>. (Many will fall away). 6. <u>Many false prophets will appear</u> and deceive many. 7. There will be <u>an increase of wickedness</u>. 8. The <u>gospel of the kingdom will be preached to all the world</u> (land, Roman world) and <u>then the end will come</u>. (See Appendix D: "Gospel to the World"). Paul states that the gospel was taken to the whole world, Col.1:23. So do many scriptures. This was accomplished by Paul and the apostles in their generation.

Then Jesus enters upon a change somewhat. He says "When you see standing in the holy place (Jerusalem) the abomination that causes desolation (Roman armies, pagans, that would defile the city) … let those in Judea flee to the mountains. Let not one on the rooftop get anything out of his house… Flee! Flee! Flee! He tells believers in so many words. From the Romans coming in and onward, the destruction would continue until all in Jerusalem was destroyed.

All of what happened until Jerusalem was destroyed would

be a time of distress unequaled in history, verse 21.

Then, in 29-31 Jesus says, "Immediately after the distress of those days (NIV) (the days up to the destruction of Jerusalem) after the distress of those days: 1. There would be signs in the heavens, the sun and moon would not shine, the stars would fall from the sky. 2. The heavens would be "shaken" (meaning judged), Lk 21:26. 3. Jesus would return, come with his angels. 4. He would blow his trumpet (1 Thess. 4:16) and gather his elect (resurrection). (cf. Lk21).

What Jesus says lays out the time sequence and events in which things were to occur. It becomes then a roadmap to help us understand where and in what time we are at in the Revelation.

THE SEALS

Verse 1. The Lamb Opened The First Seal

"I watched as the lamb opened the first of the Seven Seals. Then I heard one of the four living creatures say in a voice like thunder, 'come!' (NIV)

"The Lamb opened the first seal"

The opening of a seal was to break a seal, thus opening a book, to read what was inside. Opening what had been sealed meant that the time had come for the prophecies inside to be fulfilled, or to take place. Chapter 1:1 tells us that the revelation was of things that "must soon take place".

Rev.1:19 says it was of things that were, are, and things "about to occur".

The book of Revelation is about the fulfillment of all things. The judgments that were to come upon the Jews (and be fulfilled) start here in chapter 6. The final fulfillment of bible prophecies were tied to the destruction of Jerusalem. (We can know that the prophecies of scripture were fulfilled around that time, because they were to occur around the time of the destruction of Jerusalem.) With that destruction, the whole Mosaic system or world order would be abolished or changed. The Mosaic system included the law, the Aaronic priesthood, animal sacrifices, feast days, Jewish culture, the Jewish world order. Some of those prophecies that were to occur around the time of the destruction of Jerusalem were: the judgment of the heavens, Matt.24:29; the return or second coming of Christ, Matt.24:30; the resurrection, Jn 5:25-28; the final judgment of all those who had lived from the time of Adam and those under the Mosaic covenant, Acts 17:30-31 says (not "will judge", but Greek mellei- "about to judge"). It was about the restoration of all things, Acts 3:20-22. Revelation is about the consummation (completion) of all things. Lk.21, that tells us about the destruction of Jerusalem, says in verse 22:

"For this is the time of punishment in fulfillment of all that has been written." (NIV)

Here in Revelation 6, the punishment and judgment began.

Verse 2. A Conqueror Bent On Conquest

"I looked, and there before me was a white horse! Its rider held a bow, and he was given a crown, and he rode out as a conqueror bent on Conquest. (NIV)

"A white horse". "The horse is white", indicating a victor, a conqueror. We are not told what he actually did, but the horse represents the beginning of judgments. He rode out to battle.

We may think of the rider on the white horse here, as being Jesus, as it is in Rev.19. Jesus was raised up to the heavens, and given a crown as Lord of lords and King of Kings. He sat down at the right hand of God and began to reign. He was to reign until he put all his enemies down, 1 Cor 15:25-28. So, He Jesus, the rider on the white horse, who had been given a crown rode out to conquer his enemies and put them down. Could that be our understanding? Yes, I think so. There is a question: Could Jesus open the seals of the scroll and at the same time also be the rider on the white horse of the first seal? Does he play both roles? You, the reader, can decide.

"Horses" and their riders are symbolic of angels that are sent out from God to accomplish his purposes. This understanding is explained for us in a scene in Zechariah 6. In that text, there were four chariots with horses. An angel explains what they are, verse 5:

"…These are the four spirits of heaven going out from standing in the presence of the Lord of the whole earth." (NIV)

Why are there four spirits in Zechariah? Four represents the earth. The Bible speaks of the "four corners of the earth," Rev.7:1. That passage says,

"And after these things I saw four standing on the four corners of the earth, holding the four winds of the earth…"

In Rev. 7:1 there are four angels (There are four because they do God's bidding on the earth). The angels are standing on the four corners of the earth. They are holding the four winds (that would blow on the earth, namely North, East, South, and West). As winds, they can be understood as spirits, angels. (See Heb.1:7)

There are four horses and riders in the opening of the first 4 seals: A white one, a red one, a black one, and a pale one. These four riders seem to represent all the judgment on the earth since four is the number that represents earth.

"It's rider held a bow".

If this rider is Jesus, who is on the white horse, he had been given a crown and he had a bow. What is the significance of the bow in describing him?

The language is certainly visual. I think of Ps. 18 when the Lord comes down to rescue David. In Ps.18:14 he says,

"He shot his arrows and scattered the enemy, with great bolts of lightning he routed them." NIV.

The details of the first seal are difficult to interpret for positive identification. Our interpretation is reasonable. If we follow the outline of Christ in Matt.24, it seems to indicate the beginning of judgments as when the rider who is given a crown rides out with a battle bow to conquer. The details, if applying to the time of Matt.24, the "beginning of birth pains' ', is correct, then we have begun the time of the "distress" Christ speaks of. When did it start? There was distress with the persecution of Christians by Saul, Acts 8. There was distress in various cities during the missionary journeys. There was the distress of great famine in the Roman world predicted by Agabus, Acts 11:28. Paul speaks of the present "distress" in 1 Cor.7:26. There were the earthquakes, especially the one in 61 A.D. that destroyed the cities of Hierapolis, Colassae, and Laodicea.

These were all signs of the "beginning of birth pains" that Jesus spoke of. Then there was the horrible persecution of Christians under Nero from the great fire of Rome, July 64 A.D. to his death in June, 68 A.D. There was the struggle of the Roman empire in civil war from June, 68 A.D. until Dec. 69 A.D. There was the Jewish -Roman War from 66-70 A. D.

With the riders are we seeing symbolically the heavenly forces behind the distress and judgments? We seem to be seeing the heavenly forces, angels on horses, and the judgments they bring represented by the colors of the horses and the things they bring – namely blood - shed, famine, pestilence, scarcity, and death.

Verse 3. The Lamb Opened The Second Seal

"When the lamb opened the second seal, I heard the second living creature say 'come!'" (NIV)

Verse 4. A Fiery Red Horse

"Then another horse came out, a fiery red one. Its rider was given power to take peace from the earth and to make men slay each other. He was given a large sword." (NIV)

"The earth" here is better translated as "the land". John is not referring to the whole physical world, or globe. The word here is (Greek - ge, land). It is the word used when scripture refers to the land of Judah, the land of Zebulon, and so forth. Here, 'the land" is referring to the "promised land", Palestine. Understanding what the word really means and not "earth" helps us a lot to understand the prophecies and what the prophet has in mind, or intended, and their fulfillment.

"Earth" in scripture is not talking about the "Globe with the Eastern and Western hemispheres that we think of today. It is the land, the promised land of the Jews and the nations that are around the land. It is the Bible land, around which the action of everything in the Bible revolves and takes place. The Bible never talks about China, Australia, Indonesia, South America, North America, Antarctica or whatever. It always deals with the land that was concerning the history of the Jews and sacred history.

"Its rider was given power to take peace from the earth ("land" -T.S.)," (NIV) the land of Palestine.

"A fiery red horse." This horse brings on the battle. He takes peace from the earth, (land). He makes men slay each other. They are slain with swords, as indicated by his large sword.

The horse is red, representing bloodshed. Men were slaying each other. Jesus said there would be "wars and rumors of wars".

Prior to and during the Jewish war with Rome (66-70,73 A.D.) There were also factions of Jews fighting one another. Brothers were killing brothers. It was like a civil war among Jewish brothers. Josephus describes all the bloodshed between the warring factions of Jews. Josephus calls it a "civil war" in the city of Jerusalem when he describes three warring factions of the Jews, many zealots, who by fighting were killing many there. In Book 5, chapter 1, of the "Jewish Wars" he says,

"Dead bodies of strangers were mingled together with those of their own countrymen, and those of profane with those of the priests, and the blood of all sorts of dead carcasses stood in lakes in the holy courts." Jerusalem "became a sepulcher for the bodies of their own people, and had made the holy house itself a burial-place in this civil war."

Verse 5. The Lamb Opened The Third Seal

"When the lamb opened the third seal, I heard the third living creature say, 'come!' I looked, and there before me was a black horse! Its rider was holding a pair of scales in his hand. (NIV)

"A black horse". I think first of "death" when you say it was black. There was death by this time. This horse's rider was holding a "pair of scales." (a balance with which to weigh food) Verse 6 tells us essentially how expensive it had become to buy the simplest necessities - as food. Famine is indicated here.

In this verse, we learn of Judgment that brought great famine and scarcity. Some interpret this as in fulfillment of the prophecy of Agabus in Acts 11:28-30. There it says,

"One of them, named Agabus, stood up and through the Spirit predicted that a severe famine would spread over the entire Roman world. (This happened during the reign of Claudius.) The disciples, each according to his ability, decided to provide help for the brothers living in Judea." (NIV)

The fourth century historian Orosius mentions the famine in Syria which occurred in 46A.D. Josephus also wrote in "Antiquities", chapter 20, 1.3-2.5- says: that at the time Claudius Caesar took over the temple and its treasury, queen Helena of Adiabene "was of great help to the masses in Jerusalem for there was a famine in the land that overtook them, and many people died of starvation." It became necessary to seek food abroad and queen Helena sent her attendants with money to get food to the city of Alexandria. Suetonius mentions the famine in Claudius' time. In his book he says, "There was a scarcity of food as the result of bad harvests that occurred during a span of several years." Tacitus mentions "scanty crops, and consequent famine" also in the reign of Claudius (Tacitus, "Annals," Book XII, 43).

Such famines were predicted by Jesus in Matt. 24:7. But, does this verse refer to those predictions like that by Agabus and their fulfillment? That was the beginning of birth pains for sure. But here, I do not think so. The famine here is part of the judgment of the four horsemen. This famine followed the bloodshed of war. As war continues, food and supplies diminish. Scarcity necessarily follows. So also does pestilence and death, all as a consequence of war. It follows the red horse and the bloodshed. It is a natural sequence and result of war. The fighting that led to the destruction of Jerusalem had already begun. The famine occurs sometime during that fighting. Let us reset the scene to discover the time where we are.

Historically, the Jews had several uprisings and revolted against the Roman empire. It started the Jewish- Roman war in 66 A.D. The Roman armies under the emperor, Vespasian, and his son Titus eventually put down the Jewish rebellion, when Titus leveled Jerusalem and burned it to the ground by 70 A.D. The History is recorded by a first century Jewish historian and eyewitness, Josephus, in his book - "The Jewish Wars".

The time of famine in the city of Jerusalem, and the reason for such famine and starvation to death is recorded in Josephus.

Josephus tells us that there was grain stored in houses in Jerusalem "which would have been sufficient for a siege of many years." Titus and the Roman army had Jerusalem under siege at the time the three Jewish factions in the city were fighting one another. The factions set fire to the houses of grain in the city while fighting. Thus, it brought on great <u>famine</u> in the city. For the people in the city there was nothing to eat. They starved. However, the supplies in the temple were good. The faction in the temple was led by Eleazar. He held up in the temple with his followers. Josephus tells us there were plenty of provisions there, a great abundance of what was consecrated to sacred uses. That would include the <u>oil and the wine</u>.

Now, the people of the city could not escape the city because of the siege. They could not approach any agreement or settlement with their enemies because of the three warring factions in the city. People were hopelessly trapped, left to die by darts, the sword, starvation, pestilence.

Nothing would be reliable, predictable, or secure. It was a time of chaos, torment, fear, and death. Josephus says that the noise of fighting was incessant day and night. Only the lamentation and mourning exceeded that noise. There was no regard for those wounded, hurting and still alive. There was no care to bury the dead. The people that fought each other trod upon the heaps of dead bodies that were at their feet. (<u>Josephus, "War of the Jews," Book 5, chapter 1</u>.)

Paul spoke of the "present distress" and warned the Corinthians of harshness that lay ahead in 1Cor.7:29-31. [Paul wrote 1 Corinthians about 53-54 A. D. at Ephesus.] In the context of that chapter, "the present distress" may be referring to the "beginning of birth pains"; Paul speaks of his instructions that are given as not of necessity, but by permission, because of "<u>the present distress</u>". But he also warned of what was coming. He said "the time was short" and the "world in its present form was passing away." In verses 29-31 he says,

"What I mean, brothers, is that the time is short. From now on those who have wives should live as if they had none; those who mourn, as if they did not; those who are happy, as if they were not, those who buy something, as if it were not theirs to keep, those who use the things of the world, as if not engrossed in them. For this world in its "present form" (Greek -schemati, "order") is passing away. I would like you to be free of concern." (NIV)

The old Jewish system, its worship, temple and city were to be destroyed as prophesied. Paul spoke of what was coming in their future. Jerusalem would be cut off (besieged), war within would consume many, along with famine and disease. The city would not survive what had been prophesied. The complete destruction of the Mosaic system would happen. It would pass away. The Kingdom of Christ would open up in its place.

Even for Christians at the time - hard, trying, uncertain, and fearful times lay ahead. Could they be faithful?

Verse 6. Do Not Damage The Oil Or The Wine

"Then I heard what sounded like a voice among the four living creatures, saying, 'a quart of wheat for a day's wages, and 3 quarts of barley for a day's wages, and do not damage the oil and the wine!' (NIV)

"A quart of wheat for a day's wages." (NIV) A man could work all day just to eat that day.

"Do not damage the oil and wine." (NIV) - (see explanation in verse 5)

Verse 7. The Lamb Opened The Fourth Seal

"When the lamb opened the fourth seal, I heard the voice of the four living creatures say, 'come!' (NIV)

Verse 8. A Pale Horse

"I looked and there before me was a Pale Horse! Its rider was named Death, and Hades was following close behind him. They were given power over a fourth of the Earth to kill by sword, famine and plague, and by the wild beasts of the Earth. (NIV)

Notice here, the Pale Horse and its judgment represented an increase in judgment. Judgment started out with bloodshed, progressed to famine and scarcity, and here to all of it – sword, famine, plague, and wild beasts.

Fourth seal – perhaps was all the judgments upon the earth, as four is the number for earthly.

"A pale horse" - We don't have to guess this imagery. The rider was named Death. It was death by sword, famine, plague or wild beasts. Hades (the place for the spirits of the dead at that time), followed close behind. Those who were killed; their spirits went to the realm of the dead (hades). Their bodies - that usually in normal times would be laid in the grave; were in this war in Jerusalem, not buried; but lay in piles of dead bodies on the ground.

"A fourth of the earth" is ¼ of the earth. What does this fraction mean? The fraction, ¼, is a fraction of four. Four represents the earth. The fraction ¼, then means a "fraction of those upon the earth" were killed. It is not an exact number or portion. It is being used symbolically. It is not indicating how many, but rather tells us where the judgments are taking place - on the earth, (four) and that a fraction was killed. This is important to pay attention to, because the fraction changes when we get to the opening of the seventh seal. There, the scene of where the action occurs changes.

"Killed by sword, famine, plague and by wild beasts". The war and horrible conditions that ensued were progressively worse! They were killed by the sword and others left to starve to death. With more and more death - starvation, sickness and disease was rampant. The stench of dead bodies was by the thousands. Bodies were piled everywhere. Josephus' description serves to help us realize how terrible the judgments of these horsemen were on Jerusalem.

Verse 9. He Opened the Fifth Seal

"When he opened the fifth seal, I saw under the altar the souls of those who had been slain because of the word of God and the testimony they had maintained. (NIV)

The Fifth Seal – The number five is mentioned in scripture in connection with many different things. However, if we think about the fifth seal talking about the souls under the altar, we may get our connection. The souls under the altar are slain on the earth and now are under the altar, which symbolically represent sacrifices. The number five is often used for the sacrifices that had been offered in Numbers 7:17-83. Here the souls slain are under the altar.

"The souls under the altar." The souls are on the burnt offering as a sacrifice because they are "slain". They were slain on earth. They are not sacrifices of atonement. That was offered only once a year in the Holy of Holies. Jesus was the fulfillment once for all for the sacrifice of atonement, Heb.9:25-26. Those slain were sacrificed on the altar of burnt offering, not animal sacrifices but human. They were sacrificed for their allegiance to God and their testimony of him. They were drink offerings poured out to God. (See Phil.2:17: 2 Tim.4:6.).

In heaven there was only one sacrifice for sin offered for all time- Jesus Christ. Jesus was killed on earth but never on earth was his sacrifice offered in the temple. Rather, he was killed on earth but the offering of himself was taken into the true tabernacle of God, the one made without human hands, the tabernacle God built, the Reality in the heavens. Heb 9:23-26 says,

"It was necessary then, for the copies of the heavenly things to be purified with these sacrifices, but the heavenly things themselves with better sacrifices than these. For Christ did not enter a man-made sanctuary that was only a copy of the one; but he entered heaven itself, now to appear in God's presence for us. Nor did he enter heaven to offer himself again and again, the way the high priest enters the most holy place every year with blood not his own. But now he (Christ) has appeared once for all at the end of the ages to do away with sin by the sacrifice of himself." (NIV).

"Slain because of the word of God and the testimony they had maintained."(NIV) The souls were martyrs. They had been slain or killed for their testimony. They were faithful unto death for the cause of Christ.

"Souls". The souls under the altar had died on earth and were now in heaven. But they were still "souls". They had not received their resurrected bodies yet. 1 Thess.4:14 teaches us that when Jesus returned; he would bring with him those who had fallen asleep (died). The ones who were still alive, who remained (of Jesus' generation) when Jesus returned would not precede those who had fallen asleep. (They would not be changed to their spiritual bodies and resurrected before those whom Jesus brought with him). Of those who were alive when Jesus returned - some would be taken and others left. Of those who were alive that were taken, they would be caught up in the air with Jesus and those he brought with him and so ever be with Jesus. They would all be with the Lord forever. Those who were left, I believe were born after the Mosaic covenant legally ended, at Christ's death. They were born under the time when the New Covenant went legally into effect, "after men are dead," Heb.9:17.

Verse 10. How Long To Avenge Our Blood

"They called out in a loud voice, 'how long, Sovereign Lord, holy and true, until you judge the inhabitants of the world and avenge our blood? (NIV)

"The souls called out...how long?" Those waiting for their redemptive bodies wanted to know how long what had happened to them would go on before God avenged their death. (God avenged their blood in the heavens. It is appointed for man once to die and then the judgment, Heb 9:27. The final judgment does not take place on earth, but in heaven in the spiritual realm.) These martyrs were coming out of the first 4 seal judgments, the judgments on earth up to the destruction of Jerusalem. Their blood would be avenged in the heavens upon the wicked dead who were raised to condemnation.

Verse 11. A Little Longer

"Then each of them was given a white robe, and they were told to wait a little longer, until the number of their fellow servants and brothers who were to be killed as they had been was completed." (NIV)

"White robe". Rev. 3:4 says - if they overcame, were faithful in their earthly life, they would be dressed in white. Rev.19:8 says "Fine linen stands for the righteous acts of the saints." (NIV)

"Wait a little longer". In Lk.18:1-5 Jesus tells the story of a judge whom a widow continually asks of him to grant her justice. Finally, the judge thinks - she keeps bothering me and eventually she will wear me out with her coming. So, he grants her justice. Then in verse 6 it says, "And he said, 'listen to what the unjust judge says. And will not God bring about justice for his chosen ones, who cry out to him day and night? Will he keep putting them off? I tell you he will see that they get justice and quickly." (NIV) God's answer to the martyrs comes quickly. The next verses, Rev.6:12-17, announce the signs in the heavens and the judgment in the heavens (That is where the righteous are avenged. The wicked dead meet the wrath of the Lamb. The description of the actual action starts in chapter 8.)

I can't help but think here of Jesus in Lk. 11 and Matt.23. In those chapters, Jesus pronounces scathing woes upon the pharisees. He then says that the blood of the prophets would come upon that generation. Then in chapter 12 of Luke he tells his disciples to be ready for His coming, 12:35-48. Then he says – "I have come to bring fire on the earth, and how I wish it were already kindled." (NIV).

There, he was speaking as the Son of God so emphatically. His righteous soul had committed NO sin. Yet he was aware of a cesspool of sin. He was long suffering for us, but how He hated sin. How he must have been more than ready to punish sin and vindicate his people who in their lives had put sin to death and turned to him. God hates sin, but loves his people.

Verse 12. He Opened The Sixth Seal

"I watched as he opened the Sixth Seal. There was a great earthquake. The sun turned black like a sackcloth made of goat hair. The whole moon turned blood red." (NIV).

This verse could be very revealing as to the exact time we are at in the Revelation, if we believe the "signs in the heavens" (the sun turns black, the moon blood red, and the stars fall from the sky) are the same "signs in the heavens" in Matt.24:29. Verse 29 says, "Immediately after the distress of those days," the signs in the heavens occur, the "heavenly bodies are shaken," and then Jesus returns with his angels to earth, verse 30. Before verse 29, the destruction of Jerusalem is not described in the text. When he came the second time, he was to bring salvation to those waiting for him, Heb.9:28. That means the resurrection would take place when he came. The signs preceding his coming were the signs in the heavens and they were to "look up for their redemption was drawing near", Lk. 21:26-28. They would "see the Son of Man coming in a cloud." That resurrection took place on resurrection day, 3 ½ days after the Passover, when the two witnesses were resurrected, Rev. 11:11-12. That is how Jesus kept Philadelphia from the "<u>hour of trial</u>" (the judgment) that was about to come upon the whole world, Rev.3:10. Jesus resurrected his people and therefore his people were not there when the judgment started. His people he resurrected had been born under the Mosaic covenant. Those who were born after that covenant ended legally, 30 A.D. (at the death of Christ and the start of the New Covenant); those righteous people were not resurrected but Jesus had told them rather to flee into the mountains of Judea. Those born before 30 A.D. were resurrected. Some of them were still alive when he came the second time. After the resurrection, the judgment began. Just days after the resurrection, when the two witnesses were resurrected, Titus closed the city with a siege. Lk. says that day (the day of judgment) would come upon them "unexpectedly like a trap," Lk.21:35. It came upon all those who live on the face of the earth (Greek - ges, the land).

Josephus and Tacitus, as we have recited previously, recorded the signs in the heavens. They describe heavenly activity as seen all over, and reported as fiery chariots and soldiers in the heavens fighting. They also record that during the siege of Titus, Romans present at one point in the earthly temple of Jerusalem saw a great light in the Holy of Holies and heard voices that said, "let us be going from here." The Roman soldiers claimed that the gods (as they understood it) were leaving the temple.

This sixth seal puts us at a definite time – the signs in the heavens, just before the second return of Christ, and the resurrection and then the judgment of the Jews on earth in Jerusalem and the destruction of the temple.

Before the two judgments of chapter 9, the 144,000 are sealed, marked with the name of God in their foreheads. (This makes us recall the marks over the doorposts of God's people in Egypt before the death angel, destroyer, passed over and killed the firstborn of Egypt.) The 144,000 are marked. But where are the 144,000, and who are they? They are in heaven, the first fruits of God, redeemed from the earth, Rev.14:3-4.

In chapter 9 we see the locusts from the abyss (where demons come from). They are not allowed to touch grass, plants, or trees, or anyone who has the seal of God on their forehead. Those with the seal on their foreheads are in heaven. They are the 144,000, the first fruits unto God. They are the saints from the Old Testament period who were resurrected. But they are also those younger saints who have fled to the mountains of Judea and are kept safe there "in the desert". This sealing was just before the Day of Judgment with the siege of Jerusalem. With the saints resurrected and marked and safe, the "shaking of the heavens and earth occurs. Was the battle in heaven? Yes. The heavens were shaken. Was the battle on earth? Yes. The earth was shaken. The locusts (demons) were released to carry out the judgment of God; but, the locusts were not allowed to touch the 144,000, the people of God.

Before verses 12-13, which speak of the sixth seal and the signs in the heavens; the judgments before those verses would affect a fourth,1/4 of the earth (verse 8). In other words, a fraction of 4, with 4 being a symbolic number for the earth. But in the judgments in Chapter 9, the judgments that followed affected a third, 1/3. When Paul talks about the 3rd heaven, 2 Cor.12:2, you begin to think 3 is a number that can represent the heavens. A third then being a fraction of the whole 3, heaven. Were these judgments occurring in heaven? Yes. Were they judgments affecting a fraction of the heavens? Yes. But we have said the earth was being shaken also (at the same time). Spiritual (or heavenly -represented by 3) demons carried out judgment on earth. In the heavens, they were defeated and judged (thrown into the lake of fire, Rev.20).

There are reasons to consider this interpretation. In chapter 9, the locusts, with tails of scorpions (demons, Lk.10:19) and the army of 200 million (there has never been an army of 200 million on the earth) symbolize heavenly beings. Just because some things are said to be on "earth" (Greek-ge, the land) does not mean it is referring to "our earth". There has always been symbolized a shadow, a type on earth, of the reality and fulfillment of the type in the heavens. There exists a parallel between the spiritual world and the physical world. God used the physical world on earth to teach us about what was in the spiritual world. There was a temple on earth, but there is one in the heavens. There is a Jerusalem on the physical earth, but there is a heavenly Jerusalem. There is a promised land on the earth, but there is one in the heavens called Beulah ("married") land. The things on earth were shadows and types of what was in the heavens. The promised land in prophecy is not always talking about a place on our physical earth. Remember, there is a promised land in the heavens. (See Appendix J: "Promised Land").

In Old Testament prophecies, the prophets often switch from what is on the earth to what would be in the heavens and then back again. The prophets also switched from talking about things in their present to what would be in the future and then back to their present again. These prophecies have often been misinterpreted to mean that God was going to fulfill prophecies on the physical earth when he was talking about the future in the heavens. This is all worthy of our time here to discuss.

So, back to our question about verses 12-13. Are the signs in the heavens, the ones Jesus mentions in Matt.24:29? Do they occur before the heavens are shaken, or during their being shaken? Or, could it be used, like it is often used in the Old Testament, of simply judgment coming for people on the earth and a figurative day of the Lord? The prophets spoke often of the heavens being darkened, and darkness descended upon the peoples of the world, a day of darkness, not light, a day of judgment for them. We could say of such a judgment – "Hey, it's curtains for you. Your end day has come." But here, what Jesus refers to in Mt.24:29 were signs in the heavens, and the "<u>heavens were shaken</u>," as it says <u>in that verse</u>. Not only so, they were not just a sign of a "figurative" judgment, but the next verse says Jesus came back <u>with his angels</u> and they "<u>gathered his elect</u>" (the resurrection). He goes on to say – "Be ready". This was definitely referring to his second return.

"<u>The sun turned black like sackcloth</u>." (NIV) Or in prophecies speaking of the same thing, "the sun will not give its light". In other words - the Day of the Lord has arrived and it is a day of darkness, fear, and judgment and fiery indignation.

"The whole moon turned blood red." (NIV) This makes us think of bloodshed and judgment. It is part of the signs in the heavens. (According to some, there was a blood-red moon.) Acts 2:19-20 says,

"I will show wonders in the heavens above (Mt 24:29) and signs on the earth below (Mt 24 the signs Jesus gives), blood and fire and billows of smoke. The sun will be turned to darkness (the sun turned black like sackcloth, Rev.6:12) and the moon to blood (Rev.6:12, also Mt 24) before the coming of the great and glorious Day of the Lord." NIV. The signs of Mt 24:29 were also predicted in Lk.21:25, here in Acts 2, and described in Rev.6:12.

The context of Acts 2:17-21 is "the last days". The last days have been misinterpreted, probably because people associate the "last days" with the beginning of the Christian era announced for the first time on Pentecost. However, though Pentecost was the beginning of the Christian era, the "last days" was in "fulfillment" of the prophecy of Joel about the coming day of judgment. When Jesus died on the cross, and that started legally the New Covenant, Heb.9:17; it also marked the "beginning of the "last days" for the Old Covenant, The Mosaic covenant. That covenant, at the point of Christ's death, became old, outdated, obsolete and ready to vanish away, Heb.8:13. The Mosaic covenant was then in its "last days". The end for that covenant got closer and John then says, "it is the last hour", (NIV), 1 Jn.2:18 the final days approached near, and would end when the "great day of the Lord" (the second coming of Christ) arrived as mentioned at the text in Acts 2. (See the Appendix, the Last Days).

About the "blood moon" - the sign of the "blood moon". There are articles on-line under the subject of the sun turning black and the blood moon occurring in A.D. 69. One can read the details online.

Verse 13. Stars In The Sky Fell

"And the stars in the sky fell to earth, as late figs drop from a fig tree when shaken by a strong wind (NIV)

"The stars fell from the sky to earth". The picture given us of the sun, moon, and stars is one in which we think of our whole world falling apart. "The sky is falling! The sky is falling! says Chicken Little in the nursery story. Hey, it's curtains for you. "It's the end of everything FOR YOU". "Everything goes black"- is the message. The day of reckoning has come and who can escape it?

"Figs drop from a fig tree when shaken." (NIV) Remember Heb.12:26, "once more I will shake not only the earth but also the heavens, 27 the words once more indicate the removal of what can be shaken – that is created things – so that what cannot be shaken may remain." (NIV). The things in heaven and the earth that could be removed were removed so that the eternal kingdom, that cannot be shaken or removed remained.

Verse 14. The Sky Rolled Up

"The sky receded like a scroll, rolling up, and every mountain and Island was removed from its place. (NIV)

This is often interpreted as physical events that occur at the end of time, and the end of the physical earth and heavens. It is not. Nowhere in scripture is there ever an "end of time" itself, Gen.8:22. This is symbolic language. Such language is used in the Old Testament when God puts an end to a nation's reign and power, such as Babylon, Isa.13:10; or the nations mentioned in Amos, Amos 5:18-20. Eccl 1:4 says:

"Generations come and generations go, but the earth remains forever." (NIV) The earth will go on and on. It will remain forever.

This earth will not end. Time will not end. Jer. 33:20-21 says:

"This is what the Lord says, If you can break my covenant with the day and my covenant with the night, so that day and night no longer come at their appointed time, then my covenant with David my servant- and my covenant with the Levites who are priests ministering before me - can be broken and David will no longer have a descendant to reign on his throne." (NIV)

We have Christ, a descendant of David, on his throne who reigns forever and ever with the power of an endless life. Time and this earth will continue for ever and ever.

"The sky receded, like a scroll, rolling up" (NIV)

The picture of a scroll being rolled up suggests to us the same as "closing a book." It is the end of the book. We put the scroll (book) down. It is finished. We pick up a new scroll (book) and start reading anew. That is the idea. God has many scrolls or books within THE BOOK (the Bible). There are actually 66 books in the Bible. (Bible -means book). Here, the sky recedes, like rolling up a scroll. It does not mean the sky ends. It does mean, the sun, moon, stars, (the sky), the heavens as they once existed – changed, that scroll in the heavens was rolled up. The world order of heaven and earth changed. How, God shut the book on the Mosaic system on earth and changed how things once worked in the heavens. Jesus changed everything. He brought everything both in heaven and earth to be under his rule, Eph.1:10. In the heavens, he ruled until he brought everything - "principalities, dominion, might under his feet," 1 Cor. 15:27-28.

In this passage, the phrase "the sky receded, rolling up like a scroll," is in reference to something very specific in prophecy. The change in the heavens, also brought a change in world order on the earth. It occurred and ended with judgment on the world then. This judgment would bring about a change in the world order of things. God's people would no longer be under law and ruled by the Mosaic law. The then present world order and world conditions and requirements of that law would be removed. It would end, like rolling up a scroll and closing the book on it. That world order that God instituted way back in time would end. (Note: it was not destroyed, it was fulfilled and passed away, Mt.5:17). Everything was to be made new in the new covenant and its spiritual nature and rule by faith. The New Testament mentions the change in terms of "the heavens and earth (old system, old world order) would "pass away". That can be confusing to understand. Does it mean the physical earth and heavens, the physical world, would disappear? No. The world in Noah's time "perished"; yet the physical earth was still there, and Noah and his family lived on. 2 Peter 3:6 says,

"Whereby the world that then was, being overflowed with water, perished." (NIV). (Greek – apoleto).

"Perished" "is the same word used of heaven and earth -Heb.1:10, that "they will perish" (NIV) (Greek -apolountai) in Heb.1:11.

"They will perish, (as did the first world of Noah's time, T.S.) but you remain, they will all wear out like a garment (get old and need replacement), You will <u>roll them up</u> like a robe; like a garment they will be <u>changed</u>." [Not annihilated or brought into physical non-existence].

The old world order was useful like a garment, but it got old, outdated, no longer useful to God for his purposes. He brought in the new creation, a spiritual creation, through Christ. Everything was changed. Jesus changed everything when he came – it changed in the heavens, on earth, and under the earth. Spiritually speaking, he made everything new, Rev. 21:5. The old world order or system collapsed when God brought judgment in 70 A.D. and destroyed Jerusalem. Jesus came back, ending that world order; and He had the Kingdom ready, in its completion, to replace it.

Some scriptures help us to see this change of order: 1 Cor. 7:31 says, The world, <u>in its present form</u> (Greek- "schemati" - scheme, world order) was passing away. Hebrews 9:10-11 mentions: "They are only a matter of food and drink and various ceremonial washings-external regulations <u>applying until the time of the new order.</u> When Christ came as high priest of the good things that are already here." (NIV) (These were things of the kingdom that was coming into being and being built. Elements of that kingdom was already there.) When the kingdom of God came to completion, and the heavenly Jerusalem was ready for God's people (70A.D.), heaven opened up for God's people to live in for ever and ever with him. Rev.21:4 says: "He will wipe away every tear from their eyes. There will be no more death (those in heaven are not harmed by the second death) or mourning or crying or pain, for <u>the old order of things has passed away</u>. He who was seated on the throne said, <u>I am making everything new!</u>" (NIV) (See in Appendix G: "World passing away")

Verse 15. They Hid In Caves

"Then the kings of the earth, the princes, the generals, the rich, the mighty, and every slave, and every free man hid in caves and among the rocks of the mountains." (NIV)

"<u>Hid in caves and among rocks of the mountains</u>" (NIV). This is very specific. When Jerusalem was surrounded by the Roman army under the command of Titus, and there was so much suffering and death happening in the city – people hid in caves and among rocks from the wrath of the Lamb that was upon them. This was literally true. The Jerusalem area is known for its many limestone caves and rocky terrain. Josephus even describes the time this way - in the rebellious factions in the city trying to hide from the Romans:

"So now the last hope which supported the tyrants (the rebels in the city), and that crew of robbers who were with them, was in caves and caverns underground: where, if they could once fly, they did not expect to be searched for; but tried, that after the whole city should be destroyed, and the Romans gone away, they might come out again, and escape from them." (Josephus, The Jewish War, Book 6, chap.7, sect 3.) The rebels inside the city thought they could escape from the Romans by hiding in caves.

Josephus goes on to say, "This was no better than a dream of theirs; for they were not able to lie hid either from God or from the Romans. However, they depended on these underground subterfuges, and set more places on fire than did the Romans themselves; and those that fled out of their houses thus set on fire, fled into the ditches. They killed without mercy, and pillaged them also…"

The description of the suffering of the city by Josephus was horrendous, unimaginable and in such cringing detail. Truly, the Wrath of the Lamb, alluded to in this verse (verse 16), was upon them.

For believers, they had been warned by Jesus in Matt.24. When they saw the "abomination of desolation", the Roman armies approaching Jerusalem – they were warned to flee to the mountains.

Revelation says they were protected in the desert, from the Dragon during that time, Rev.12:14.

Verse 16. Hide Us From The Face Of Him

"They called to the mountains and the rocks, 'fall on us and hide us from the face of him who sits on the throne and from the Wrath of the Lamb!' (NIV)

The passing of the "old world order" (The Mosaic system), took place with the destruction of Jerusalem in 70 A.D. The collapse of the city came with the Wrath of the Lamb – coming in vengeance upon those who had killed the prophets,

Mt. 23:35-36; and upon those who had rejected the son of God and crucified him. Jesus had told those who condemned him at his trial – "In the future you will see the Son of Man sitting at the right hand of the Mighty One and coming on the clouds of heaven." Mt.26:64. Yes! Some of those who had condemned Jesus would see his return and experience the Wrath of the Lamb.

The words of verses 15-16 are spoken of in Luke. In the context it is referring to judgment upon the earth at the time of the destruction of Jerusalem. Verses 15-16 are a reference to Luke 23:28-31. There, women were following Jesus mourning and wailing for him as he carried his cross. Jesus turned and said to them,

"Daughters of Jerusalem, do not weep for me; weep for yourselves and your children. 29 For the time will come when you will say, 'Blessed are the barren women, the wombs that never bore, and the breasts that never nursed.' 30 Then 'they will say to the mountains, fall on us! And to the hills, cover us.' 31 For if men do these things when the tree is green, what will happen when it is dry?' (NIV)

These verses in Luke are also like Hosea 10:8 and Isa. 2:19,21. The prophetic language used in all three places - here, and in Hosea and Isaiah, refer to judgments of Israel on different occasions. In Hosea 9:1 God says, "Do not rejoice O Israel. Do not be jubilant like other nations for you have been unfaithful to your God… They will not remain in the Lord's land." (NIV) In Hosea 10:8 it says "the high places (the idol shrines on the mountains) of wickedness will be destroyed– it is the sin of Israel. Thorns and thistles will grow up and cover their altars. Then they will say to the mountains and to the hills, 'fall on us!'…(NIV)

Isaiah 2:19 speaks of the day "when the Lord rises <u>to shake the earth</u>" – that men would flee to caves in the rocks and to holes in the ground from the dread of the Lord…verses 10,19, 21. (NIV)

The words are in reference to the Lord shaking the earth, not the heavens. They hid in caves and rocks because of the "<u>wrath of the Lamb</u>". 2 Thess. 1:5-7 says,

"All this is evidence that God's judgment is right, and as a result you will be counted worthy of the kingdom of God, for which you are suffering. God is just: <u>He will pay back trouble</u> to those who trouble you and give relief to you who are troubled, and to us as well. This will happen when the lord Jesus is revealed (the 2nd coming, his return to the earth) from heaven in blazing fire with his powerful angels. <u>He will punish those who do not know God</u> and <u>do not obey the gospel of God</u>." (NIV)

The <u>wrath of the Lamb</u> occurred on earth – the destruction of Jerusalem. It would also be revealed when he came. Was that judgment on earth? Perhaps. He returned in flaming fire taking vengeance, 2 Thess.1. Was there punishment while men were on the earth? We know there was. But, was there not also punishment in the heavens? What of the great day of judgment in the heavens when he separated the sheep from the goats? There is everlasting punishment then in the lake of fire. There was judgment on the earth and in the heavens, Heb.12:26. "Once more I will shake not only the earth but also the heavens." (NIV). There is more to understand.

His judgment on the earth was very severe. Jesus said the judgment would be a time of distress so terrible that there had not been anything so terrible since the beginning of the world or never to be equaled again, Matt. 24:21. Isa. 30:28 says,

"He (the Lord) shakes the nations in the sieve of destruction." (NIV). The nations were judged, punished and removed. Heb.12:26 says, "Once more I will shake not only the earth but also the heavens". (NIV). God would remove the things that could be shaken- he would remove the things and destroy them.

That "shaking" in Hebrews was in relation to the "order of things" in the heavens and earth. Then he tells us- "we (those to whom the letter was written - in the book of Hebrews) <u>are receiving a kingdom</u> that cannot be shaken." (NIV). They were in the process of receiving the kingdom. The kingdom came to its complete state in 70 A.D. when Jesus came back. The Kingdom in the heavens has been open in the heavens ever since that time with all nations flowing into it by faith.

A note here - we cannot say "the kingdom is but not yet." By that, people mean that Christians are in the kingdom, so in a sense it is here, but because, as some believe, that Jesus has not come back yet (a serious error), and has not yet set up his kingdom on earth, then the kingdom is not fully here yet. Such Christian still pray for the "coming" of the kingdom, believing that it has not yet been fulfilled. Such a view denies that Jesus came in 70 A.D. (Matt.16:27-28; Matt. 24:29-31). It denies that the kingdom is fully here and has been ever since 70 A.D. (See the appendix on the topics of the "Coming of Jesus", "the Kingdom" and the "Fulfillment of prophecies").

Verse 17. The Great Day Of Wrath Has Come

"For the great day of their wrath has come, and who can stand?' (NIV)

"Who can stand before the wrath of the Lamb?" No one. It's an easy and obvious answer. But – it was very excruciating beyond comprehending the experience on earth. Now what about the wrath of the Lamb in the heavens at the judgment? Best they were on the right side and that we are on the right side.

Here we answer the question, "who can stand?" Psalms 15 says,

"Lord, who may dwell in your sanctuary? Who may live on your holy hill? He whose walk is blameless and who does what is righteous, who speaks the truth from his heart and has no slander on his tongue…" (NIV)

Psalms 5:4-6 says,

"You are not a God who takes pleasure in evil; with you the wicked cannot dwell. 5 The arrogant cannot stand in your presence; you hate all who do wrong. 6 You destroy those who tell lies; bloodthirsty and deceitful men the Lord abhors. (NIV)

[Note the underlined words. They are either wrong in the verse and God contradicts himself elsewhere; or a person's understanding is very wrong to say that God does not hate anyone (See Ps.11:5-6) and God loves us unconditionally even as sinners. (Or is it – "while we were yet sinners"?). See the comments on the church of Thyatira in 2:20].

Isaiah 33:14-15 says,

"The sinners in Zion are terrified; trembling grips the godless; who of us can dwell with the consuming fire? Who of us can dwell with everlasting burning? 15 He who walks righteously, and speaks what is right…" (NIV). Witness the saints that walked with God in the fire of the furnace, Dan.3:25.

They walked with him in the fire – not touched by the flames and had not even the smell of smoke on them. They could dwell with a consuming fire.

When the great day of the wrath of the Lamb came – Jesus and the apostles had warned- be ready, be vigilant, be on your guard, don't be caught unaware.

CHAPTER SEVEN

144,000 SEALED

<u>Who is the 144,000?</u> Answer —All believers born under the Old Testament Period up to 30 A.D. Let's look:

In this chapter we see 144,000. That is a very Jewish number. Immediately we think – "Israel." But it is <u>not Physical Israel</u>. It is <u>Spiritual Israel</u>, the nation that was born on a day when Jesus resurrected them, Isa. 66:7-8. Let us examine things here closely.

1. Gal.3:16 teaches us that the promises to the patriarchs were not to "seeds as of many" (the physical descendants of Abraham) but to <u>ONE SEED</u>, Jesus Christ. It was through Jesus ONE SEED, that "all nations of the earth would be blessed," Gen12:3; 22:18. (NIV) It was through that ONE SEED a "spiritual nation" in the heavens would be born. Those who sprang from the ONE SEED Jesus, would be blessed. "If you belong to Christ, then you are Abraham's seed (of the ONE SEED) and heirs according to the promise," Gal.3:29. (NIV)

2. Rom.9:6-8 teaches us that <u>not all Israel is of Israel</u>. It was not the natural physical descendants that were Israel in prophecies, but children of Promise. It would be children by grace. John 1:12-13 speaks of this in saying, "Yet to all who received him, to those who believed in his name, he gave the right to become sons of God -<u>children born not of natural descent</u>, nor of human decision or a husband's will, but <u>born of God</u>." (NIV) Those born of God are the <u>True Israel</u>!

3. In Rom.11:5 there was a "remnant (of Israel) chosen by grace". Verse16, "If the <u>part </u>of the dough (the remnant) <u>offered as first fruits</u> is holy, then the whole batch is holy." (NIV) Then he tells Gentiles – if

you being "a wild olive shoot, have been grafted in among the others and now share in the nourishing sap" (NIV) (of the olive tree, true Israel). Gentiles (believers) were grafted into the true Israel of God. So, all Israel (True Believers) will be saved, verse 26.

All of what was said above was very quick perhaps, without good explanation. The point is – God sees the saved as the Spiritual Israel of God. When we see the 144,000, John is talking about the all saved believers, born under the Old Testament period, Spiritual Israel.

In Rev.14:4 the 144,000 are "offered as first fruits to God and the Lamb". (NIV)

Rom.11:16 the remnant (believers in Israel), were "offered as first fruits." (NIV)

James 1:18 says, "He chose to give us birth through the word of truth, that we might be a kind of first fruits of all he created." (NIV) That was Christians!

In Rev.14:4 the 144,000 were "purchased from among men." (NIV)

From the teaching of all scripture – Jesus "purchased us" (all believers- Old and New Testament). No one was saved any time until Jesus "purchased us with his own blood."

The 144,000 are the "servants of our God", verse 3 (NIV)

Verse 1. Four Angels At The Four Corners Of The Earth

"After this I saw four Angels standing at the Four Corners of the Earth, holding back the Four Winds of the Earth to prevent any wind from blowing on the land or on the sea or on any tree." (NIV)

"After this" gives us a break from the action. We end with the opening of the sixth seal in 6:12-17. Then we have an interlude in Chapter 7, so the prophet can inform us of some things. Then, in chapter 8, it begins with the opening of the 7th seal and takes up from the end of chapter 6 where the prophet John had already seen the sixth seal opened.

"Four angels...holding back the four winds". They are holding back judgments. Why? Before those judgments could come, God wants his people marked so they are not part of it. God's people are protected from the judgments. Thus, we see the sealing of the 144,000 in chapter 7.

Verse 2. Angel From The East

"Then I saw another angel coming up from the East, having the Seal of the Living God. He called out in a loud voice to the Four Angels who had been given power to harm the land and sea;" (NIV)

"Given the power to harm the land and sea". The angels had the power to bring judgment. The Judgment would not include land, sea, or trees. It would not include those sealed with the seal of God in their foreheads (in the next verse). This judgment was selective.

Verse 3. Do Not Harm Land, Sea, Or Trees

"Do not harm the land or the sea or the trees until we put a seal on the foreheads of the Servants of our God." (NIV)

When we hear of the seal of God we immediately think of the seal of the Holy Spirit, Eph.1:13-14. We are marked by the Spirit when we become Christians during our life on earth as an earnest guaranteeing our inheritance. However, this is referring to the sealing of the 144,000. They were sealed so that the judgment about to take place would "pass over them." This was like when the houses of the Israelites that were marked by the lamb's blood were passed over in the death of the firstborn of Egypt in Exodus12. Like the believers were passed over in Ex. 12, so here, the 144,000 who were the "servants of our God ", would not be included in the judgment that is described later in chapter 9 of the locusts.

Verse 4. The 144,000

"Then I heard the number of those who were sealed, 144,000, from all the tribes of Israel. (NIV)

Let us deal with the symbolism of numbers here. I do not believe they are literal numbers because it is hard to believe an exact 12,000 were saved out of each tribe. The numbers are symbolic and represent ideas.

"12,000" is 12 x 1000. 12 could be 4 (earth) x 3 (heaven). Those who lived on earth from that tribe that went to heaven. 1000 is "all". (God owns "the cattle on a 1000 hills,"

Ps. 50:10-12. (NIV) The meaning is God owns all of them. In verse 12 of that psalm he says, "the world is mine, and all that is in it." (NIV)

"144,000" is, of course, the number when all the tribes are added together - 12 tribes x 12000 from each tribe. Perhaps it means 12 tribes x 12 months (a year) x 1000 meaning all. With this idea it would mean all the saved ones from all the tribes of all the years.

My interpretation:

I think the 144,000 represents "Spiritual Israel" (all believers saved who were born under the Old Testament period until 30 A.D.).

I think of 12 in scripture as always representing "God's People". There were 12 patriarchs or 12 tribes (Old Testament); 12 apostles (New Testament); 12 foundations of the city of God's people.

Now we have:

144,000 is 12x12x1000 = 12 tribes x 12 apostles x1000 = all the saved. "All Israel will be saved!" Rom. 11:26. The apostles were born under the Mosaic period and chosen by Christ before his death. They were included, even though we think of them as the beginning of the New Covenant.

Verse 5. Judah, Reuben, Gad

"from the tribe of Judah 12000 were sealed,
  from the tribe of Reuben 12000,
  from the tribe of Gad 12000,"
  (NIV)

Verse 6. Asher, Naphtali, Manasseh

"from the tribe of Asher 12000,
  from the tribe of naphtali 12000,
  from the tribe of Manasseh 12000," (NIV)

Verse 7. Simeon, Levi, Issachar

"from the tribe of Simeon 12000,
  from the tribe of Levi 12000,
  from the tribe of issachar 12000,"
  (NIV)

Verse 8. Zebulin, Joseph, Benjamin

"from the tribe of Zebulun 12000,
  from the tribe of Joseph 12000,
  from The Tribe of Benjamin 12000." (NIV)

Notice the list of the tribes. The 12 sons are listed in Gen.49. They are: Reuben, Simeon, Levi, Judah, Zebulun, Issachar, Dan, Gad, Asher, Naphtali, Joseph, and Benjamin. In verse 17 of that text Jacob prophesied, "Dan will be a serpent by the roadside, a viper along the path." (NIV) The tribe of Dan did become a servant of the Serpent, the Devil. The tribe of Dan, in Judges 17, took Micah's idol and his priest with their tribe and moved north. They took over the city of Laish and changed the city's name to Dan. They became very idolatrous.

The city of Dan in the north was near Tyre, as indicated by 2 Chron. 2:14. Tyre was on the coast of the Mediterranean Sea, a great seaport of world trade. Ship traffic and caravans from the East and all over came through Tyre. Isaiah called Tyre the "marketplace of the nations", Isa.23:3. (NIV) She would return to her hire as a prostitute (idolatry) and ply her trade with all the kingdoms of the face of the earth, Isa.23:17. The tribe of Dan was right there near Tyre. Both Dan and Tyre became the area through which idolatry was spread all over the world.

Here, in Rev.7, Dan is not listed among the tribes. I believe all of Dan was lost due to idolatry. How terrible. A whole tribe condemned. Of the 12 tribes, 1, the tribe of Dan, was lost. Of the 12 disciples of Jesus,1, Judas was lost. Strange parallel. No. The Old foreshadows the New. In the list, the tribe of Manasseh (a son of Joseph) is listed in Dan's place. In Acts 1:20 it says it is written in the Psalms – "May another take his place", (NIV) and they chose Matthias in the place of Judas.

What about Ephraim? The tribe of Joseph was represented as part of the 12 tribes as half tribes – the half tribe of Manasseh and the half tribe of Ephraim, Josh.14:4; Joshua13:29;16:5;17:1. However, Ephraim was later often used as referring to the northern 10 tribes, Ezek.37:16; Hos.5:3. Here in revelation, instead of using the name Ephraim to stand for the half tribe, God uses "the tribe of Joseph" to stand for the half tribe. Ephraim is not used because it often refers to the 10 tribes. So, in the list of the 144,000 Ephraim and Manasseh are both represented. I have a hunch that the tribe of Dan was the only tribe in which everyone was lost.

From all the other tribes a remnant was saved. Of the remnant of each tribe, "all" were saved as indicated by the figurative meaning of the number 1000. That they were Jewish believers is represented by the number 12. Christian believers are represented by 12 also since Christians are "grafted in", Rom.11:17.

Another thought about why Ephraim is not listed by name in Revelation is this. Jeroboam was an Ephraimite, and rebelled against Rehoboam in Judah. To keep Israelites from going to Jerusalem to worship and perhaps go back to Rehoboam, Jeroboam set up places of idolatrous worship at Dan and Bethel, 1 Kings 12: 28-31. Ephraim was responsible for the spread of Idolatry in Israel through Jeroboam. Perhaps God was not honoring the name of Ephraim here in Revelation. In referring to the remnant (the saved) from Ephraim John refers to them as from the tribe of Joseph. The honor went back to Joseph (Ephraim's father) in stating those who were saved from Ephraim. The whole tribe was not lost as with Dan but the honor of those saved from Ephraim could not be mentioned with Ephraim's name. Ephraim was disgraced.

THE GREAT MULTITUDE IN WHITE ROBES

Verse 9. The Great Multitude

"After this I looked and there before me was a great multitude that no one could count, from every nation, tribe, people, and language, standing before the throne and in front of the Lamb. They were wearing white robes and we're holding palm branches in their hands." (NIV)

"After this I looked," again indicates a separate vision. The great multitude is seen by John in the vision at a separate time. John is shown both the 144,000 and the great multitude in heaven. So, one follows another, but at separate times. The 144,000 are first fruits. They arrive in heaven at Jesus' ascension. They do not have resurrection bodies yet, but they are the righteous dead from the Mosaic period. In Revelation 14:3-4, the 144,000 have been "redeemed from the earth", "purchased from among men". (NIV) The great multitude "come out of the great tribulation", 7:14. (NIV) The "great tribulation" occurs during the time of the "birth pains", and the distress that occurs before the siege and destruction of Jerusalem, Matt.24:21; Luke

21:22-26. The great multitude followed into heaven in the resurrection. We see them separate from the "souls under the altar who were slain." The souls under the altar were martyrs coming out of the great tribulation. The great multitude came out of the time of the great tribulation, but some of them fled to the mountains and were kept safe from the dragon's reach, Rev. 12:14. The souls under the altar came to heaven as they were killed throughout the great tribulation as they were slain for the cause of Christ. They were mentioned in the opening of the fifth seal. Here. The Great Multitude is mentioned in the interlude between the sixth seal and the opening of the seventh seal. John sees them in a vision perhaps before they actually arrive in heaven. Why? John is shown the first fruits in heaven and the Multitude of the saved to be at the end, before it happens.

Verse 10. Salvation Belongs To God And The Lamb

"And they cried out in a loud voice: salvation belongs to our God, who sits on the throne, and to the lamb." (NIV)

Remember, at Jesus' second coming, on his return to the earth, He was "to bring salvation to those who were waiting for him", Heb.9:28. They were those who would "still be alive" when he came, 2 Thess. 4:15. (NIV)

Verse 11. All The Angels Worshiped

"All the Angels were standing around the throne and around the elders and the four living creatures. They fell down on their faces before the throne and worshiped God," (NIV)

There is going to be a lot of worshiping in heaven – and guess what, we are going to love it. We will drench ourselves fully in it – worshiping our God and Savior.

Verse 12. Praise, Glory, Wisdom, Honor, Power, Strength Be

"Saying, 'Amen! praise and glory and wisdom and thanks and honor and power and strength be to our God forever and ever, amen!'" (NIV)

Verse 13. Who Are They

"Then one of the elders asked me, 'these in the white robes- who are they and where did they come from?'" (NIV)

Silly angel. He knew the answer. Why ask John? Perhaps as a way to draw John's attention to it. Perhaps he wanted John to realize what God was going to do and the end result before he did it. Don't you love the different scenes God describes of all the forces or armies that mount up - the evil against the good – and then NO BATTLE! God blows them away with the breath of his mouth. NO CONTEST. We are on the WINNING SIDE. We win! I like the way God shows us what is going to happen and the End before it happens. Anybody worried? Anybody concerned when we are on God's side? Nah. Not at all. It's totally foolish to be evil and unrepentant. I only feel pity. I cry for them. Sinners who don't repent – you are so blind. You do not have a smidgen of a chance with God unless you repent and turn to Him. He will blow you away like chaff. He will toss you in the lake of fire like a weed. Please, please, wake up and repent!

Verse 14. The Great Tribulation

"I answered, 'sir, you know.' And he said, 'these are they who have come out of the Great Tribulation; they have washed their robes and made them white in the blood of the Lamb. (NIV)

Heb.9:22 says, "the law required that nearly everything be cleansed with blood, without the shedding of blood there is no forgiveness." (NIV) Only the blood of the Lamb can truly make us clean. What a strange thought, that by applying blood we cleanse. Spiritually speaking, applying the blood of the Lamb to make us clean accomplishes for God both the justice of God in the shed blood of the Lamb, and the mercy and love of God in applying it to us so that we can be clean. What a mystery. God's way is righteous and loving in all that he does.

Verse 15. Will Spread His Tent Over Them

"Therefore, they are before the throne of God and serve him day and night in his temple; and he who sits on the throne will spread his tent over them." (NIV)

The heavenly Jerusalem is referred to in Isa.33:20: "Look upon Zion, the city of our festivals; your eyes will see Jerusalem, a peaceful abode, a <u>tent</u> that will not be moved." (NIV) Psalms 5:11-12 speaking of

God says, "spread your protection over them," and he "surrounds them with your favor as with a shield". (NIV) A beautiful passage is in Isaiah 54:1-2 where the heavenly Jerusalem is pictured as a mother having children. The text says: "Enlarge the place of your <u>tent</u>, stretch <u>your tent curtains wide</u>, do not hold back… spread out to the left and the right." (NIV)

God is saying to the heavenly Jerusalem, who is our mother, (Gal. 4:26), spread your tent flaps wide and let my children come in. God loves having children. Isaiah 66:9 continues the thought – would I(God) "bring to delivery and then close the womb (of the heavenly Jerusalem, the bride of Christ) up again? (NIV) Of course not. God loves children and he seeks them throughout all the generations forever. PRAISE be to God. Jesus has a glorious Bride. (See the description of her in Rev. 19-20.)

The great multitude is here in the heavenly Jerusalem, and God spreads his tent over them. Isa.4:5 says –

"Then the Lord will create over all mount Zion and over all those who assemble there a cloud of smoke by day and a glow of flaming fire by night; over everything the glory will be a canopy. It will be a shelter and a shade from the heat of the day, and a refuge and hiding place from the storm and the rain." (NIV) What a prophecy! And what is now a fulfilled prophecy – for us!

Verse 16. The Sun Will Not Beat Upon Them

"Never again will they hunger; never again will they thirst. The sun will not beat upon them, nor any scorching heat. (NIV)

This thought is repeated in chapter 22. Heaven is the place Jesus ascended to and prepared a dwelling place for his people, for his Bride, the heavenly Jerusalem. What he prepared is beyond imagining. The spiritual world and wonders are inexpressible – and waiting, prepared for us.

Verse 17. Their Shepherd

"For the lamb at the center of the throne will be their <u>Shepherd</u>; He will lead them to Springs of Living Water. and God will wipe away every tear from their eyes. (NIV)

"Lamb ... their Shepherd"

The concept of Jesus being their shepherd is very important. In Ezekiel 34 God condemns the shepherds of Israel. He says there in 3-5, "you did not take care of the flock. You have ruled them harshly and brutally so they were scattered." (NIV) In verse 10 he says, "I am against the shepherds, and I will hold them accountable for my flock." "I will remove them from tending my flock." Then in verse 11 the Lord says something very special, "I myself will search for my sheep and look after them." (NIV) Wow!

Ezekial 37:24 predicts, "My servant David will be king over them, and they will all have One Shepherd." (NIV) This passage is fulfilled in John 10:16 which says, "there shall be one flock, and one shepherd." (NIV) Jesus says, "I am the good shepherd." (NIV) Here in Rev. 7:17 Jesus is their shepherd, the good shepherd, the One shepherd. Jesus looks after his sheep and works with them through his indwelling Holy Spirit. He is the One Shepherd. All earthly shepherds may not be appointed by him anymore and few qualified according to 1 Tim.3 and Tit.1. The verdict is still out for me. I do not know. What I do know is that if there are still shepherds in the churches – they still wreak the same havoc of God's flock that the O.T. shepherds did when the prophet said – "I will remove them from tending my flock so that the shepherds can no longer feed themselves", Ezek. 34:10 (NIV). He said "I (the Lord) myself will search for my sheep and look after them," Ezek 34:11, (NIV). I believe that the shepherds of the first century were miraculously gifted, as were all the gifts given in Eph. 4:11. They were given, verse 13, "until we all reach unity in the faith…attaining to the whole measure of the fulness in Christ", (NIV). I believe that verse points to the completion of all things, the restoration of all things, Acts3:21, the things God had purposed to be accomplished in Christ. Jesus is the good shepherd – with one flock and he is the ONE SHEPHERD, Jn 10:16. Yes, they had qualifications for bishops or elders in the first century, I Tim.3; Tit.1; and they appointed elders in every city, Tit.1:5. The miraculous was at work because God's plan and purpose would not fail. Yet, gifts as knowledge and prophesy ended. They were part by part gifts for the revelation of the mystery, 1 Cor. 13:8-10. "But when the complete thing came, the thing in part (revelation gifts – knowledge and prophesy) were abolished (Greek – katargethesontai)." (NIV). We do not have apostles now either. Jesus chose the apostles. They accomplished with the prophets the revelation of the mystery, Eph.3:5, and the ministry of their office. The word of God was presented in its fullness, Col.1: 23-25. Once the mystery was revealed and they had taken the gospel to the world (the Great Commission), their job, like the gifts of knowledge and prophecy were complete. The first century required the working of the miraculous because it was the time of the fulfillment by God for everything he had purposed. Could God have also ended the "office of bishop"? Jesus, our Shepherd and King, now rules in each Christian's heart through his indwelling Spirit. Through the indwelling Spirit we receive understanding when we pray, Eph.1; we walk with the Spirit; we do the things that please the Spirit, Rom.8; we are "transformed by the Spirit from glory to ever increasing glory", 2 Cor.3:18, (NIV).

If we still have elderships today in the organization of the church – how are we benefited? How are we different from the corrupt shepherds who fed themselves in Ezek.34? Do not the elderships of the 300+ different denominations ("divisions") of Christ's body and cults spearhead the division between all the different churches? They promote division, not the "oneness" Jesus prayed for in Jn 17. They want their members to conform to their brand of "truth." Those who would think differently from those of an individual denomination get an unenthusiastic "half-fellowship". They are not really open to all believers. They have a tight knit group. The denominations bring confusion and strife. They continue to peddle and push forward their human understanding of doctrines and division. Yet they send the message out – "Come here. Believe and practice our way. We are the right ones." They are nearly all denominations (divisions). Do you know a rare exception? Do they not demand conformity to their group, their statements of faith, their leaders, or you don't belong? Shame on them.

Most of their elderships I am convinced are not qualified according to the qualities listed in 1 Tim.3, and Tit.1. Many in the elderships have never really even read the Bible. They do not trust the "teaching of the indwelling Spirit," or maybe do not even know how to participate with the Spirit. They walk by their own effort and not with the help of the Spirit of God. They follow the theologians and seminaries, the Bible universities who trust in doctor degrees, and try to attract followers with human programs and earthly ideas. They approach "running God's people like a business." With human promotions and attractions. It is prominent men of the communities that are usually chosen for elderships, not for their spiritual understanding and maturity in Christ, but because they have doctor degrees, thriving businesses, and lots of influence. The assemblies do not choose them "by the guidance of the Holy Spirit" but usually by the popularity of the candidates with the congregation. That is my observation and experience with many churches.

If we still have elders today, we are no better off than the situation that God predicted he would change in Ezek.34. I personally find people who by faith are trying to follow God in nearly all the churches. They are somewhere on the journey of faith. I can have fellowship with them. I will not, however, support the divisions of denominations and their practices. I trust THE ONE SHEPHERD of my life, Jesus Christ, and the lead of His Holy Spirit. He will not lead me astray. He will not fail me. He totally cares about me. I trust Him fully! The Lamb at the center of the throne is THE ONE SHEPHERD!

In the book of Ezekiel, the shepherds divided his flock - as do the leaders of the denominations (divisions) that bring confusion and strife among God's people today. The <u>true believers</u> among the churches are led by Christ's Spirit and they follow the Lamb because they know his voice. They are led by the True and One Shepherd.

<u>"He will lead them to springs of living water"</u>.

In John 4: Jesus talks to the woman at the well. He asks her for a drink. Then he tells her if she knew who it was who asked her for a drink, she would ask him for a drink. She replies that he has nothing to draw the water with. Then Jesus replies, verses 13-14, "Everyone who drinks this water will be thirsty again. But whoever drinks the water I give him will become in him a spring of water welling up to eternal life." (NIV). Of course, by this he meant the indwelling Spirit that he gives to those who believe in him and receive him. The indwelling Spirit is central to the life of the believer and his being sanctified, made Holy, by God.

The Lord predicted what he was going to do with the Spirit in Ezekiel 36:26-27,

"I will give you a new heart and put a new spirit in you. I will remove from you your heart of stone and give you a heart of flesh. And I will put my Spirit in you, and move you to follow my decrees and be careful to keep my laws." (NIV) Verse 29 – "I will save you from all your uncleanness." (NIV)

Roman 8 describes the spiritual working of God's Spirit in our hearts. God uses his Spirit to sanctify us, make us like his Son, Jesus. What <u>we do not find the power to do</u>, in what we know is right, Rom. 7, his indwelling <u>Spirit enables us to do</u>, Romans 8. Verse 4 of Chapter 8 says: "the righteous requirements of the law might be fully met in us, who do not live according to the sinful nature but <u>according to the Spirit</u>." (NIV) The indwelling Spirit of God in our hearts is God's answer. Cooperation with the indwelling Spirit is God's spiritual process to accomplish our sanctification.

One last comment about the Spirit's work in us. Do you want to understand the Word of God? Do you want to understand the Revelation book? You must have and must rely on the indwelling Spirit. 1 John 2:20 says, "You have an anointing from the Holy One, and all of you know the truth." Verse 27, "But the anointing which ye have received of Him abides in you, and ye need not that any man teach you but as the same anointing teaches you of all things, and is truth, and is no lie, and even as he hath taught you, ye shall abide in him." (NIV)

CHAPTER EIGHT

THE SEVENTH SEAL AND THE GOLDEN CENSER

Verse 1. He Opened The Seventh Seal

"When he opened the seventh seal, there was silence in heaven for about half an hour. (NIV)

Silence can be deafening. It can speak so loud without a single sound. The opening of the seventh seal left everyone speechless for about half an hour. We can assume the silence was the result of what everyone saw when the seventh seal was opened and revealed. It was the seventh and last seal. We can only believe the seal revealed judgment now at its very worst, terribly awful! Jesus had said, "there will be great distress unequaled from the beginning of the world until now," Matt.24:21, (NIV).

Verse 2. Seven Angels Were Given Seven Trumpets

"And I saw the seven angels who stand before God and to them were given seven trumpets. (NIV)

The seven trumpets remind me of the story of the fall of Jericho in Joshua 6. There were 7 priests who were given trumpets. On the seventh day they were to march around Jericho seven times, blowing their trumpets. With a shout, the walls fell down. Here in Revelation, seven trumpets were blown. At the last one, the seventh trumpet, the earthly Jerusalem (figuratively Babylon) fell, Rev.14:8. This reminds us of when Jericho fell in Judges 6. There were seven priests who carried seven trumpets for seven days in front of the ark of God and marched around Jericho. On the seventh day the priests marched around Jericho seven times with trumpets blowing and the city collapsed. Here, Babylon 9earthly Jerusalem) fell at the blowing of seven trumpets by seven angels.

Verse 3. The Prayers Of All The Saints

"Another angel, who had a golden censer, came and stood at the altar. He was given much incense to offer, with the prayers of all the saints on the golden altar before the Throne. (NIV)

Here we are reminded of the souls under the altar,6:9-11. Many had died and come out of the great tribulation as martyrs, killed for their testimony of Christ. Their concern – "how long before you avenge our blood?" The answer – "not long, a little longer, till the rest who were to be martyrs were killed in the great tribulation." Many prayers were going up. The conditions on earth were the worst they had ever been. God's people were struggling horribly and wanted relief. Some more would die. They cried out to God; their prayers rose before God.

Verse 4. Incense With The Prayers Rose

"The smoke of the incense, together with the prayers of the saints, went up before God from the angel's hand. (NIV)

Verse 5. Fire From The Altar Hurled To The earth

"Then the angel took the censor, filled it with fire from the altar, and hurled it on the Earth; and there came peals of thunder, Rumblings, flashes of lightning and an earthquake. (NIV)

What was the answer to the prayers of the saints, and his martyrs? God brought fire and judgment upon their enemies and quickly. Luke 18:8 – "He saw they got justice quickly." (NIV)

There is a beautiful Psalm that David shares in chapter 18. Verse 5 says, "The cords of death entangled me (David)" (NIV). In verse 3 he says God is worthy of praise. He saves David from his enemies. Then the picture is dramatic. From heaven, in God's temple God hears David's voice. The earth trembles, the foundations shake, smoke rises from God's nostrils, consuming fire comes from his mouth. God parts the clouds and comes down and rescues David. God loves his people.

Here in verse 5, God is quick to answer the cry of his martyrs. He loves them. He responds to their enemies with fire from the altar.

THE TRUMPETS

The sounding of the 7 trumpets occurs with the opening of the 7th seal. We have already seen many judgments in the opening of the first six seals. Why the trumpets? I believe these 7 trumpets represent even more severe judgments that accompany the final seal. The very end is even much worse. Verses 7-12, may offer some detail that we can interpret from the symbolic language. However, I do not believe God intended for us to interpret every detail. Even though God is "revealing, unveiling" these events to us – there still remains a certain mystery, un-approachableness, unreachable-ness, incomprehensibleness about God. We remain finite and vulnerable, helpless before our awesome God.

I think in much of the description, God wants us to experience it emotionally. It is fearful, it is overwhelming and shaking. God does not want us to analyze every detail with our intellect. He wants us to experience the judgments by appealing to our imaginations and be emotionally moved. God is a consuming fire. God is in control of the universe and all things. Fear Him. Reverence him. Acknowledge Him.

Verse 6. Trumpets Prepared To Sound

"Then the seven angels who had the seven trumpets prepared to sound them." (NIV)

Judgments were about to proceed at the sounding of each trumpet. These judgments, I believe, represent God's Judgment Day on the earth. It began when they were besieged by Titus, "unexpectedly like a trap." Lk.21:34, (NIV). It ended when the temple and Jerusalem were destroyed. However, the completion of the Judgment may have extended to the destruction of Masada also, A.D. 73. When the judgment day began, all repenting, changing, second thoughts were too late, all was set and determined. "Let him who does wrong, continue to do wrong; let him who is vile continue to be vile; let him who does right continue to do right; and let him who is holy continue to be holy." Rev.22:11, (NIV).

Verse 7. A Third Burned Up

"The first angel sounded his trumpet, and there came hail and fire mixed with blood, and it was hurled down upon the Earth. A third of the Earth was burned up, the third of the trees were burned up, and all the grass was burned up." (NIV)

"Hail and fire mixed with blood"

Could this be figurative of the stones and darts that were hurled into and back and forth inside the Jerusalem walls? Could it refer to the many fires set inside the walls of Jerusalem by the three factions inside, to burn each other out and burn up the others' food and supplies.? That, mixed with the slaughtering of each other with swords and all manner of weapons so that blood ran in the streets and bloody bloated dead bodies were piled high in heaps and walked over, exposed to the world? The scene was horrible in Jerusalem, as described by Josephus.

Hail"

Hail was the seventh plague that God sent upon Egypt. It fell on "men and animals and on everything growing in the field," Ex.9:22, (NIV). Of course, the hail beat down everything growing in the field and hurt or killed men and animals.

"Fire"

In Judges 15:1-5, Because Samson's Philistine wife had been given to someone else, he retaliated in anger toward the Philistines. During the time of wheat harvest, he tied 300 foxes' tails together, set them on fire and let them run through the wheat fields of the Philistines. He burned up their fields and grain and also their vineyards and olive groves. Fire consumes crops.

Even today we find examples of using fire to destroy people's crops. In Sudan, the Muslims of the North come to the South and machine gun down whole families. Christians try to escape to the mountains. But then, the Muslims set fire to their fields and crops and the Christians starve to death. Famine and death have been experienced several times in Sudan because of this.

In the siege in Jerusalem, the storehouses of grain were burned up and all supplies. There could be no care for the wounded. There were no extra clothes or dishes to eat from. Clothes were stolen off dead bodies. The dying were sometimes eaten for food. The sound of death and killing never ended day or night. The stench took breath away and totally all hope had been extinguished.

"Mixed with blood"

This happened inside Jerusalem as the three rebel Jewish forces that took over the city fought and set fire to places in the city. There were those who died in the fires and fire was mixed with bloodshed.

The sounding of the trumpets point to the latter time of the judgments. The sounding of the trumpets occurred with the opening of the seventh seal. However, even before the opening of the seventh seal, and Rome had besieged the city of Jerusalem, the Romans marched down through Palestine and set fires to villages and cities that resisted them or did not immediately surrender and even turn on their brothers. Many thousands of Jews were killed. Josephus tells us in detail in book 3-6 of his "The Jewish Wars".

"a third". What does a third represent? First, we look again at ¼. In 6:8 power was given over a fourth of the earth to kill with sword, famine…etc. There, we observed that ¼ was a fraction of four. Four represents the earth, as the four corners of the earth, or the four winds that blow on the earth, meaning north, east, south, west. So, we might conclude that ¼ represents a fraction of those on the earth.

What is a third? I believe it is a fraction of 3. Three refers to the heavens, the spiritual world. Paul speaks of the third heaven in 2 Corinthians 12. The heavens were viewed as having 3 levels. One third would be a fraction of 3, or heaven.

Now if these judgments are on the earth, (in Jerusalem) why is 1/3 used here which indicates heaven? Perhaps, the explanation is that judgments that came from the earth, i.e. - earthly armies, killed a fraction that are represented by ¼. But then, took on a new element, the judgments on the earth came from spiritual beings also from heaven, from demons, and that is represented by 1/3. It does appear that the judgments described in chapter 9 are from spiritual beings, not an earthly army. The locust are demons, and the army of 200 million is no earthly army; nor are their horses in the description. This interpretation would further make sense, when remembering what Jesus had said in Mt.12:43-45. We will discuss this more in chapter 9.

Noticing further 1/3, I do not believe it was a literal 1/3, just as earlier it was not a literal 1/4, as in 6:8. The fractions would not add up if we were tracking each judgment and adding the number of thirds and fourths. These fractions are figuratively used. They tell us where the judgment occurred or the source of where the judgments came from.

Verse 8. A Huge Mountain Was Thrown Into The Sea

"The second Angel sounded his trumpet, and something like a huge mountain, all ablaze was thrown into the sea. A third of the sea turned into blood." (NIV).

"a huge mountain, all ablaze."

Again, nothing specific to interpret the judgment. Normally, a huge mountain would represent in symbolic language a great nation such as Babylon or Egypt. But wait. Maybe there is more here than meets the eye. This is a spiritual book. This verse may remind us of what Jesus said in Mark 11:22-23 where he said, 'Have faith in God', Jesus answered. 'I tell you the truth, if anyone says to this mountain, Go throw yourself into the sea, and do not doubt in his heart but believes what he says will happen, It will be done for him." (NIV).

Is there something in that passage that relates here? Let's look at the passage. Mark 11 (NIV) describes his triumphal entry into Jerusalem. As he entered, there were those who shouted, "Blessed is the coming kingdom of our father David. Hosanna is the highest." When Jesus entered Jerusalem; he went to the temple. He looked around at everything. It was getting late, so He and the Twelve left and went out to Bethany. As they left Bethany the next day, Jesus was hungry, and walked to a fig tree for fruit. The tree had only leaves, but no fruit. It was not the season for figs. Jesus cursed the tree – "May no one ever eat from you again". (NIV) (Why did he curse the tree?)

On reaching Jerusalem, he entered the temple and drove out the money changers. He taught them – "My house will be called a house of prayer for all nations." (NIV) But you have made it a den of robbers. The chief priests and the teachers of the law began to look for a way to kill him. Jesus and his disciples again went out of the city. The next morning as they went along the fig tree had withered from the roots. Peter, at that point said, "Rabbi, look the fig tree you cursed has withered!" Then, verse 22-23, "Have faith in God," Jesus answered. 23 And he tells Peter if you say to a <u>mountain</u>, go throw yourself into the sea, it will be done for him.

But then he goes on to say, verses 24-25 "Therefore (here is the application) I tell you, whatever you ask for in prayer, believe that you have received it, and it will be yours. And when you stand praying, if you hold anything against anyone, forgive him, so that your Father in heaven may forgive you your sins." (NIV)

Now, be patient. In order to see the big picture to understand this we must let the Spirit help us here. The temple and the Jerusalem on earth stood for the old Mosaic system, Gal.4:24-25. That system represented the covenant that brought condemnation. It was a "ministry that brought death," 2 Cor. 3:7, (NIV). The law was holy, righteous and good, Rom.7:12. But the law condemns us because we all violate the law. It was a ministry of death. The problem was with people. What about the money changers? They had turned God's house, which was holy, righteous and good, into a den of robbers. (The people did not follow the law. They violated it. They corrupted it.)

Why did Jesus curse the fig tree? Because it had no fruit. The Mosaic system, that covenant, represented by the temple and Jerusalem had bore no fruit unto God. That system had taught us what righteousness was; but the result of that covenant is that it brought death.

What about the mountain being thrown into the sea? What was that about? Prophecy also refers to a mountain, (not as a nation as in some places in scripture) but in many places in the O.T. The mountain is referring to the Lord's house, on a mountain in Jerusalem. For example, Isaiah 2:3 says, "Come, let us go up to the mountain of the Lord, to the house of the God of Jacob …".

The mountain of the Lord's house then, the old Mosaic covenant was about to be thrown into the sea. It bore no fruit. It instead had brought death. Man needed forgiveness; God's forgiveness.

So then, why the "therefore"? Why the lesson on prayer about forgiveness? Forgiveness was the real focus of what Jesus was about to accomplish for all nations. God's house would be a house of prayer for all nations. Those who would come to him from any nation could receive forgiveness for the condemnation they were under through the Law. That Law, that stood over everyone, and condemned everyone – could be thrown into the sea. Its condemnation could be destroyed.

Now, let's read a beautiful prophecy, Isa. 25:6-8.

"On this mountain the Lord Almighty will prepare a feast of rich food for all peoples, a banquet of aged wine- the best of meats and the finest of wines. On this mountain he will destroy the shroud (you were wrapped in a shroud at death) that enfolds all peoples, the sheet that covers all nations: he will swallow up death forever. The sovereign Lord will wipe away the tears from all faces; he will remove the disgrace of his people from all the earth." (NIV)

Remember, verse 8, is a judgment. Perhaps we could understand it like this: Jerusalem and the temple (which stood for the Mosaic covenant, a covenant of death) was cast all ablaze (the entire city was burned historically in a terrible judgment) into the sea. It was destroyed in judgment and the covenant that it represented.

Verse 9. A Third Of Living Creatures Died

"A third of the living creatures in the sea died, and a third of the ships were destroyed." (NIV)

When Jerusalem ("the great mountain all ablaze") was destroyed, it had far-reaching effects. Many living then died from it. Related commerce and wealth were ruined.

Verse 10. A Great Star Blazing Fell

"The third Angel sounded his trumpet, and a great star blazing like a torch, fell from the sky on a third of the rivers and on the Springs of water". (NIV)

"a great star, blazing like a torch, fell from the sky".

Usually, in prophecy, a star represents an angel, as it did in Rev.1:20. If the star is an angel here, he was "blazing like a torch". Angels are "his servants" and they are "flames of fire", Heb.1:7. John describes the angel he saw as "blazing like a torch" as he fell (descended to the earth from heaven) from the sky. To John it probably appeared that the star was "a falling star" or a "shooting star". Of course, we understand that it was an angel shooting through the sky to the earth.

Jesus predicted Satan's fall. In Lk10:18 He said he saw Satan fall like lightning from heaven. Jesus conquered the power of evil that Satan had worked -the condemnation of man through the law, that stood against us, (the mountain set all ablaze and cast into the sea). He despoiled the evil powers by his death on the cross. Now we see when he ascended into the heavens that Satan is cast out and "a great star like a blazing torch, fell from the sky." His name is "Wormwood". The name describes his character – He is BITTER!. Watch out below earth, for he has come down to the earth.

Does Isa.14:12 refer to this verse? "How you have fallen from heaven morning star, son of the dawn! You have been cast down to the earth!" compare Rev.12:8-12.

Verse 11. The Name Of The Star Is Wormwood

"The name of the star is Wormwood. A third of the waters turned bitter, and many people died from the waters that had become bitter." (NIV)

The angel's name was "Wormwood." Often in the O.T. people's names meant something about them: what they were, did, or would become. Abraham's name was changed from Abram to Abraham – meaning "father of many," Gen.17:4-5. In the case of an angel, they too wear names that describe who they are or what they do. In the case of Manoah and his wife an angel came to tell them they would have a son (Samson). Manoah asked the angel – "what is your name that we may honor you? Judges 13:17, (NIV). The angel replied – "it is Wonderful." (NIV). That name means – "beyond understanding or knowing." Of course, that is the name used in Isa.9:6 "And he will be called Wonderful, Counselor,

Mighty God…" (NIV). Names tell you things. Angels have a name. Here, the angel's name is Wormwood (meaning - bitterness).

What could this mean? Was he an angel sent by God to poison springs of water? Maybe. More likely, Satan was cast down and he was bitter and poisoned much around. God used his actions in punishing the corrupt and wicked generation of Jesus.

The people of Israel were idolatrous in the O.T. and the N.T. In Jer.9:15, after God speaks of their idolatry – "they have followed the stubbornness of their hearts; they have followed the Baals." (NIV) Then God says – "See, I will make these people eat bitter food and drink poisoned (bitter) water. I will scatter them among the nations." (NIV). He says the same thing in Jer.23:15.

Num. 5:11-31 speaks of the woman suspected of infidelity. She was made to drink the bitter water. When she was guilty, the water made her belly swell and her thigh to rot. There may be an allusion here to that idea. Israel was unfaithful to God, and worshiped idols under every spreading tree. God sent the angel, Wormwood, to poison their water supplies.

Here in this verse, it is the same idea. I am going to make them drink from this cup of suffering. I am going to make them drink this bitter water. I will poison their springs and their water. It would be the most bitter of judgments. God's flaming servant, Wormwood, carried out the judgment. We know this angel would bring great bitterness into their judgment.

Verse 12. A Third Of The Sun, Moon, And Stars Were Struck

"The fourth Angel sounded his trumpet, and a third of the sun was struck, a third of the Moon, and a third of the Stars, so that 1/3 of them turned dark. A third of the day was without light, and also a third of the night." (NIV)

I think that this judgment indicates that even the creation was agreeing with and participating in the judgments of God. The creation was a witness to the oath the Israelites took to obey the covenant. Deut.4:26, (NIV). The creation responded, if they disobeyed, with a curse – their crops would fail, their streams would dry up, their offspring would die, disease would overtake them and so on. Their lives would be bitter, cursed because of their disobedience. Creation responded!

"A third of the day was without light"

This reminds me of the day Jesus was crucified. Matthew records –

"From the sixth hour until the ninth hour darkness came over the land" (NIV), (Palestine, "the promised land"). There was darkness in the middle of the day, from our 12 o'clock until three. Creation could not hold back, the death of Jesus was too much to bear, and the sun would not give its light.

In the ten plagues on Egypt, the ninth plague was darkness, just before the tenth, the death of the firstborn. Darkness preceded the worst and final plague of Egypt. In Ex.11:21-29, the plague of darkness, a darkness that could be felt, spread over all Egypt for three days. No one could see anything else or leave his place. This was an attack on the Egyptian's chief god, the sun god Ra. He was depicted as a bird with a man's body and an orange sun disc over his head. All the plagues attacked the various Egyptian gods, Ex.12:12. In this plague of darkness – the sun nor the moon would give its light.

"A third of them turned dark."

It is true that the sun, moon, and stars in prophecy often represent rulers. It is true also that it says the sun, moon, and stars were struck -so that they did not give their light anymore. They turned dark. Perhaps it is in reference to the rulers who were guilty, who were responsible for condemning and crucifying Jesus. Not all of the rulers had agreed to his condemnation. Luke tells us Joseph of Arimathea was a member of the Council, but that he had not consented to their decision, Lk.23:50-51. Rather, he was waiting for the kingdom of God and he buried Jesus in his own tomb. Nicodemus, a Pharisee, and a member of the Jewish ruling council, sought out Jesus, and called him a teacher who had come from God. Jn.3:1-2. Yet, we know that Jesus told his accusers at the trial – "In the future you will see the Son of Man sitting at the right hand of the Mighty One and coming in the clouds of heaven." Mt.26:64, (NIV). They saw the "Wrath of the Lamb". Perhaps then, this verse, verse 12, is saying – their lights were struck and their lights went out. Many of them would have been in Jerusalem, officiating as priests, and many lived there. They would have been trapped by the siege of the Romans and killed. Josephus tells us that many priests were killed in the temple by the rebels who had taken over the city.

It is true that in Matt.24:29 it predicts that "Immediately after the distress of those days (the distress during the days of the destruction of Jerusalem) – the sun will be darkened, and the moon will not give its light; and the stars will fall from the sky" (all figurative language). But here, the stars do not fall, but rather do not give their light. The description is similar, but different. It also says in Matthew, - "the heavenly bodies will be shaken." It does not then follow that they are talking about the same thing. What is here described, in verse 12, is not what Matt. 24:29 is describing.

Verse 13. An Eagle Flying In Midair

"As I watched, I heard an eagle that was flying in midair call out in a loud voice:

'Woe! Woe! Woe! to the inhabitants of the Earth, because of the trumpet blasts about to be sounded by the other three angels!'" (NIV)

The last three trumpets are bringing about things most woeful, most terrifying, most excruciating. Oh - inhabitants of the earth, your most unimaginable and horrifying nightmares are about to be lived out.

CHAPTER NINE

This chapter is challenging. Our impression of what is symbolized by the locusts is difficult. It might be at first, we think that the locusts represent the Roman army. Because of verse 9 - "their wings were like the thundering of many horses and chariots rushing into battle," (NIV) we have the impression of an army. There is a similar description of locusts in Joel 2 where in verse 4ff we have "they have the appearance of horses; they gallop along like cavalry", (NIV) and so forth. That the description is like unto horses and cavalry does suggest an army, but it does not have to suggest an earthly army, does it?

Our objection to the locusts symbolizing an <u>earthly</u> army is verses 4 and 5 of this chapter. This army of locusts, whatever they symbolize, "<u>cannot harm</u> the earth, <u>plants or trees</u> nor <u>those who have the seal of God in their foreheads</u>" (The seal in our life on earth is the Holy Spirit, Eph.1:13-14; 2 Cor.1:22; 5:5. Here the seal is the name of the Lamb and the Father written in their foreheads, 14:1. It is a sign of ownership - they belong to God.) (We are to understand from the 144,000 being sealed, that they are protected from this locust army.) Not only so, those who the locusts can touch, (those who do not have the seal of God) are tortured, and are tortured so intensely that they seek death as a result, but cannot find death, 9:5-6. Also, did not the Roman army burn peoples' houses and crops (plants and trees) as they punished Jews while advancing down through Palestine? Did not the Romans cut down trees and build siege works against Palestinian cities and Jerusalem?

Can we take the locusts to represent the Roman army? We have trouble making that interpretation work right away. Did the Roman soldiers "not harm plants or trees?" Were they selective so that they did "not harm those who had the seal of God in their foreheads," God's people? What of the persecution of Christians (God's people) by Nero from the time of the burning of Rome in 64 A.D. until his death in 68 A.D.? Were the locusts (Roman army?) held back from harming them? What of those Christians who died as martyrs between 68 -70 A.D? Did the locusts

(Roman army?) not harm them? The locusts only harmed those who were not Christians? And those who were not Christians they were not allowed to kill? What of the 144,000 who were sealed? Weren't they already in heaven? They were the first fruits unto God, taken to heaven when Jesus ascended, Eph.4. How would the Roman army on earth affect them up in heaven? The army was only to torture those who did not have the seal of God. Could the Roman army be so selective? They were only to torture them but not kill them. Where did the Roman army just torture people only? Where did they only torture those who did not have the seal of God? The locusts do not represent the Roman army.

Another observation is that these locusts come from the <u>abyss</u> (the bottomless pit) and their king is called Abaddon in Hebrew, or Apollyon in Greek. What their king is called means "<u>destroyer</u>." Who do we know who was a king of demons and a destroyer?

In Luke 8:26-33, Jesus casts out the Legion of demons that possessed the man from the region of the Gerasenes. They begged him repeatedly not to order them to go into the <u>abyss</u>. (The abyss was the prison for demons).

Here in chapter 9, I believe demons (represented by the locusts) were let out of the abyss. The powerful horrifying description of the locusts fit the description of spiritual beings, or demons. They were not allowed to enter Christians or harm them. God put a limit on them. What they could do was both selective and limited (they could not kill). However, they were allowed (by God) to torture those who did not have the seal of God.

How real is this symbolism here? Perhaps very real and literal and historical. The first century certainly was a time of demon possession. During Jesus' ministry, there is recorded in Matt. 15:21-22, that Jesus withdrew to the region of Tyre and Sidon. "A Canaanite woman from that vicinity came to him, crying out. 'Lord, Son of David, have mercy on me! My daughter is suffering terribly from demon-possession." (NIV) Demons could torment people. They could suffer terribly from demons. The Gerasene man in Lk. 8 lived in the tombs, driven to solitary places by the demons that lived in him. There was the terrible case in Mark 9:17-26 where a man's son, possessed by a demon, was robbed of his speech, often thrown to the ground and caused to have convulsions. The demon, in verse 22, often threw him into the fire or water to kill him. Demons, without any doubt, tortured people.

A very interesting passage relates to this discussion in Matt. 12:43-45. Jesus tells us here:

"When an evil Spirit comes out of a man, it goes through arid places seeking rest and does not find it. 44 Then it says, 'I will return to the house I left. When it arrives, it finds the house unoccupied, swept clean and put in order. 45 Then it goes and takes with it seven other spirits more wicked than itself, and they go in and live there. And <u>the final condition of that man is worse than the first.</u> That is how it will be with this wicked generation." (NIV)

Jesus said that is how it would be with "<u>this</u> wicked generation" (his generation). How would it be? Their latter end would be worse than at the first. Jesus predicted "the wickedness would get worse" in (Matt.24:12). Toward the end, "this generation" was characterized as being like the man having 7 demons coming to live in their corrupt house (bodies).

In the beginning, there was a favorable reception of Jesus. In the beginning of the New Testament, we have the opening scene of John the Baptist preaching. Pharisees came to him to be baptized. They were responding to his preaching. His answer to them was 'who warned you of the judgment to come? First bring forth fruit in keeping with repentance.' (Mt. 3. NIV)

When Jesus started his ministry, many people, crowds, and multitudes followed him. They liked his teaching. He taught as one having authority and not as the scribes. The Jewish leaders were jealous because of his popularity. But, as Jesus' ministry progressed, people fell away. In John 6:55 when Jesus taught "that except you eat my flesh and drink my blood you have no life in you," (NIV) many turned back and no longer followed him. Jesus asked his disciples, "Do you want to leave me too?" (NIV)

In the passion week, Jesus entered Jerusalem and the people had much enthusiasm and delight. In Matt.21 the people lay down their cloaks for him and cut branches and lay them down. They yelled, 'Hosanna (save) …Blessed is he who comes in the name of the Lord'. (NIV) It was the "Triumphal entry" as we refer to it. By the end of the week the same people were crying out in Matt. 27:22 "Crucify him", verse 25 - "His blood be upon us and on our children!" (NIV)

The people started out following, listening to Jesus. They were joyous. No doubt, some had responded to Him. But, in the end many rejected him. They became even more wicked.

Not only this, But Jesus had predicted that before the end, at the time of the destruction of Jerusalem, that -"at that time many will turn away from the faith and will betray and hate each other," Matt. 24:10. (NIV) The "falling away" was predicted in 2 Thess.2:1-3 and in many places.

Now how does all this fit together and help us see what is happening in Revelation? Let us look at 2 other passages.

2 Peter 2:20-22 says, "If t<u>hey have escaped the corruption of the world, by knowing our Lord Jesus Christ</u> and are <u>again entangled</u> in it and overcome, they are worse off at the end than they were at the beginning." (NIV) (Recognize the phrase? "<u>The latter end is worse than the first</u> of Matt. 12.) It would have been better for them not to have known the way of righteousness, than to have known it and then turn their backs on the sacred command that was passed on to them." 2 Pet.2:21,1(NIV)

What of those in Hebrews 6:4?

"It is impossible for those who have once been enlightened, who have tasted the heavenly gift, who have shared in the Holy Spirit, 5 who have tasted the goodness of the word of God and the powers of the coming age, 6 if they fall away, to be brought back to repentance…" (NIV)

Now, an explanation of Revelation 9. There was to be a falling away - those who turned away from Christ, rejected him, to follow him no more. This would happen and judgment would follow. It would be much worse for them. Their houses (hearts) had once been cleaned, swept. But they again got entangled in the world. They were wide open for the demons to enter. They and all who rejected Christ. This was the time for punishment. The demons could not enter Christians who had the seal of God on their foreheads. The demons could only do what God allowed them to do. Demons were allowed to torment, but not kill those who had rejected our savior. God used the Romans to kill, put to the sword, burn cities, starve, bring horrendous suffering, death and destruction to the unbelieving Jews and apostates. God also allowed their punishment through demons who tortured them, but did not kill them. They sought death. They wished they could die, but could not find death. This was a time of distress unequaled before or after.

If the interpretation of what I am suggesting is correct, truly this would be the time of the worst distress since the beginning of the world. Jesus said – "there will be great distress unequaled from the beginning of the world until now – and never to be equaled again". How is it possible that it would be the worst ever for all time? Wouldn't the suffering and abuse of man in prison camps, in slaughter and confusion on battlefields, in torturing spies, in torturing Jews in the Holocaust of W.W.II – wouldn't they equal such torment? Surely what Jesus said is hyperbole. Or was it?

Can you imagine having demons living inside you, having no control over them, but they having control over your body and torturing you. Yet, they did not kill you. That would be a "living hell". And then, in addition to demons tormenting from within, the people suffered in all the ways that man could inflict pain and suffering on them too. They would seek death, but could not find it.

Josephus makes statements that add weight to how bad and evil the Jews had become by the time judgment arrived.

Again, we may object to this interpretation because we may think God does not use evil spirits for his purposes. In 1 Sam. 15 God rejects Saul as King over Israel. In chapter

16:14-15 it says: "Now the Spirit of the Lord had departed from Saul, and <u>an evil spirit from the Lord</u> tormented him. Saul's attendants said to him, 'See, <u>an evil spirit from God</u> is tormenting you." (NIV) God can work all things after the counsel of his will. Nothing can resist him. Even evil spirits have to obey the boundaries and limitations he puts on them. He uses them as he wills.

Another passage that points out that God uses all things in working out the counsel of his will is in 1 ki.22:20-23, where after God had already rejected king Ahab and determined that he should die (1 Ki.20:42). Then in 22:20-23 God says – "Who will entice Ahab into attacking Ramoth Gilead and going to his death there? One suggested this and another that. Finally, a spirit came forward, stood before the Lord and said, 'I will entice him.' 'By what means?' the Lord asked. 'I will go out and be a lying spirit in the mouths of all his prophets,' he said. 'You will succeed in enticing him,' said the Lord. 'Go and do it.'" (NIV) This perhaps is a hard passage to swallow or to understand. We are repulsed by the thought. God was using a lying spirit (a demon) to accomplish what he had willed for Ahab, namely his death. We must not lean unto our own understanding and expectations. If we walk by faith, we must let the Spirit tell us, teach us what to believe. In prophecy, we are always trying to interpret the prophecies to fit what God is going to do "in our world", the physical realm we live in. God is trying to tell us about things even in the spiritual world. We do not have spiritual senses to "see" the spiritual world. We believe them by faith. But we are body, soul, and spirit. We are members of the spiritual world. Someday we will understand when we are in that world.

Verse 1. The Star Was Given The Key To

"The fifth angel sounded his trumpet, and I saw a star that had fallen from the sky to the Earth. The star was given the key to the shaft of the Abyss. (NIV)

When the fifth angel sounded his trumpet and let loose the locusts plague (demons), what a terrible judgment. They were tormented by them, sought death and could not find it.

"<u>Star</u>." The star here that fell from the sky is in a few verses identified in the chapter. The star was given the key (authority, power) to the shaft of the abyss and verse 11 says the king over them was the angel of the abyss. His name was Abaddon in Hebrew and Apollyon in Greek. The name means Destroyer. The star is an angel, a fallen angel, a king over the locusts, and his name is Destroyer, verse 11.

<u>Stars</u> are often used to represent angels or rulers in scripture. In 12:4 the dragon, Satan, sweeps a third of the stars (angels) out of the sky and flings them to the earth. In 1:20, the text tells us clearly, "The seven <u>stars are the angels</u> of the seven churches…"

Verse 2. He Opened The Abyss

"When he opened the abyss, smoke rose from it like the smoke from a gigantic furnace. the Sun and Sky were darkened by the smoke from the abyss." (NIV)

This is a very vivid scene. The star (angel), the Destroyer, opened the abyss (a bottomless pit) and it was like a giant furnace. Smoke rose from it like the smoke of a giant furnace.

<u>"The sun and sky was darkened by the smoke"</u>. It was the day of the Lord. It was the time of his judgments. In Revelation, different judgments came forth as each seal was opened. In Isaiah 13:9, it says, the day of the Lord is a cruel day as God exhibits his wrath. In verse 10 of Isaiah, as in many passages, the stars will not give their light, the sun is darkened, the moon will not give its light. The day of the Lord is a day of Darkness for the wicked, Amos 5:18. When the Day of the Lord came – the day went dark in judgment. It was curtains for them; play ended. It was the end (close) of their world. The blackness of the smoke from the furnace came boiling out and brought darkness upon the world – upon all who knew not God.

Verse 3. Locusts Given Power Like Scorpions

"And out of the smoke locusts came down upon the earth and were given power like that of scorpions of the earth." (NIV)

Out of the smoke came scorpions. The whole scene is foreboding. The arrival of locusts upon the earth streaming out from the smoke of a huge furnace - our imagination cringes from the scene. These locusts could bring great pain. They had power in their tails to sting like scorpions, verse 5.

Our impression of what is symbolized by the locusts is difficult. It might be at first, we think that the locusts represent the Roman army because of verse 9 "their wings were like the thundering of many horses and chariots rushing into battle." There is a similar description of locusts in Joel 2 where there, in verse 4ff, it says "they have the appearance of horses; they gallop along like cavalry", and so forth. We know that in the Old Testament, locusts often symbolized invading armies that descended upon the land, Jer.51:14; Nahum 3:13-15. I am tempted to think at first the locusts represent the Roman armies under Vespasian as they bring judgment to Palestine. But the following verses convinced me to change my understanding.

Verse 4. Harm Only Those Who Do Not Have The Seal

"They were told not to harm the grass of the Earth or any plant or tree, but only those people who did not have the seal of God on their foreheads." (NIV)

Our objection to it being the "Roman army" is in verses 4-6 of this chapter. This army of locusts, whatever they symbolize, "cannot harm the earth, plants or trees nor those who have the seal of God in their foreheads" (NIV) (For us, the Holy Spirit, Eph.1:13-14; 2 Cor.1:22; 5:5. But, here it is the name of God and the Lamb in their foreheads, Rev.14:1). The locusts would cause men to seek death, but they could not find it. These locusts are limited from hurting the land and cannot hurt God's people who are sealed. Even those who were not sealed, they could only torture but not kill.

The Roman army harmed the grass and trees. They burned cities. They cut down trees and built siege works against Jerusalem. Those who were sealed by God were killed, martyred by both Jews and the Romans. They massacred many as they came down with the armies of Vespasian through Palestine. In Jerusalem, Romans surrounded the city and starved the people there, put them to the sword and burned the city. The people whom the Romans came upon wanted to live, to survive, to escape the Romans. The people did not seek death, but they did experience death. The

Romans killed thousands of them. The Roman army does not fit any description here of the locusts. Finally, the Romans had not lived out their life yet. They had not gone to the spiritual world yet. They had not been judged nor thrown into the lake of fire. The locusts come from the abyss, the great furnace. They were already in the spiritual world. God brought the evil spirits out of the abyss to bring judgment on the earth.

Another observation is that these locusts come from the abyss (the bottomless pit where demons had been condemned, 2 Pet.2:4) and the angel, their king, verse 11, is called Abaddon in Hebrew, or Apollyon in Greek. Their king's name means "destroyer." If their king was an angel, would the locusts represent angels, fallen angels? Demons?

To identify who the locusts represent, let us think about what we know.

1. They come from the abyss. They were already in hell fire (the furnace).
2. Their king is an angel. His name means Destroyer.
3. They have the power to sting like a scorpion.
4. They cannot harm the land nor God's people who are sealed. (They were sealed in 7:3)
5. They can torture those who do not have God's seal, but they cannot kill them.
6. They make people want to die, seek death, but cannot find it, 9:6

We deal with our first observation that they come out of the abyss. In Luke 8:26-33, Jesus casts out a Legion of demons that possessed the man from the region of the Gerasenes. They begged him repeatedly not to order them to go into the abyss. (The abyss was the prison for demons.) Fallen angels were held in chains for judgment there until the Great Day, Jude 1:6. 2 Peter 2:4 says,

"For God did not spare the angels when they sinned, but cast them down to hell (Greek - is for Tartarus) and delivered them into chains of darkness, to be reserved unto judgment." (NIV)

Satan was seized and bound with a great chain and thrown into the abyss and it was locked and sealed for a thousand years in Rev. 20:1-3. The abyss was a bottomless pit that contained Tartarus, the place for fallen angels. It was a great furnace. The fallen angels, demons, were released from there by their king, the destroyer, and allowed to torture those who did not have the seal of God in their foreheads. The abyss was the place for imprisoned demons. (The destroyer might be another name for Satan. He was the god of this world. Here, he is called the king over them. He led the angels into sin, 2 Pet.2:4. He destroyed everything that is good.)

So far then, with the sounding of the fifth trumpet and the judgment it brought forth, demons were released to torture those who did not have the seal of God in their foreheads. These demons were limited by God in what they could do. But, did God use these demons to bring judgment upon those who would not follow him?

Let us consider the words of Heb. 10:29:

"How much more severely do you think a man deserves to be punished who has trampled the son of God under foot, who has treated as an unholy (common) thing the blood of the covenant that sanctified him, and who has insulted the Spirit of Grace?" (NIV)

Luke 19:12-27 tells of a noble (Jesus) who went to a far country to have himself appointed king. His subjects hated him and refused that he be their king. He was made king however and returned home. The day came when the king judged his servants. Verse 27 says –"Those enemies of mine who did not want me to be king over them – bring them here and kill them in front of me." (NIV) I cannot help but imagine Jesus on his throne. He can view all things on the earth. Just like Jesus was standing in front of his throne in the heavens watching, looking down as Stephen was stoned (Acts 7:55-59); So also I believe from his throne he watched as his enemies were destroyed on earth in front of him.

Verse 5. They Were Not To Kill Them

"They were not given power to kill them, but only to torture them for 5 months. And the agony they suffered was like that of the sting of a scorpion when it strikes a man." (NIV)

"Not given power to kill them." (NIV)

God had put his limitations upon the demons. This was just like he had put his limitations upon Satan concerning Job – "The Lord said to Satan, 'Very well, then, everything he has is in your hands, but on the man, himself, do not lay a finger," Job 1:12. God had put a limit upon Satan. Then in Chapter 2, Satan comes before God again – "Skin for skin!" Satan replied. Verse 6 – "The Lord said to Satan, 'Very well, then, he is in your hands; but you must spare his life." The demons here could "torture men", but they could not kill them.

"Torture them for five months." (NIV)

This might indicate the time in which the demon possession and torture may have taken place.

It may mark the time historically. The Roman armies did surround Jerusalem and lay siege to it for five months; from April 14 to Sept.8, 70 A.D. People in the city were trapped. They could not get out. Jesus had said – "Be careful, or your hearts will be weighed down with dissipation, drunkenness, and the anxieties of life, and that day will close on you unexpectedly like a trap. For it will come upon all those who live on the face of the whole earth (the land). Be always on the watch, and pray that you may be able to escape all that is about to happen," Luke 21:34-36.(NIV)

Verse 6. Death Will Elude Them

"During those days men will seek death; they will long to die, but death will elude them." (NIV)

These demons could torture those who did not have the seal of God for five months, but they could not kill them. Realizing that demon possession was having a demon living with you in your body. You could not control your body, but the demon could. They could make you have convulsions, have excruciating pain in your body, take away your speech or sight, throw you in a fire, and anything they liked, but they could not kill you. Talk about a living hell! That is why verse 6 says - "men will seek death; they will long to die, but death will elude them"(NIV)

Remember where we are in our context. The judgments began to be released when the first seal was opened, 6:1. It seems, as we progress toward the last, the seventh seal, the judgments get more severe. At the opening of the sixth seal the sun turns black. The moon turned blood red. The stars in the sky fell. (These were the signs in heaven before the coming of the Lord, Matt.24:29-30.) Seeing what was coming, kings, princes, generals, rich and mighty hid in caves and among rocks. They called out to mountains and rocks - "Fall on us and hide us… from the wrath of the Lamb, Rev. 6:15-16. (NIV) The 6th seal finishes. There is an interlude in the action before the seventh seal is opened. In chapter 7, the servants of God are sealed by the seal of God. Then in chapter 8, the opening of the seventh seal begins. The seventh seal is the sounding of the 7 trumpets. The opening of the seventh seal is the last, and the last 3 trumpets of the seventh seal are the three Woes of the final and most horrible of the judgments. When the 7th trumpet of the seventh seal was sounded, 11:15, Jesus had come, and then, the "time had come for judging the dead", 11:18.

The sounding of the fifth trumpet, during the time of the seventh seal, is toward the end of judgments. Four trumpets had been sounded and the judgments delivered. Then before the last 3 trumpets sounded bringing the end, an eagle is seen calling out in a loud voice – "Woe! Woe! Woe!" To the inhabitants of the earth. The next 3 judgments announced by the sounding of the last three trumpets, the 5th, the 6th, and the 7th trumpets, were particularly horrible. Here, in the releasing of the locusts upon the earth, we are at the sounding of the 5th trumpet. The judgment was particularly horrible as we would expect.

In the following verses we see a description of these locusts, verses 7-10. They were awesome and terrible. They were horrifying.

Verse 7. Their Faces Resembled Human Faces

"The Locust looked like horses prepared for battle. On their heads they wore something like crowns of gold, and their faces resembled human faces." (NIV)

"They were like horses prepared for battle" (NIV) - perhaps all decked out in leather, armor, and stately array.

"They wore something like crowns of Gold"(NIV) - suggests they were royal and majestic. These were no ordinary group of horses.

"Their face resembled human faces"(NIV) - They were intelligent, full of great thought and action.

In Ezekiel chapter 1, the description of the four living creatures had 4 faces, the face of a man, the face of a lion, the face of an eagle, and the face of an ox. They were the face of the rulers of each part of the earthly creation. Man was the crowning of creation.

Verse 8. Hair Like Women, Teeth Like Lions

"Their hair was like women's hair and their teeth were like lions' teeth." (NIV)

"Their hair was like women's hair. (NIV) A woman's hair is her glory, 1 Cor. 11:15. It speaks to a man. It adorns her beauty, her attractiveness, her softness. It draws a man. What a deception to draw you in. One is allured to her and then she opens her mouth as a devouring lion. Ouch, Yikes. No! More than that. Instant terror! It reminds me of the movie "The Lost Ark," where Indiana Jones exclaims - "Don't look at her!" Then the camera shows you this angelic figure gliding through the air. She looks like a beautiful woman with long flowing hair in white. "Then all of a sudden there is a roar as she reveals her true self as a devouring skeleton-faced figure that pierces through all who were looking upon her with fire.

These demons have an appearance that draws a man, perhaps fascinates him, but they can pierce with terrible, unrelenting agony. Man would cry out with an excruciating plea - "God help us!" But it is too late. This is the time for judgment.

Verse 9. Breastplates Of Iron

"They had breastplates like breastplates of iron, and the sound of their wings was like the Thundering of many horses and chariots rushing into battle." (NIV)

"Breastplates of iron" – (NIV) They were fully equipped and very well equipped. They were equipped with breastplates of iron and who could defeat them? "Oh God, deliver us?" No. It's too late. Judgment has already begun. The time to repent had passed.

"The sound...thundering...like chariots rushing into battle." (NIV) When they came, doom and torture rushed upon those who were not sealed by God with thundering and relentless purpose. Who could escape?

Verse 10. Torment For Five Months

"They had tails and stings like scorpions, and in their tails, they had power to torment people for five months." (NIV)

"Sting like scorpions". (NIV) That was the power to torment those in the flesh (who did not have the seal of God). As demons, they could torment the body and mind in unimaginable ways, and the people could still live. A living hell!

Note: there are some commentators that believe this is evidence that the locusts are the Roman armies. They explain that the "sting of scorpions" is describing the siege works used by the Romans that could launch huge stones and darts. They point out that the catapults used by the Romans were actually called "scorpions" and that the hurling darts and stones of the catapults were like a scorpion's sting. This is interesting, but it does not fit. These darts and stones killed people. It was a war. The Romans killed thousands. In the text, the locusts could torment, but not kill.

We may make another observation. In prophecy, symbols suggest and represent certain things, but the context still controls how the symbol is to be understood. Mountains in prophecy often represented kingdoms. Many of these mountains represented kingdoms on earth. But the mountain of the Lord's house represents a spiritual kingdom, "not of this world". So too, locusts could represent in prophecy human armies. But locusts can also represent an army in the spiritual world. We tend to want to make everything fit our earthly existence. Yet, both worlds, the physical and the spiritual have existed and operated alongside each other for all of time. We are just normally "aware" of our own world. We need the eyes of faith to open our eyes to what has been there all along.

"Torment people five months"(NIV) I don't know what 5 actually symbolizes here or in scripture. Perhaps, the decalogue, five commandments each on two tables of stone suggests the right balance, as the first 5 commandments regarded our relationship with God and the next 5 with man. The law suggests proper balance and order. The creation may suggest the proper balance and order. Man has 5 fingers on each hand and 5 toes on each foot. Perhaps, if this idea is even close, then unbelievers are tortured for just the right balance of time to be just.

Verse 11. King Abaddon/Apollyon

"They had as king over them the angel of the Abyss, whose name in Hebrew is Abaddon, and in Greek Apollyon. (NIV)

"Abaddon and Apollyon" (NIV)

Knowing that Abaddon and Apollyon mean "destroyer" we recall the story of the plagues of Egypt. The children of Israel were delivered from most of the plagues that came upon Egypt. The plagues came upon Egypt, but not upon the land of Goshen where the Israelites lived. God's people were protected. Then, before the last and most horrible plague, God marked his people. Their doorposts were marked by the blood of the lamb. Then the last most horrible plague, the death of the firstborn, came upon Egypt. The "Destroyer" was not permitted to enter the houses of those marked with the blood of the lamb, Ex.12:23. The word for "destroyer" there however is "olothreuo" in the Septuagint, not Apollyon. The word "olothreuo" is used in Heb.11:28 where it says, "By faith he kept the Passover and the sprinkling of blood, so that the destroyer of the firstborn would not touch the firstborn of Israel." (NIV)

Here in Rev.9, the "destroyer angel" releases the locusts. But the locusts could not enter the houses(bodies) of those who had been marked by the seal of God. Those whose houses (bodies) they could enter, the locusts could not kill, but the locusts (demons) made them wish they could die. "The people sought death and could not find it".

I believe the "destroying angel" of Exodus 12, that killed the firstborn of Egypt, is the "destroying angel" of Rev.9 who opened the abyss and let out the locusts (demons). There was a "band of destroying angels" that brought the other plagues on Egypt, Ps.78:49. An interesting verse, about this destroyer, is in Isaiah 54:16-17:

"And it is I who have created the destroyer to work havoc; no weapon forged against you will prevail." (NIV)

The destroyer was an instrument in God's hand, an angel under his control, to do God's bidding.

In Exodus 12:23, we read of this destroyer in Egypt:

"When the Lord goes through the land to strike down the Egyptians, he will see the blood on the top and sides of the doorframe and will pass over the doorway and <u>he will not permit the destroyer</u> to enter your houses and strike you down." (NIV). Wow. God is in control! He protected his people. Amen!

Verse 12. Two Woes To Come

"The first Woe is passed; two other Woes are yet to come." (NIV)

The sounding of the 5th trumpet and the judgment it brought was completed and past. Now the second Woe, the sounding of the 6th trumpet is sounded. The judgment was quickly coming to its final consummation. The sixth trumpet starts another judgment.

Verse 13. A Voice From The Golden Altar

"The sixth Angel sounded his trumpet, and I Heard a Voice coming from the horns of the golden altar that is before God." (NIV)

<u>"The voice came from the horns of the golden altar.</u>" (NIV) Remember with the opening of the fifth seal we saw the souls under the altar who cried out – "How long - until you judge the inhabitants of the earth and avenge our blood?" 6:9-10. In 8:3 an angel offers incense with the prayers of the saints on the golden altar. The prayers and incense went up before God. Then the reply - an action by the angel. The angel took his censer and filled it with fire from the altar and threw it upon the earth, 8:5. Judgments on the earth were the response of God because of the prayers of God's people. God would avenge his people.

Evidently, the angel has not moved from the golden altar. He was still standing by the souls under the altar. The souls were witnessing the angel's actions and presence. Now, in this verse, the angel calls out in a loud voice - "release the four angels" that have been held back. The result is more judgments are released upon those who are on the earth. God has not forgotten the prayers of his people. God's hand is still upraised (as the phrase is used in the O.T. where God's hand is raised in judgment until it is finished. When it is finished, when it is completed, "It is enough.")

Verse 14. Four Angels At The Great River Euphrates

"It said to the sixth angel who had the trumpet, 'release the Four Angels who are bound at the great river Euphrates." (NIV)

"bound" (NIV) This verse does not say what bound them, or "held them back". The point is, even though bound, at the proper time determined by God, verse 15, they are released to do their work.

"The Great River Euphrates" (NIV) These angels are at the river Euphrates. This reference is to the north end of the river. Judgments that came upon Palestine and the Jews normally came from the North, from the north end of the river Euphrates. It was the northeast border of the promised land, the land of Israel. Judgments that historically came from the north were like Babylon, Assyria, and Greece, all and crossing the Euphrates. An example of such judgments from across the river is in Isaiah 8:7-8,

"Therefore, the Lord is about to bring against them the mighty floodwaters of the River (Euphrates) the king of Assyria with all his pomp; It will overflow all its channels, run over all its banks and sweep into Judah, swirling over it, passing over it and reaching up to the neck." (NIV) The judgment comes from the North.

The "four angels" (NIV). In Rev. 9:14, the judgment is from four angels. These are not the four living creatures around the throne, 4:6. Perhaps it is the four angels in 7:1, who are "holding back the four winds" (of judgment) "to prevent wind from blowing on the land",7:1, (the promised land, land of Palestine). They had been given power to harm the land and the sea, 7:2. In 7:3, they hold back the four winds until the servants of God are sealed. In 9:14 we find the angels are also held back, or bound (perhaps by the word of God, the order of God). So, until the order from God, the four angels have held the judgments back. In verse 14, the order is "release the four angels" (and therefore their judgments). The time had come.

They are released. The releasing of the four angels at the river involved the releasing of an army, verse 16, an army of 200 hundred million mounted troops. Such a number never existed in the Roman army. (Even today, no army has ever had such numbers.) Yet, angels and armies of the heavens are unlimited.

Historically there were several legions of the Roman armies. In the area of the Euphrates that swept down into Palestine to put down Jewish revolts and help Titus subdue Jerusalem, there were four legions specifically: the fifth, tenth, twelfth, and fifteenth, (Josephus, Wars of the Jews, Book III, 4,2 and V, 1,6. Josephus records what happened in the Jewish-Roman war that started in 66 A.D.) But, are there facts in the text that can tie the 6th trumpet to activities of the Roman army? No. Especially verse 16, prohibits such an interpretation. In verse 16, it was an army of 200 million. Whoops. The Roman army does not fit the narrative.

Verse 15. The Four Angels Were Released

"And the Four Angels who had been kept ready for this very hour and day and month and year were released to kill a third of mankind." (NIV)

"Ready for this very hour and day and month and year" (NIV)

This is an interesting verse. It emphasizes that the events to happen with the 6th trumpet had been kept ready for a long time, before the time arrived for them to happen. The very hour, day, month, and year had been determined, appointed by God. Deut.29:29 says,

"The secret things belong to the Lord our God, but the things revealed belong to us." NIV

We do not know the appointed time of things, God does. They happen at the time and in the way he has determined. (Cf Matt.26:54). Does that then mean we do not really have choice? No. Not at all. But he works all things after the counsel of his own will. Even the fallen angels, the demons, all creation God uses as he wishes, (cf. 1 Kings 22:19-23; 1 Sam.16:14-15).

Isaiah 46:11 says, "What I have said, I will bring about: what I have planned, that will I do." (NIV)

Isaiah 48:3 says, "I foretold the former things long ago, I announced them and I made them known; then suddenly I acted, and they came to pass." (NIV)

Isaiah 46:9-10 "I am God, and there is no other; I am God and there is none like me. I make known the end from the beginning, from ancient times, what is still to come. I say" my purpose will stand, and I will do all that I please." (NIV)

Isaiah 45:7 "I form the light and create darkness, I bring prosperity and create disaster; I the Lord, do all these things." (NIV)

God reminds us here in this verse, everything he does is according to his purpose, what he planned, and according to his appointed time. He brings it about. It occurs when he acts.

There are many appointed times in scripture. They did not just happen. God controls them all.

Verse 16. 200 Million Mounted Troops

"The number of the mounted troops was 200 million. I heard their number." (NIV)

This is a very large number. Symbolically or with biblical reference, I do not know anything the number could represent. Therefore, it may be an actual number and not symbolic. John was impressed with the number. So are we! The number does not represent any army ever assembled on earth. Therefore, I have to shy away from any interpretation again that it was symbolic of the Roman army. So where can we find such an army? In heaven? Angelic? I believe so. Let us look at the description of the army, especially their horses.

Verse 17. Horses And Riders

"The horses and Riders I saw in my vision looked like this: their breastplates were firey red, dark blue, and yellow as sulfur. The heads of the horses resembled the heads of lions, and out of their mouths came fire, smoke, and sulfur." (NIV)

Similarities between the locusts and the horses.

Here we see the similarities between the locusts and the horses. The locusts were given power to torture, but not kill. The horses were given power to kill a third of the men. The locusts had power in their tails. The horses had power in their mouths and tails. The locusts had as their king, the angel of the abyss. The horses and army had the four angels over them.

The locusts had teeth like lions. The horses had heads like lions.

The locusts had breastplates of iron. The horses had breastplates that were "fire-colored, dusky red, and sulfurous" (Marshall's Interlinear Greek-English N.T.) In other words, their breastplates were like different shades of red with fire. The locust had the sound of wings like thunderous horses.

Is it not reasonable here to believe that we have angelic beings that are being described? Were they used in this judgment to kill a third (a fraction) of the men? I think so. Remember, it was a very miraculous time and a very significant time in which the world order both in heaven on earth was about to change. Some may object, thinking God would not allow angelic beings to bring such a judgment; it must be symbolic of men's activity on the earth. I ask - Why must it? We should not force the interpretation to make chapter 9 symbolic of the Roman army and its judgment on the Jews. It is an historic fact that the Roman army killed thousands of the Jews in the Jewish-Roman war between 66 and 70 A.D. and that The Romans completely leveled Jerusalem and burned it. But the text here should not be forced to fit what we think it "should" represent. The details in the text are counter to that interpretation. Stick with the text and reason from the details. We should never read into the text what we think should or should not be there. We should not go "beyond that which is written".

This could have represented a spiritual army under God's orders that put to death thousands at the time of the Judgment of God in 70 A.D. So many were killed, missing, displaced; chaos reigned - who would know what happened to anybody else or where they went? They would be dealing with their own situation. Times were desperate. This was a divine judgment in which God may have employed both human and heavenly armies to accomplish his will. This was a time of both human and heavenly forces. Look at all the demon possession in the first century. Look at all the miracles performed in the first century. This was a battle of human and spiritual forces. What did Paul tell the Ephesians? "For our (wrestling) struggle is not against flesh and blood, but against the rulers, against the authorities, against the powers of this dark world (human) and against the spiritual forces of evil in the heavenly realms." (NIV) (Spiritual forces). Paul said it. I believe it. That was the struggle.

That is what we are seeing in the book of Revelation – the struggle of man with both human and spiritual forces. Do not try to explain everything in Revelation as exotic symbols of human activity only. This is a spiritual book. It takes the eyes of faith to see it and believe it. There is a spiritual world. Believe it. Lift your eyes up, off this world, and look at things above where Christ is seated.

Verse 18. Three Plagues Of Fire

"A third of mankind was killed by the three plagues of Fire smoke and sulfur that came out of their mouths." (NIV)

"Fire, smoke, and sulfur." (NIV) Fire burns up. Smoke destroys by inhalation. Sulphur both burns and suffocates. It's a fire you cannot escape.

"A Third" (NIV) is used again here as probably a fraction of the whole, a fraction of mankind was killed by heavenly beings.

Verse 19. Power In Mouth And Tail

"The power of the horses was in their mouth and in their tails; for their tails were like snakes, having heads with which they inflict injury." (NIV)

These horses could kill. They had tails like snakes (I would guess vipers – who could kill. Not like scorpions that just sting and torture.)

Verse 20. Still Did Not repent

"The rest of mankind that were not killed by these plagues still did not repent of the works of their hands; they did not stop worshiping demons and Idols of gold silver bronze Stone and wood- Idols that cannot see or hear or walk." (NIV)

"Still did not repent" (NIV) What a terrible, horrible, disgusting thing - those who were not killed by the plagues "still did not repent." They rejected the goodness of God, the good news of God, the grace and forgiveness of God. Now, they could not be turned from their hardness even by the severity of God. How we need to truly fear sin, the influence of sin, the addiction of sin. When the addiction of sin has firm hold of a man, he cannot turn it loose even though he knows it will kill him. You have seen it. Addiction of many kinds destroys a life. All sin can become addictive.

Let us be warned. The people could not repent, even after the locusts and the army of 200 million. Even with torture and death all around they could not find in themselves to repent. Remember Esau, who for a single meal sold his inheritance. Later, he wanted to inherit the blessing but he could not bring about a change of mind even though he sought it with tears, Heb. 12:16-17. All we have to do is give in to the flesh, let its desires lead us, and we become trapped.

How many people use sin as a crutch to get temporary relief or a temporary pleasure. Every time they feel stressed or unhappy, they reach for a temporary fix of food. It becomes so fixed in their habits and lifestyle that they cannot turn from it. It is sin. Why? Because instead of turning to Jesus and trusting him, letting him fill them, they try to fix themselves.

What of those who are stressed from a job or a relationship and they turn to alcohol to relax them, to mellow them out. They too are choosing sin. They have turned to alcohol instead of Jesus and trusting Jesus to guide them, strengthen them. What of seeking money for power or security. If the reliance in life is there instead of Jesus it is sin. What of drugs, gambling, lying, sex or any other reliance on the flesh rather than Jesus. It is deceptive. It takes away the understanding. It builds a habit that cannot be broken. It cannot be repented of. Dear heart, sin is a nasty horrible business. Repeat a sin often, and it will get so established you can't break free from it, even if you seek to be free with tears, you may not find strength to repent.

In Proverbs 5:22-23 it says, "The evil deed of a wicked man ensnares (trap) him; the cords of his sin hold him fast." (NIV). I can picture a man sitting in a chair. The cord of sin is wrapped around him a wrap at a time. At first, he may easily wiggle free. But, as each wrap (participation in that sin) encircles him over and over again, it becomes impossible for that man to break free. He cannot repent. The cords of sin hold him fast. We should never let the devil have a foothold, an opportunity. We should fear sin in all its forms. Practicing any sin over and over will ensnare (trap) you. You become what you live. Your life becomes the product of the choices you make every day. They could not repent.

Verse 21 Nor Did They Repent Of

"Nor did they repent of their murders, their magic arts, their sexual immorality or their thefts." (NIV)

CHAPTER TEN

Again, there is another interlude here, 10:1-11:14, separating the sounding of the 6th trumpet in 9:13 from the sounding of the 7th trumpet in 11:15. In the interlude we see "The Mighty Angel and the little scroll," 10:1-9; and "the Two Witnesses," 11:1-14.

THE ANGEL AND THE LITTLE SCROLL

Verse 1. A Mighty angel - His Face Like The Sun

"Then I saw another Mighty angel coming down from heaven. he was robed in a cloud, with a rainbow above his head; his face was like the sun, and his legs were like fiery pillars." (NIV)

"Mighty angel"

Many would deny this is Jesus because he is called here a "Mighty Angel". Yet, in the Old Testament there is "the angel" of the Lord. He appeared to Moses in the flames of the burning bush, Ex.3:2 and in verse 6 he said, "I am the God of your father..." (NIV) When Abraham was about to offer his son on mount Moriah, the angel of the Lord called out to him, Gen.22:11-12, "Do not lay a hand on the boy...you have not withheld from me (God) your son." (NIV) In Zech. 3:1-4, Joshua the high priest stands before the angel of the Lord and Satan is standing at his right side to accuse him. The Lord (the angel) said to Satan, 'The Lord rebuke you Satan. The Lord who has chosen Israel rebuke you". (NIV) The wording is like that of "The Lord said to my Lord," sit thou here at my right hand until I make your enemies a footstool for your feet." Acts 2:34. (NIV) Then the angel in Zechariah tells those around him to take off the filthy clothes of Joshua. The angel then tells Joshua – "see, I (the angel) have taken away your sin." (NIV) There is no one who can remove sin or forgive sin but God. Who then is the angel? God, the son. There are up to 50 scriptures in the Old Testament that reveal that the angel of the Lord was the pre-incarnate Son of God. He received worship, Judges 13:13,16-23, that his name was "Wonderful", meaning "beyond knowing", Judges 13:19; Isa.9:6; that he was the pre-incarnate Jesus with the Old Testament people, 1 Cor. 10:4; that he is Michael, meaning "who is like unto Jehovah" or "who is like God, the archangel, the chief prince, Daniel 10:13, Israel's prince, Daniel 12:1. When Jesus came, he spoke with the voice of the archangel, 1 Thess. 4:16. The Old Testament Jesus was "the angel of the Lord"; He was Michael. The whole study of Jesus pre-incarnate in the Old Testament is called the "Christology of the Old Testament."

How can that be? Jesus is what God the Father wants him to be in his creation. To us, Jesus is a man. He humbled himself and became a man, born of Mary. Yet he is God. "For in Christ all the fullness of the deity lives in <u>bodily form</u>," Col. 2:9. That is how God reveals himself to his physical creation. But what of the world we cannot see, the spiritual world? He is Michael meaning "like God", the archangel. There is no Being in the heavens like him or higher. God manifest himself to his angels by becoming one of them in bodily (spiritual body) form. But Jesus <u>is</u> God. He is God in bodily form manifesting himself to his creation. Jesus is a man. He is a mighty Angel. He is God bodily manifesting the fulness of deity to his creation. We see the son, but no one has ever seen the Father (Spirit), Jn.1:18. Yet, if you have seen the Son, you have seen the Father manifesting himself in bodily form.

We are made in the image of God. We are body, soul and spirit. So is God. There is only One God, not Three. God manifests himself through his body, Jesus. In the Old Testament, God always does everything through his right arm. Jesus is his right arm, Isaiah 53. God does everything through Jesus. But, just as my body is obedient to my Spirit, and subject to my Spirit, so Jesus is subject to the Father. Jesus was to reign until he put his enemies down, 1 Cor. 15:25. God was doing his work through Jesus. But when the work was finished, Jesus was himself subject to the Father, 1 Cor.15:28.

Jesus reveals a lot about his relation to the Father in John. Listen to these verses:

"The Son can do nothing of himself; he can only do what he sees the Father doing, because whatever the Father does the Son also does." John 5:19 (NIV)

"As the Father has life in Himself, so he has granted the Son to have life in himself." Jn. 5:26. (NIV)

"My Father, who has given them to me is greater than all… I and the Father are one. Jn.10:29-30. (NIV)

We live in our physical bodies. Our bodies are us, yet someday we will die. We will be raised with spiritual bodies because then we will be living in the spiritual world. Our existence will change from the physical world to the spiritual. But we will still be us, ourselves. We have no control over when that change happens. God, who is ONE, is eternal. He can manifest himself in the physical world, then to the spiritual world, then back to the physical and back again. He can change worlds any time he pleases. God is not three persons. He is one person and we are made in his image.

Well, then what of the Holy Spirit. The Spirit belongs to both the Father and to the Son, the three are ONE. That is a lot to think about. Yes, it is a mystery beyond our fully comprehending.

"The Mighty Angel" here is not an angel imitating or impersonating Christ. He is Christ.

"Robed in a cloud" (NIV)

In Ps.18:11 God wraps the dark rain clouds around him.

In Ps. 104:3 God makes the clouds his chariot and rides on the wings of the wind." (NIV)

"Rainbow above his head" (NIV)

In Rev.4:3, God is on his throne, and a rainbow is above his head. Just as the rainbow there represents God's glory, so the glory of the Father is also the Son's. You see a rainbow of glory above the Son's head.

"His face was like the sun" (NIV)

In Rev.1:16, the Son's face was like the sun shining in all its brilliance. This is Jesus.

"His legs were like fiery pillars" (NIV)

In Rev.1:15, the same description is used there of the Son.

Verse 2. A Little Scroll

"He was holding a little scroll, which lay open in his hand. He planted his right foot on the sea and his left foot on the land." (NIV)

"A little scroll", "which lay open in his hand" It was a little scroll, not big. There was a few more things to reveal, to "prophesy again," verse11. John was not done yet. It was a prophesy in the middle of what was "about to happen."

"He planted his right foot on the sea and his left on the land" (NIV)

Jesus planted his foot on the sea (the nations) and his foot on the land (Israel, Palestine). Each was under his feet. Jesus was in complete control of both. This alludes to Zech.14:3-4. There, Christ stands on the Mount of Olives that splits into. His feet are on the two parts of the mountain and God's people will flee through the valley between. Then, Jesus comes with his angels in judgment upon the earthly Jerusalem. Then, living water will flow from the heavenly Jerusalem. Jesus will be king over the whole earth. Jerusalem will be raised up (to heaven – the heavenly Jerusalem).

Verse 3. Voices Of Seven Thunders

"And he gave a loud shout like the Roar of a lion. When he shouted, the voices of the seven Thunders spoke." (NIV)

"a loud shout like the roar of a lion" (NIV)

In Rev.1:10, Jesus gives a loud shout like a trumpet. That is like 1 Thess. 4:16.

Because he is the lion of the tribe of Judah, here he gives a loud roar like a lion.

But, when Jesus speaks, because his is God, his voice is as thunder. Job 37:4-5 says,

"After that comes the sound of his roar; he thunders with his majestic voice. When his voice resounds; he holds nothing back. God's voice thunders in marvelous ways; he does great things beyond our understanding." (NIV)

"When he shouted, the voices of the seven thunders spoke" (NIV)

Jesus is the word. He is God. His voice is like thunder. When he speaks the seven thunders speak.

Jesus said to his disciples, "But when he the Spirit of Truth comes, He will not speak on his own: he will speak only what he hears, and he will tell you what is yet to come. He will bring glory to me by taking from what is mine and making it known to you." That is what is happening here. Jesus speaks, and the Spirit "echoes" (thunders) his words to John.

"<u>The seven thunders</u>". The Holy Spirit is represented as seven of many things. Think on these verses.

"He had seven horns and <u>seven eyes which are the seven spirits of God</u> sent out into all the earth," Rev.5:6. (NIV)

"grace and peace … from the seven spirits before his throne," Rev.1:4. (NIV)

"Before the throne <u>seven lamps</u> were blazing. <u>These are the seven spirits of God</u>," NIV. Rev.4:5 (NIV)

Verse 4. Seal up The Seven Thunders

"And when the seven Thunders spoke, I was about to write; but I Heard a Voice from Heaven say, 'seal up what the seven Thunders have said and do not write it down.'" (NIV)

<u>He was about to write what the seven thunders spoke</u> – (NIV)

Something was revealed to John by the seven thunders (the Spirit, the deliverer of the Word to man)

"<u>Seal up what the seven thunders have said and do not write it down</u>." (NIV)

Seal it up. Do not make it known. Do not write it down. But what? Perhaps verse 7 is a hint. "There will be no more delay." It was time for Jesus to return to the earth, to get his own, those waiting for him, Heb.9:28. He was also coming in flaming fire with his powerful angels to take vengeance on his enemies, 2 Thess. 7-8. The appointed time of the Father had come. Perhaps the Spirit heard the hour and the day and thundered it to John. But wait John. Do not write that down. It is time. There will be no more delay. But the <u>day</u> and the <u>hour</u> no man is to know – for Jesus was to come as a thief in the night and those who were not watching, those who were not ready, it would come upon them like a trap. It would be too late. (And so, John did not tell us what was said. He did not write it down). The day and the hour were not revealed to them. But we know he came because he said he would.

Verse 5. The Angel On The Sea And Land

"Then the angel I had seen standing on the sea and on the land raised his right hand to heaven." (NIV)

"Raised his right hand to heaven." (NIV)

Jesus had taught man in Matt.5:34-35 – "Swear not at all, neither by heaven nor by earth."

The Angel, only because of who he is - God, raises his Hand to swear. God can swear by no one but himself, Heb.6:13. So he does here. He was assuring us of what he said - like no other being can. What he says is absolute.

Verse 6. He Swore by Him

"And he swore by him who lives forever and ever, who created the heavens and all that is in them, the Earth and all that is in it, and the Sea and all that is in it, and said," (NIV)

Verse 7. No More Delay

"There will be no more delay! but in the days when the seventh angel is about to sound his trumpet, the mystery of God will be accomplished, just as he announced in his servants the prophets."

"There will be no more delay." Jesus would come in judgment.

"Seventh angel is about to sound his trumpet." That was the last trumpet; when Jesus returned.

"Mystery of God will be accomplished." The mystery (God's eternal plan) was being revealed. At Jesus' coming it would be accomplished or completed. (NIV)

Verse 8. Take The Scroll

"Then the voice that I had heard from heaven spoke to me once more" 'go take the scroll that lies open in the hand of the angel who is standing on the sea and on the land.'" (NIV)

"The voice"

Remember, John had been caught up in the Spirit on the Lord's Day (Judgment Day), chap 1:10 and the voice that spoke to him there was from Jesus. Here, it is the same voice. The voice was from heaven because John was in spirit viewing and hearing things there.

"<u>Go take the scroll that lies open in his hand.</u>" (NIV)

Verse 9. Take It And It Eat

"So I went to the angel and ask him to give me the little scroll. he said to me, 'take it and eat it. it will turn your stomach sour, but in your mouth, it will be as sweet as honey.' (NIV)

"<u>Eat it</u>"

When we eat the word of God, we chew on it, we swallow it, we digest it. It becomes part of us.

It may be sweet in our mouth. The concepts are beautiful to us: God's glory, his holiness, his forgiveness, and so forth. But when we swallow it to digest it, it may turn sour. Why? When the Spirit applies it to us, Heb.4:12, He reveals the intentions, the thoughts, the attitudes of our heart. That can be unpleasant. Like David we might discover – "if there is any offensive way in me"- lead me in the way everlasting." Ps.139:24

(NIV) God's word for the Christian can be sweet, but become bitter when we digest it.

For the prophet, the words of God may be sweet at first to his taste, but as he learns its message – if it is of judgment and destruction for a people – it sours in his stomach. Sometimes, he has to deliver a very hard message.

"<u>It will turn your stomach sour, but in your mouth, it will be sweet as honey.</u>" (NIV)

This sounds just like Ezekiel 3:1-3.

Psalms 119:103 says,

"How sweet are your words to my taste, sweeter than honey to my mouth!" (NIV) (cf. Prov.16:24; Jer.15:16).

But then the words turn sour in our stomach when the words speak of judgment:

Poor Ezekiel. God's words he ate were at first sweet. But then we read this: "The house of Israel is not willing to listen to you because they are not willing to listen to me, for the whole house of Israel is hardened and obstinate. But I will make you as unyielding and hardened as they are. I will make your forehead like the hardest stone, harder than flint." (NIV) His message would not be fun. His work was hard.

In Revelation, even though John is writing to churches that need repentance, he is also writing to a hardened unrepentant people who crucified our Lord. His message is amazing, but still a message of doom for the wicked. But John did get to enjoy the message about heaven and to some of God's people.

Verse 10. It Tasted Sweet, but My Stomach Turned Sour

"I took the little scroll from the Angel's hand and ate it. It tasted as sweet as honey in my mouth, but when I ate it, my stomach turned sour." (NIV)

The prophet cannot refuse. He is a prophet of God. He must speak the words of God. Witness the reluctant prophet - Jonah. He did what God told him. There is no indication here that John was reluctant. He ate it.

Verse 11. Prophesy Again

"Then I was told, 'prophecy again about many peoples, nations, languages and kings." (NIV)

"Prophesy again about many peoples..." (NIV)

I do not know yet, but I do have a theory of what this verse is about. First, to review the history. John was exiled under Domitius Nero, according to Irenaeus and Tertullian. He was exiled or banished to Patmos, one of four islands in the Aegean Sea, off the coast of Asia Minor, used for the purpose of exiles of Rome. He began writing the Book of Revelation while in exile on the island of Patmos, Rev.1:9. In Rev.17:10 it says, "Five have fallen." That was after the death of Nero, the 5th emperor. Nero died June 9, 68 A.D. "one is, the other has not yet come." ("The other" was Titus, 10th emperor, who reigned only 2 years, "a little while", verse 10. His reign was from June 24, 79 A.D. to Sept, 81 A.D.) Before him, Vespasian, 9th emperor, reigned Dec, 69 A.D. to June 2, 79 A.D. Before him was the year and a half of the civil war in Rome where three emperors reigned only a few months each: Galba from the death of Nero, June 8-9 to Jan.15, 69, Otho until April 69 and Vitellius until Dec. 69.

"One is" of Rev.17:10, does not refer to Vespasian, but rather Galba. Why? "Five had fallen". Even though it was a civil war, and that three emperors died in only a few months, they were emperors. Galba was the sixth, Otho the seventh, and Vitellius the eighth. Vespasian was the 9th emperor, who stabilized the kingdom, and reigned for ten years.

Now, the theory. John was exiled to Patmos under Nero. When Nero died, civil war broke out. I think this verse may be a prophecy that during the time of the civil war, John would be released from exile, and John would "prophecy (predict and teach) again about many peoples." In exile, on an island, John would be limited. If he was released and could go to the mainland, Asia Minor, he could deliver his message to the seven churches and others before the main trial and punishment of the Jews in Jerusalem and the city's destruction. If John was released after Nero's death, He would likely return to Ephesus. In 64A.D. Paul had been decapitated outside the city wall of Rome. Peter was likely crucified, Jn.21:18-19, at that time. That was the beginning of Nero's persecution of Christians. After Nero's death, June 9, 68 A.D., if John was released and he returned to Ephesus, he would again resume leadership at Ephesus. It has been believed John lived at Ephesus. Irenaeus wrote in "Against Heresies", book 3, chap.3 section 4 –

"There are also those who heard from him (Polycarp) that John, the disciple of the Lord, going to bathe at Ephesus, and perceiving Cerinthus within, rushed out of the bath house without bathing, exclaiming, 'Let us fly, lest even the bath house fall down, because Cerinthus, the enemy of the truth is within." [Note: Polycarp is said by Tertullian (Prescription Against Heretics, chap 32) to have been appointed a bishop of Smyrna by John.]

Clement recorded in his work - "Who is the rich man that will be saved? XLII" these words – "And that you may be still more confident, that repenting thus truly there remains for you a sure hope of salvation, listen to a tale, which is not a tale but a narrative, handed down and committed to the custody of memory, about the Apostle John. For when on the tyrant's death, he returned to Ephesus from the isle of Patmos, he went away, being invited to the contiguous territories of the nations, here to appoint bishops, there to set in order whole churches, there to ordain such as were marked out by the Spirit." (The tyrant was

Nero. On his death, John left the island of Patmos for Ephesus. TS)

I believe John was probably released at the death of Nero, went back to Ephesus, and from there communicated with the churches of Asia Minor. [That is what this prophecy is about. He would again prophesy to the nations.] At the resurrection (probably about Apr.7,70A.D. See commentary on 11:11) John would have been taken up to heaven with Jesus. That is why we have no historical record of John after that time.

CHAPTER ELEVEN

THE TWO WITNESSES

Verse 1. Go And Measure The Temple

"I was given a reed like a measuring rod and was told, 'go and measure the temple of God and the altar, and count the worshippers there," (NIV)

"I was given a reed like a measuring rod" (NIV) – to measure the Temple with.

"Measure the temple of God and the altar, (NIV)

This passage is important in determining the date of the authorship of the book. The temple still existed. John was told to go measure it. That means that John was writing the Book of Revelation before the temple was destroyed in 70 A.D. That is very important. The Book of Revelation was about things that would happen (must soon take place, Rev.1:1) before or by 70 A.D. Scholars today say the book was written between 94-96 A.D. during the end of the reign of Domitian. That's 24-26 years later. They miss the crucial events of historical and spiritual history by 24-26 years. Scholars have already missed the events of the book with such a late date. They cannot interpret the book correctly because they start at the wrong time, too late. They are searching for events to fit the book that will never fit the book. The correct date of the book and that the events would "soon take place are crucial to understanding the book.

This reminds me of what modern scholars do with the history of the time of the patriarchs through the time of Israel being brought out of Egypt. They say that those people and events cannot be found in secular history, so they must be mythological.

Ted Stewart in his book, "the Exodus Mystery" argues that the scholars have the wrong Pharaoh ruling Egypt at the time of Moses. Because of that, they are searching for the events of the patriarchs and the Exodus of Israel in secular history and cannot find Biblical history and characters because the scholars are 300 years off. Ted argues and shows that when you line up the secular and biblical histories correctly, there are over 400 verifications of the biblical history with secular. The scholars were searching in the wrong period of time. So, also with the Book of Revelation. Scholars do <u>not</u> have the dates right.

"<u>Measure the temple</u>." (NIV)

The temple was about to be destroyed (in 70 A.D.) Before God was willing to destroy it, he wanted it measured. Lam. 2:8 it says:

"The Lord determined to tear down the wall around the daughter of Zion. He stretched out a <u>measuring line</u> and did not withhold his hand from destroying." (NIV)

God's judgment and destruction is not arbitrary. It is not without exact purpose. By God stretching out a measuring line He is letting us know – his judgment is just. It is purposeful. God stretches out a measuring line before he destroys.

Other verses of scripture teach us the same thing:

Isa.34:11 "God will stretch out over Edom the <u>measuring line</u> of chaos and the <u>plumb line</u> of desolation." (NIV) ("destruction". Mt. 24:15 mentions the "abomination that causes desolation")

Amos 7:7-9 "This is what the Lord showed me: The Lord was standing by a wall that had been built true to plumb, with a <u>plumb line</u> in his hand. And the Lord asked me, what do you see Amos? 'A plumb line,' I replied. Then the Lord said, 'Look, I am setting a <u>plumb line</u> among my people Israel; I will spare them no longer." (NIV)

In this verse, God is measuring the temple and its people. He is about to destroy it and them.

"<u>And count the worshippers there</u>." (NIV)

The people were included in the measurement. They were to be judged and then destroyed.

In 2 Sam.8:12 it says,

"David also defeated the Moabites. He made them lie down on the ground and <u>measured them off with a length of cord</u>. Every two lengths of them were put to death, and the third length was allowed to live." (NIV)

Of course, when God judges people individually, ultimately in heaven – it is totally just. When God judged on earth, in regard to nations; it was also just and purposeful. But it was done on the scale of a nation, not in regard to individuals. Genesis 15:16 helps us understand:

"In the fourth generation your descendants will come back here, for the sin of the Amorites has <u>not yet reached its full measure</u>." (NIV)

God was not willing to use the Israelites to judge the Amorites yet, at that time, because the sin of the Amorite had not reached its full measure. God is patient. He is long-suffering with us. He is not willing for any to perish but that all come to repentance. But when a nation becomes so corrupt (reaches its <u>full measure</u>) God will judge it and destroy it. Even righteous individuals may be killed in the judgment of nations. Do not despair. God knows those who are his. They will be honored and eternally with him in heaven.

Verse 2. Exclude The Outer Court

"But exclude the outer court; do not measure it because it has been given to the Gentiles. They will trample on the holy city for 42 months.(NIV

"<u>But exclude the outer court</u>"; "<u>do not measure it</u>." "<u>Because it has been given to the Gentiles</u>." (NIV)

The outer court was a rectangular area enclosed by curtains supported on pillars. Within the entrance to it stood the altar of burnt offering, where sacrificial animals were brought in and killed. The fire of the altar was to never go out, Lev. 6:12-13. Toward the opposite end, still within the court stood the enclosed Holy Place and Holy of Holies. Only the High Priest could go into the Holy of Holies. Priests could enter the Holy Place.

The "fence" of the outer court, made of white linen, separated the outer world from the Tabernacle of God within. "White linen" in scripture, signifies righteousness; and in Rev.19:8 "it stands for the righteous acts of the saints." (NIV) Those accepted into the tabernacle of God are the righteous.

Priests who served in the Tabernacle were to wear "white linen", Ex.28:39-42.

The second temple was built by the Jews when they returned from exile. It was built under the decree of Cyrus the Great, Isa. 44:28. during the time of Nehemiah and Ezra. Herod rebuilt the second temple and enlarged it in 37 B.C.

In Herod's Temple there were four separate courts, each designed for a separate purpose. There was: 1. the court of the Gentiles, 2. the court of the women, 3. the court of Israel (or the men) and 4. The court of priests. The court of the Gentiles was accessible by Gentiles, or foreigners. It was the only place where non-Jews were allowed. It was there that even Gentiles could come and exchange money from other nations with the money-changers of the temple. Sacrifices were also sold there. It was there that Jesus the first time drove out animals and the money-changers, Jn. 2:13-16; Isa.56:7.

"<u>Do not measure the outer court.</u>" (NIV)

Here, in verse 2, Jesus says, "do not measure the <u>outer court, because it has been given to the Gentiles</u>. In other words, during that time, in the Temple of Herod, there had been built an "outer court", "the court of the Gentiles" where they were allowed to come in and interact with the money-changers of the day. This "court" was not from the plan of God for the temple. It had been added by man. It was a corruption of what God had given the Jews. The "court of the Gentiles" represented a compromise with the world. The people of God had allowed the "world" to come into the "Church" or house of God (the saved people of God wearing white linen). Through that addition, the Jewish money changers could interact with the world and profit nicely off of them. It was being "friends with the world and a part of the world".

"<u>Do not measure the outer court.</u>" (NIV)

Salvation was to come "first to the Jew, Acts 2; then the Gentile," Acts 10. (Cf Rom.1:16; Acts 13:46)

Judgment also, was to come first to the Jew, then to the Gentile, Rom. 2:9-10.

The judgment of the Jews was to be first. The destruction of Jerusalem and the Temple was their (the Jews') judgment. The court of the Gentiles was to be excluded from measurement because they were not to be part of this judgment. Their judgment would come later.

Some feel the outer court was exempt from being measured because it was already desecrated. In other words – it was not a holy place.

"They will trample on the holy city for 42 months." (NIV)

1. Some equate the "time of the Gentiles" to this "42 months" that they trample the city and beyond. This is incorrect. (See Appendix Q: "Time of the Gentiles")

2. Some equate the "time of the Gentiles" from the time the Jews began to be under the rule of Gentile nations (under Nebuchadnezzar, the Babylonian king) until the Gentile rule over God's people ended when Christ opened his kingdom in heaven in 70 A.D.

"42 months" (we will say more about the time period in the next verse.)

Notice the time is expressed as 42 months that the Gentiles trample the Holy City, Rev. 11:2.

It is also 42 months that the beast out of the sea (Roman empire) was given (by the dragon) a mouth to blaspheme and exercise his authority. He was given power to make war against the saints, Rev.13:1-2,7.

42 possibly could stand for what is earthly, or even of the flesh; and 2 stands for when 2 agree together (Satan and the roman rulers). We do not answer it here.

Verse 3. Two Witnesses

"And I will give power to my two witnesses, and they will prophesy for 1260 days clothed in sackcloth. (NIV)

"Two witnesses." It was two witnesses that were supposed to bear witness to the truth, Matt.18:16; Deut.19:15. Jesus sent out the Twelve and the 72 two by two to witness to the truth, the good news of the kingdom. In the case of Jesus – He is a prophet, priest, and king. His truth is established through three witnesses - three different offices.

"Witness" - comes from the Greek word, "martus or matur"; English martyr. He bears witness to truth by his death. These witnesses are killed and lie in the streets, verses 7-8.

Who are the two witnesses? At first, I thought the answer was going to be in Zech.3-4. There, the prophet talks about Joshua the high priest, representing the Aaronic priesthood, and Zerubbabel, the governor, representing the David line, who built the second Temple, Ezra 3:2. They were men symbolic of things to come, Zech.3:8. Not only that, but they are called in Zechariah two olive trees (sons of oil) on the right and left of the gold lampstand, Zech.4:3. The lampstand (Jesus) has 7 branches (seven lamps blazing, Rev. 4:5 - figurative of the Holy Spirit.) The two witnesses here are called two olive trees and two lampstands. The Prophet, priest, and king are all called witnesses in scripture. Could the two witnesses be symbolic of the two offices which Jesus holds, as priest and king? Could Jesus represent both of the two witnesses? Many things mentioned in the text are similar to Zech.3-4. John makes use of some of it. But, do the details bear out just a figurative interpretation. No, such cannot explain the passage.

The details of chapter 11 do not support that understanding. Verse 8 says: "their bodies lie in the street of the great city (Jerusalem – "where also their Lord was crucified." NIV. Jesus did not die in the streets of Jerusalem nor lay dead on the streets, not buried. Jesus died "outside the camp", outside the city - on Golgotha, and he was buried in a rock hewn tomb of the rich man Joseph of Arimathea. Neither can we explain that the office of priest and the Davidic line died in the streets. We cannot make that make sense. Verse 9 says their bodies lay there in the streets 3 ½ days and people gazed on their bodies. Jesus was buried and in the heart of the earth 3 days. No, the details do not work. We cannot ignore the details. The details always fit in scripture. They always fit perfectly. If it does not fit – do not follow your own knowledge and guess. Stay on track. Follow the lead of the Spirit. Follow his details. Stay with him. Pray to him for understanding. He is there to be our helper. He will teach you, 1 Jn. 2:27. Trust him.

We shall share a more reasonable explanation of the two witnesses in verse 11.

"They will prophesy for 1260 days." (NIV)

The "1260 days" is equal to "3 and one - half years" ("times, time, and half a time) is equal to "42 months". The variation in expressing the same length of time - is a way to *emphasize* the time in different passages.

This time period is expressed in relation to many different scriptures related to Revelation: (ALL the passages below are from the NIV)

Daniel 7:25 "He will speak against the Most - High and oppress his saints and will try to change the set times and the laws." (NIV) "The saints will be handed over to him for a time, times, and half a time." (NIV)

Daniel 12:7 "It will be for a "time, times, and half a time (3 ½ years) when the power of the holy people has been finally broken (Jerusalem and Temple destroyed 70 A.D., T.S.), all these things will be completed." (NIV)

Dan.9:27 "In the middle of the seven (seven = 3 ½ = 3 ½) he will put an end to sacrifice and offering. And on a wing of the temple he will set up an abomination that causes desolation, until the end that is decreed is poured out on him." (NIV)

Rev.11:2 "Gentiles. They will trample on the city for 42 months." (NIV)

Rev. 11:3 "my two witnesses and they will prophesy for 1260 days, clothed in sackcloth." (NIV)

Rev.12:6 "The woman fled into the desert to a place prepared for her by God, where she might be taken care of for 1260 days. (NIV) (In verse 14 it says the woman was taken care of for a time, times and a half time).

Rev.13:5 "The beast (out of the sea) was given a mouth to utter proud words and blasphemies and to exercise his authority for 42 months." (NIV)

A lot happens during that time period as indicated in these scriptures above. The period of time represents something different for each group considered. The amount of time itself (3 ½ years) is experienced by all the groups but some at a different time.

"For the saints" – it means the world will try to persecute them, but they are protected and nourished in the desert.

It means some will be persecuted, but they are given strength to endure.

It means some will be killed during this time, but they are raised victorious.

For the Gentiles – It means they will be given power to trample the city for that period of time, but they themselves will come to nothing. They will be defeated and punished.

For the Jews – they would experience the Wrath of the Lamb without mercy.

What does the period of 3 1/2 years symbolize?

Notice that:

Dan.7:25 – the saints would be oppressed, persecuted for a time, times, and half a time.

This is the "fiery trial" of Christians in 1 Pet.4:12. This was the persecution of Christians by Nero from 64-68 A.D. (That fiery trial ended with the death of Nero; and at his death the Roman empire was thrown into a civil war of Nero's generals fighting each other over the throne).

Dan.12:7 – It would be for time, times, and half a time before the power of the holy people (Israel) would be broken (Jerusalem and the Temple destroyed in 70 A.D. This would correspond to the judgment and punishment of the Jews or the Jewish Roman War from 67 ½ A.D. to Sept.8,70 A.D.

Rev. 11:2 – the Gentiles would trample the holy city (Jerusalem) for 42 months. This also corresponds to the period of the Jewish Roman War, a period of suffering.

Rev. 11:3 – the prophets would prophesy for a period of 1260 days. That would be when they were alive in Jerusalem, and correspond to the period they preached warning Jews of the judgment coming upon them.

Rev.12:6 The woman (the church, believers) fled into the desert where she would be taken care of, protected for 1260 days. Christians were to flee from Jerusalem to the mountains of Judea (a desert), Matt.24, so that they would not become part of the suffering meant for the Jew and the period of the Jewish punishment from 671/2 A.D.- 70A.D.

Rev.13:5 The beast was given authority to exercise 42 months. The context in that chapter, verse 7, is "he was given power to make war against the saints." The beast at that time was represented by Nero and corresponds to the persecution of the saints by Nero from 64 to 68 A.D. However, it was the beast (the Roman Empire) that brought judgment, suffering upon the Jews also from 67 1/2 A.D. to Sept.8, 70 A.D. Most of that persecution was under Vespasian as emperor and the destruction by Titus, his son.

What did 3 ½ years symbolize? It symbolized a period of suffering. It was a period of trial and suffering for the saints. It was a period of suffering and punishment for the wicked Jews who rejected Jesus. The period of 3 ½ years did not have to all be the same period. It occurred at different times for the saints and the wicked Jews. But it represented a period of suffering for both.

When did this time period (3 ½ years) occur?

The Jewish-Roman War started in 66 1/2 A.D. and essentially ended with the fall of Jerusalem on Sept. 8, 70 A.D. The time of that war is close to the time of 3 ½ years. More specifically, this period (3 ½ years) matches more closely to when the Jewish – Roman war was taken to Jerusalem in the summer of 67A.D. One named John, a tyrant and a rebel fled the city of Gischala from the Romans and came to the city of Jerusalem. John, being ambitious for power and a tyrant brought war to Jerusalem. Along with him, a group that called themselves zealots who were rebels and tyrants also came to Jerusalem and took over the Temple and the sanctuary. Josephus explains that —Jerusalem, the royal city, and the principal city of the whole nation, ended up with the rebellious and tyrants who had fled to the city from the conflicts with Rome in other places. (Josephus, book 4, chapter 2, section1) As it occurred, the zealots who had taken the Temple area killed the high priests and their families. They appointed unknown and ignoble persons to the office. Ananus, of the royal lineage and the most powerful in the whole city, joined with John in fighting the zealots who were fortified in the Temple and sanctuary above them. Later at the death of Nero and the civil war that followed, a third Jewish faction, led by one named Simon, entered Jerusalem. Jerusalem was divided into three major factions that warred and fought each other. This was for a period of 3 ½ years.

It would be for a time, times, and half a time when "the power of the holy people (Israel) was broken (with the destruction of the Temple and Jerusalem)" Dan. 12:7.(NIV)

"Clothed in sackcloth" (NIV)

Zech.13:4 says: "On that day every prophet will be ashamed of his prophetic vision. He will not put on a prophet's garment of hair in order to deceive." (NIV). From the verse we learn that Prophets wore a garment of hair.

In speaking of the prophet Elijah, king Ahaziah recognized his description in 2 Ki.1:8: "He was a man with a garment of hair and a leather belt around his waist." (NIV)

Matt.3:4 describes John the Baptist as "John's clothes were made of camel's hair, and he had a leather belt around his waist." (NIV)

"Sackcloth" –

Sackcloth was a coarsely woven fabric usually made of goat hair. Sackcloth was not only what prophets wore; but it was worn also as a sign of mourning and deep humbling of oneself - as in the times of repentance.

Jesus said in regard to the towns of Korazin and Bethsaida, "If the miracles that were performed in you had been performed in Tyre, and Sidon, they would have repented long ago, sitting in sackcloth and ashes." (NIV)

Verse 4. Two Olive Trees And Two Lampstands

"These are the two olive trees and the two lamp stands that stand before the Lord of the earth." (NIV)

"These are the two olive trees and the two lamps"

The two witnesses of verse 3 are called here "two olive trees and two lamps.

Verse 5. Fire Comes From Their Mouths

"If anyone tries to harm them, fire comes from their mouths and devours their enemies. This is how anyone who wants to harm them must die." (NIV)

"Fire come from their mouths and devours their enemies" (NIV)

Of course, the language is figurative but testifies to the power of these witnesses. The prophets speak the word of God. It is the two-edged sword. For the Christian, it pierces the heart and reveals the thoughts and intents of the heart. For the enemies of God, it will judge them and consume them with fire, Jn 12:48; Jer.23:28-29. The word is the fragrance of life to the believer and the smell of death to the wicked, 2Cor.2:16.

The text seems to also confirm the reality of the power of these prophets. They had miraculous powers like certain prophets of the Old Testament. Elijah, in the Old Testament, called down fire from heaven to consume the king's messengers, 2 Kings 1:10. Here, God protected the witnesses until, verse 7, their testimony for God was complete. Many times in the New Testament, especially in Acts, we see the deliverance of the apostles and prophets by angels from jails, stoning, and death.

Verse 6. The Power To Shut Up The Sky

"These men have power to shut up the sky so that it will not rain during the time they are prophesying and they have power to turn the waters into blood and to strike the Earth with every kind of plague as often as they want." (NIV)

"These men". (NIV) The text seems to indicate <u>real men</u>, men living at the time. It does not just seem figurative. They are compared to prophets of the Old Testament. Who had the power to shut up the sky so that it would not rain? Elijah did that, Js.5:17, Lk.4:25. Who had the power to turn water into blood and send plagues on the earth? Moses! Book of Exodus. These men had powers of both of those prophets.

Verse 7. The Beast Would Kill Them.

"Now when they have finished their testimony, the Beast that comes up from the abyss will attack them, and overpower and kill them." (NIV)

"<u>The beast that comes up from the abyss</u>" (NIV)

This phrase is very close to 17:8: "<u>The beast</u>, which you saw, once was, now is not, and <u>will come up out of the abyss</u> and go to his destruction."

The beast comes up out of the sea (the world, the nations) in chapter 13. We can identify the beast as the fourth kingdom of Dan.7:23. The beast then is the Roman empire. Each emperor of Rome represents the beast while he is ruling. The emperor (the beast) of 17:8 "who once was, now is not" was Nero. He is described in the phrase of verse 10 as "five have fallen" – five emperors had fallen, or died. Nero was the fifth king, he "was not' (he had died, or "fallen"). He was a very wicked emperor who had persecuted and killed thousands of saints from 64 A.D. to his death in June, 68 A.D. Where did he go? To the abyss, the bottomless pit (where the fiery furnace was, 9:1-2); the same place the locusts (demons) came out of. He would come up out of the abyss (where the wicked was kept) and go to his destruction (in the lake of fire, 20:10,15). The abyss was like a fiery furnace. The wicked dead were also kept there, like the rich man, in the story of the rich man and Lazarus. Lk.16:19-31. The rich man "was in torment", verse 23. The rich man asked Lazarus to "cool his tongue, because I am in agony in this fire," verse 24. (NIV) The laws of heaven are not like the laws on earth. On earth, things burn up. When the laws of heaven are applied to the nature of fire, it is different. For example, Moses and the burning bush. The bush did not burn up. God is a figure of fire, Ezek.1. Yet, he nor the angels who are "flames of fire" (Heb.1:7) burn up. They are fiery figures who control the fire and can use it at their will. In the abyss, the fire torments, but they are not burned up. In Rev.17:8 where the beast comes up out of the abyss (torment as in a furnace); and goes to destruction (Greek – apoleian, destruction). Rev.20:10 tells us the beast had been thrown into the lake of burning sulfur. Ouch! Ouch! Ouch! Things got even hotter! It's kind of like our saying "to go from the frying pan into the fire." If one goes from the torment of a furnace to a lake of burning sulfur and if I know- that it was even much worse – Lord, I cannot comprehend it. I cannot imagine it. Does it mean destruction - meaning extinction, annihilation or non-existence? (Review the meaning of the Greek word - APOLLUMI and where it is used on this subject.) Or, does it mean you exist – in total absence of well - being; without any good thing from God; shut out totally from his presence? Does it mean total darkness, total burning, continually forever? If so - Enough! I do not want to even think about it anymore.

The two witnesses were real people.

Verse 7 indicates further that the witnesses were real people. If the two witnesses were just symbols – what would it mean to kill them and leave them lying in the street, verse 8, and people gloating over them in verse 9? The Beast (Rome) would attack them and kill them. After verse 11, let's look closely at who the two witnesses could be. I believe the details of the text are describing two real people in Jerusalem.

Verse 8. Their Bodies Will Lie In The Street

"Their bodies will lie in the street of the great city, which is figuratively called Sodom and Egypt, where also their lord was crucified, (NIV)

Jerusalem is figuratively called Sodom, (Deut. 32:32; Isa.1:8,10; Isa.3:8-9; Jer.23:14; Ezek.16:44-49).

In a song recited by Moses to the assembly of Israel in Deut.32, in verse 32 he says: "Their vine comes from the vine of Sodom and from the fields of Gomorrah." (NIV)

In Isaiah 1 the prophet addresses "the Daughter of Zion", verse 8 as "Hear the word of the Lord, you rulers of Sodom; listen to the law of our God you people of Gomorrah." (NIV)

Jerusalem was to receive the plagues of Egypt, (Deut.28:27,60; Amos 4:10). Israel had learned idolatry while in Egypt from the Egyptians. They built the golden calf. They wanted to go back to Egypt.

"Where also their Lord was crucified." (NIV) This is a very definitive statement. The "Great City" (11:8), that is referenced over and over in Revelation is definitely identified here. The Lord Jesus was crucified in Jerusalem. Jerusalem is the "Great City"! The woman, the Great Prostitute, of chapter 17, is in verse 18 identified: "The woman you saw is the Great City that rules over the kings of the earth." (NIV) Earlier in that chapter, the woman is called "Babylon the Great, the mother of Prostitutes," verse 5.

Verse 9. For 3 ½ Day They Refuse Them Burial

"For three and a half days men from every people, tribe, language and nation will gaze on their bodies and refuse them burial." (NIV)

"For three and a half days"

I do not know for sure what 3 ½ days symbolized. It is probably a literal 3 ½ days.

Because these saints had been killed, their bodies lay in the streets for 3 ½ days. (See comments, verse 11)

"People…gaze on their bodies", "and refuse them burial"

It was a disgrace not to be buried. (God predicted that the wicked Queen Jezebel the dogs would eat, and there would be none to bury her, 2 Ki.9:10. In regard to sinful Israel God said: "even if Moses and Samuel were to stand before me, my heart would not go out to these people," (NIV) Jer.15:1. Then in 16:4 he says: "They shall die grievous deaths: they shall not be lamented; neither shall they be buried; but they shall be as dung on the face of the earth." (NIV)

But these two witnesses were not wicked. Yet they were treated with disgrace by the wicked. Those who had killed them refused their burial. God decided the things in the verses above. But in verse 9 wicked men decided that these two witnesses would not be buried and that their bodies would lie in the streets. The wicked disdain and detest the righteous. Even our savior they spit on and mocked and beat, Mt.27:27-31.

Verse 10. They Will Gloat Over Them

"The inhabitants of the earth will gloat over them and will celebrate by sending each other gifts, because these two prophets had tormented those who live on the earth." (NIV)

Ever notice how when the enemies of God think that they are winning, they want to gloat? They are disrespectful even over the righteous dead? They can act despicable. What evil they do they feel is ok. But when it concerns the righteous, they can point out every pretense of a flaw with a spin, a twist, a deception, an outright lie. The righteous vex them, irritate them, anger them! I guess they even "send each other gifts" when the righteous are dead! Is that an exaggeration? Remember - the head of John the Baptist was sent on a platter to the daughter of Herodias (like a trophy), Mk.6:25-28.

"These two prophets had tormented those who live on the earth." (NIV) (Tormented by preaching the word of God.).

Verse 11 The Breath Of Life Entered Them

"But after the three and one - half days a breath of life from God entered them, and they stood on their feet, and terror struck those who saw them." (NIV)

Who are the two witnesses? Let's list what we know from the text:

1. They are prophets who prophesy for 1260 days. (Verses 3,6)
2. They are clothed in sackcloth. (Verse 3)
3. They are called two olive trees and two lampstands. (Verse 4)
4. They have miraculous powers like Moses and Elijah. (Verses 5-6)
5. They are killed by the beast (Roman empire, under Nero at the time). (Verse 7)
6. They are killed in the great city (the city where our Lord was crucified - Jerusalem).
7. They are not buried, but are left to lie in the streets.
8. After 3 ½ days, they are resurrected, they "went up to heaven in a cloud while their enemies looked on", Rev.11:12 (NIV) (The resurrection took place when the Lord returned, 1 Thess.4:16, etc.) "a loud voice from heaven said – 'come up here.' (verse12) (NIV)
9. The two prophets tormented those on the earth. (verse10)
10. That very hour a severe earthquake killed 7000 people and survivors gave glory to God. (Verse 13).

What 2 prophets prophesied 1260 days (the full time of the Jewish War with Rome, clothed in sackcloth, who were two olive trees and lampstands who were anointed before the Lord (alluding to Zech.4:11-14), living in the city of Jerusalem, who had the gift of miracles as great as Moses and Elijah, who were martyred for Christ, and taken to heaven? I think we have narrowed down our search quite a bit. Seems obvious – James and Peter! No surprise. They were apostles and very close to Jesus.

They were in Jerusalem. There was James, the brother of Jesus, (Mt.12:46;13:55; *Gal.1:19*) and an apostle (Mt.10:2-4; Mk 3:13-19; *Gal.1:19*). (It was not the James, an apostle, and the brother of John, who was killed with a sword by Herod, Acts12:1) It was James, the Lord's brother, an apostle, who spoke up and gave his judgment at the Jerusalem council of the apostles and elders (verse 22) in Acts 15, see verses 13-21. Peter had also got up and addressed the group, verse 7-11 at Jerusalem.

Peter in Jerusalem:

Peter preaches on Pentecost in Jerusalem, Acts 2.

Peter represents the church before the Sanhedrin of Jerusalem, Acts 4:1-12.

The apostles stayed in Jerusalem when the church was scattered at the death of Stephen, Acts 8:1.

Peter leaves Jerusalem to share the gospel to the Samaritans, Acts 8:14; but then returns to Jerusalem, verse 25.

Peter goes to Caesarea to preach the gospel to Cornelius, and then returns to Jerusalem, Acts 11:2.

Peter is imprisoned by king Herod in Jerusalem after Herod kills James, brother of John, Acts 12.

Peter is seen by Paul who goes up to Jerusalem to get acquainted with him, Gal.1:18.

Peter is again seen by Paul 14 years later in Jerusalem, Gal.2:1 and in verse 9 James, Peter, and John were reputed to be pillars there.

Peter and James were the main speakers at the Jerusalem council of apostles and elders, Acts 15.

They were apostles and elders. Peter mentions being a "fellow elder" in 1 Pet.5:1. Of what church? I believe he was an elder of the Jerusalem church. He started there and he worked from there. James also. The scriptures strongly indicate they were apostles, prophets, elders of the Jerusalem church.

Their letters James, and 1,2 Peter were written near the time and about the time of the end (Js. 5:7-9 and 1 Pet 4:7; 2 Pet 3).

The death of Peter:

"Early church tradition says that Peter died by crucifixion (with arms outstretched) at the time of the Great Fire of Rome in the year 64. This took place three months after the disastrous fire that destroyed Rome for which the emperor (Nero) wished to blame the Christians." (https://en.m.wikipedia.org.) The second epistle of Peter – "Scholars consider the apostle to be between A.D.60 -130, with a favor for a date between 80-90 and so contend that it is pseudepigraphical." (https://en.m.wikipedia.org).

I do not believe either quotation by wikipedia. The time of Peter's death is not known. However, I present my reasons here why I believe that Peter and James were the two witnesses. There is reason to believe they were killed on the Passover and were resurrected 3 ½ days later.

Josephus records the <u>death of James</u>:

"But this younger Ananus (the son of Ananus, the high priest, appointed by Caesar), who, as we have told you already, took the high priesthood, was a bold man in his temper, and very insolent; he was also of the sect of the Sadducees, who are very rigid in judging offenders, above all the rest of the Jews, as we have already observed. When therefore Ananus was of this disposition, he thought he now had a proper opportunity [to exercise his authority]. Festus was now dead, and Albinus was but upon the road; so he assembled the Sanhedrin of judges, and brought before them the <u>brother of Jesus</u>, who was called Christ, whose name was <u>James</u>, and some others [or some of his companions]; and when he had formed an accusation against them as breakers of the law, he delivered them to be stoned." (Josephus, "Antiquities of the Jews", book 20, chapter 9, section 1.) Note: It was this Ananus, the son of Ananus, who excited the people in Jerusalem against the zealots * who had taken the temple area. He was in the big middle of the fighting of the three factions who were "tyrant rebels" who provided the occasion for the total destruction of the city, Jerusalem. *(see Josephus, "The Jewish War," book 4, chap.3, sect.9).

Another account of the <u>death of James</u> is provided by Hegesippus (110 – about 180 A.D., also known as Hegesippus the Nazarene). Eusebius records him, (H.E. 2,23).

In regard to James, he said – "And by his preaching to them Jesus as the Christ, so many of them believed on him that, many of the rulers also believing, there was a tumult of the Jews and of the scribes and Pharisees, saying that all the people were in danger of expecting the coming of Jesus the Christ. On this they invited James to deter the people from being thus deceived, <u>standing on the wing of</u>

the temple at the Passover, that he might be seen and heard by all. But the story proceeds, when he was set there, and appealed to by them to undeceive the people, he answered with a loud voice, why ask ye me concerning the Son of Man? For he is sitting in heaven at the right hand of the Almighty Power, and will come in the clouds of heaven. (A quotation of Mt.26:64) On this, many were confirmed in their belief, and glorified God for his testimony and cried "Hosanna to the son of David. Whereat the scribes and Pharisees said to on another, We did wrong in affording such testimony to Jesus: but let us go and throw him down, that they may be deterred by fear from believing him. So, they cried out, saying, Oh! Oh! The Just one has gone mad. So, they went up and cast him down, and said to one another, let us stone James the Just. And they began to stone him, since he was not killed by the fall."

It is interesting that in Dan.9:27, talking about this very time, the text says: "And on a wing of the temple he will set up an abomination that causes desolation, until the end that is decreed is poured out on him." (NIV)

Could this be talking about when James was cast down from the wing of the temple and then stoned. Could it be by spilling the righteous blood of James, a martyr for Jesus, that the abomination that caused the desolation of Jerusalem began?

Hegesippus proceeds to say that - immediately upon the death of James, Vespasian (Titus) formed the siege of the city! Luke 21: 34 says "that day will fall on you like a trap." (NIV) The Jews could not escape the judgement! Historically, Josephus tells us, Titus laid siege to the city five months and no one could escape. At the end of the siege the city of Jerusalem was leveled and destroyed. (Josephus, book 7, chap1).

We also see in Rev.11:13, after the two witnesses were killed and raised in 3 ½ days, what happened next - "At that very hour" - there was a judgment - "there was a severe earthquake and a tenth of the city collapsed. 7000 people were killed in the earthquake..." Judgment upon the Jews started immediately at the death of James the Just One, the brother of Jesus. Josephus confirms the earthquake:

"And now did the Idumeans make an acclamation to what Simon had said: but Jesus went away sorrowful, as seeing that the Idumeans were against all moderate counsels, and that <u>the city was besieged on both sides</u>. Nor indeed were the minds of the Idumeans at rest; for they were in a rage at the injury that had been offered them by their exclusion out of the city; and when they thought that the zealots had been strong, but saw nothing of theirs to support them, they were in doubt about the matter, and many of them repented that they had come there. But the shame that would attend them in case they returned without doing anything at all, so far overcame their repentance, that they lay all night before the wall, though in a very bad encampment; for their broke out a great storm in the night, with the utmost violence, and very strong winds, with the largest showers of rain, with continued lightnings, terrible thundering, and amazing concussions and bellowings of the earth, that was in an <u>earthquake</u>. These things were a manifest indication that some destruction was coming upon men, when the system of the world was put into this disorder; and anyone would guess that these wonders foreshadowed some great calamities that were coming." (Josephus, Book 4, Chap 4, Sect 5).

It was by this storm and earthquake that the Idumeans, the third violent Jewish faction, (in addition to John's group and the zealots) gained entrance into the city and helped tear it apart. Josephus above confirms the severe earthquake of Rev.11:13.

But wait, There's more! We go back and notice that Hegesippus tells us that James spoke on the wing of the temple <u>AT THE PASSOVER</u>! Then, he was stoned. What happened to Jesus? He died on the Passover. What happened to James? He died on the Passover. What happened to Jesus three days later? He was RESURRECTED! What happened to the two witnesses whose bodies lay in the streets of Jerusalem 3 ½ days? They were RESURRECTED! Jesus was resurrected early in the morning. The witnesses must have been resurrected in the middle of the day (corresponding to 3 ½ days.) (Where everyone could see it!) When was the Passover? In our English calendar, the Passover is March 27 - April 4. Three days later would be the Resurrection! (MAYBE April 7?) The resurrection of the first century took place in April! It was right before the siege that history records took place from April 14 to Sept.8 of 70 A.D.

[Note: the days, months and year I supply in my text correspond to what they would be in the year 2021, the year of my writing. The dates vary a little, changing with each year, because of the differences in the Jewish and Gregorian calendars. The dates do fit within a range – that fulfill the time the events occurred. The dates and their fulfillment were exact in 70 A.D., in fulfillment of God's appointed times; but how they translate into a date for our time with our calendar varies some from year to year.]

From Revelation 11 we figure out that the resurrection took place when the two witnesses were resurrected (in April, 70 A.D.) – before the 5 months of the siege where the Jews were trapped in judgment. What else do we know? It explains what Jesus was saying to the church in Philadelphia in Rev.3:10: "I will keep you from the hour of trial that is going to come upon the whole world" (NIV). I was thinking – how would he keep them from an "hour of trial"? I thought – the hour of trial is obviously a judgment or suffering. Would he keep the Romans from coming through their city somehow and slaughtering many? No. The answer is: Jesus would resurrect them and remove them from the "hour of trial" that would come upon the whole world" (NIV) (Greek -oikoumene, "inhabited earth"). Jesus only told the church of Philadelphia that because they were faithful, he would resurrect them. He could not tell the rest that. The rest he told to repent.

I thought at first, from the context of Luke 21:35, that "the hour of trial" corresponded to the "five months of the siege," until Jerusalem fell. That is when the "hour of trial" began and the church of Philadelphia and the saints were rescued from the "hour of trial" by the resurrection. Jesus had wanted to deliver the saints from "the worst part of the judgment of the Jews, the time the Jews were trapped, besieged for five months until the city collapsed. (The persecution of Jews was during the Jewish-Roman Wars from 66-70 A.D.)

Jesus had told his followers to flee to the mountains, Mt.24:16. Well, if that was what he told them to do, how do you explain "they were to flee" and yet there was the "resurrection of the saints"? Answer – in speaking of his coming and the resurrection, Jesus said – "one will be taken and the other left", Mt 24:36-42. Not all would be resurrected. Not all living then, belonged to the Mosaic period that was being closed out and judged. Some believers (and unbelievers) would be left on earth for the future. With Jerusalem being destroyed, this was the main judgment of the Jews. They were to be judged first. The judgment of the Gentiles came later.

The persecution of saints stopped with Nero's death. It resumed under Domitian, the 11th emperor, "the eighth"- "like unto the seven", 17:11. The judgment of the Jews was to come first; then the judgment of the Gentiles, Rom.2:9-10.

The worst judgment was certainly the judgment of the siege of Jerusalem for five months. That is the focus of the prophecy of Jesus in Mt.24; Mk.13; and Lk.21. The judgment of the Jew was not fully over, even with the fall of Jerusalem. The siege by the Romans of Masada and it's fall was in 73 A.D. However, Jesus focused on the fall of Jerusalem, the center of operations for the whole Mosaic system. The Mosaic system fell with the fall of Jerusalem. Christians were heavily persecuted under Domitian from 89 to 96 A.D. Domitian died, Sept 18, 96 A.D. The "hour of trial" seems to have started with the siege of Jerusalem, but it was to come "upon the whole world". It must have included the judgment of the Gentiles as well as the Jews. When did the judgment of the Gentiles take place? Perhaps, Mt 25:31-46 is the answer. At the final judgment, "all nations (ethnos – Gentiles) are gathered before Jesus, verse 32. He separated the sheep from the goats, and the wicked who are cursed, are cast into the eternal fire, verse 41. They "go away to eternal punishment", verse 46.

Now, isn't it great that Jesus removed his people from earth in the resurrection before "the wrath of the Lamb" came upon that generation! God's people were not there! What did he tell them? 2 Pet.2:9-10 says:

"The Lord knows how to deliver godly men from trials and to hold the unrighteous for the day of judgment NIV ("hour of trial on the whole world," specifically the five months they were held, trapped) while continuing their judgment. This is especially true of those who follow the corrupt desire of the sinful nature and despise authority…" (NIV)

Gal.1:4: "who gave himself for our sins to rescue us from the present evil age." (NIV) (their generation – the ones Jesus said was a "wicked and adulterous generation," Mt.16:4.)

Someone thinking about the scriptures here may say – "I can see how those who remained alive were 'rescued' by the resurrection; but how were the two witnesses who were martyred 'rescued'. If the witnesses were James, he was stoned to death; and if the other was Peter – he was killed also. How were they rescued?" The reply is – true, the witnesses were not rescued from death. (But great is their reward in heaven!) And we also leave you with the words of Isaiah 57:1-2 "The righteous perish and no one ponders in his heart; devout men are taken away and no one understands that the <u>righteous are taken away to be spared from evil</u>. Those who walk uprightly enter into peace; they find rest as they lie in death." (NIV) Again, in the words of 2 Chron.34:27-28 "Because you were responsive and you humbled yourself before God when you heard what he spoke against this place and its people, and because you humbled yourself before me and tore your robes and wept in my presence, I have heard you, declares the Lord. Now I will gather you to your fathers, and you will be <u>buried in peace</u>. <u>Your eyes will not see all the disaster I am going to bring on this place and on those who live here</u>." (NIV)

But wait! There's more! If the resurrection took place with the two witnesses going to heaven – then that means <u>Jesus returned</u>! Jesus had promised that he would come back in the lifetime of some standing before him. They would see him in his glory, with his angels, Mt.16:27-28. Paul says, "According to the Lord's own word, we tell you that we who are still alive; who are left till the coming of the Lord, will certainly not precede those who have fallen asleep. For the Lord himself will come down from heaven with a loud command, with the voice of the archangel and with the trumpet call of God, and the <u>dead in Christ will rise first</u>. After that we who are <u>still alive and are left</u>" (NIV) (not all believers, nor all who were still alive, but those of Jesus' generation who were still alive and were left) would be caught up together with them in the clouds to meet the Lord in the air.

The witnesses, after 3 ½ days being dead on the streets, "the breath of life from God entered them, they stood on their feet" (NIV). "<u>A loud voice</u> (Jesus' loud voice. He was in the clouds to meet them). "A loud voice from heaven said to them, 'come up here' and they went up to heaven in a cloud <u>while their enemies looked on</u>." (NIV)

Did their enemies see it? Yes. Some were those who had condemned Jesus and they condemned James also (the Sanhedrin and the high priests). Jesus had told them some of them would see him on his return. Mt.26:64 says, "I say to all of you: 'In the future you will see the Son of Man sitting at the right hand of the Mighty One and coming on the clouds of heaven." (NIV). Jesus predicted his return at his trial before the high priests, the scribes, the council, etc. Jesus' enemies saw his return!

<u>The death of Peter</u> is not recorded in secular history that I know. I reject as unhistorical the lying legends that claim Peter went on to be the first bishop of Rome and was martyred there.

Jesus predicted the death of Peter in Jn 21. He would not "remain alive" like John until Jesus returned, 21:22. Rather, Jesus predicted that when Peter was old "he would stretch out his hands" (as on a cross) and "lead you where you do not want to go". "Jesus said this indicating the kind of death by which Peter would glorify God," 21:18-19. NIV. Peter would be a martyr.

Peter had just said, "The end of all things is near," 1 Pet.4:7 (NIV). Then in 17 he says, "For the time is come", KJV or "For it is time" NIV – "for judgment to begin with the family of God: and if it <u>first begin at us</u>, what shall be the end of those that obey not the gospel of God." (NIV). Is Peter saying it would start with him? Was he about to die as a martyr?

In 1 Peter 5:9 Peter writes, "stand firm in the faith, because you know that your brothers throughout the world are undergoing the same kind of suffering." (NIV)

**In 2 Peter 1:13-15 he writes, "I think it is right to refresh your memory <u>as long as I live in the tent of this body</u>, because <u>I know I will soon put it aside</u>, <u>as our Lord Jesus Christ has made clear to me</u>. And I will make every effort to see that <u>after my departure</u> you will always be able to remember these things." NIV. Yes, I believe Peter knew his "departure" from this life as a martyr was very close. I think he was the other of the two witnesses (martyrs).

James and what we can know about him fits the description of the two witnesses very well. Because we do not know about the details of the death of Peter, we have less to go on. Peter may not be the other witness. However, I believe then it was another, in Jerusalem, that was comparable to Peter in the church there that could fit.

Verse 12. Come Up Here

"Then they heard a loud voice from Heaven saying to them, 'come up here.' And they went up to heaven in a cloud while their enemies looked on." (NIV)

"Went up to heaven in a cloud" (NIV) – Paul taught they would be "caught up together with them in the clouds to meet the Lord in the air." 1 Thess. 4:17

Verse 13. A Severe Earthquake

"At that very hour there was a severe earthquake and a tenth of the city collapsed. 7000 people were killed in the earthquake, and the survivors were terrified and gave glory to the God of heaven." (NIV)

"a severe earthquake." (NIV) I do not believe the earthquake here was just symbolic. The Jews had killed James, the Just, one of the three of Jesus' inner-circle of friends.

I believe this was a real earthquake, just like on the day Jesus died. On the day Jesus died there was an earthquake: the rocks split and graves opened up, Mt.27:50-52.

"7000 were killed." (NIV) Why 7000? I do not know the explanation. I think of the time of Elijah who was despondent and God told him "I have reserved for myself 7000 who have not bowed the knee to Baal." 1 ki.19:18; Rom.11:4. But how are we to understand the number here? Is it literal or figurative?

In both cases 7000 is 7 x 1000. The number 7 is all like 7 days of a week, all the days; but also points to what God does or is as the 7 Spirits or the 7 eyes upon the Lamb. 1000 is also representative of all. He owns all the cattle on all the hills, etc. So, 7000 that had not bowed the knee would be all that God reserved for himself. The 7000 that were killed would again be all killed that God determined. I believe the number is figurative.

Verse 14. The Third Woe

"The second Woe has passed; the third Woe is coming soon. (NIV)

We are at the start of the third and final woe! We have ended the second woe. We are at the beginning of the siege of Jerusalem. That siege started on April 14, 70 A.D. It lasted to Sept. 8, 70 A.D. It lasted 5 months. The siege was by far the worst of the punishment of the Jews. The Romans, under Titus, the son of Vespasian, the emperor, laid siege to the city. No one could get out. They were trapped, Lk.21:34. There was no running away. No one could try to seek an agreement with the Romans. The three rebel Jewish factions slaughtered people brutally throughout the city, without cause and without mercy. Bodies were not buried, but piled high in putrid piles. Famine was so bad people ate each other, even their own. Disease and stench were so overbearing that it was often hard to even breathe. If we are right about the locusts being demons who possessed people and tortured them for five months – we cannot imagine the horror. Josephus describes the details so horrendously that we are left shocked and speechless. God paid them back for what they had done. They had killed his prophets, murdered his saints, and crucified his son. They had rejected the love and forgiveness offered by his son and for many who once knew grace, they did despite unto the Spirit of grace, Jesus' chief gift given to indwell the hearts of his people.

Jesus had opened the seventh seal in 8:1. With it appeared seven angels with seven trumpets. Judgments followed with the sounding of each of the first four trumpets. Then before there was more, three Woes were announced to come with the fifth, the sixth, and seventh trumpet. The fifth trumpet was the releasing of the locusts. The sixth trumpet was the releasing of the army of 200 million. Now, in the next verse, the seventh angel sounds his trumpet. But we do not see immediately the Woe of the seventh trumpet.

First, we see what John wants the saints to see and to be made aware of.

THE SEVENTH TRUMPET

Verse 15. The Seventh Trumpet Sounded

"The seventh angel sounded his trumpet, and there were loud voices in heaven, which said, 'The kingdom

of the world has become the kingdom of Our Lord and of his Christ, and he will reign forever and ever.'" (NIV)

(Remember, Jesus was to come back, return, with the sounding of the trumpet, 1 Thess. 4:16; at the sounding of the "last trumpet", which is the seventh trumpet, 1 Cor. 15:52).

Verse 16. They Fell On Their Faces

"And the 24 elders, who were seated on their thrones before God, fell on their faces and worshiped God," (NIV)

If we were in the presence of God, we would be on our faces too. We would be in high praise and worship of God. We cannot imagine it.

Verse 17. You Did Reign

"Saying, 'we give thanks to you, Lord God Almighty, the one who is and who was, because you have taken your great power and have begun to reign." (NIV)

"**Have begun to reign.**" (NIV) (Greek - ebasileusas, "**didst reign**" – Marshall's Interlinear; aorist indicative active) "The aorist tense is the Greek grammarian's term for a simple past tense. The aorist simply states the fact that an action has happened."

"You have taken your great power and didst reign." When Jesus ascended into the heavens, he came with those whom he had rescued from captivity in the lower earthly regions, Eph.4:7-10. He took them to Paradise. He then offered himself, his blood, in the True tabernacle of God (in the heavens) made without hands, Heb.9.24-25.

He then sat down at the right hand of God on his throne and began to reign. During his reign, he was active in ruling upon the earth through his Spirit. The Spirit was to take what was Jesus', and make it known to his people on the earth, Jn.16:14. He was to reign until he had put all his enemies under his feet, 1 Cor.15:25. Jesus would come back, resurrect his people from the dead and those still alive waiting for him, 1 Thess. 4:15-17. Then death would be swallowed up in victory. How and when was the last enemy, death, 1 Cor. 15:26 destroyed? Answer in verse 54, "When the perishable has been clothed with the imperishable, and the mortal with immortality, then the saying that has been written will come true: 'Death has been swallowed up in victory". Death was the last enemy to be conquered. 1 Cor. 15:51-54. Once Jesus accomplished that, verse 28 says "When he has done this, then the Son himself will be made subject to him who put everything under him, so that God may be all and in all." (NIV) Jesus reigned until the last enemy -death, was destroyed by the resurrection!

Here, <u>at the seventh trumpet</u>, it says that Jesus had taken his power and <u>didst reign</u>. He had been reigning ever since he had taken the throne in heaven. What he had already done was "action that had happened", "he didst reign." The first part of chapter 11 was of the two witnesses. The return of Jesus and the resurrection happened with them, 11:11-12. Now in verses 15-17, with the sounding of the seventh trumpet, there was the proclamation of the 24 elders – "you have taken your power and <u>didst reign</u>."

Verse 18. The Time Has Come For Judging

"The nations were angry; and your wrath has come. The time has come for judging the dead and for rewarding your servants, the prophets, and your saints, and those who reverence your name, both small and great, and for destroying those who destroy the earth." (NIV)

"<u>The nations were angry</u>" (NIV)– This phrase is in reference to many O.T. scriptures. Ps. 2 says, "Why do the nations rage, and the people plot a vain thing?" "The kings of the earth set themselves, and the rulers take counsel together against the Lord, and against his anointed." They did in the first century. They crucified the Lord's anointed, and sought to defeat his followers. In application, the Nations still do that today.

"<u>Your wrath has come</u>" (NIV) – the time for his wrath had come. It was time for his wrath to be unleashed. This more specifically refers to the "hour of trial", the "day of the Lord", the "five months" that the Jews were trapped by the siege and would be punished. It was the "time of punishment" Lk.21:22

"<u>The time has come for judging the dead</u>" (NIV) - What dead? All of those who lived under the Old Mosaic Covenant and before. All of those who had died in time up to that time. All of those who lived under the "old world order" (the "present form that was passing away", 1 Cor.7:31) before the opening up of the kingdom in heaven. God was ending that Mosaic covenant and judging those who had been under it. It was to end with a judgment just like he ended the "first world" – "that perished by water" 2 Pet.3:6. He was going to end that (Mosaic) world order with judgment. That whole system of the mosaic world order affected things both in the heavens and earth and under the earth (the place of the dead). With the change in world order (Mosaic) the whole world in heaven and on earth would be changed, removing what could be removed, that the things of the New spiritual kingdom would remain, Heb.12:26-28. Jesus changed the universe!!!!!

"The time has come for rewarding your prophets, and saints". (NIV) Jesus would reward his sheep, the True Israel of God, Rom.9:6; Rom.2:29.

"The time has come for destroying those who destroy the earth." (NIV) [Destroying (Greek – diaphtheirai) those who destroy (Greek – diaphtheirontas) the earth.] does not mean annihilation nor extinction. The word comes from "portheo" – (to "ruin by laying waste, to make havock of" ("Expository Dictionary of New Testament Words, by W.E. Vine, p.303.) They are thrown in the lake of burning sulfur, Rev.20:15.

Verse 19. God's Temple In Heaven Was Opened

"Then God's temple in heaven was opened, and within his Temple was seen the Ark of his Covenant, and there came flashes of lightning, rumblings, peals of thunder, an earthquake and a great hailstorm." (NIV)

"God's temple in heaven was opened" (NIV) – After the judgment of that world order (that got old and antiquated, Heb.8:13, T.S.) under Moses and the people under it, so that that order of things "passed away" - then God opened up the New spiritual Kingdom in the heavens. He made everything New, Rev. 21:5.

"Within his Temple was seen the Ark of his Covenant" (NIV) - the ark of the covenant was called "the ark of his might", Ps.78:61; the "ark of the Testimony", Ex.30:26; the "ark of the covenant", Josh.4:18. When the ark set out and traveled, the people set out and traveled behind it. Where the ark went, they went. On top of the ark was the atonement cover with two Cherubim facing each other over the cover. God's presence was above the atonement cover.

For the ark of the covenant to be seen in the temple in heaven, it would mean that God's presence had left the earthly sanctuary in Jerusalem and had been lifted up to the heavenly sanctuary in the New Jerusalem. God's presence would be in the temple in heaven now, no longer in the earthly temple because it had been destroyed.

Josephus writes something interesting connected to this verse. In his context, he is telling his reader about the temple and how strange things occurred in the temple and then God's presence left the temple. He says,

"A certain great and incredible phenomenon appeared: I suppose the account of it would seem a fable, were it not related to those who saw it. And were not the events that followed it of so considerable a nature as to deserve such signals; for, before sun setting, chariots and troops of soldiers in their armor were seen running about among the clouds, and surrounding cities. Moreover, at that feast which we call Pentecost as the priest were going by night into the inner court of the temple, as their custom was, to perform their sacred ministrations, they said that, in the first place they felt a quaking, and heard a great noise, and after that they heard a sound of a great multitude, saying, "Let us remove from here." (Josephus, "The Jewish Wars," Book 6, Chapter 5, Section 3) The whole section reveals really the second coming of Christ and his Presence leaving the Temple, though Josephus did not understand what he was recording.

Pentecost, (meaning 50 days after Passover, Lev.23:15-16) also called Shavuot ("weeks"), "Feast of Weeks", the second harvest - was the celebration of the beginning of the early weeks of harvest. (This was after the "First fruits", Shabbat, the first harvest, a "wave offering," Lev.23:9-12 and Deut.16:1-7. First fruits took place during Passover.) (Pentecost 50 days later was the beginning of the general harvest. For the church, it marked the descent of the Holy Spirit on the disciples and the beginning of the harvest of God through the preaching of the gospel, the start of the Great Commission.) Here in this passage by Josephus, what happened represented the beginning of the harvest of the earth. The resurrection, April 7, had taken place 3 ½ days after the Passover, April 4. Pentecost would be fifty days after that. The angelic beings, multitudes in the clouds, said "Let us remove from here." If the resurrection took place April 7, 70A.D. and the saints were caught up with Jesus and angels in the air; then 47 days later (50-3=47), May 23, they would "remove from the clouds" on earth? Why? The first fruits had been taken, lifted up (From Passover to Pentecost.)

Now, the heavenly Jerusalem was opened up, verse 19. The ark of the covenant had moved from earth to heaven, verse 19. The start of the 2nd or general harvest Pentecost began (that began then and continues on). The second harvest, "Feast of Weeks" was on the 6th of Sivan. (It fell between May 15 and June 14). The "Feast of Weeks" marks the wheat harvest, Ex.34:22.

"There came flashes of lightning, rumblings, peals of thunder, an earthquake and a great hailstorm." (NIV)

CHAPTER TWELVE

THE WOMAN AND THE DRAGON

Verse 1. A Woman Clothed With The Sun

"A great and wondrous sign appeared in heaven; a woman clothed with the Sun, with the moon under her feet, and a crown of twelve stars on her head." (NIV)

"sign appeared" (NIV) – Here, the sign is the Woman and the dragon. In Chapter 15, he sees a sign – seven angels with seven last plagues.

"A woman – the harlot, chapter 17. Israel in the Old Testament is depicted as a woman. She is the woman of God's choice, he picked her. An allegory in Ezekiel 16 tells of how God found her. Her ancestry and birth were in the land of the Canaanites. God passed by, covered her nakedness, clothed her, dressed her beautifully with jewelry and a crown. She rose to be a queen. But she trusted in her beauty, and became adulterous, following idolatry with the nations. That is what Israel had become. This was "unbelieving, worldly Israel."

"A woman clothed in the sun," (NIV) here in chapter 12. Prophetically, the Old Testament prophecies of the woman, "spiritual Israel," "the faithful remnant" of God's wife. Here she is depicted as "a woman clothed with the Sun." Remember that Jesus is represented prophetically as the "sun," Lk.1:78. Jesus is the "morning star," 2 Pet. 1:19. Jesus brings the day. He brings the light into the world, Jn 1:8. "Jesus is the true light, that gives light to every man." In heaven, there will be no more need of the sun or moon – for God and the Lamb will be its light."

To be clothed with the sun – is to be clothed with Jesus. Rom. 13:14 says, "clothe yourselves with the Lord Jesus Christ." Jesus "is our righteousness, our holiness and redemption, 1 Cor.1:31. To be clothed with Jesus is to be clothed with righteousness, purity, holiness. Rev.19 describes the bride of the Lamb who is clothed in fine linen. "Fine linen stands for the righteous acts of the saints," verse 8. The woman clothed in the sun is "spiritual Israel", the bride of Christ, the church.

"With the moon under her feet." (NIV) In Genesis 1:16 we read: "God made two great lights – the greater light to govern the day, and the lesser light to govern the night." (NIV) The lesser light, of course, is the moon. The moon is "under her feet". When Jesus conquered his enemies, they were to be "put under his feet", 1 Cor.15:25. Here is a woman clothed with the sun, Jesus, and has conquered the things of the night. She rules over the wickedness of the night (not participates in, but has conquered over) as the moon is the lesser "light" over the night. Paul says in 1 Thess.5:4-5:

"But you, brothers, are not in darkness, so that this day should surprise you like a thief. You are all sons of the light and sons of the day." (NIV)

"and a crown of twelve stars on her head." (NIV) In Genesis 37 Joseph has a dream in which his parents and brothers bow down to him. His brothers are represented as "stars". There are 11 stars, Joseph would be the twelfth star." The twelve stars represent the 12 sons of Jacob, or the twelve tribes of Israel. She is "spiritual Israel." The woman clothed in the sun, with the moon under her feet, and a crown of 12 stars on her head represents the Jewish church. She has a crown because she is royalty, the wife of the King of kings, Jesus.

Verse 2. She Was About To Give Birth

"She was pregnant and cried out in pain as she was about to give birth." (NIV)

"The woman was pregnant and cried out in pain." (NIV)

The woman (Mary) cried out in pain as she was about to give birth. Verse 5 tells us she had a male child who will rule all the nations with an iron scepter, Gen.49:10; Ps.2:9. From these scriptures we see that this child was Jesus. Mary, who had Jesus, certainly cried out in pain giving birth to him. The woman (the nation of Israel) gave birth to Jesus. Jesus was born "under the law", Gal.4:4, born of a woman (Mary, but not of the seed of man). He lived a life without sin and so fulfilled the demands of the law perfectly. He lived and died under the Mosaic covenant. Because he willingly died for us, taking our place, he can offer his life for ours, for everyone who believes. By his death, he is the mediator of a new covenant. It became legally of force after his death, Heb.9:17.

Now, I have emphasized that <u>Mary cried out in pain</u> with the birth of Jesus. But prophesy had something else going on for the woman (Israel). She was barren (she bore no children "under the Mosaic covenant".) Isa.26:17-18 says –

"As a woman with child and about to give birth writhes and cries out in her pain, so were we in your presence O Lord. We were with a child, we writhed in pain, but we gave birth to wind. We have not brought salvation to the earth; we have not given birth to people of the world." (NIV.)

Yes, Jesus was born "under the Law", under the Mosaic covenant. His mother cried out in pain to give him birth. But she had not borne any children under the New Nation, the spiritual nation. The heavenly Jerusalem did not exist yet.

In Isaiah, chapter 53 is the famous prophecy about Christ. Read it. Then, in Isaiah 54, it tells of this woman. Her husband (Jesus), verse 5, is her Maker, the Lord Almighty. She was barren, but it predicted that she would have more children than the woman who had a husband (physical Israel of the old covenant). (This is an allusion to the story of Hagar and Sarah that represents two covenants, Gal.4:21-27. There in Gal.4, verse 27, It quotes Isa.54:1 and says this: "Be glad, o barren woman, who bears no children; break forth and cry aloud, you who have <u>no labor pains</u> because more are the children of the desolate woman…") (NIV). Then, in Isaiah 66:6-8, it says, "Hear that uproar from the city, hear that noise from the temple! It is the sound of the Lord repaying his enemies all they deserve. (NIV). (This was during the five months they were trapped, and the Jews were punished in the judgment of the destruction of Jerusalem.) But wait, the resurrection had taken place right before that. So, in Isaiah 66, the next verse reads – "Before she goes into labor, she gives birth;

before the pains come upon her she delivers a son. Who has ever heard of such a thing? Who has ever seen such things? Can a country be born in a day or a nation be brought forth in a moment? Yet no sooner is Zion (the heavenly Jerusalem) in labor than she gives birth to her children." (NIV)

What does it all mean? The spiritual woman (heavenly Jerusalem) clothed in the sun was barren until the resurrection. The woman is the Heavenly Jerusalem. When the "completion" of the saints took place, namely when they inherited spiritual bodies and were resurrected to heaven, a whole spiritual nation was born in ONE day, the day of the resurrection. The woman, "who is our mother," Gal. 4:26-27, the Jerusalem which is above, did not even go into labor, and yet was born to her a whole nation in a single day. Wow! What a thought. What wonderful things God has worked for us!

There were the birth pains in regard to the judgment coming upon the Jews, described in Mt.24. The beginning of birth pains in 24:8. The prophets often described judgment as having birth pains, Jer.13:19-21; Jer.30:6-7; and many more. There would be judgment and those pains in judgment were also the pains of starting over and producing a new offspring. The new sprang out of the old. The pains of death were also the pains of bringing new life. Even though God brought "birth pains" and punished wickedness; he also brought new life. Chastisement or punishment can bring life – Prov.23:13-14,

"Do not withhold discipline from a child; if you punish him with the rod, he will not die. Punish him with the rod and save his soul from death." (NIV)

It is interesting that with all the judgments that took place with the seals, Chap.9:21 says, "Nor did they repent of their murders, their magic arts, their sexual immorality or their thefts." (NIV) They were "past feeling", Eph.4:19, unable to repent, Heb.6:6. We are to discipline while there is hope, Prov.19:18.

Verse 3. An Enormous Red Dragon

"Then another sign appeared in heaven; an enormous Red Dragon with seven heads and ten horns and seven crowns on his heads." (NIV)

"Another sign appeared". First the woman - a sign; now the dragon – a sign.

"An enormous red dragon" (NIV)

We do not have to read far to know who this is. Verse 9 of chapter 12 says- "The great dragon was hurled down – that ancient serpent called the devil, or Satan, who leads the whole world astray. How enormous was he? I believe he was huge like Leviathan. In Ps.74:14, we read of Leviathan, a sea serpent with many heads. If he ruled the seas (seas are the Nations -symbolically), he was like Satan (who ruled the nations, as the god of this world). In Job 41 he says, "Can you pull in the Leviathan with a fish hook? Or tie down his tongue with a rope? Can you put a cord through his nose or pierce his jaw with a hook?" Verses 1-2. (NIV) "Can you fill his hide with harpoons or his head with fishing spears? If you lay a hand on him, you will remember the struggle and never do it again! Any hope of subduing him is false; the mere sight of him is overpowering. No one is fierce enough to rouse him," verses 7-10, (NIV). Then he goes on …verse 15 – "His back has rows of shields, tightly sealed together", Verse 19 –"Firebrands stream from his mouth; sparks of fire shoot out"…verse 21- "His breath sets coals ablaze"…verse 24 "his chest is as hard as rock"…verse 26 "The sword that reaches him has no effect"…verse 27 "iron he treats like straw and bronze like rotten wood," (NIV) etc. Leviathan is called the "monster of the Sea".

Now, read Isa. 26:20-27:1 "Go, my people, enter your rooms and shut the door behind you: hide yourselves for a little while until his wrath has passed by." (NIV) (Like in Ex.12, at the "first Passover," till the destroyer passed over the houses marked with the Lamb's blood.) "See, the Lord is coming out of his dwelling to punish the people of the earth for their sins. The earth will disclose the bloodshed upon her; she will conceal her slain no longer." (NIV) In chap. 27 - "In that day, the Lord will punish with his sword, his fierce, great and powerful sword, Leviathan, the gliding serpent, Leviathan the coiling serpent; he will slay the monster of the sea." (NIV) Hmmm. What is he talking about? Read the rest of chapter 27.

From that thought Isaiah goes on to say "in that day" (the day of judgment), Leviathan also would be punished. Is there a parallel of Satan in Revelation to Leviathan in Isaiah 27?

Here in Rev.12, the dragon was with "With seven heads and ten horns and seven crowns on his heads." What a monster!

Satan had seven heads. Why seven? First, he imitates God. The Lamb has seven horns and seven eyes which are the seven Spirits of God," Rev.5:6, (NIV). There are seven lamps blazing which are the seven Spirits of God – Rev. 4:5. "Seven" - represents things of God. Satan is the deceiver. He makes himself as an angel of light, 2 Cor.11:14. Satan has always pretended to be something he is not. He pretends to be the Christ, but he is the anti-Christ and supported the many anti-Christs, 1 Jn. 2:18. He pretends to bring light, but he brings darkness. He pretends to be as God, but he is a sham, a phony, a pretender, a deceiver.

In chapter 13 we run into "the beast out of the sea". He imitates Satan and gets his power from him, v.2. The beast's seven heads represent seven emperors, as we shall see. The beast also has ten horns and ten crowns. He serves the dragon and draws his power from him.

"The ten horns of Satan." Horns represent power, and therefore authority. Ten is a number which can represent wholeness, or stand for the whole, as the Ten Commandments represent the whole of God's law. Egypt experienced the Ten Plagues, therefore all, the whole, of plagues.

"The seven crowns" correspond to the seven heads and add a description. Crowns suggest royalty, kings. When we see these kings come against the earthly Jerusalem, the earthly Jerusalem loses big time. It is these kings that bring God's judgment upon physical, earthly, ungodly, sinful Israel. But, in the heavens there is a parallel battle. There, these earthly hordes lose big time and are buried all over. No harm comes to the heavenly Jerusalem, God's true Jews, Rom.2:29. This battle, in heaven, is the battle of Gog and Magog in Ezek.38-39 and Rev. 20:7-10. That battle in heaven will be fun to study when we get there.

Verse 4. His Tail Swept A Third Of the Stars

"His tail swept a third of the stars out of the sky and flung them to the Earth. The dragon stood in front of the

woman who was about to give birth, so that he might devour her child the moment it was born." (NIV)

"His tail swept a third of the stars out of the sky". (NIV)

We have read in Joseph's dream that the twelve stars represented the 12 sons of Jacob. Stars can represent men. But we have also read in Rev.1:20, "The stars are the angels of the seven churches." (NIV) In this verse, the stars are angels, fallen angels. The dragon brought with him a fraction (1/3) of the heavenly hosts. It is a symbol, but not an exact fraction. It is 1/3 because it is a fraction of heavenly or spiritual beings. Remember the 3 heavens of 2 Cor.12:2? Things of the spiritual world are represented with 3.

"And flung them to the earth". (NIV) When did this happen in this text? Before the birth of the son, verse 5. Then what does this tell us? Satan was trying to destroy the Christ who was coming into the world. [Satan had tried to destroy the "seed of the woman" in Noah's time when the "sons of god" married the daughters of men and created the Nephilim.] Satan again got help in the heavens from his followers and flung them to the earth to get ready to destroy the woman's child. [This child – Christ was made from the "seed of woman" only, a virgin]. There was demon possession and great wickedness in the world when Jesus was born. I do not know how long before Jesus was born that there was demon possession. I do not know exactly when Satan flung them to the earth. Perhaps, when God went silent for 430 years at the end of the writing of Malachi. The

The Medo-Persian empire ruled Israel at the time, and the temple had been rebuilt. Nevertheless, the Jews in Malachi's time were mistreating their wives and marrying pagans, and not teaching the word of God. I've often wondered what was going on after the Greeks took power over Israel in 333B.C. What was Greek mythology about? Was there something in life that spawned such tales? Hmmm. All of this before Jesus was born.

This getting ready of the dragon to defeat the man child, Jesus, that was coming into the world – this effort had been done before by Satan. "There was the prophecy in Gen.5:29 about Noah, "He will comfort us in the labor and painful toil of our hands caused by the ground the Lord has cursed."

(NIV) Satan realized what it may mean. He wanted to defeat the prophecy of Gen.3:15 that the "seed of woman would crush his head." So, he thought to corrupt the "seed of women". In Gen.6:1-2, The sons of God (angels, see 2 Pet.2:4; Jude 6) came down and married the daughters of men, any of them they pleased. The offspring of the unions were the Nephilim, or giants. The corruption of the seed line did corrupt man at the time. Man's thoughts became evil continually. So, God brought on the flood, and "that world perished by water", 2 Pet.3:6. Now, in this verse, before the man child, Jesus, is born, Satan flings his followers to earth and they inhabit man with demon possession. They made the world of that time very wicked. Jesus says over and over how wicked and evil that generation had become. Satan was trying to defeat the seed line again and destroy it. Instead, it was God working his plan to work out the salvation of mankind. Yes, that generation ended in a judgment also. That judgment again is described as a judgment of the whole world. The world judgments are contrasted in 2 Pet. 3. Each time, it was not the physical world that was annihilated, but the inhabited world that was judged. The last judgment, in the first century, then ushered in the Kingdom of Christ.

"Dragon stood in front of the woman, that he might devour the child, as soon as it was born." (NIV) Historically, this happened. Herod sought the child, Jesus, to kill him, Mt.2:13. Herod even killed all the boys two years old and younger, verse 16.

Verse 5. A Son, A Male Child

"She gave birth to a son, a male child, who will rule all the nations with an iron scepter. And her child was snatched up to God and to his throne." (NIV)

Mary gave birth, not to just a son, but the son, Immanuel, "God with us". He was the promised son of thousands of years, the hope of the world! Jesus was born, he would rule the nations. He is the Lord of lords, and the King of Kings, both of heaven and earth!

"He was snatched up to God and his throne" (NIV) (at the ascension).

He (as a man) was snatched up, out of the Dragon's reach. He was raised – "far above all rule and

Verse 6. The Woman Fled Into The Desert

"The woman fled into the desert to a place prepared for her by God, where she might be taken care of for 1260 days." (NIV) (1260 days = 3 ½ years)

"1260 days" (NIV) - is the 3 ½ years, the "time, times and a half time." The period of time represents a period of trial and suffering. (see comments on chap.11:3) In this verse, the woman fled to escape the suffering. She is protected from it for that period of time and taken care of.

"The woman "fled into the desert to a place prepared for her by God." (NIV) When was this? Was it after the male child was snatched up to God and his throne? Verse 5 says "He will rule…" speaking of what would happen to him in the future in that text. Though verse 5 speaks of what would happen (to help us identify who he is) the text in verse 6 goes back to the time of his being a child. The woman fled with him.

Mt.2:13 says, "An angel of the Lord appeared to Joseph in a dream. 'Get up', he said, 'take the child (Greek – paidion, "a little or young child") and his mother and escape to Egypt." (NIV) Later, in verse 19-20, it says, "After Herod died, an angel of the Lord appeared in a dream to Joseph in Egypt and said, 'Get up, take the child and his mother and go to the land of Israel, for those who were trying to take the child's life are dead." (NIV)

Jesus was born about 4 B.C. He died in 30 A.D. when he was 33 years old. When he was born, Herod the Great (born about 72 B.C and died, Apr.4, 4 BC.; reigned 37-4 B.C.) the king in Judea tried to kill him. It must have been soon after Jesus and his family escaped that Herod the Great died at age 69. (It is interesting, scholars say that Herod the Great died of chronic kidney disease and that a complication of it was a case of maggot-infested gangrene of the genitals.) Yet, being still a child in Egypt, the Bible says here in Mt.2:19-20 that Herod (the Great, had died and that the family could return to Israel. How long were they in Egypt? Perhaps 3 ½ years? They fled to a desert prepared for them. Where is the desert of Egypt? It is just southeast of the Nile River delta. The desert is called the Arabian desert. Perhaps they fled there. (Note: Herod the Great was the king who started the rebuilding of the Temple in 20B.C. (Josephus, "Jewish Antiquities", Book 15, Chapter 11 and Book 16, Chapter 1). The Temple was not completed for 46 years. Herod the Great's eldest son was Herod Antipater (born 21 B.C. and died 39A.D.) (Josephus, Jewish Ant., Book 16, chap 3). Jesus referred to Antipater as "that fox", Lk.13: 31-32. He wanted to kill Jesus too.

Verse 7. War In Heaven

"And there was war in heaven, Michael and his angels fought against the Dragon, and the dragon and his angels fought back." (NIV)

This verse takes up the thought again of what happened when Jesus was snatched up unto his throne.

"And there was war in heaven". (NIV) When did this happen? In the context we find a clue. In verse 10 It says, "the accuser of our brothers…has been hurled down." (NIV) Satan was always coming before God accusing man of sins. Man's sins stood against him. God allowed this for a long time. But then Jesus died for man's sin. Jesus ascended into the heavens and offered his blood there, to appear for us in God's presence, Heb.9:23-26. Jesus then took the throne beside God the Father and began to reign. He threw Satan out. This war would have been right after Jesus ascended into heaven and took his throne.

Rom. 8:32-34 says, "He who did not spare his own Son, but gave him up for us all – How will he not also, along with him, graciously give us all things? Who will bring any charge against those whom God has chosen? (Even Satan the accuser!) It is God who justifies. Who is he that condemns? Christ Jesus who died- more than that, who was raised to life – is at the right hand of God and is also interceding for us." (NIV) Satan had no place in heaven anymore. He was hurled to earth.

"Michael and his angels". (NIV) Remember, the name Michael means – "who is like God".

Michael is Jesus, the chief prince, the son of the ruler who is God. (See comments on Michael in Revelation 10:1).

"The Dragon and his angels fought back" (NIV) I have never understood how Satan, a created angel, ever thought he could defeat God who created him and everything else. Michael appears as the archangel, but he was not a created being, He is God (Jesus) taking on an angelic bodily form to relate to his spiritual creation above. Jesus is God. Satan, do you really think you could overpower God? What blinding ambition and arrogance!

But then I remember man. Man rails against God, denies God exists, makes himself gods of stone and wood, or makes himself out to be God. How ridiculous! But, man does it? Was Satan so ridiculous? God's creation rebels. His creation wants to be in charge. What a mess his creation can make.

Verse 8. They Lost Their Place In Heaven

"But he was not strong enough, and they lost their place in heaven." (NIV)

Of course, Satan was not strong enough! So, he lost his place in heaven. Satan goes from being able to be in the presence of God in the heavens to his "time short" on the earth, to his final abode – cast into the lake of fire, Rev.20:10. He lost everything and gained everlasting burning.

Verse 9. The Great Dragon Was Hurled Down

"The Great Dragon was hurled down- that ancient serpent called the Devil, or Satan, who leads the whole world astray. He was hurled to the earth, and his angels with him." (NIV)

"The Great Dragon" (NIV)

Here, we see who Satan is – Satan, is a Greek form 'satanas', derived from the Aramaic 'Satan', meaning "adversary, opposer". Devil (Greek- diabolos) means "accuser, slanderer." He is the Dragon, the ancient serpent that deceives the whole world.

"He was hurled to the earth and his angels with him". (NIV) In other words, "they lost their place in heaven." They could no longer go to the earth and back to heaven again, as in Job 1:6-7.

Verse 10. The Accuser Has Been Hurled Down

"Then I heard a loud voice in heaven say: 'Now have come the salvation and the power and the kingdom of our God, and the authority of his Christ. For the accuser of our brothers, who accuses them before our God, day and night, has been hurled down." (NIV)

"Accuser ... hurled down." (NIV)

When Jesus ascended into heaven and began to reign, he threw Satan and his angels out. In the heavens, he was "preparing a place for us," Jn.14:2. He was building his kingdom in the heavens for his people, his coming bride. When he got it built, (In 70 A.D) He would return and get his bride (His return and the resurrection). He would take his bride to the place he had prepared for her (in the heavens). Then you see the Wedding Supper of the Lamb, Rev. 19:9. Jesus was preparing for his bride by cleansing the heavens, restoring all things both in heaven and on earth to under his control. So, he threw Satan out. Satan and his angels lost their place. They could not share (come and go to) the heavens, now the place for Jesus' bride.

Some confuse the wording of the KJV where here, 12:13, Satan "was cast" to the earth; and in Jn.12:31, "Now is the judgment of this world: now shall the prince of this world be cast out." The two passages are not referring to the same thing. In Revelation, Satan is "cast out of heaven" to the earth. In the judgment, Satan is cast out of this world and judged, ending up in the lake of fire.

"Now have come salvation, power, and the kingdom, and the authority of Christ" (NIV)

Jesus' kingdom and reign began when he ascended and sat down at the right hand of God in the heavens. His covenant went into force after he had died, Heb. 9:17. The new Covenant had to be administered – its terms announced in the gospel, and the gospel had to be spread to all the world (the great commission) before the end (Mt.24:14) of the Old Mosaic system was closed out with the destruction of the Temple and Jerusalem in 70 A.D. The New Covenant and the Old Covenant existed at the same time, side by side, while the terms of the New Covenant was being made known and the kingdom being built till it's completion in 70 A.D. During the 40 years that the two covenants existed side by side, people were being saved (salvation) daily through the gospel. The kingdom was being built. Jesus was reigning.

Verse 11. They Did Not Love Their Lives So Much

"They overcame him by the blood of the Lamb and by the word of their testimony; they did not love their lives so much as to shrink from death." (NIV)

Saints overcame the devil. They overcame death by the blood of the Lamb and forgiveness. They overcame deception and lies by the word. They did not count their lives more important so as to pull back from death for what they believed.

Verse 12. Woe To The Earth

"Therefore rejoice, you heavens and you who dwell in them! But woe to the earth and the sea because the devil has gone down to you! he is filled with fury, because he knows that his time is short." (NIV)

"Rejoice you heavens!" (NIV) The heavens were rid of Satan and his angels. Yay! The heavens could be cleansed, ready for the bride.

"But woe to the earth and sea" (NIV)

Satan was going to wreak havoc and pain. He is the destroyer of all that is good.

"He is filled with fury, because he knows that his time is short." (NIV)

How I wish Christians today understood this verse and believed it! Satan's time was short. He did not have long upon the earth (40 years) before he himself would be judged and thrown into the lake of fire, Rev.20:10. Jesus took care of everything for us, including taking care of Satan for us, meaning destroying him in the lake of fire. (cf. Rom.16:20)

I hear Christians talking about all the terrible things Satan is doing today – "Look what he is doing in China! Look what he is doing in the United States and Russia! Look what he is doing in the Middle East!" They fear Satan! They refer to 1 Pet.5:8 "You know Satan is like a roaring lion seeking to devour us!" They do not know that verse is speaking to Peter's time, when Satan was furious and his time was short. Christians continue with their fear – "You can tell it is the 'end times' because the world is getting so bad." Christians act like Satan is everywhere doing terrible things. It's like to them that Satan can read minds and know the future. In their minds he has powers like God himself. No, he was a created angel. He was not omnipresent nor omniscient. Every generation has believed they lived at the "end time. Every generation has predicted Jesus was coming again in their generation. Research it and you will find it's true. What a misunderstanding because of the doctrines of men. So many Christians today do not know – SATAN IS DESTROYED! They still live in fear of him. They do not know what Jesus accomplished in 70 A.D., and the completion of all things God had purposed in Christ. Christians live way below their privileges in Christ!

Satan was destroyed. Remember the prophecy of Gen. 3:15, "That he (Jesus) would crush Satan's head." It was soon to be fulfilled in the book of Romans. Rom.16:20 says, "The God of peace will soon crush Satan under your feet." To "crush" him, is the Greek word suntripsei – "to shatter, to break in pieces by crushing." Heb.2:14 says, "...so that by his (Jesus') death he might destroy him who holds the power of death – that is, the devil." It does not say here Jesus destroyed his power (though Jesus did do that -He destroyed the works of the devil,1 Jn.3:8). (The NIV, 2011 edition has changed what they said from "destroy him", 1984 edition, to "destroy the power of him," 2011 edition. The change is wrong. The Greek says he "destroyed the One who had the power of death"). Here, it says he was to destroy HIM – that is, the devil. Jesus said in Jn.12:31 "Now is the time for judgment on this world: now the prince of this world will be driven out." Satan was driven out. He is not in the world anymore. Quit worrying about him. Satan was judged and stood condemned, Jn.16:11.

Then, you may ask, "how do you explain all the evil in the world?" Js.4:1-2 answers, "From whence come wars and fighting among you? Come they not hence, even of your lusts that war in your members? Ye lust and have not: Ye kill and desire to have, and cannot obtain: ye fight and war, yet ye have not because ye ask not." Man's fallen nature can account for all the evil in the world. Man is capable of doing any and every evil thing to one another – even without Satan. The evil imaginations of the heart, if not stopped by repentance and faith in Christ, get worse and worse through life. Evil is never satisfied!

Verse 13. The Dragon Pursued The Woman

"When the dragon saw that he had been hurled to the Earth, he pursued the woman who had given birth to the male child." (NIV)

When Satan had been thrown out of heaven by Jesus on the throne, and hurled to the earth, He was furious. He was especially furious at the woman, the Jewish remnant of believers, who had given the male child birth. Satan pursued her to persecute her.

Verse 14. The Woman Was Given Two Wings Of A Great Eagle

"The woman was given the two wings of a great eagle, so that she might fly to the place prepared for her in the desert, where she would be taken care of for a Time, times, and a half time, out of the serpent's reach." (NIV)

Verse 14-16 is <u>not</u> a repeat and amplification of the thoughts in verse 6. This is after Satan was hurled to the earth and thrown out of heaven. He pursued the woman (spiritual Israel).

"<u>A place prepared for her in the desert</u>." (NIV)

The <u>wilderness</u> is a symbol of a place of testing, as in the case of Israel that was tested for 40 years in the desert, Heb.3. But it is also a place of God where he protects and provides for his people. God guided Israel in the desert and provided food (manna from heaven) and water (from the rock).

Historically, this may refer to spiritual Israel, the church which started in Jerusalem and was "provided for" by the outpouring of the Holy Spirit on Pentecost. The Indwelling Spirit was given, and miraculous gifts as well. There were apostles, prophets, teachers, pastors and much more given to care for the church. But soon persecution broke out under Saul. He was sent to different cities to drag men and women back to Jerusalem to be condemned. The <u>persecution was like a "river" spewed out to overtake the woman</u> and her offspring. But the earth helped. Rulers of that time dismissed charges brought up by the Jews against Christians. And God fought for them. God turned the threatening and slaughter of Saul around and changed him into an apostle born out of due season. God stopped the persecution for a time, and was with the apostles in their ministry. The edict of the emperor Claudius, somewhere between 41 and 54 A.D., Acts 18:2; also served to protect Christians from persecution and so the church grew by multitudes and thousands.

Verse 15. The Serpent Spewed Water

"Then from his mouth the serpent spewed water like a river, to overtake the woman and sweep her away with the torrent." (NIV)

Verse 16. The Earth Helped The Woman

"But the earth helped the woman by opening its mouth and swallowing the river that the dragon had spewed out of his mouth." (NIV)

(See verse 14 comments)

Verse 17. The Dragon Was Enraged

"Then the dragon was enraged at the woman and went off to make war against the rest of her offspring- those to obey God's commandments and hold the testimony of Jesus." (NIV)

Jesus was born under the Law. He lived it perfectly and died in our place. Then, the heavenly Jerusalem could begin. Jesus was the first born from the dead. "This day have I begotten thee," Heb. 1:5-6. Jesus is the first born of the New Creation, the spiritual creation. Jesus was the start of a godly offspring, a spiritual nation. At the resurrection, a whole nation was born in <u>one day</u>, Isa.66:8. A whole nation was born from the dead – the heavenly Jerusalem. Jesus is the <u>One seed</u> of Gal.3:16, the fulfillment of the Abrahamic promise. A whole spiritual nation would spring from that One seed. Who are Jesus' offspring? "Those who obey God's commands and hold to the testimony of Christ." Who is the mother of those righteous offspring? The heavenly Jerusalem, the bride of Christ, the woman who represents the beginning of the New Covenant, Ga.4:26.

CHAPTER THIRTEEN

THE BEAST OUT OF THE SEA

Verse 1. The Beast Out Of The Sea

"And the dragon stood on the shore of the sea. And I saw a beast coming up out of the sea. he had ten horns, and seven heads with ten crowns on his horns and on each head a Blasphemous name." (NIV)

"The sea". Is figurative for the nations, the Gentile nations, (Greek – ethnos).

"But the wicked are like the tossing sea," Isa.57:20. (NIV)

"Oh the raging of many nations- they rage like the raging sea," Isa.17:12. (NIV) (cf. Ps.65:7; Ezek.26:3)

"The waters you saw, where the prostitute sits, are peoples, multitudes, nations, and languages," Rev.17:15. (NIV)

In Daniel 7: 2-3, Daniel sees "Four great beasts (world empires) each different from the others, came up out of the sea." (NIV)

"A beast coming up out of the sea." (NIV)

In Daniel 7:2-6, Daniel sees four great beasts representing four world empires or kingdoms (Dan.7:14) coming up out of the sea. One, the first, was like a lion with the wings of an eagle, verse 4. (We know from Dan.2:37, that Nebuchadnezzar, of the Babylonian kingdom was of that first kingdom, a king of kings, the ruler over all, Dan.2:38.) Continuing in Dan.7:5, we learn the second world kingdom was like a bear. (This was the Medo-Persian kingdom that followed in time the Babylonian Kingdom). The next or third world kingdom looked like a Leopard. (This was the

Grecian kingdom of history started by Alexander the Great). Both the Medo-Persian and the Grecian empires are also identified in Daniel, see Dan.10:20. The fourth kingdom is not identified in Daniel but it follows the Grecian kingdom. Daniel tells us the fourth beast is a fourth kingdom, Dan. 7:23.

"He (the beast) had ten horns and seven heads with ten crowns on his horns." (NIV)

Rev.17:9 interprets the "seven heads" for you – "The seven heads are seven hills on which the woman (earthly Jerusalem) sits. They are also seven kings." (NIV) The seven heads are the 7 kings (emperors) of the beast (The Roman empire). The harlot (chap.17) is earthly Jerusalem. She rides on the 4th beast of Daniel's prophecy (which is the fourth world empire) coming up out of the sea. In 13:1, it says that each head had a "blasphemous name." The emperors were blasphemous toward the true God and claimed to be a god (emperor worship).

The heads (emperors) have "ten horns" to which they give power. In the Roman empire, each emperor had vassal kings which had been conquered earlier. To these conquered kings, or vassal kings, they gave them authority or "power" over a certain area of the empire to govern it. These kings had their "kingdom", their domain to rule in power. They ruled as lesser kings in the empire. At first, then, we may think these ten horns are vassal kings. The ten horns (powers) wore ten crowns (indicating kingship). But we cannot name or even point to ten vassal kings in the roman empire. Not only so, but notice what the text 17:12 says about these "horns":

The text of 17:12 says – "the ten horns you saw are ten kings who have not yet received a kingdom". (NIV) These "kings" had not been given a territory by Rome to govern. They were not vassal kings.

The Romans, rather than getting them to surrender to them, fight them. In fighting them, they actually, with those they were fighting, accomplish God's plan to destroy the Temple and Jerusalem, as predicted by Christ in Matt.24. Rev.17:12 goes on to say of these kings -"but who for one hour will receive authority as kings along with the beast" (NIV) These ten horns were given "power" as kings for one hour to work with the beast. They did not already have the power as a vassal king would have.

The kings had one purpose – "to give their power and authority to the beast" (Roman empire), Rev.17:13, (NIV). In that effort, what did the beast and the ten horns who gave their power to the beast do? The next verse. 17:13 says – "They will make war against the Lamb."

The ten horns were ten Jewish leaders who were chosen in the Jewish- Roman War to lead against the Romans in defending the temple and Jerusalem. (See details in chapter 17).

[To help understand what all this symbolism leads our minds to see is this – God used "ten chosen Jewish leaders" (horns) and their conflict with the Romans to bring about his purpose - the destruction of the temple and Jerusalem in A.D, 70. The ten Jewish leaders (named in chapter 17 notes) had been given power temporarily along with the beast, NOT power by the beast, to "make war with (resist) the Lamb." Jesus had predicted that the temple and Jerusalem would be destroyed in Mt.24. The Jews and their leaders resisted that destruction and fought to defend the temple and Jerusalem. But the Jews were also divided into three factions and fought each other in Jerusalem. The Jewish leaders and Jewish factions then fought the Romans (in the Jewish war with Rome) to resist the temple being destroyed, but also fought each other. By fighting the other, the Jews actually brought about the temple's destruction and the destruction of the city. Jesus' prophetic words and purpose was fulfilled. The Jews and the Romans fighting, though opposing each other in war, nevertheless together brought about the destruction of the temple and Jerusalem. They together were responsible for fulfilling the purpose and prophecy of Jesus.] (See comments and details in chapter 17).

Let's compare the heads, horns, and crowns of the Dragon with the heads, horns, and crowns of the beast that comes up out of the sea:

The Dragon has:

With Satan,12:3, the ten horns are on seven heads. The horns stand for powers. Satan has control over and gives power to horns through the heads. He has "seven crowns on the seven heads." (Notice, with the dragon, *the crowns are on the heads.* With the beast, *the crowns are on the horns.*) Satan has control over seven heads- "emperors" of Rome, with seven crowns (kings of Rome). They are kings of Rome.

The Beast has:

The beast that rose out of the sea, in 13: 1, is Rome (the fourth world kingdom as identified in Daniel 7:17,23). With the beast, there were seven heads. There were also "ten crowns on the ten horns", 13:1. Rev.17:12 interprets the ten horns for us –

"The ten horns you saw are ten kings" (NIV) (kings because they had crowns on those horns,13:1)

1. "who have not yet received a kingdom" 17:12, (NIV)
2. "who for one hour will receive authority as kings along with the beast" 17:12, (NIV)
3. "They have one purpose and will give their power and authority to the beast" 17:13, (NIV)
4. "They will make war with the Lamb" 17:13, (NIV)
5. "The lamb will overcome them" 17:14, (NIV)

(The ten horns were kings, but NOT emperors. The emperors were the seven heads). Perhaps at first, you may have thought – they were vassal kings of Rome, kings who had been conquered by Rome. Vassal kings were given ruling power in parts of the Roman empire by the emperors. Vassal kings to not fit the descriptions of 1-5 above:

1. Vassal kings already had a territory or kingdom. The ten horns had not been yet given a kingdom.
2. Vassal kings had already been given the authority by Rome to rule or govern their territory for some time, not just for one hour.
3. Vassal kings had multiple duties in ruling their territories, not just "one purpose". They did not give their authority to Rome, rather Rome gave authority to them.
4. Some vassal kings did join Rome in making war against the rebellious Jews.
5. The Lamb did overcome them and thus destroyed the temple and Jerusalem. The Romans did not want to ultimately do that. The Romans did want to put

down the Jewish rebellion, and did win over the Jews in Jerusalem and took captives back to Rome. Vassal kings do not then fit the descriptions that are given. (See who the "ten horns who were ten kings" were in chapter 17.)

Notice here, a difference between Daniel and John in how they are using similar prophetic language:

Daniel talks about ten horns of the beast in Dan.7:20-25. Daniel tells us the ten horns of the beast (the Roman empire) are ten kings: "the ten horns are ten kings who will come from this kingdom," Dan.7:24. (NIV)

Daniel speaks of 10 kings, (where horns = emperors) (not 7 Heads as emperors, as in Revelation).

The "ten horns" of Dan.7 is not the same as the "ten horns" of Rev.13 and 17. The contexts use the symbol differently.

"The ten horns are ten kings that will arise from this kingdom." (4th kingdom) in Dan.7:24. He goes on to say, "Three would be subdued", verse 24. The three would be "rooted up" (killed), Dan.7:8. That would leave seven (10-3=7) horns or kings, (emperors). Seven emperors is the number in Revelation where it speaks of 7 heads (emperors).

We shall explain more in chapter 17.

"On each head a blasphemous name."

The Romans had many gods: Mars/Ares, Jupiter/Zeus (king of the gods), Neptune/ Poseidon, Venus (Aphrodite), Juno/Hera (queen to all deities), Vulcan, Ceres/Demeter, Mercury/Hermes, Minerva/Athena, Apollo, Diana/Artemis, Vesta, Saturn, Janus, Faunus, Fortuna, Proserpina, Terra, Flora, Sol, Bellona, Victoria, Liber. The Romans were very polytheistic.

These gods are mentioned throughout the New Testament and had temples in cities everywhere: Zeus - Acts 14:12; Hermes – Acts 14:11-12; Diana/Artemis – Acts 19:35; Castor and Pollux – Acts 28:11. Aphrodite shows up in the name Epaphroditus – Phil.2:25.

The different emperors were highly polytheistic, and even made themselves out to be gods and to be worshiped. They "spoke against God" and his Temple and thus "blasphemed", Rev.13:6.

There were several times rulers blasphemed the God of heaven. Three were:

Sennacherib, king of Assyria, blasphemed God, 2 Ki.19. God's angel killed 185,000 of his men.

Antiochus IV Epiphanes, king of Greece, blasphemed God and desecrated the Temple of Jerusalem (in 167 B.C.), Dan.11:31-37; 1 Macc.1:54: Josephus, "Jewish Wars", Book 1, chap.1.

Titus, the Roman general that destroyed Jerusalem in 70 A.D. blasphemed God.

Jewish writings about Titus' pompous words say,

"Vespasian sent Titus who mocked, where are their gods, the rock in whom they sought refuge (Deut. 32:37). This was the wicked Titus who blasphemed and insulted heaven. What did he do? He entered the Holy of Holies and with his sword slashed the curtain. Through a miracle blood spurted forth and he thought he had killed God himself. He brought two harlots and spread out a scroll beneath them, transgressed with them on top of the altar. He began to speak blasphemies and insults against heaven, boasting, 'One who wars against a king in a desert and defeats him cannot be compared to one who wars against a king in his own palace and conquers him." Dan.7:25 alludes to the pompous words of Titus. Titus is the "little horn" of Daniel.7:8. We shall study this in chap.17.

Verse 2. The Beast I Saw

"The Beast I saw resembled a leopard, but had feet like those of a bear, and a mouth like that of a lion. the dragon gave the Beast his power and his throne and great Authority." (NIV)

"The beast I saw resembled a leopard...a bear...a lion." (NIV) The fourth kingdom resembled the first three world kingdoms. Here, John reverses the order in Daniel of the three kingdoms as if looking back through time. The fourth kingdom (the Roman empire) is like the first three. By mentioning the first three, he helps us know this is the fourth kingdom, the fourth beast.

"The Dragon gave the beast his power and his throne and great authority." (NIV)

Immediately we know the nature of this kingdom was evil. It drew its power and authority from the Dragon. Satan gave power to Rome.

Verse 3. The Beast Had A Fatal Wound - Healed

"One of the heads of the Beast seemed to have had a fatal wound, but the fatal wound had been healed. The whole world was astonished and followed the Beast." (NIV)

"One of the heads... had a fatal wound" (NIV) (The head had died.)

The head that received a fatal wound was Nero. This is further amplified by John in Rev.17:10:

"They are also seven kings." (NIV) "Five have fallen" (NIV) (The first 5 emperors of Rome were dead: 1. Augustus, 2. Tiberius, 3. Caligula, 4. Claudius, 5. Nero.)

But "the fatal wound had been healed" (NIV)

This does not mean the wound had been healed at the time of this writing of John. The statement was predictive. John was describing what "he saw", verse 2, in a vision. Remember, in his visions, he would see things in the past, the present, and what was "about to occur," Rev.1:19.

What does it mean "the fatal wound had been healed?"

Let's read verse 3 again - "One of the heads of the Beast seemed to have had a fatal wound (Nero), but the fatal wound had been healed (under Vespasian, the ninth emperor). The whole world was astonished and followed the Beast." Remember the beast is the 4th kingdom of Daniel.7:23. The beast is the "Roman Empire."

When did the Roman Empire receive a fatal wound? With the death of Nero, June 9, 68 A.D. At that point in history, the empire went into a civil war. Everyone at the time wondered if the Empire was going to survive. Men fought for the throne of the Empire. Three men briefly claimed the throne. These three were: 1. Galba, who was the general in command of the upper German army and Spain. He claimed the throne and reigned from June 8, 68 A.D. to Jan. 15, 69 A.D. 2. Otho allied himself with

Galba. In the civil war upheaval, he murdered Galba. Otho assumed the throne and reigned for 3 months, from Jan. 15, 69 A.D. to April 16, 69 A.D.

3. <u>Vitellius</u>, was the commander of the army in Germania Inferior. Otho fought Vitellius' army at the battle of Bedriacum and 40,000 died. Otho then committed suicide rather than fight on. Vitellius assumed the throne, reigned 8 months, from Apr.19, 69 A.D. to Dec.20, 69 A.D.

Vitellius was killed ----------------

These three emperors reigned briefly, took the throne, but did not have the power (nor backing of the people and military legions), and therefore the authority needed to rule. During the time of these three, Rome was in civil war, from June 9, 68 A.D. to Dec. 20, 69 A.D. These 3 were "broken off", "uprooted," Dan.7:8. Nero was the 5th emperor. He died. In the civil war, Galba was the 6th; Otho the 7th; and Vitellius the 8th. Vespasian followed as the 9th, and his son, Titus, as the 10th. But, these three of the civil war were "broken off" or "uprooted" according to Dan.7:8. The three "ruled" briefly when the empire was struggling. It had received a death blow and everyone wondered if the empire would survive. Those three were eliminated before Vespasian came along and the empire "came back to life". The empire revived.

Now read verse three again: "One of the heads of the Beast seemed to have had a fatal wound (Nero), but the fatal wound had been healed (- after three emperors were uprooted. Vespasian stabilized the empire and brought it back to life.). The whole world was astonished and followed the Beast" (the revived empire).

"<u>Three were broken off</u>" - during the "civil war" Of Rome (68-69A.D.) - fighting for the throne after Nero's death. <u>These three</u> were emperor #'s 6,7 and 8. Of the 10, "<u>3 were broken off</u>" meant: 10-3=7. Recalculating then, the 5th was Nero, (and with the 3 broken off) the 6th would be Vespasian; the 7th Titus. Now we have the seven heads of Revelation's beast.

Verse 4. Men Worshiped The Dragon

"*Men worshiped the dragon because he had given authority to the Beast, and they also worshiped the Beast and* asked, 'who is like the Beast? Who can make war against him?" (NIV)

"Given authority" (NIV)

Vespasian would be the emperor (when the wound "healed"). The Dragon (Satan) gave him authority (and power). Remember, the three emperors who were "uprooted" took the throne; but they had no backing, no power or authority to rule. Vespasian did have the backing. It was even his army that insisted he become emperor and the other legions came over to him. Even Egypt, under Alexander, who supplied grain to Rome, readily became his ally. (Josephus, "the Jewish War", Book 4, Chap.10, Sections 4-5.) Vespasian had the power and ruled for ten years, from July 1, 69 A.D. (when he was declared emperor by the armies, but in December affirmed by the Senate in Rome) to June 23, 79A.D. He died at age 69.

"Who is like the beast?" (NIV) The people were shocked when the Roman Empire "came back to life." Then, they asked the question: "Who is like the Beast?

"Men worshipped the Dragon … and the Beast." (NIV)

The Dragon. – We have mentioned the Roman gods and all the temples of the various gods in various cities. Rome was very polytheistic. The worship of false gods existed: first – on the level of the official Roman gods; second, with the state – the worship of emperors; third on the municipal level; and fourth, in private groups. Worshiping false gods was worshiping Satan.

Worshiping the Beast. This was the worship of the emperor. This started with Augustus Caesar, the first emperor, who reigned from 31 B.C. to 14 A.D. He started the Imperial Cult. Imperial rulers had state divinity. They were "divi". They were considered divine. They were the Dea Roma. Because they were divinely sanctioned, their authority was absolute. Augustus had changed Rome from a republican system to a De Facto monarchy. Emperors were viewed as gods and could decide all things over religious, political and moral choices.

Vespasian was worshiped as a god. Part of allegiance and obedience to Rome was Caesar worship. The Imperial Cult was inseparable from Rome's official deities.

Verse 5. Exercise His Authority 42 Months

"The Beast was given a mouth to utter proud words and blasphemies and to exercise his authority for 42 months." (NIV)

"Beast... utter proud words and blasphemies" (NIV) The Caesars were polytheistic. They "SPOKE AGAINST God" or blasphemed. To them, the God of the Jews was just another god of many. They ridiculed the Jews – "Where is your God now?" as Titus did when he conquered Jerusalem. Domitian's normal title was - your "Lord and God" (Suetonius, The Twelve Caesars, Domitian)

"Authority for 42 months." (NIV) Here again is the "3 ½ years", "1260 days", "time, times, and a half time." The Romans were given power to cause the "period of suffering" that came upon Christians and Jews.

Verse 6. He Opened His Mouth To Blaspheme

"He opened his mouth to blaspheme God, and to slander his name and his dwelling place and those who live in heaven." (NIV)

He ... blasphemed God, his dwelling, those who live in heaven." (NIV)

He (Vespasian, represented the Roman Empire). Vespasian and his son Titus spoke against the true and only God, and his sanctuary, the Temple, at Jerusalem. (This statement shows the Temple was still standing. They blasphemed the Temple. It was therefore before 70 A.D.)

"They blasphemed those who live in heaven." This may mean saints in heaven. It may mean celestial beings, Jude 1:8; 2 Pet.2:10. It probably is both saints and celestial beings.

Verse 7. War Against The Saints

"He was given power to make war against the Saints and to conquer them. And he was given authority over every tribe, people, language and Nation." (NIV)

"Was given power to make war against the saints." (NIV) Usually, this is interpreted as Christians. "Christians" (called Christians first at Antioch, Acts11:26) is the Greek word - "cristianous". The word for saint is the Greek, - "agios".

The word for church in Greek is – "ecclesia," ("called out"). This is referring to "saints," "saints" as Daniel understood the term to mean when he prophesied. To him it referred to his people, the Jews.

I believe verse 7 here is referring to Daniel's prophecy in Dan. 7:23-26:

"The saints will be handed over to him for time, times, and half a time." Dan.7:25:

"He gave me this explanation: The fourth beast is a fourth kingdom that will appear on earth. It will be different from all the other kingdoms and will devour the whole earth, trampling it down and crushing it. The ten horns are ten kings (Caesar Augustus through Titus, T.S.) who will come from this kingdom. After them another king (Vespasian, T.S.) will arise, different from the earlier ones; he will subdue three kings (Galba, Otho, and Vitellius, T.S.). He will speak against the Most - High, and oppress his saints (Vespasian was sent to put down Jewish uprisings in Jerusalem. Then he set his son Titus to finish the job, T.S.) and tried to change the set times and the laws." (NIV)

What can we learn from that chapter in Dan.7?

1. "Another horn, a little one, which came up among them," 7:8:7:20. (NIV) (Why was it a little horn? He was a prince, Titus. His father Vespasian was the emperor at the time. Titus had power, but he was not emperor yet, so he was a little horn, T.S.)

2. "Three of the first horns were uprooted before it." 7:8 (NIV) (The civil war occurred where 3 emperors fell before Titus and his Father, T.S.)

3. He had "a mouth that spoke boastfully." 7:20 (NIV) (That is what he does in Rev.13:5 - "proud words and blasphemies".)

"Vespasian sent Titus who mocked - Where are their gods, the rock in whom they sought refuge (Deut. 32:37). This was the wicked Titus who blasphemed and insulted heaven. What did he do? He entered the Holy of Holies and with his sword slashed the curtain. Through a miracle blood spurted forth and he thought he had killed God himself. He brought two harlots and spread out a scroll beneath them, transgressed with them on top of the altar. He began to speak blasphemies and insults against heaven, boasting, 'One who wars against a king in a desert and defeats him cannot be compared to one who wars against a king in his own palace and conquers him.'"

(Josephus, "The Jewish Wars")

4. "His look was bolder than the rest." 7:20. (Septuagint Interlinear Translation).

5. "Made war with the saints and prevailed against them" – until the Ancient of Days came". 7:21 (Sept. Interlinear Trans.)

Rev.13:7 - "given power to war against the saints and conquer them." (NIV). (Titus did defeat the Jews and Jerusalem and took them captive. He conquered them. At the end of that time the "Ancient of Days came", Dan.7:26 and set at court, Rev.4.)

"and pronounced judgment in favor of the saints of the Most -High, and the time came when they possessed the kingdom." Dan.7:22 (NIV).

6. "Who shall exceed all the former ones in wickedness" 7:24 (Septuagint Interlinear Translation) (How did he, Titus, exceed in wickedness? He destroyed the former people of God).

7. "Shall wear out the saints of the Most - High." 7:25 (Septuagint Interlinear Translation) (With a siege of Jerusalem – famine and war)

8. "Shall think to change times and law." 7:25 (Septuagint Interlinear Translation) (Titus thought he had defeated the God of the Jews, the ruler of heaven and earth).

9. "Power... given to him for a time, and times, and half a time." (Sept. Interl. Trans.) (That is the 42 months of Rev.13:5) (He was directly involved in putting down Jewish revolts in the 3 ½ year war with the Jews.)

10. "The wild beast was slain and destroyed, his body burned with fire." 7:11 (Septuagint Interlinear)

11. "The dominion of the wild beasts were taken away; but a prolonging of life was given them for certain times (a time and a season", The New English Bible, 1970; also NRSV).

#8 "Shall think to change times and laws." (Septuagint. Inter. Transl.) God had set a time for judgment,

Acts 17:31. God had predicted through Jesus that Jerusalem and the temple would be totally torn down, Mt 24; Mk 13, Lk.21. God had set times and laws that He determined. Titus tried to work against God's plan and change it. Josephus records much of Titus' intentions:

"So, Titus retired into the tower of Antonia, and resolved to storm the temple the next day, early in the morning with his whole army, and to encamp around the holy house. But **as for that** house, God had, for certain long ago doomed it to the fire; and now that fatal day was come, according to the revolution of ages; it was the tenth day of the month Loios [Ab] upon which it was formerly burned by the king of Babylon; although these flames took their rise from the Jews themselves, and were occasioned by them; for upon Titus retiring, the rebellious lay still for a little while, and then attacked the Romans again, when those that guarded the holy house fought with those that quenched the fire that was burning the inner court of the temple; but these Romans put the Jews to flight, and proceeded as far as the holy house itself. At that time one of the soldiers, without staying for any orders…snatched something out of the materials that were on fire, and being lifted up by another soldier, he set fire to a golden window, through which there was a passage to the rooms that were around the holy house…a certain person came running to Titus and told him of this fire…he rose up in great haste and as he was, ran to the holy house, in order to have a stop put to the fire…Then did Caesar, both by calling to the soldiers that were fighting, with a loud voice, and by giving a signal to them with his right hand, order them to quench the fire. But they did not hear what he said…thus the holy house burned down without Caesar's approval." (Josephus, "The Jewish Wars," Book 6, Chap 4, Sections 5-7.).

Titus tried to stop the destruction of the temple; but what God had determined happened, right on the day, the day of the 10th of the month [Av]. (about Aug.30, 70 A.D.) This was the exact day the temple had burned under Nebuchadnezzar. God determines the times and the seasons, Acts 1:7; Dan.2:21; Eccl.3:1ff; Isa.46:9-10. Both temples were destroyed on the tenth of Av. Jer.52:12 says: "And in the fifth month, on the tenth day of the month," verse 13 –"he set fire to the temple of the Lord…and every great house he burnt with fire." (Septuagint Interlinear Translation)

Who was the "wild beast" in Dan.7:11?

"until the wild beast was slain and destroyed", 7:11 (Septuagint Interlinear Translation)

"And the dominion of the rest of the wild beasts was taken away." (Septuagint Interlinear Translation)

What about Nero? Does he fit the description "the wild beast was slain"?

Does Nero fit the description above? Certainly, he fits as a "persecutor of the saints" He killed Christians and persecuted them from the time of the fire of Rome, Jul.18 – Jul.23, 64A.D. to the time of his death, Jun.9,68 A.D. The context of Dan7:8-11 is not talking about Nero, but rather the "little horn". The little horn is Titus.

Again, this is not about Nero. He died before the civil war and the three kings that followed and fell in the civil war. In the description above and Dan.7:8, the little horn came up among the horns and the three were plucked up "to make room for it." See NRSV, NEB. The little horn followed the death of the three that were uprooted. This refers to Titus – "the wild beast". Notice, verse 12 says the dominion of the "wild beasts" was taken away. All the emperors were "wild beasts". They were the kings of the "beast (Rome) that came up out of the sea."

There is a popular theory that Nero, "persecutor of Christians" was resurrected in the person of Domitian, and that "Domitian persecuted Christians". The impression is that "persecution of Christians" had stopped between the emperors Nero, the 5th, and Domitian, the 11th. A modern scholar, Brian W. Jones, refutes the special claim of the "Domitian persecution of Christians" and says it was spun by Eusebius. Whatever! Yes, I believe Domitian probably persecuted Christians just as did all the emperors. We earlier looked at Vespasian. He persecuted Christians. Titus did too.

The major emphasis in the text of Revelation about the Beast is that he imposed "worship of the beast" on the people. Rome's evil, corrupt character was beastly; but his claiming to be God and imposing his worship on others - was the most beastly attribute of all! God is first. He is the First commandment in the Law – "to have no other gods before him".

"War against the saints <u>and conquer them</u> (conquer the saints)"

When and where did a ruler of this world ever "conquer a Christian?" Christians are "more than conquerors." They could never be "conquered" in a spiritual sense. But "God's people" of that time, the Jews were conquered with the leveling of the temple and Jerusalem by Titus. Rome "conquered them" and carried the riches and captives back to Rome. There exists even today the "Arch of Titus"(in memorial of Titus' victory in 70 A.D.) that still stands in Rome and attests to that fact of history.

Verse 8. All Worship The Beast Whose Names Are Not Written

"All inhabitants of the earth will worship the Beast- all whose names have not been written in the Book of Life belonging to the lamb that was slain from the creation of the world." (NIV)

"<u>All the inhabitants of the earth</u>" will worship the beast (NIV) – (except the saved, T.S.)

This phrase is used by Jesus in Lk.21:34-35 "That day will close on you unexpectedly like a trap (when Jerusalem was besieged by Titus). For it will come upon <u>all those who live on the face of the whole earth</u> (Greek – ges. "land"). Again, Jesus refers to it in Rev. 3:10. He told the church of Philadelphia: "I will also keep you from the hour of trial that is going to <u>come upon the whole world</u> (Greek – oikoumenes, "inhabited earth") to test those who live on the earth (Greek – ges, "land").

"<u>Will worship the Beast</u>". How difficult of a circumstance! Worship the Caesar as god, showing allegiance to the State or DIE! Swallow hard Believer. YOU must confess Caesar as god. Your wife must confess Caesar as god. Your children must confess Caesar as god. Or, your whole family dies! I'm horrified! Live or die? Lie and confess the Caesar? Save your family? God may understand? What do you say? What do you decide? Where is your ultimate love and loyalty?

"<u>The Book of life</u>" – Those that are saved, their <u>names</u> are written in the Lamb's (Jesus') "Book of Life". Remember the amazing and very special fact - We will each be given our own special name by God himself, Rev. 2:17; Isa.56:5; Isa.62:2

Rev. 2:17 "To him who overcomes… I will give him a white stone, and a new name written on the stone which no one knows but he who receives it." (NIV)

Isa. 56:5 "to them I will give in My house and within My walls a memorial, and a name better than that of sons and daughters; I will give them an everlasting name which will not be cut off." (NIV)

Isa.62:2 "… You will be called by a new name which the mouth of the Lord will designate." (NIV)

"Lamb slain from the foundation of the world."

Some believe this is referring to God's foreknowledge – that God's plan was known from the very beginning of the creation of this world. This is true. But does this verse mean that?

The Lamb was slain at the beginning of the "New Creation".

It can be referring to the "slaying of the Lamb " (Jesus being crucified) thus – creating the "new spiritual world," Rom.5:18-19. The New Spiritual Creation through Christ is contrasted to the old earthly creation that came through Adam in Rom 5. (Paradise lost versus Paradise regained). There is the physical creation of man that came through Adam and the spiritual re-creation of man that comes through Christ. "If anyone is in Christ, he is a new creation," 2 Cor.5:17. All the prophecies of the Old Testament, (veiled in "earthly symbols' ') were fulfilled in Jesus' "New Creation", his "spiritual Creation". How beautiful! The whole "Spiritual World" Christians have been made a part of. It all started with the "slaying of the Lamb". The Book of Life belongs to the Lamb. There is life in the Son. "He that has the Son has life. He that has not the Son, does not have life," 1 Jn.5:12.

Verse 9. Let Him Hear

"He who has an ear let him hear." (NIV)

God holds us accountable for how we hear! If we do not understand, God holds us accountable for that too! Jesus said:

"You will be ever hearing but never understanding; You will be ever seeing but never perceiving, for this people's heart has become calloused…", Mt.13:14-15.

Verse 10. If Anyone Is - Will Be

"If anyone is to go into captivity, into captivity he will go. if anyone is to be killed with the sword, with the sword he will be killed." (NIV)

This is referring to the time of Judgment. Everything will remain "at that time" as they are. It's too late to repent! It's too late to change your mind! It's too late to be rescued! All has been decided.

THE BEAST OUT OF THE EARTH

Verse 11. The Earth Beast

"Then I saw another Beast coming up out of the Earth. He had two horns like a lamb, but he spoke like a dragon." (NIV)

"Beast coming up out of the earth." Who is he?

In this section of chapter 13, John gives us several descriptions of the earth Beast:

1. He comes out of the earth."
2. He had two horns like a Lamb
3. He spoke like a Dragon.
4. He exercises all the authority of the first Beast on his behalf.
5. He makes earth's inhabitants worship the first Beast.
6. He performs great miraculous signs.
7. He deceives the inhabitants of earth.
8. He orders them to set up an image of the first beast.
9. He gives breath to the image.
10. He kills all those who do not worship the beast.
11. He forces everyone to put the mark of the Beast on his hand or forehead.

If the Sea Beast is the 4th Kingdom, the Roman Empire, then who would the "beast that comes up out of the earth" be?

"He had two horns like a Lamb, but spoke like a Dragon."

Verse 12. Made The Earth's Inhabitants Worship The First Beast

"Exercise all the authority of the first beast on his behalf, and made the Earth and its inhabitants worship the first Beast, whose fatal wounds had been healed." (NIV)

"Exercised all the authority of the first beast on his behalf." (NIV)

This has to have been some authority more local who got their power and authority from Rome. Rome was the Sea Beast, the national authority. Under the authority of Rome was the governor of Syria or Palestine and more locally under him would be the governor over Judea.

The high priest Ananias and his sons that were appointed by Rome at different times to be high priests, would also answer to authorities under Rome.

"Made …inhabitants worship the first Beast" (NIV)

Under Caius Caesar (who reigned 37 to 41 A.D.), Caius (Gaius) took himself to be a god and desired himself to be so called. He sent out Petronius with an army to Jerusalem to place his statues in the temple in Jerusalem and to slay those who opposed it. At Ptolemais, the Jews opposed him and were willing that they, their wives, and children be killed rather than submit. Josephus says Ptolemais thought the Jews opposition and petition was –

"unreasonable, because while all the nations in subjection to them (the Romans) had placed the images of Caesar in their several cities, among the rest of their gods, for them (the Jews) to oppose it was almost like the behavior of revolters, and was injurious to Caesar." Petronius went on to ask – "Will you make war against Caesar?" [Josephus, "The Jewish War," Cap.10, Sections 1-4.]

Before that stand off continued to develop into war, Gaius Caesar died. Under the fourth Caesar, Claudius, such demands were not made of the Jews. However, under Caesar Nero, a procurator of Judea, Gessius Florus proved to be a very unjust man, who for money ruled very openly cruel and unjust toward the Jews. Lest the kind of man he was be complained about by the Jews to Caesar ; Florus did many things to induce the Jews to a rebellion so that Rome would not listen to the Jews. The result was the Jewish War did break out, the twelfth year of the reign of Nero in the month of Artemisuis (Jyar). [Josephus, "The Jewish Wars," Chapter 14, Sections 1-4.]

Those who represented the Roman government as the "Earth Beast" were the procurators of Judea. The one that would fit the description the most was Gessius Florus. This is what description he fits:

1. The Earth beast rises up out of the land.
2. He only has two horns (not as much power as the Sea Beast) and they are like a lamb's (to some he appears good).
3. But he speaks like a dragon (He is a liar and deceiver).
4. He is clothed with the authority of the Sea Beast.
5. He makes men worship the Sea Beast (Caesar Worship).
6. He pretends to exercise miraculous powers.
7. He rules with force, unjustly, and with cruelty.
8. He refuses any rights to those who refuse him.

"First Beast, whose fatal wound had been healed." (NIV)

The first Beast, Rome, appeared to have received a fatal wound when Nero died. The empire was plunged into civil war from the time of Nero's death, June 9, 69 A.D., through the quick fall of three rulers: Galba, Otho, and Vitellius, (all who were generals of Nero) until Vespasian was put in and confirmed by the senate as the Caesar of Rome in Dec. 69 A.D.

The Beast, Rome finally was healed under Vespasian.

Verse 13. Causing Fire to Come Down

"And he performed great and miraculous signs, even causing fire to come down from heaven to earth in full view of men." (NIV)

"He performed miraculous signs."

"Even causing fire to come down from heaven to earth."

I do not know if the Earth Beast actually could perform miraculous signs or if they were false signs. In Biblical history, God did allow the magicians of Pharaoh to duplicate the miracles of Moses and Aaron for the first three times. When Aaron threw down his staff and it became a snake; the magicians threw down their staffs and they became snakes, Ex.7:11-2. Of course, Aaron's snake swallowed their snakes. When Aaron struck the waters of the Nile and it became blood – the magicians did the same things by their secret arts, Ex.7:20-22. When Aaron stretched out his hand over the waters of Egypt and the frogs came up – the magicians did the same things by their secret arts, Ex. 8:6-7.

The first century was a miraculous time. Demons possessed people and caused them to hurt themselves and even hurt others. The powers of evil that were allowed in the first century are really not clear. I do not know of New Testament scriptures that address it. We do know, the power of God used such things to demonstrate the superiority of God over all creation. Demons could possess a man; but they could not resist Christ and his apostles. These may be areas God has not revealed to us an answer or revealed to us for our understanding.

Verse 14. He Deceived The Inhabitants Of The Earth

"Because of the signs he was given power to do on behalf of the first feast, he deceived the inhabitants of the Earth. He ordered them to set up an image in honor of the Beast who was wounded by the sword and yet lived." (NIV)

"He deceived the inhabitants of the earth."

"He ordered them to set up an image in honor of the beast." (Gessius Florus did that -demanding it of the Jews. T.S.)

Again, the Earth Beast, the local power with Rome's authority, was in direct conflict with the Jews. Caesar worship was mandated and it was looked upon at showing allegiance to the Roman Empire. Those who did not comply were viewed as in rebellion against Rome.

"Beast who was wounded by the sword and yet lived."

The Beast (Rome's empire), we are reminded, was wounded (Nero died and the empire fell into a civil war) and yet it survived.

Verse 15. He Gave Breath To The Image Of The First Beast

"He was given power to give breath to the image of the first beast, so that it could speak and cause all who refused to worship the image to be killed." (NIV)

"He was given power to give breath to the image of the first beast."

This may simply be a poetic way of saying that the power of Rome "came alive" through the local authorities and their actions.

"So that it could speak"

The local authorities gave Rome a voice among the population. They could not communicate all over the empire like we do today through radio, T.V., phones, etc. Local authorities gave the Roman empire a local voice.

"all who refused to worship…killed"

Nero sent Vespasian, one of his generals at that time, to make war with the Jews. Vespasian was to punish the Jews for their rebellion. Vespasian conquered several cities of Palestine and killed thousands of Jews. The Jews fled to other cities. Men fled to Jerusalem. Jerusalem was a strong city on a hill, fortified in many ways and having three walls around it. Thus, many of the rebellious Jews were funneling into Jerusalem.

Verse 16. Forced Everyone To Receive A Mark On His Forehead

"He also forced everyone, small and great, rich and poor, free and slave, to receive a mark on his right hand or on his forehead," (NIV)

"He also forced everyone …to receive a mark on his right hand or on his forehead". [see next verse].

Verse 17. No One Could Buy Or Sell

"So that no one could buy or sell unless he had the mark which is the name of the Beast or the number of his name." NIV

"So that no one could buy or sell unless he had the mark."

Historically I could find no actual mark that was used on people during the Roman rule that allowed them to buy or sell. However, since this is a picturesque description of symbols we may understand it this way. Jesus is prophetically referred to as "the right hand of God or the right arm of God". The Father does everything through him. [See Isaiah 53:1; 51:5; 59:16] Jesus sits at the right hand of the Father. [See Heb.1:13 and many more passages.] Jesus sits at the position of authority or power at God's right hand. The Lord was said to be at a person's right hand. Psalms 16:8 says –

"I have set the Lord always before me. Because he is at my right hand,

I will not be shaken." NIV [see also Isa.41:13].

If someone figuratively speaking had the "mark of the beast" on his right hand, that would indicate who his LORD was. He followed the beast or submitted to him as Lord. The beast would work through him because he would be his servant.

If he had the mark on his forehead, that would indicate he followed the beast in what he thought, believed, and submitted to.

Exodus 13:9 speaks of the consecration of the firstborn and says –

"This observance will be for you like a sign on your hand and a reminder on your forehead that the law of the Lord is to be on your lips." NIV

Deut.11:18 says -

"Fix these words of mine in your hearts and minds; tie them as symbols on your hands and bind them on your foreheads."

"The mark which is the name of the Beast or number of his name."

[see next verse].

Verse 18 His Number Is 666

"This calls for wisdom. If anyone has insight, let him calculate the number of the Beast, for it is man's number. His number is 666." (NIV)

"The number of the Beast is man's number."

The number is man's number. His number seems to be 6. He is less than seven. Seven represents God – the seven eyes of the Lamb that was slain are the seven spirits, Rev. 5:6. Man's number is 6, less than God. He was made upon the sixth day. Man is a fallen creature and in his natural state follows the flesh.

"The number is 666."

A number repeated 3 times is emphasized that way. Repeated three times stresses the quality and character of that number in a complete way. As 10x10x10 = 1000, the number makes a cube, a complete dimensional representation of its character. So, the number 6 here is emphasized in the same way, intensifying the character of fleshly man.

Some have interpreted the number by the system of Gematria, a system in which numbers represent letters in an alphabet. Words, names, and so forth can be represented by numbers. If this is a correct approach to interpreting the number 666, then we could try to figure it out. Remember, Revelation is a book written to Jewish Christians in seven churches. They were in persecution by the Romans. The possible names the number might represent would not be in the Roman tongue -Latin. It would be too easy for the Romans to understand it and the Romans would persecute Christians more. It would not be in the Greek tongue. That was too well known and used at that time. Perhaps, to hide it from the Romans, the Jewish Christians used both the Greek and Hebrew language. The Greek letters of Nero Caesar are Neron Kaisar. But in Hebrew it is Neron Kesar. Adding the Hebrew letters would equal 666. My computer does not have Hebrew so I cannot write it out here in Hebrew.

Nero's reputation of being very evil was certainly recorded by Josephus, Tacitus and Suetonius. Suetonius has a whole chapter on the life and character of Nero. [Suetonius, "The Twelve Caesars, Nero]. Tacitus records murders by Nero, his character of lasciviousness and debauchery included all types of evil.

CHAPTER FOURTEEN

This chapter is very interesting. It helps us to understand the three scenes of this chapter to become aware of three Jewish Harvests celebrated in a year, mentioned in Ex.23:14-17 and Lev. 23. These three harvests give us the background information we need to orient to the three scenes we see in chapter 14.

The three scenes in this chapter are:

1. Jesus with the 144,000, verses 1-5;

(An interlude of 3 angels making announcements).

2. Those who were harvested by the angel who was like the Son of Man, verses 14-16;

3. Those harvested by another angel and the angel in charge of the fire, verses 17-20.

The three Jewish harvests in the O.T. were:

1. The Passover; 2. Pentecost; 3. Feast of Tabernacles.

Now let us look at how these three harvests related to the three scenes of Chapter 14:

1. The Passover. (Heb. -Pesach). The first harvest. At this feast the lamb was sacrificed; and the first grain harvested was offered, by waving the sheaf before the Lord. This feast is called the "Feast of the First Fruits", Lev.23:4-14. The lamb was offered to the Lord. The first fruits were offered to the Lord.

In regard to the fulfillment of this festival and offering of the first fruits in the New Covenant, we read:

"For Christ, our Passover lamb has been sacrificed," 1Cor.5:7. Jesus is the Passover lamb.

"Look, the Lamb of God, who takes away the sin of the world," Jn.1:29.

Note: The Day of Atonement took place later, on Yom Kippur, Oct.4-5 in 2022, "the tenth day of the seventh month", Lev.23:26, (NIV).

"God presented him as a sacrifice of atonement, through faith in his blood," Rom.3:25.

Heb.9:23-24 "It was necessary then, for the copies of the heavenly things to be purified with these sacrifices, but the heavenly things themselves with better sacrifices than these. For Christ did not enter a man-made sanctuary that was only a copy of the true one; he entered heaven itself, now to appear for us in God's presence". (NIV) Jesus died on earth as the Passover Lamb for our sins; but his blood was offered in the heavens after his ascension on the day of Atonement. The Day of Atonement, our Oct.4-5 this year, 2022, will follow the Passover, April 15-23.

The Passover was linked to the Feast of unleavened bread (bread without yeast, yeast being symbolic of sin). Paul says, "For Christ our Passover lamb has been sacrificed for us, therefore let us eat…bread without yeast, the bread of sincerity and truth." 1 Cor.5:8.(NIV)

"Jesus said, I am the bread of life." Jn.6:48. (NIV)

"Unless you eat the flesh of the Son of Man and drink his blood, you have no life in you." Jn.6:53. (NIV)

The Passover had the offering of the first fruits, the first grain of the wheat harvest. The priest was to wave a sheaf before the Lord as an offering.

"But Christ has indeed been raised from the dead, the first fruits of those who have fallen asleep," 1 Cor.15:20. (NIV) Jesus is the firstfruits.

As an explanation of first fruits, we can bring in the thought of Jn12:24-25:

"Except a grain of wheat fall into the ground and die (first fruit offered at Passover), it abideth alone: but if it die; it bringeth forth much fruit (first fruit comes to life, resurrects – 1 Cor.15:20). He that loveth his life shall lose it; and he that hateth his life in this would shall keep it unto eternal life." Jn.12:25 (NIV). I believe the first fruit (grain offering) of the Passover spoke of Jesus' death and His Resurrection 3 days later.

Jesus' life-blood was the sacrifice for all the O.T. saints as well as Christians, Rom.3:24-26.

2. <u>Pentecost</u> (50 days later after the Passover) (Heb.- Hag Shavuot – "festival of weeks"), or "<u>Feast of Weeks</u>". This was the <u>second harvest</u>, Lev.23:15-22. The second harvest represented the main harvest of the wheat (of the three harvests) during the year.

The fulfillment of Pentecost in the N.T. occurred 50 days later, after Jesus' death.

In the NT., Jesus blesses the coming harvest by pouring out living water, the Holy Spirit from heaven in Acts 2. That day, on Pentecost, the Gospel was preached for the first time and Christians began to enter the Spiritual kingdom. The harvest of God's people into the kingdom had begun. This harvest, which <u>started on Pentecost</u>, would <u>continue for the next 40 years</u> through the preaching of the gospel to all nations, the Great Commission, Mt.28:18-20 and Mk. 16:15-16. When the gospel had been preached in the whole world, then the "end" would come, Mt.24:14. (That "end" would be the end for the Jewish system to exist, Jerusalem would be destroyed and the Mosaic system would collapse with Jerusalem's destruction). The "last days", as Peter mentions in Acts 2:17 was the "last days" of the Mosaic system. After Jesus' death, His New Covenant legally was put into effect. The Mosaic Covenant at that point became obsolete, old, and ready to vanish away. Paul says it was "passing away" 1 Cor.7:31. The harvest of the people who lived under the Mosaic covenant certainly began when the Mosaic covenant became outdated. Jesus actually started the harvesting when he sent out the twelve and the seventy-two into the fields.

Jesus had taught that the fields were "already white unto harvest, Jn.4:34-36. John the Baptist and Jesus taught, "repent, for the kingdom of heaven was at hand." Their ministries prepared the way for Pentecost. It was on Pentecost, that for the first time, people could be baptized "in the name of the Lord Jesus" and receive the "gift of the Holy Spirit", Acts 2:38. It was for the first - time people could enter the New Covenant. Pentecost was also the time of the second harvest, preparing for the closing of the Mosaic covenant in 70 A.D. For forty years both the New covenant and the practice of the

Mosaic covenant existed side-by-side, at the same time. It was a transition period from the practice of the Mosaic covenant, which had existed for hundreds of years, 1400 years earlier, and the beginning of the New Covenant of faith under Christ.

3. The Feast of Tabernacles. Hebrew – sukkot, meaning "huts or booths." This was the <u>third and final harvest of the year</u>. It was also called the "Feast of Ingathering." <u>It commemorated the 40 year journey of the Israelites in the wilderness</u>, Lev.23:43. (This would be at the end of their journey or the end of life.) This was the third and final harvest of the year. It was celebrated on the 15th day of the 7th month, Tishrei. (In 70 A.D, I think the harvest started on the 2nd of October and would last 1 week, the 9th.) It is interesting, as a parallel, that the "Last Days" for the Jews was forty years.

In Jn.7:2, the <u>Feast of the Tabernacles</u> was near. John says, verse 1, the Jews were waiting to take his life. Jesus says, verse 7, "the world hates me because I testify that what it does is evil. Verse 30, the people try to seize him (to kill him) but no one laid a hand on him because his time had not yet come. Chap 8, the Jews show their hypocrisy with the "woman taken in adultery". Later the Jews claim they are slaves to no one, but Abraham's descendants, 8:33. Jesus tells them they are of their father, the devil, 8:43. In chapter 9 Jesus heals the man born blind. The Jews tell the blind man later, we don't know where this man (Jesus) comes from. The blind man answers: "Now that is remarkable! You don't know where he comes from, yet he opened my eyes." The entire feast – Jesus was dealing with the unbelieving Jew.

This feast commemorated the 40 years in the wilderness. That was a wicked generation that came out of Egypt. The Hebrew writer, in Heb.3, calls them – "the <u>rebellion</u> during the time of testing in the desert". (NIV) God was angry with that generation and swore <u>they would never enter his rest</u>, Heb.3:11. Why? Because of their <u>unbelief</u>, 3:19. Did the Feast of Tabernacles represent a harvest of weeds to be burned in the fire?

When you look at the third group in Rev.14:17-20; the grapes that are harvested are thrown into the great winepress of God's wrath. They are trampled in the winepress "outside the city" where the refuse was.

Historically, the judgment of the Jews on earth by Rome was worst during the siege of 5 months, by Titus, from April 14 to Sept.8. (This had just followed the resurrection of saints, Rev.11:12 and 2 Pet.2:9) By Sept. 8, 70 A.D., the Temple and Jerusalem were burned and leveled. (Josephus, book 7, Chap.1). The final judgment of God, the "harvest of the weeds" and burning them in the fire ("Feast of Tabernacles" -unbelievers) took place the week of Oct. 2. It is not clear that the final judgment ended then, but it had started. The Jews were not fully destroyed until the judgment of the Jews at Masada, A.D. 73-74.

Summary:

The first harvest of Christ and the first fruits occurred during Passover, 30 A.D.

On Pentecost, 30 A.D. The beginning of the second harvest began, and lasted for the next 40 years. In 70 A.D., God resurrected his people (as we shall see) on Resurrection day (on April 20, 70 A.D.). They were harvested by Jesus, (the "angel like unto the "son of Man".) "He swung his sickle and the earth was harvested," Rev.14:16.

The Judgment, by Titus, on earth- started on the day of the siege of Jerusalem, April 14,70 A.D. and lasted 5 months, to Sept.8, 70 A.D. The third and final harvest, "Feast of Tabernacles" began on Oct.2.-9, 70 A.D and may have lasted until Masada was judged. Another angel swung his sickle and the earth's vine was harvested, and the grapes were thrown into the great winepress of God's wrath, Rev.14:17-20.

These three scenes in Rev.14, are related to the 3 harvests.

Now - Let's look at the chapter.

THE LAMB AND THE 144,000

Verse 1. The 144,000

"Then I looked, and there before me was the lamb, standing on Mount Zion, and with him 144,000 who had his name and his father's name written on their foreheads." (NIV)

"Mount Zion" is the prophetic name for the "Mountain of God", the "Heavenly Jerusalem".

Heb.12:22, "But you have come to Mount Zion, to the heavenly Jerusalem, the city of the living God."

John saw the Lamb (Christ), standing on the Mount of God in the heavens.

"With him 144,000 who had his father's name written on their foreheads." (NIV) We identified them and saw them sealed in chapter 7.

Verse 2. The Harpist Playing Their Harps

"And I heard a sound from heaven like the Roar of rushing waters and like a loud peal of thunder. The sound I heard was like that of the harpist playing their harps." (NIV)

"roar". "The lion has roared; who will not fear? The Lord God has spoken; who can but prophesy," (NIV), Amos 3:8. God's voice roars! In Rev. 5:5, Jesus is the lion of the tribe of Judah. Jesus roars like a lion.

Yet here, the roar is not fearful, but loud and majestic, filling and inspiring! It was the roar of rushing waters, and like a peal of thunder. Have you ever heard an orchestra in a concert hall when the orchestra reaches a crescendo and the cymbals crash in acclamation? What a climatic movement! What grand emotion held in abrupt suspension, the pause, the inspiration! Breathless pause! Then –

"The sound I heard was like harpist playing their harps." (NIV) What an absolutely gorgeous sound – so full, so harmonious, so pleasant and even soothing and filling.

Verse 3. They Sang A New Song

"And they sang A New Song Before the Throne and before the four living creatures and the elders. No one could learn the song except the hundred and forty-four thousand who had been redeemed from the Earth." (NIV)

"And they sang a New Song." (NIV) This was not just a new song. This was in a new body, not earthly. This was in the heaven of heavens, not the world. This was with myriads of angels and myriads of believers in countless numbers. This was about salvation! This was about glorification! This was about Transformation! This was Yes -Yes -Yes, being in the presence of The Eternal One as one of his Redeemed Sons – Sing! Sing! Sing! Sing it out! Shout it out! Rejoice!!!!!

No one could have ever, ever have sang like this!

"No one could learn the song except the 144,000."

"Who had been redeemed from the earth." (NIV)

Redeemed – such a big word. "I've been redeemed" – the popular song.

We use the word to mean - "I've been forgiven". My sins have been paid for. I have been redeemed from my debt of sin. God has done so much more, given us so much more, now that we are sons in his family.

In Rom. 8:23 Paul says, "Not only so, but we ourselves, who have the first fruits of the Spirit, groan inwardly as we wait eagerly for our adoption as sons, the "redemption of our bodies." (NIV)

As long as we are in this body, there is a war going on between the desires of the flesh and the Spirit. They are contrary one to the other, Gal.5:17. Our outward man is perishing, 2Cor. 4:16.

Because of the sin of Adam – "dying we shall die." We want eagerly for our bodies to be changed, our mortality to put on immortality. We wait eagerly for the "redemption of our bodies." We want a full transformation!

The 144,000 had been REDEEMED (transformed) from the earth. Yay! Rejoice! We made it! They had been made complete, perfected in Christ.

Verse 4. Those Who Do Not Defile Themselves

"These are those who did not defile themselves with women, for they kept themselves pure. They follow the lamb wherever he goes. They were purchased from among men and offered as first fruits to God and the lamb." (NIV)

AND:

Verse 5. They Are Blameless

"No lie was found in their mouths; they are blameless." (NIV)

"not defile themselves with women" Of all things, why does he say this? Many things can defile.

In the New Covenant, all Christians are "priests unto God". In the O.T., a special requirement of a priest was Lev.21:7:

"They must not marry women defiled by prostitution or divorced from their husbands, <u>because priests are HOLY to their God</u>." (NIV) The "priest must have kept himself pure!" (NIV) The emphasis in this verse is that the <u>first fruits</u> were <u>HOLY to their God</u>.

There was the prohibition in Deut.7:3-4 "Do not intermarry with them (the nations). Do not give your daughters to their sons or take their daughters for your sons, for they will turn your sons away from following me to serve other gods." (NIV). Even priests did that in Ezra 10:18ff.

<u>"Offered as 'first fruits' to God and the Lamb"</u> (NIV)

Ps.78:51 says, "He struck down all the <u>firstborn</u> of Egypt, the <u>first fruits</u> of manhood in the tents of Ham." (NIV) (cf. Ps.105:36.) The Bible uses first fruits as the firstborn.

In the last plague of Egypt, God struck down the <u>firstborn</u> of Egypt. Because he had spared the lives of the firstborn of Israel (by the blood of the lamb on their doorposts),

God said Israel's firstborn belonged to him. Ex.13:12 says, "you are to give over to the Lord the first offspring of every womb. All the firstborn males of your livestock belong to the Lord. Redeem with a lamb every firstborn donkey, but if you do not redeem it, break its neck. Redeem every firstborn among your sons." NIV

God was teaching then that the life of the firstborn could be redeemed by the blood of the lamb.

First fruits were offered during the Passover, and (symbolically redeemed by the blood of the Lamb). (The first fruits that were redeemed got their life back at the resurrection).

<u>Jesus was the first fruits of God the Father.</u> (NIV) Jesus died (sinless) on the Passover of 30 A.D. (So, death had no hold on him, Jn. 14:30) He was raised as the <u>"First" - Born</u> from the dead in 3 days on Resurrection Day. Jesus had died (physical death). He was begotten (born – from the dead) at the resurrection. He was begotten, "came back to life" into the "spirit world." That is what Heb.1:5 is referring to: "You are my Son; today I have become your Father." (NIV) He was his Father

on earth, born of Mary and the Holy Spirit. Once he died, Jesus was born again from the dead.

The 144,000 were redeemed by the Lamb. (NIV) When they died, they were born again on Resurrection Day, A. D. 70. They were the First fruits of Jesus. That is why John says – they were the "first fruits to God and the Lamb." Rev.14:4 (NIV). Jesus was the first fruit "unto God the Father" in 30 A.D. The 144,000 were the first fruits "unto God and the Lamb" in 70 A.D. They were the "first-born" of Jesus from the dead. How did Jesus have so many First-borns? When the resurrection took place in 70 A.D., they were all "born from the dead" at the same time. Isaiah speaks of the marvel of this in Isa. 66:8-9: "Who has ever heard of such a thing? Who has ever seen such things? Can a country be born in a day? (The heavenly Jerusalem) Or a nation be brought forth in a moment? (a holy nation, a spiritual nation.) Yet no sooner is Zion (the heavenly Jerusalem) in labor that she gives birth to her children." (NIV)

All the firstborn of Egypt were God's. Num.3:11-13 says, "The Lord also said to Moses, I have taken the Levites from among the Israelites in place of the first male offspring of every Israelite woman. The Levites are mine, for all the firstborn are mine. When I struck down all the firstborn of Egypt, I set apart for myself every firstborn in Israel, whether man or animal. They are to be mine. I am the Lord." (NIV). What can we understand? The firstborn have always belonged to God and were dedicated to the service of God. They were "set apart" unto God. That is what "holy" means – "to be set apart." The firstborn's service unto God in the Old Testament was substituted by the Levites who were priests "unto God." In the New Testament – the "firstborns from the dead" are "priests unto God. to offer up spiritual sacrifices unto God. Isn't it amazing how God's word fits together so perfectly? Who could ever weave together so perfectly, the Old Testament system of types, shadows, events, peoples, generations – so perfectly to foreshadow the fulfillment of all of it in Jesus Christ and his kingdom. God is amazing beyond knowing!

Were the Jewish times of Harvests symbolic of resurrections? The Passover was. The first born were new grains that had sprung up (for us-born again spiritually, Jn. 3) and were harvested from the earth. (They would be "first-borns" from the dead).

1. Jesus was the first fruits of the Passover, 30 A.D.

2. The main harvest of the year began on Pentecost.

When were the 144,000 (first born) resurrected? I believe it was on Resurrection Day, the same day as Christ (just not A.D. 30 but A.D.70). The Two Witnesses could testify. James, the brother of Jesus, spoke on "the wing of the temple" - Dan.9:27, on the Passover, 70 A.D., was stoned, and 3 ½ days later the two witness of Rev.11 "came to life", our "Easter" (were resurrected) Rev.11:11-12. Their resurrection day was the same day as Jesus was raised – three days after the Passover when Jesus, the Passover Lamb was crucified, only 40 years later to the day, in 70 A.D.

Those born during the O.T. period who were saints were resurrected on Resurrection Day. They were all given spiritual bodies; being raised from the graves. Those saints had to wait for their inheritance until Christ died for them, and Christ then created a New covenant. I believe that is indicated in Heb. 11:39, "… only together with us would they be made perfect." The "O.T. saints were made perfect (complete with spiritual bodies) on Resurrection Day with N.T. believers (who were born during the end of that Old covenant). Resurrection Day was just before the siege of Jerusalem started. The siege started April 14, 70 A.D. and lasted until Sept.7, A.D. 70. The Passover started April 17. The Lamb was sacrificed on the 1st day, Deut.16:1-4). The resurrection was 3 ½ days later. That was the "First Resurrection," Rev.20:5. Those who had died in the Lord, as mentioned in 1Thess. 4:16, would be brought back with the Lord to receive their resurrection bodies.

"Blessed and Holy are those who take part in the First Resurrection," Rev.20:6.

[Note: It is understandable, fitting God's "appointed time" for Resurrection Day, that both the First Fruits - Jesus, and those who belong to him, would be resurrected on the same day (but different years: 30 A.D. and 70 A.D.). Paul writes, "each in his own turn: Christ, the first fruits, then, when he comes, those who belong to him." (NIV), 1 Cor.15:23.

The NIV can be understood two ways:

One as - the order: 1. Christ, 2. First fruits, 3. Those who belong to him;

Two as – the order: 1. Christ who is the first fruit, 2. Then when he comes, those who belong to him.

I agree with Christ who is the first fruit, the first one raised from the dead to die no more. All the rest were resurrected on resurrection day (3 days after the Passover) in 70 A.D. They were raised when he came in 70 A.D., the day the two witnesses were raised, Rev. 11:11-12.

There is more to see or understand:

1 Thess. 4:15, "We who are still alive, who are left to the coming of the Lord, will certainly not precede those who have fallen asleep." (NIV)

Then he goes on to say, 16-17, "the dead in Christ will rise first, after that, we who are still alive and are left will be caught up together with them in the clouds to meet the Lord in the air."] (NIV)

What Paul is saying in Thessalonians is the same as in 1 Corinthians: "each would be resurrected in his order" – those who were still alive would not precede those who had died.

John 5:28-29 speaks of two resurrections: "Do not be amazed at this, for a time is coming (a time is coming and has now come, verse 25) when all who are in their graves will hear his voice and come out: those who have done good will (1.) rise (resurrection) to live, and those who have done evil (2.) will rise (resurrection)to be condemned." (NIV)

In Rev.14:14-16, it is Jesus (the angel seated on a cloud "like a son of man") who takes his sickle and harvests the earth. Who does he harvest? The righteous believers. It is the "resurrection unto life." Heb. 9:28 says he would come the second time (his return to earth. That was in A.D. 70) to bring salvation to those who were waiting for him. 1Cor.15:23 says, "when he comes, those who belong to him." (NIV) Jesus came back to get his own. "Christians are very special!"

In Rev.14:17-20 tells us there were two other angels who reaped the earth of grape vines (weeds) and put them in the winepress of the wrath of God. That is the "Second Resurrection".

It is the "resurrection unto condemnation" of those who have done evil. When did it happen?

If the three Jewish harvests tell us anything, they were "resurrected unto condemnation" at the "Feast of Tabernacles." The small huts or tents camped around the tabernacle of God meant they were "outside his Holy Tabernacle" or outside his fellowship. They had been excluded. They could not enter.

Ps.5:4, "You are not a God who takes pleasure in evil; with you the wicked cannot dwell." (NIV)

Ps.15: "Lord, who may dwell in your sanctuary? Who may live on your holy hill? (NIV)

SMILE! YOU KNOW!

The First Fruits were HOLY unto God.

Notice that the resurrection of A.D. 70 is prophesied in Ezek..37 in the prophesy of the "Valley of Dry Bones. The bones (long dead – "dry") are made to live. They are, in 37:11, "the whole house of Israel." (NIV) In 37:12 he says, "I am going to open your graves (Resurrection Day) and bring you up from them; I will bring you back to the land of Israel." (NIV) This is prophesying of the Resurrection and that God would take them back to "the land of Israel", the fulfillment of that type in the "promised land" in the heavens. After the prediction of the resurrection takes place in chapter 37; the final battle and judgment of "Gog and Magog" is prophesied. The resurrection "*precedes*" the Judgment!

John had seen the scene in his vision of: the Lamb and the "144,000 redeemed from the earth," (NIV) verses 1-5. Next, "The three angels" are introduced as, "Then I saw" -.

THE THREE ANGELS

Why the announcement of this first angel at this point? John has shown us the 144,000 redeemed from the earth in verses 1-5. Now, the next thing to happen was the Judgment. So, John sees the angel flying in midair; his message? "The Hour of his judgment has come," (NIV) Judgment followed the resurrection. The Day of the Lord was a Day of Light (the resurrection) for the righteous. The Day of the Lord was a day of darkness for the wicked (the judgment and resulting punishment). Cf.1Thess.5:1-4.

Verse 6. Another Angel Flying In Mid-Air

"Then I saw another Angel flying in mid-air, and he had (Greek – echonta, "having,") the Eternal Gospel to proclaim (or preach good news, evangelize) to those who live on the Earth - to Every Nation, tribe, language and people." (NIV)

"He had the <u>Eternal Gospel</u> to proclaim." The word here for Gospel is the Greek word – "euangelion," meaning the gospel – "good news" of Christ. The angel possessed the Eternal Gospel, the Gospel that is to be preached for ever and ever. It is the Eternal Gospel. However, in mentioning the Gospel to be preached, John is reminding the saints of what Jesus had said, "the <u>gospel of the kingdom will be preached in the whole world as a testimony to all nations, and then the end will come.</u>" Mt.24:14, (NIV). Paul makes it clear that the gospel had been preached in all the world, Col.1:23. (see also Rom.10:16-18; Rom.15:17-21; Titus 1:1-3.).

Verse 7. The Hour Of Judgment Has Come

"He said in a loud voice, 'fear God and give him glory, because the hour of his judgment has come. Worship Him who made the heavens and the Earth the sea and the Springs of water." (NIV)

"<u>The hour of his judgment has come.</u>"

Time was up. The gospel had been taken to the world of Paul's day. The appointed time of the end had come (or arrived.)

Verse 8. Fallen! Fallen! Is Babylon The Great

"A second Angel followed and said, Fallen! Fallen! is Babylon the Great, which made all the nations drink the maddening wine of her adulteries." (NIV)

"<u>Fallen! Fallen! Is Babylon the Great!</u>" The second angel's announcement is a proclamation of what had arrived, the judgment then to occur –"Babylon" (the harlot - earthly Jerusalem, "the great city" -Rev.11:8;18:10) was seen as fallen. Jerusalem and the Jewish system were to be destroyed, A.D. 70. The appointed time had arrived. The second angel announces its doom.

Verse 9. If Anyone Worship The Beast

"The third Angel followed them and said in a loud voice: 'if anyone worships the Beast and His Image and receives his mark on the forehead or on the hand," (NIV)

The third angel announces who would be included in the judgment of Babylon: "if anyone worships the Beast and His Image and receives his mark on the forehead or on the hand." (NIV) Was it an actual mark? Historically I do not know of any mark used. One is mastered by what he thinks (the forehead) and what he does (the hand). Some were mastered by the beast (Rome and Caesar worship).

Verse 10. The Wine Of God's Fury

"He too will drink of the wine of God's Fury, which has been poured full strength into the cup of his Wrath. He will be tormented with burning sulfur in the presence of the Holy Angels and of the Lamb." (NIV)

"God's Fury, which has been poured *'full strength'* into the cup of his wrath." For God's wrath to be "full strength" means to be "unmixed", not mixed with anything else. His pure wrath: without mercy, without compassion, without longsuffering. His compassion had been shown. His longsuffering had been endured. His offer of mercy and forgiveness through his Son had been made. The time for those things had passed. They had been ignored and rejected. Now, God's wrath "in full strength" was to be poured out on them.

God had done this before. When God was ready to destroy Jerusalem and destroy those in the promised land by Nebuchadnezzar; God did it without mercy. Jer.13:14 says –

"I will smash them one against the other, parents and children alike, declares the Lord. I will allow no pity or mercy or compassion to keep me from destroying them." (NIV)

"He will be tormented with burning sulfur." (NIV)

Those waiting in Hades, as the rich man, were waiting in a hot place. The rich man wanted relief to cool his tongue. But, now all those, like the rich man, would be cast into the fire. As it were- "they went from the frying pan into the fire." Things got really, really, hotter! (So also, the fallen angels went from the furnace of the abyss to their destruction (the lake of fire) Rev:17:8.

"in the presence of the holy angels and of the Lamb." (NIV)

The wicked being "tormented with burning sulfur in the presence of the Lord" of Rev.14:10 does not contradict 2 Thess1:9 which says, "They will be punished with everlasting destruction and shut out from the presence of the Lord and from the majesty of his power on the Day he comes to be glorified in his holy people." NIV

During the punishment of the wicked – "tormented with burning sulfur in the presence of the Lord" – you see God's vengeance upon the wicked as he punishes them, and the saints witness this, as in Ezekiel 38. God "fights for the righteous and vindicates them".

In 2 Thess.1:9, "" the wicked are shut out from (excluded from the presence of the Lord, T.S.) the face of him and from the strength of him (to transform us at the resurrection, T.S.) whenever He comes to be glorified (his second return to earth, T.S.) (NIV).

Here in Rev. 14:10 – they are in heaven and at the end result of the judgment: being "tormented in the presence of the Lord." What does that mean? Both blessings and judgment come FROM the Lord. God is a "consuming fire for the wicked. He is a savior with eternal life and blessings for the righteous. God sits on his throne, a figure of fire from the waist up, and from the waist down, Ezek.1:27. If it is judgment, his throne is flaming fire, and its wheels (under the platform that he sits on is all ablaze, and we see a "river of fire" flowing, coming out from before him." Dan.7:10.

But if it is a blessing for the righteous, we see "the river of the water of life, as clear as crystal, flowing from the throne of God and of the Lamb," Rev.22:1.

The wicked, here in verse 10, are in the presence of God as "a consuming fire" a "river of fire".

Jesus too, is mentioned here. Jesus is pictured as a "Lamb", the sacrifice for his people. But for the wicked at judgment he can look like God the Father. In Rev.1:13ff, Jesus is said to have hair white like wool (like the Ancient of Days- Daniel.7:9); His feet are like bronze glowing in a furnace, his eyes are like blazing fire. We don't get to see him fully because he is dressed in a robe reaching down to his feet. But Jesus is God, Jn.1:1. He is the Father in bodily form. "For in Christ all the fullness of Deity lives in bodily form," Col.2:9. (NIV) God is NOT three persons in one; any more than you are Three Persons. You are made in God's image and likeness and you are ONE person, made up of - 1. Body, 2. Soul. 3. Spirit. We have ONE God, not Three! Jesus is in subjection to the Father, 1Cor.15:28, just as your body is in subjection to your spirit. Your body acts out the will of your spirit, just as Jesus is the "right arm of God" and does the Father's work. God and Jesus are ONE and act as ONE - in blessing the righteous and punishing the wicked.

Verse 11. Their torment rises forever

"And the smoke of their torment rises forever and ever. There is no rest day or night for those who worship the Beast and His image, or for anyone who receives the mark of his name." (NIV)

"And the smoke of their torment rises for ever and ever (Greek-aionas aionon, "ages of ages) (NIV)

Some try to claim that it is the "smoke" that lasts for ever and ever; but not the torment. Perhaps. It says in the Greek – "the smoke of the torment of them unto ages of ages goes up." (Marshall's Interlinear Translation). Jesus said, (in Marshall's Greek Interlinear Translation) "And will go away these into punishment eternal, but the righteous into life eternal." Mt.25:46. If life is not eternal (i.e.-forever) for the saint; then we can say punishment is not eternal for the wicked. In this text in Matthew, the word for eternal is the same (aionion – "eternal") for both the righteous and wicked.

Perhaps there is a different understanding of the punishment of the wicked that still fits. We could understand their destruction as like what is stated in 2 Peter 2:6:

"If he condemned Sodom and Gomorrah by burning them to ashes, and made them an example of what is going to happen to the ungodly." (NIV)

The destruction is to reduce them to a pile of ashes – and they exist no more. They are destroyed. That would agree with the teaching of the Old Testament – they will be remembered no more, they live no more, Isa.26:14. Their punishment and thus end - would last forever, be final forever.

Then, after the Great day of God's judgment in Revelation, there is no one day that judgment takes place from then on. Rather, judgment from then on continues after men die, and their fate is decided right after they die. For the righteous – "Blessed are those who die in the Lord from this time and forever more", Rev.14:13. But for the wicked, they are immediately judged and destroyed and the smoke of the wicked who are judged and destroyed – the smoke of them rises continually through the generations as each is judged and destroyed. We are not held in the grave and waiting for the future to receive judgment. That changed. Now judgment occurs continually and immediately when and as men die.

"There is no rest day or night" (NIV)

Either, there is no break from the torment (one interpretation and men are tortured forever which is hard to comprehend as just) or the wicked of different generations and their judgment does not rest. That latter interpretation makes more sense to me.

Verse 12. Remain Faithful To Jesus

"This calls for patient endurance on the part of the saints to obey God's commandments and remain faithful to Jesus." (NIV)

"This calls for patient endurance on the part of the saints"(NIV)

Oh the wisdom of "keeping on keeping on". Saints can never quit before the end of their earthly life is over. Saints must "set their mind on the goal". Nothing can detract; nothing can take us out of the race; nothing can we allow to defeat us. We MUST finish the race set before us. Endure! Endure! Endure! What's the watch word? Endure! REMAIN FAITHFUL to Jesus!

Verse 13. Blessed Are The Dead Who Died In The Lord

"Then I Heard a Voice from Heaven say, 'write, blessed are the Dead who died in the Lord from now on. 'yes,' says the Spirit, 'they will rest from

their labor, for their deeds will follow them." (NIV)

"Blessed are the Dead who die in the Lord from NOW on!" (NIV)

For all time up until Jesus'+ death, this could not be fully so. The righteous dead remained in Hades (the place of disembodied spirits) because even though they lived by faith, their sins had not been atoned for yet. Jesus had not died for them yet. They were held captive in the place of the dead. When Jesus died, he descended into the lower earthly regions and brought the righteous dead out, Eph.4:8; Ps.66:15-18. Jesus took them to paradise where they waited for the Resurrection. They (from the Old Testament times could not inherit without us (Christians of the generation of Christ when they would inherit -at the resurrection when Jesus returned, 70 A.D.). Heb.11:39-40.

But now, in this verse,13; those who die from now on (then, when John wrote) can die and inherit their blessings. There is NO WAITING! The Old Testament saints waited in Hades for centuries and centuries. We today have been given "everything" in Christ Jesus!

THE HARVEST OF THE EARTH

Now, in the two next scenes, we see the harvest (resurrection) of the two groups of John 5:29: "those who rise to live and those who rise to be condemned." Jesus harvests his people, the righteous, verses 14-16, in the resurrection; and then, two other angels harvest the wicked in verse 17-20. There are two scenes of two different harvests. Jesus is the harvester of the first group, the saints, who rise to life. Two other angels are the harvesters of the second group, the wicked. They rise to condemnation.

Verse 14. Seated On The Cloud Was One Like The Son Of Man

"I looked, and there before me was a white cloud, and seated on the cloud was one 'like a son of man' with a crown of gold on his head and a sharp sickle in his hand." (NIV)

"seated on a cloud" (NIV)

The disciples would see his return, "coming on a cloud," like he went, Acts 1:9. (NIV)

Jesus told those who tried and condemned him, they would see him "coming on the clouds of heaven", Mt 26:64. (NIV)

God rides on a cloud, Psa.18:9.

"one like the son of Man" (NIV)

The same phrase is used,1:13, of Jesus walking among the 7 candlesticks." (see notes there.)

Verse 15. Take Your Sickle And Reap

"Then another angel came out of the Temple and called in a loud voice to him who was sitting on the cloud, 'take your sickle and reap, because the time to reap has come, for the Harvest of the earth is ripe'." (NIV)

God's appointed time for reaping had come. Eccl.3 says, "There is a time for everything, and a season for every activity under heaven:" (NIV) Then Solomon tells us many of these appointed times of God – "a time to be born and a time to die, a time to plant and a time to uproot, a time to kill and a time to heal, a time to tear down, and a time to build..." Eccl.3:2-3, (NIV) God has appointed a time for everything under the sun. Everything God was going to do in fulfilling his plan had an appointed time. It was foreshadowed and prophesied in the Old Testament, even to the day. Remember when Jesus taught, "my time is not yet", Jn.2:4? Or, when Jesus told his brothers before the Feast of Tabernacles, "The time for me has not yet come." Jn.7:7. (NIV) (Look at John 7:30; Jn.17:1; Jn.13:1.) Here, The time for reaping had come.

Verse 16. The Earth was Harvested

"So he who was Seated on the cloud swung his sickle over the Earth, and the Earth was harvested." (NIV)

Jesus came back to reap his own. In 1 Cor.15:22, "In Christ all would be made alive...when he comes (he came in 70 A.D.) those who belong to him." In Heb. 9:28 he says, "He will appear a second time not to bear sin, but to bring salvation to those who are waiting for him." Why were they waiting for him? Because he had told them he was going to come back (in that generation, before some had tasted death; in the clouds he would return as he went, etc.) They expected him! They were ready and waiting.

Now - begins the next scene of a separate harvest: the harvest of the wicked.

Verse 17. Another Angel To Reap

"Another angel came out of the temple in heaven, and he too had a sharp sickle." (NIV)

Verse 18. Earth's Grape Vine Is Harvested

"Still another angel, who had charge of the fire, came from the altar and called in a loud voice to him who had the sharp sickle, take your sharp sickle and gather the cluster of grapes from the Earth's Vine, because it's grapes are ripe." (NIV)

The two angels are told to gather the grapes from earth's vine.

There is a prediction of this judgment. It starts in a prophecy by Jacob about Jesus, Gen.49:10-12. There, Jesus is of Judah, he has the scepter, and the "obedience of nations is his" (that is in heaven when every knee will bow and confess him as king). He washes his garments in wine, his robes (royal robes) in the blood of grapes. (This speaks of the King of Kings. Jesus metes out justice.) This prophecy is expanded and Jesus is again seen administering judgment in Isa.63:1-6:

"Who is this coming from Edom, from Bozrah, with his garments stained crimson? Who is this, robed in splendor, striding forward in the greatness of his strength? It is I, speaking in righteousness, mighty to save. Why are your garments red, like those of one treading the winepress? I have trodden the winepress alone; from the nations no one was with me. I trampled them in my anger and trod them down in my wrath...for the day of vengeance was in my heart..." (NIV)

These prophecies foreshadow the judgment here. The grapes are harvested by two angels. Jesus (in heaven) will bring judgment down on them in his wrath, next verse – "the winepress of God's wrath."

We will see the scene more fully when we look at the rider on the white horse, Rev.19:11-21. The armies of heaven were following him 19:14. This is also the battle of Gog and Magog in Ezek.38-39.

Verse 19. Grapes Thrown Into The Winepress Of God's Wrath

"The angel swung his sickle on the Earth, gathered its grapes, and threw them into the great winepress of God's Wrath." (NIV)

It is clear, this is the harvest of the enemies of God; when the angels throw the grapes into the great winepress of God's wrath.

Verse 20 They Were Trampled

"They were trampled in the winepress outside the city, and blood flowed out of the press, rising as high as the horses' bridles for a distance of 1600 stadia." (NIV)

"They were trampled in the winepress outside the city." (NIV)

The enemies of God are trampled outside the city – because God is a wall of fire around the heavenly Jerusalem, Zech.2:5, the city of the living God. God protects his city and no enemy could ever get through. Also, God never allows any wicked to gain entrance into his city. No wicked can dwell there. Joel 3:12-14 has similar language –

"Let the nations be roused; let them advance into the Valley of Jehoshaphat, for there I will sit to judge all the nations on every side. Swing the sickle, for the harvest is ripe. Come and trample the grapes, for the winepress is full and the vats overflow- so great is their wickedness." Verse 14 says – for the day of the Lord is near, in the valley of decision." (NIV)

"1600 stadia" - about 180 miles. That is a lot of dead bodies and blood was as high as horses' bridles, for 180 miles. Who can imagine it? It would be a sea of blood! The point is – it was horrible beyond imagination! God WILL judge the wicked! God will bring vengeance on his enemies! It may seem like an an exaggeration. Perhaps! But this happened in heaven. We don't know the laws that govern the spirit world, the heavenlies. And remember, this is God's judgment of all the wicked who lived through the centuries up to that time, (A.D.70). This is the judgment of them all, the enemies of God gathered to do the last Battle with Jesus, the rider on the white horse. He who has a sharp two-edged sword coming out of his mouth, the King of all kings.

CHAPTER FIFTEEN

SEVEN ANGELS WITH SEVEN PLAGUES

Verse 1. The Last Seven Plagues

"I saw in heaven another great and marvelous sign: seven angels with the seven last plagues- last, because with them God's Wrath is completed." (NIV)

"I saw" He starts a new vision, or at least a new scene.

"Another great and marvelous sign." He has already told us about two signs: The woman clothed in the sun, 12:1; and the Dragon, 12:3. Now, he tells us another sign. What is it Lord?

"Seven angels with the seven last plagues." (NIV)

We have already seen the opening of the seventh seal, 8:1. With that opening, we were introduced to "seven angels with seven trumpets", 8:6. Now we are looking at "seven angels with the seven last plagues." Did these seven angels with the plagues follow the seven angels with the seven trumpets; or are we looking at the same seven angels again but from a different viewpoint? Even though these two texts are very similar – they are different events. We will look at them in detail at the beginning of Chapter 16. There, we will first look at their similarities, and then why they are different events.

Here, John introduces us to the seven angels with the seven last plagues but does not develop what happens. Instead, he wants us to first see the saints who are victorious in heaven.

"With them God's wrath is completed." (NIV) The completion of punishment is announced.

This statement is in the context of completing the judgment of the nation. God says in Jeremiah 50:20 –

"In those days, at that time, declares the Lord, search will be made for Israel's guilt, but there will be none. And for the sins of Judah, but none will be found, for <u>I will forgive the remnant I spare</u>." (NIV)

The judgment will be over for those of the remnant whom God spares. But what happens to those whom God judged without mercy? Even if their judgment ends on earth, what of the afterlife? They will not be forgiven, neither will they have life again after physical death occurs on earth. They have no future after death. They are raised to condemnation and are cast into the lake of fire. Perhaps we could say – when the wicked die, they are dead all over. They have no future, no life. There is no memory of them. (See Appendix R: Death).

Verse 2. Those Who Had Been Victorious

"And I saw what looks like a sea of glass mixed with fire, and standing beside the sea, those who had been victorious over the Beast and his image and over the number of his name. They held harps given to them by God." (NIV)

It is interesting here that you see a <u>sea of glass mixed with fire</u>. In judgment there is a flow of blessings for the righteous (sea of glass) and for the wicked a "river of fire."

John sees the victorious (those who had been faithful even unto death) and not submitted to the image of the beast or his name in their lifetime.

Verse 3. The Song Of Moses And The Lamb

"And sang the song of Moses the servant of God and the song of the Lamb: 'Great and marvelous are your deeds Lord God Almighty. Just and true are your ways, King of the ages'." (NIV)

They sang the song of Moses (Ex.15) - which were O.T. saints; and the song of the Lamb (Rev. 5:9-10,12) - which were the N.T. saints. The songs are both to the ONE LORD – the Lord God Almighty.

Verse 4. You Alone Are Holy

"Who will not fear you, oh Lord, and bring glory to your name? for you alone are Holy. All nations will come and

worship before you, for your righteous acts have been revealed." (NIV)

Only God is holy, and righteous all-together. Christians are only accounted (reckoned) righteous and made holy by Christ. Jesus is our righteousness, sanctification and redemption, 1 Cor.1:31.

Verse 5. The Tabernacle Of The Testimony Was Opened

"After this I looked and in heaven the temple, that is, the Tabernacle of the testimony, was opened." (NIV)

Chapter 11:19 tells us also the temple in heaven was opened and the "ark of the covenant was seen." In that chapter it meant that the "ark of the covenant" (the presence and abode of God, Ex.25:22) had lifted from the earthly temple in Jerusalem and ascended to the heavenly Jerusalem and was seen there. Here, the statement – "the Tabernacle of the testimony" was opened. The Tabernacle of the testimony is referring to the "tent of meeting" (Ex.40:2,6) that housed the ark of the covenant in the Most Holy Place. Above the "ark of the covenant", between the two angels, God met with his people. Now, the ark of the covenant was in heaven, the true tabernacle of God not made by human hands, (Heb.10:24); not an earthly sanctuary, (Heb.9:1). The temple in the heavens was opened. However, the seven angels with seven last plagues had to finish their judgment before anyone could enter, Rev.15:8.

Verse 6. Seven Angels With Seven Plagues

"Out of the temple came the seven angels with the seven plagues. They were dressed in clean, shining linen, and wore golden sashes around their chest." (NIV)

Seven again and again refers to what is divine or the activity of the divine, God himself. These seven angels with seven last plagues would carry out the divine judgment of God. The seven angels who stand before God are mentioned in 8:2.

Verse 7. Seven Golden Bowls Filled With The Wrath Of God

"Then one of the four living creatures gave to the seven angels 7 golden bowls filled with the wrath of God, who lives forever and ever." (NIV)

The four living creatures were cherubim, (Ezek.10:20). The glory of God was above the four living creatures and the commands of God went out from before his throne. Here, one of the four living creatures gives the seven angels the bowls full of God's wrath to finish or complete his judgments.

Verse 8. No One Could Enter The Temple

"And the temple was filled with smoke from the glory of God and from his power, and <u>no one could enter the temple until the seven plagues of the seven angels were completed</u>." (NIV)

Why could they not enter before? God's judgments had to be completed, the heavens completely cleansed. Christ's enemies had to be defeated and dealt with, before letting his people enter the heavenly Jerusalem. Nothing unclean could ever enter there.

CHAPTER SIXTEEN

Let's compare the seven angels with the seven trumpets, 8:2-9:21; 11:15-19 – with the seven angels with the seven last plagues:

[Note: the quotations below come from the NIV.]

Another angel with seven angels and seven trumpets -"...fire from the altar and hurled it on the earth",8:5.

Angel which said, "pour out the seven bowls of God's wrath on the earth," 16:1.

1st Trumpet – "...hail and fire mixed with blood... hurled down upon the earth.

1st Vial – "poured his vial on the land, painful sores broke out on the people.

2nd Trumpet – "huge mountain thrown into the sea ... a third of the sea turned to blood."

2nd Vial – "poured out his bowl on the sea, and it turned into blood. All living things in the sea died."

3rd Trumpet – "a great star fell from the sky...third of the waters turned bitter...many people died."

3rd Vial – "...poured out his bowl on the rivers and springs...became blood (A statement in the text: "You are just in your judgments... for they have shed the blood of your saints and the prophets, and you have given them blood to drink as they deserve." Yes, Jesus speaks this against Jerusalem, Mt.23:37, but the JEWS killed the saints and prophets everywhere. The judgment was not just upon Jerusalem, but all the Jews who were guilty.)

4th Trumpet – "a third of the sun... the moon... the stars were struck."

4th Vial – "the sun was given the power to scorch the people …the people refused to repent."

These judgments sound very similar. Let's notice the differences:

With the Trumpets – a THIRD of things was affected by the judgments. In other words, the judgment was partial. God's judgment was not on all of them. It was not complete.

With the Vials, the second vial says ALL or EVERY living thing in the sea died.

With the third Trumpet MANY people died.

With the third Vial God gives THEM blood to drink.

With the fourth Trumpet, a THIRD of the sun, moon, and stars are affected. It was again partial, not all or complete.

With the fourth Vial, the sun was given power to scorch them (all affected) but they refused to repent.

With the fifth Trumpet, locusts are let out of the abyss and can torture only the wicked, for 5 months.

With the fifth Vial, the throne of the beast and his kingdom are thrown into darkness.

With the sixth Trumpet, 4 angels bound at the Euphrates are released and 200 million demon army.

With the sixth Vial, was poured out on the Euphrates, the river dried up so the armies of the East could cross, then demons with deception of the dragon, the beast, the false prophet- gather the nations for the battle on the great day, Armageddon. (An announcement – "Behold I come like a thief.")

With the seventh trumpet, voices said, "the kingdom of this world has become the kingdom…of Christ." This statement does not seem to include all judgment yet.

With the seventh Vial, voice from the throne said, "It is done." Babylon the Great had been given the cup of God's wrath. This statement seems to complete the judgment of Israel, the Jews on earth, and

REVELATION EXPLAINED

the destruction of the Temple and Jerusalem.

THE SEVEN BOWLS OF GOD'S WRATH

The bowls of God's wrath are certainly indicating judgment being poured out on the land.

Verse 1. Go Pour Out The Bowls Of God's Wrath

"Then I heard a loud voice from the temple saying to the seven angels, 'go pour out the 7 bowls of God's Wrath on the Earth'." (NIV)

No one could enter the temple until the seven plagues were completed, 15:8.

The plagues, or punishment must be completed upon the Jews, before the New Temple could be opened. The Old Temple must be destroyed first. Heb.9:8 says,

"The Holy Spirit was showing by this that the way into the Most Holy Place had not yet been disclosed as long as the first tabernacle was still standing." (NIV)

Rev.18:4 says, "come out of her, my people ("flee Jerusalem", Mt.24:16) so that you will not share in her sins, so that you will not receive any of her plagues." (NIV) Jerusalem was to suffer seven last plagues, and then God's judgment of her would be done, 16:17. Then, the temple of heaven could open up.

Verse 2. The First Angel Poured Out His Bowl

"The first Angel went and poured out his bowl on the land, and ugly and painful sores broke out on the people who had the mark of the beast and worshiped His image." (NIV)

"The land" – would more likely be pointing to the land of Judea with Jerusalem, the focus of God's judgment.

"Painful sores broke out on the people who had the mark of the beast and worshipped his image," (NIV) - Unbelievers/ the unfaithful. In the forehead (in thoughts) and mark on the hand (actions) the people yielded to the beast. They worshiped the image of the beast (the Caesar) even if only to show compliance with and obedience to Rome and not to appear rebellious to the empire. The righteous had to refuse such gestures rather they were self-preserving or to protect others. Which are we? Isaiah 1:5-6 has very descriptive verses –

"Why should you be beaten anymore? Why do you persist in rebellion? Your whole head is injured, your whole heart is afflicted. From the sole of your foot to the top of your head there is no soundness – only wounds and welts and open sores, not cleansed or bandaged or soothed with oil." (NIV)

The people being afflicted with sores was representative of the corrupt character of their whole spiritual condition.

Verse 3. The Second Angel Poured Out His Bowl

"The second angel poured out his bowl on the sea, and it turned into blood like that of a dead man, and <u>every living thing in the sea died</u>." (NIV)

"<u>Poured out his bowl on the sea</u>" (NIV) The sea represents the nations, the peoples of the earth. They also would be those who had the mark of the beast and worshipped his image. The nations were made to "drink blood", verse 6 (bloodshed, death) because they had shed the blood of the saints and prophets. This was God's vengeance on the wicked.

"<u>Every living thing in the sea died</u>." (NIV) All those marked for God's judgment would be punished in it. No one escaped. This was not discipline and a partial judgment. This was judgment determined by God and appointed for that time.

Verse 4. The Third Angel Poured Out His Bowl

"The third Angel poured out his bowl on the rivers and springs of water, and they became blood." (NIV)

"<u>On the rivers and springs of water</u>." (NIV) The blood shed was not just on a national level. Even on a local level, a personal level, the wicked would drink of the cup of judgment they deserved. ALL the wicked, guilty of shedding the blood of the saints and the prophets died. All the wicked, appointed for judgment, would be included. All the levels and sources of water would be turned to blood [bloodshed/punishment].

Verse 5. You Are Just

"Then I heard the angel in charge of the waters say: 'You are just in these

judgments, you who are and who were, the Holy One, because you have so judged." (NIV)

"The angel in charge of the waters." (NIV) God had made the waters bitter. The waters were filled with stench and polluted. The blood which filled them represented the shedding of blood they deserved. They had left the "living waters."

Jesus had judged them and he was just in these judgments. They got what they deserved. Remember the cries of the Jews? "His blood be on us and on our children." Mt.27:25, NIV. Verse 6 gives additional reasons it was just.

Verse 6. Blood To Drink As They Deserve

"For they have shed the blood of your Saints and Prophets, and you have given them blood to drink as they deserve." (NIV)

Verses 5 and 6 can be taken together. God's judgments were just. He had given them blood to drink as they deserve. How did they deserve it? They shed the blood of the saints and the prophets, Mt.23:35-37. For that, "her sins were piled up to heaven, and God remembered their crimes." Rev. 18:5. (NIV)

It is good to remember here – God is longsuffering, not willing that any perish, but that all come to repentance 2 Pet.3:9. But he "had" set a day for judgment, in which he was "about", Greek – mellei, to judge the world (Acts 17:31). (See Appendix E: "Judgment"). Not only so, but it has always been that when the iniquity of a nation was full ("piled up to heaven", as in Rev.18:5) he would judge and punish it, Gen.15:16.

Verse 7. True And Just Are Your Judgments

"And I heard the altar respond: Yes, Lord God Almighty, true and just are your judgments." (NIV)

Verse 8. The Fourth Angel Poured Out His Bowl

"The fourth Angel poured out his bowl on the sun and the sun was given power to scorch people with fire." (NIV)

I do not believe this is referring to the "signs of heavens" mentioned in Mt.24:29. Those signs were to take place just before Jesus' coming and "immediately after the distress of those days." Jesus also said in Lk.21:11, "There will be great earthquakes, famines, and pestilences in various places, and fearful events and great signs from heaven." In that context of Lk.21, it is not until verse 20 that Jesus brings in "When you see Jerusalem surrounded by armies you will know that its desolation is near." The signs in this verse are the "great signs from heaven" of Lk.21:11.

"power to scorch people with fire." (NIV) Judgment is often depicted with "fire". It can be figurative and sometimes literal.

Verse 9. They Were Seared By The Intense Heat

"They were seared by the intense heat and they cursed the name of God, who had control over these plagues, but they refused to repent and glorify him." (NIV)

"The intense heat" (NIV) or severity of God, did not lead them to repentance. They had stubborn and unrepentant hearts, Rom.2:5. Some people have been so hardened by sin they are "past feeling," Eph.4:19. Some people are "impossible …to renew unto repentance", Heb.6:6. Whichever it was here – too hard to repent, or couldn't be renewed to repentance, "THEY REFUSED TO REPENT!"

We may think, "how can that be?" How after such judgments, can people not be brought to repentance? It may be because the very wicked cannot see those events as judgments. We have but to think of the ten plagues on Egypt and their effect on Pharoah. Pharoah got harder and harder. Even his officials realized that Moses was a snare to Egypt and pleaded to let the Israelites go. They said, "Do you not realize that Egypt is ruined?" Ex.10:7, NIV. Yet Pharaoh would not repent. He could not learn. He hung onto his power and fought with God. He could not see or understand what was happening.

The unrepentant seems to refer to the Jews here because they were held responsible for shedding the blood of the saints and prophets.

The next verse seems to shift the focus of the judgments that were on the Jews' (vials 1-4) to the Roman empire, the Beast, and his throne.

Verse 10. The Fifth Angel Poured Out His Bowl

"The fifth angel poured out his bowl on the throne of the Beast and his kingdom was plunged Into Darkness. Men gnawed their tongues in agony." (NIV)

The vial was specifically poured out on the "<u>THRONE OF THE BEAST" and his kingdom was plunged into darkness.</u>

Historically, this happened when Nero died, June 9, 68 A.D. The "throne of the beast" (Rome) the Roman empire was plunged into darkness. The Roman empire went into a civil war. During the chaos of the war, it went through the death of 3 kings who struggled to take power: Galba, Otho, and Vitellius, from June 9, 68 A.D. until December, 69 A.D. That would be a year and a half of civil war and then a period of trying after the civil war to stabilize the Roman Empire by Vespasian. (Josephus, "The Jewish War, Book 4, chapters 9-10.) It was during this civil war, all the people wondered if the Roman empire would even survive.

Verse 11. They Refused To Repent

"And cursed the God of Heaven because of their pains and their sores, but they refused to repent of what they had done." (NIV)

The unrepentant here seems to be the Romans because the vial was poured out on the throne of the beast and his kingdom.

Again, there is a shift in judgment. First, the focus was on the judgment of the <u>Jews</u>. Then the focus shifted with the pouring out of the fifth vial onto the "<u>throne of the beast.</u>" The Roman empire was temporarily plunged into darkness, struggling to exist. There was judgment on the Jews, then the Gentiles, the Romans. Now, starting in verse 12, there is a shift of judgment from earthly scenes to judgment in the heavens. That shift to the heavens is with the sixth vial that is poured out. Let us attempt to orient our understanding to this transition.

In the prophets of the Old Testament, God moves through the prophecies effortlessly – speaking of events that would occur in the lifetime of a generation, and then adding a few verses about far future events, and then back again. Just as we can speak of events in our past and weave them into our current conversation, so God can speak of the distant future and then back to our present again. God in his "normal" conversation can speak of the past, the present, the future, the distant future, and then back to the present again. God does do that in scripture. For those who want to use the scholarship of man, and the wisdom of man, this can be very confusing. With man's rules we insist on following the "context" of a passage (which is reasonable), but not always reliable. The Bible is a spiritual book, and it does not always yield itself to the hermeneutical rules of men. Only the Spirit of God knows the mind of God. We are given the Holy Spirit as Christians to enlighten us or give us understanding. God does not just move from past to present to future and back again. He moves in thought from earth to heaven and back again also. He moves from our earthly physical world to the spiritual unseen world and back again. He is boundless.

The passage here can be explained this way. Judgment Day was not just for the earth. Heb.12:26 says he would shake (judge) not only the earth, but the heavens also. Jesus was to restore "all things", Acts 3:21. He was to reconcile all things to himself both in heaven and on earth. The whole universe he was to "set in order again" (restore). He was to restore it; not replace it. On the Day of Judgement, there was judgment of the whole world (heaven and earth). God was doing it all at the same time. The battles on the earth were not the only ones. There was judgment in the heavens also. The heavenly bodies were being shaken, Mt.24:29. "Men will faint from terror, apprehensive of what is coming on the world, for the heavenly bodies will be shaken." Lk.21:26. (NIV) Perhaps, as I would expect, God was seeing the Day of Judgment as all one event, viewing heaven and earth at the same time and what was happening in both places. Is it any surprise that he would describe judgments on earth and then tell us what was happening in the heavens? After all, he is God. Easily, he could do that. Prophetically, he has told us all kinds of things that are beyond our earthly capability; but if he tells us, it is not beyond our earthly understanding. I say- let God be God. Do not demand your own way to understand things.

Verse 12. The Sixth Angel Poured Out His Bowl

"The sixth Angel poured out his bowl on the great river Euphrates, and its water was dried up to prepare the way for the Kings from the East." (NIV)

The vial is poured out on the Euphrates and - "its water was dried up." (NIV)

Some explain this verse as referring to historical events on earth. They explain the following:

The River Euphrates was crossed at the northeast of Palestine. Armies from the East had to cross the Euphrates River to come into Palestine and invade the land of the Jews. Historically, after the "civil war" of Rome was over, ("the waters dried up", the Roman civil war) the agenda of the Empire was resumed. Vespasian undertook to finish putting down the uprisings of the Jews and ending the Jewish-Roman war. Vespasian sent his son Titus to put down the rebellion in Jerusalem. Titus waited at Caesarea for the legions from the north (vassal kings of the East) to join him before marching on to Jerusalem to put down the Jewish rebellion.

(See Josephus, "The Jewish Wars", Book 4, chapter 11 and Book 5, Chapter 1).

Historically the above is true. However, why not the mention of the other kings and forces that came up with Titus from the South, from Egypt? Does this interpretation fit with the context? Verses 12-16 are about the pouring out of the sixth vial. What does that include?

1. The Euphrates is dried up to prepare the way for the kings of the East, verse 12.

2. Three evil spirits come out of the mouths of the dragon, of the beast, and of the false prophet, verse 13.

3. The evil spirits perform miraculous signs and gather the kings of the earth for battle on the great day of God Almighty, verse 14.

4. Jesus announces – "Behold, I come like a thief!" Verse 15.

5. The kings of the whole world are gathered in a place called Armageddon, verse 16.

Let's look at each of these verses. #1. Normally, when a nation from the East crosses the Euphrates and invades the land of Palestine, the prophetic imagery is of the Euphrates overflowing its banks and flooding down into Palestine, (Isa.8:7-8). It is a picture of judgment like a flood. In Rev,16:12, the waters are "dried up". Why? Does it represent the drying up of the power of these military forces? God enables them to cross, but not by their power.

#2 and #3. The three evil spirits come out of the mouths. They deceive the armies or <u>hordes</u>. (We assume they deceive the people of Palestine, the Jews; but is that what is happening? Are not the kings and their hordes "being gathered for battle"? How are they gathered? By the influence of the three evil spirits? #3 The battle is on the <u>Great Day of Almighty God</u>. The Great Day is prophetically, the Day appointed by God for judgment. It is seen and pointed to all through scripture. This was Judgment Day. This is when the wicked are faced down by Christ and judged. #4 Jesus announces he is coming – for the wicked, it is like a thief. Again, this points to Judgment Day. #5. The kings of the whole world are gathered for the battle of Armageddon (a place where they would be slaughtered.). Is that what happened historically on earth? Were the armies of Titus slaughtered? Or were they victorious? Did Titus go back to Rome with his captives and erect the Arch of Titus to commemorate his victory? Then how is the pouring out of the sixth vial referring to an <u>earthly</u> historical event? <u>It is not</u>!

"<u>The kings of the earth</u>" raging against Christ is prophetically mentioned in Psalms 2 and the various scriptures we have listed. It refers to the final battle in heaven where Christ brings judgment upon all those generations of evil hordes who had opposed him.

Verse 13. Three Evil Spirits That Looked Like Frogs

"Then I saw 3 evil spirits that looked like frogs; They came out of the mouth of the Dragon, out of the mouth of the Beast, and out of the mouth of the false prophet." (NIV)

<u>Why did the three evil spirits look like frogs</u>?

Maybe we can make a good guess. First, we can describe our theory. The spirits go out to deceive the nations. Remember, the three evil spirits come out of the mouth of the Dragon, Satan. Rev. 20 :7-8 says "Satan will be released from his prison and will go out to deceive the nations in the four corners of the earth - Gog and Magog - to gather them for battle." (NIV) How does Satan deceive the nations ("the kings of the whole world", verse 14) and gather them for battle? Three evil spirits come out of his mouth to deceive the nations. On the earth, they are deceiving spirits of the Beast,(Rev. 13:1,-2) and the false prophet (13:11). That is the battle going on on the earth (Rome - a world empire and the nations aligned with it.) In the spiritual world, the heavenly realm, a battle raged also. Those nations over all of time who persecuted God's people and were then dead, who were about to be judged, are gathered also to come against the rider on the white horse and his heavenly armies, Rev. 19:11-14. The heavenly battle is the battle of Gog and Magog.

Now, why are the three spirits like frogs? What if the frogs are poisonous frogs. When they come out of the mouth of Satan, they are like poisonous lies to deceive the nations. Does that understanding fit? It seems to fit so far. Psalms 140:3 says, "the poison of vipers is in their lips." (KJV) Satan is a serpent, a viper, and poison is in his lips. James 3:8 says, "No human being can tame the tongue. It is a restless evil, full of deadly poison.

The frogs of the plague of Egypt, Exodus 8, do not seem to be poisonous, but into everything and very destructive. Because the Bible does not make a frog a symbol for something poisonous, we cannot insist on this theory. However, the frog was viewed as slimy and unclean. Unclean spirits came out of the mouth of Satan.

The workers, the emissaries of the Evil One are sent out to gather the armies. They have to deceive even their own, for these 3 evil spirits must convince those in the grave they still have a chance in fighting against God. The armies are very large. Ezekiel calls them "hordes", Ezekiel 38:4,7,13.

Ezekiel says God would "turn you around, put hooks in your jaws and bring you out with your whole army", Ezek.38:4. (NIV) This army (of the already "dead" in the realm of the dead) was a very reluctant army to come out against God. They were going to their destruction. Somehow, I think they knew it; but what choice did they have - but to crazily try again?

Verse 14 The Kings Of The Earth To Gather For Battle

"They are spirits of demons performing miraculous signs, and they go out <u>to the kings of the whole world</u>, to gather them for the battle of the great day of God Almighty." (NIV)

"<u>They are spirits of demons performing miraculous signs</u>." (NIV)

Can demons (fallen angels) perform miraculous signs? Yes, it would seem so. Why? They are very powerful, being of the spiritual world. Miracles are things not natural to the laws of the physical realm. Evil spiritual beings could possess a man and cause him to do things that he would hurt himself. A possessed man was made very strong and could break chains, Lk.8:29. What else could be done? I do not know, but here it says they performed miraculous signs. Were they "false miracles"? It does not say so. However, in this context, I think we are talking about the battle to take place in heaven, Gog and Magog, for they <u>go out to the kings of the earth</u> (I understand as dead, Ezek.32:17-32, and from other passages) to gather them, as Ezekiel 38; Psalms 2. The action in heaven and on earth may be shown to us back and forth by the prophet. To God, he could view it all at the same time and as the same judgment happening both in heaven and on earth at the same time. The judgment time appointed for heaven and earth had arrived.

"<u>They go out to the kings of the whole world, to gather them for the great day of God Almighty</u>" (NIV)

Ezek.38:4 says it was a "whole army" and a "great horde". (See the explanation of Ezek.38-39 under "Gog and Magog").

Verse 15. I Come Like A Thief

"'Bold I come like a thief! Blessed is he who stays awake and keeps his clothes with him, so that he may not go naked and be shamefully exposed." (NIV)

Following the Battle about to be fought in the heavens in the previous verse, then comes Jesus "like a thief" in the second coming. There were to be signs in the heavens and the heavenly bodies SHAKEN (that is - judgment), Matt. 24:29 and then in Matt.24:30 the sign of the Son Of Man would appear and they would see him coming in the clouds, with power and great glory, and he would send out his angels. That is the second coming. He came "immediately after the distress of those days" when the temple and Jerusalem were destroyed.

Why would Jesus' second coming be a sign? I believe that it marked the total end for the Mosaic period and the opening up of his kingdom in the heavens. His coming marked the final transition from the first covenant to the New Covenant.

"Behold I come like a thief!" (NIV) The saints did not have to be caught off guard that the judgment day caught them by surprise, 1 Thess.5:4. They were to be ready.

"Blessed is he who stays awake." (NIV) They were to be alert, watchful, spiritually ready.

"And keeps his clothes with him, so that he may not be naked." (NIV) This is like the day the first born were killed in Egypt and God's people were to be ready with "cloak tucked into their belt, their sandals on their feet, and staff in hand, and to eat in haste" Ex.12:11.

Verse 16. Armageddon

"Then they gathered the Kings together to the place that in Hebrew is called Armageddon." (NIV)

"The kings gathered together." (NIV)

In Ps.2, the kings of the earth take their stand and the rulers gather together against the Lord and against his Anointed One. Verse 4, God in heaven laughs. Verse 6 – "I have installed my king on Zion, my holy hill." (This shows that Jesus is already in heaven – installed as king.) Verse 7 – "you are my son, today I have become your Father". (Jesus was begotten, born from the dead, quoted in Heb.1:5). Verses 8-9 – "I will make the nations your inheritance, the ends of the earth your inheritance. You will rule them with an iron scepter; you will dash them to pieces like pottery." (NIV) Ps.37:13 -The Lord laughs at the wicked, for he knows their day is coming." What happens on that day, the appointed day of judgment? Zech.12 is a great passage to read to answer that.

This gathering was in the heaven of all the kings and armies (that had died through the generations up to that time) from the places of the dead (the sea and hades). The final battle and judgment was about to occur as they were gathered in the heavens in the spiritual world. The battle is described in Ezekiel 38-39.

It is also described in Rev.19:11-18. These kings of the earth, or "hordes" as Ezekiel calls them, go up against the rider on the white horse whose name is the "Word of God", Rev. 19:13. There is no contest for these kings. They are slaughtered.

"Armageddon" is ONLY mentioned in scripture here in Rev.16:16. John uses the word I think for its symbolic meaning to the Jews of a battle of unrivaled bloodshed and slaughter. The word was associated with great lament and mourning. We will look closer at it.

Modern writers and theologians claim that the evil forces of this world will be gathered together in our future by the Anti-Christ. Then a great battle (Armageddon) will be fought on earth and the forces of evil defeated. From the way that modern writers talk and write, you would think the Bible and the Old Testament prophets prophesied about Armageddon and talked about it all over the scripture. That is just not true. The word is mentioned ONLY once in scripture, here in Re.16:16. It does not have the widespread claims and teachings in the Bible that modern scholars have dreamed up. Not only so, but John taught the Anti-Christ was already existing in his day and that there were "many Anti-Christs", 1 Jn.2:18. John defined the Anti-Christ as "whoever denies that Jesus is the Christ," 1Jn.2:22, (NIV). The spirit of the Anti-Christ was already in the world in his time, 1 Jn. 4:3. There are multiple errors of the modern theorists. The biggest one is that they ignore that Revelation was to "soon take place", Rev.1:1:22:6, (NIV) after John wrote it. It was soon to be fulfilled.

"Armageddon." Is either from Hebrew "har megiddo" and means a mountain or mount of Megiddo or "ar megiddo" and means the city of Megiddo. Megiddo itself may come from the Hebrew word "gad" – a troop, (gad- "a plundering troop", Gen.49:19), and from a verb "gadad" – to cut to pieces. The meaning of the word Armageddon then suggests that troops were slaughtered or cut to pieces. Historically, at the valley of Megiddo, that is what happened several times. What historically often took place there becomes an emblem for how it is used later. It is used here in Revelation as an emblematic reference to the final battle with Christ. The kings that were gathered together (in the spiritual realm in the heavens) against Christ and his heavenly hosts were cut to pieces.

It is interesting to point out some of the history where Megiddo is involved. This area is where other battles were historically fought and great slaughter took place. It was a crossroads where Eastern culture and armies met Western culture and armies. Great battles were fought there. In Judges 5:19-21 Israel (under Deborah and Barak) fought against Sisera. The verses say –

"Kings came, they fought; the kings of Canaan fought at Taanach by the waters of Megiddo, but they carried off no silver, no plunder. From the heavens the stars (angels, T.S.) fought, from their courses they fought Sisera. The river Kishon swept them away." (NIV).

Both the angels and nature itself fought Sisera. (What a strange passage.) God fought for the Jews both with angels and nature itself.

In the final battle in heaven between those (gathered from the graves) the kings and their armies ("hordes" in Ezekiel); they came against Christ and his army, heavenly hosts, Rev. 19:4. They fought the battle. Of course, Christ and the angels decimate the hordes.

Isaiah 24:14-23 is a parallel passage to Ezekiel 38 and 39 and also Rev. 19:11-21, and Zech.12. All of Isaiah 24- 27 (prophecy of the event of the final battle with Christ and final judgment). In Isaiah 26:20, the Lord tells his people to go to their room and shut the door and hide themselves for a little while because the Lord is coming out of his dwelling to punish the people of the earth (the kings and armies of the earth that were held for judgment of the Great Day). In other words, God's people in heaven were to go to their rooms until the fighting and judgment was completed. <u>God fought for them</u> – just like in the story of Deborah and Barak fighting Sisera. Read the chapters of Isaiah 24-27 carefully and you can see all kinds of details that let you know it was the time and event of God's judgment. (For more information on Armageddon, see Appendix S – Armageddon).

The <u>slaughter</u> indicated by the meaning of the word – "Armageddon" is seen in the Ezekiel 38-39 passage.

Ezekiel 38:21 says – "I will summon a sword against Gog on

all my mountains" and "will execute judgment upon him…" Ezek.39:12 "For seven months the house of Israel will be burying them in order to cleanse the land." (NIV)

Zechariah 12:11 suggests <u>great lamentation and weeping associated with Megiddo</u> – "as like the weeping of Hadad Rimmon in the plain of Megiddo." (NIV) Israel lamented Josiah's death many years, even down through the death of Ezra. Josiah was killed by Pharoah Neco at Megiddo, 2Kings 23:29; 2 Chron. 35:22-25. The saying in Zechariah became an expression for Israel for what was greatly lamentable. Even the lament is used to describe the lament for the Christ, "the one whom they have pierced" and mourning for him, Zech.12:10-11.

So, Armageddon is emblematic of a day of great slaughter and bloodshed, of great lament and mourning, and maybe of even a day in which God himself fights and judges.

Verse 17. The Seventh Angel Poured Out His Bowl

"The seventh angel poured out his bowl into the air, and out of the temple came a loud voice from the throne, Saying, 'it is done!'" (NIV)

"<u>The seventh angel poured out his bowl into the air</u>." (NIV) This is the final plague. We do not get to see what happens with the seventh plague. The announcement just comes forth "It is done." Notice, we do not get to see the destruction of Jerusalem in this chapter, nor do we get to see the battle in the heavens. We do see the battle in the heavens in Chapter 19:11-21.

"<u>Out of the Temple came a loud voice from the throne</u>," (NIV) The official announcement from the throne; it is loud for all to hear -

"<u>Saying, It is done!</u>" (NIV) The seven last plagues were last – because with them the wrath of God was completed, 15:1. NIV. No one could enter the temple until the seven plagues were completed, 15:8. The temple was opened with the sounding of the seventh trumpet. Now with the last plague, the temple could be entered.

Verse 18. No Earthquake Like It Has Ever Occurred

"Then There came flashes of lightning, rumbling, peals of thunder, and a severe earthquake. No earthquake like it has ever occurred since man has

been on Earth. so tremendous was the quake." (NIV)

The reaction of the heavens responded in appropriate thunders and a tremendous shaking, "an earthquake not like it has ever occurred. Nature, in heaven and earth, in total connection and agreement with the acts of God – exactly respond.

This may point to the historical event of a severe earthquake recorded in Josephus. The Idumeans had been excluded from the city. The Idumeans lay all day and all night before the wall of Jerusalem and could not gain access. That night, there was a severe earthquake and by it the Idumeans were able to enter Jerusalem. The Idumeans were one of three Jewish warring factions that destroyed the city from within. Josephus records the earthquake as so severe that there were "amazing concussions and bellowings of the earth… These things were a manifest indication that some destruction was coming upon men, when the system of the world was put into this disorder; and anyone would guess what these wonders forshadowed some great calamities that were coming." [Josephus, "The Jewish War," Book 4, chapter 4, Section 5].

Verse 19. The Great City Split Into Three Parts

"The great City split into three parts, and the cities of the nations collapsed. God remembered Babylon the Great and gave her the cup filled with the wine of the fury of his Wrath." (NIV)

"The great City split into three parts." (NIV)

This may be alluding to the historical fact that Jerusalem was divided by three Jewish factions that took over three different sections of the city and ripped it apart. The "great city" refers to the "earthly" Jerusalem, that here in Revelation is the "great prostitute. The "great city" is earthly Jerusalem "where also their Lord was crucified", Rev.11:8, (NIV).

Josephus speaks first of 2 factions of rebel tyrants who fought in Jerusalem: John and the zealots, and later added the faction of Simon's followers. At that point, 3 main factions brought the city of Jerusalem into bloody war, brothers against brothers – destroying, killing and burning. The city collapsed and with it, the Mosaic system it represented. (Josephus, Book 4, Chapters 3-4).

"The cities of the nations collapsed." (NIV) What could this mean? The cities of the Roman empire and the surrounding nations were still there. Are we speaking spiritually? Dan 2:44 predicted that "In the days of these kings" (Roman kings) the God of heaven would set up a kingdom that would never be destroyed and that it would break in pieces and "consume all other kingdoms." Did it conquer all other kingdoms? No, not in the sense of a conquering ruler in the physical world. Speaking of spiritual power though, the kingdom of God has spread throughout the world ("broke into pieces" and spread) and "consumes all other kingdoms. The kingdom of God cannot be stopped because (here on earth) it crosses all national borders and cultures. It spreads into the hearts of men and cannot be stopped. No earthly kingdom can stand against it. The cities of the nations fall to its power for every man whom it reaches and who believes. This could be referring to the collapse of the old Mosaic system in a figurative allusion. The domination of sin reigning in death by using the law to condemn man – that power was broken. Now, in Christ, grace could reign through righteousness, Rom 5:21.

"God remembered Babylon the Great and gave her the cup...wrath." (NIV) Babylon (the earthly sinful Jerusalem, the unfaithful harlot, Rev. 17; the woman in bondage to sin with her children, Gal.4:25) she was punished for her sin, filth, murders of the prophets, Christ, and the saints.

Verse 20. Every Island Fled

"Every island fled away and the mountains could not be found. (NIV)

This is now figurative language of the removal of the "old order" of things. The "world" as they knew it changed. The Jewish system under Moses fled.

Verse 21. Huge Hailstones Of About A Hundred Pounds Fell

"From the sky huge hailstones of about a hundred pounds each fell upon men. And they cursed God on account of the plague of hail, because the plague was so terrible." (NIV)

"From the sky huge hailstones of about a hundred pounds."(NIV)

This could easily allude symbolically to the historical experience of the Jews in Jerusalem when Rome was taking the city. Josephus says in regard to the taking of the Galilean city of Jotapata, that the Romans set 160 engines round about the city. These engines could throw huge stones as big as a talent (75 to 100 pounds, some put it at 114 pounds) with a range of 2 furlongs (440 yards). Here is what Josephus said:

"At the same time such engines as were intended for that purpose at once lances upon them with a great noise, and stones the weight of a talent were thrown by the engines that were prepared for that purpose, together with fire, and a vast number of arrows, which made the wall so dangerous that the Jews dared not only not come upon it, but dared not come to those parts within the walls which were reached by the engines." (Josephus, The Jewish War, Book 3, chap.7, sect.9.)

These symbolized "hailstones" could be nearly 20 inches or more in diameter and travelling 370 miles per hour when they hit.

"They cursed God on account of the plague of hail." (NIV)

The judgment did not bring repentance, (as also in verse 11). It brought the cursing of God. They were more than adamant, they were unreachable, evil, and unrepentant.

CHAPTER SEVENTEEN

THE WOMAN ON THE BEAST

Verse 1. The Punishment Of The Great Prostitute

"One of the Seven Angels who had the 7 bowls came and said to me, 'Come I will show you the punishment of the great prostitute, who sits on many waters." (NIV)

"The punishment of the great prostitute" (NIV) -

Historically, throughout the Old Testament, Israel and Judah are depicted as being unfaithful. In Jer.3:6-8, there prostitution (unfaithfulness to God) is clearly stated. In Ezek.16, there is an allegory of unfaithful Jerusalem - whose birth was in the land of the Canaanites. Her father was an Amorite and her mother a Hittite. God found her as a child, cleaned her up. She grew. He dressed her in beautiful clothing and put a crown on her head. But she trusted in her beauty and became a prostitute. She did terrible things with the nations. (The chapter is well worth your time to read. It is very descriptive.) Historically, the unfaithful nation, and the city of Jerusalem are depicted as a prostitute over and over. The symbol of a prostitute well fits Israel and Jerusalem in the Bible.

"Who sits on many waters".(NIV)

Israel was in Palestine. Its capital was in Jerusalem. Ezek. 5:5 says – "This is Jerusalem, which I have set in the center of the nations, with countries all around her." Jerusalem sat in the center of the nations (figuratively -"many waters").

Verse 2. Intoxicated With The Wine Of Her Adulteries

"With her the kings of the earth committed adultery and the inhabitants of the earth were intoxicated with the wine of her adulteries."(NIV)

"With her the kings of the earth committed adultery" (NIV)

Jerusalem (representing Israel) practiced idolatry (spiritual adultery against God) with the nations around her. This was true when God destroyed the temple the first time. It was still true in Jesus' day. Jesus called his generation – "a wicked and adulterous generation", Mt.12:32; 16:4: Mk. 8:38. They were still an adulterous and unfaithful nation and they rejected God when he sent his son. In a very real way, the kings were corrupt with the leadership of Israel. Even, by the time of Christ, it was the Caesar, or his representative that (Josephus tells us) chose the high priests for Israel. The high priest's family was corrupt, and in the narrative of the gospels and Acts we see the high priest directly involved the plot to kill Jesus, and to persecute his apostles and the disciples. The leadership of Israel was intertwined with Rome, influenced by Rome, and made appeals to Roman rulers to have Jesus crucified and his followers killed.

"The inhabitants…intoxicated with the wine of her adulteries" (NIV)

Verse 3. A Woman Sitting On A Scarlet Beast

"Then the angel carried me away in the Spirit into a desert. There I saw a woman sitting on a Scarlet Beast that was covered with blasphemous names and had seven heads and ten horns." (NIV)

"Into a desert" (NIV) Why was she in the desert? Remember verse 1, "the punishment of the great prostitute"? God was going to judge sinful Israel. Ezek.20:35-36 tells us – "I will bring you into the desert of the nations, and there, face to face, I will execute judgment upon you. As I judged your fathers in the desert of the land of Egypt, so I will judge you." (NIV)

God judged the Jews in the desert when he brought them out of Egypt. They refused to believe and follow him. Then, God again in Ezekiel "judged Israel in the desert of the nations" and destroyed the temple.

Later the temple was rebuilt as we read in Nehemiah and Ezra. Now, in the time of Jesus, they had crucified the Son of God and killed apostles and disciples of Jesus. God again, was ready to judge them "in the desert" and destroy the temple and Mosaic system once for all. That judgment happened in A.D.70. That is what is happening here in Revelation.

"Woman sitting on a scarlet beast that was covered with blasphemous names." (NIV)

The woman (sinful Israel, centered in Jerusalem the capital) was riding on the scarlet (symbol of royalty, rulership) beast (The Roman empire). She was in the middle of the empire and being carried along by its rule and influence. The beast was covered with "blasphemous names". The Caesars claimed to be gods and demanded worship in order for people to demonstrate loyalty to Rome. The Caesars were blasphemous pagans. Rome was a pagan empire that ruled over the nations.

"Had seven heads and ten horns." (NIV)

The beast, that is, had seven heads (Seven Caesars the prophet focuses on, and then an eighth in this chapter. See verse 12 ff.). The ten horns – see verse 12.

Verse 4. A Golden Cup Filled With Abominable Things

"The woman was dressed in purple and Scarlet, and was glittering with gold, precious stones and pearls. She held a golden cup in her hand, filled with abominable things, the filth of her adulteries." (NIV)

"The woman was dressed in purple and scarlet, glittering with gold, precious stones and pearls." (NIV)

She had been blessed by God. She had become very prominent among the nations because of her history. She had even risen to be called a queen, Ezek.16:13. She was prominent in the time of Christ and Jews that had been scattered among the nations traveled to Jerusalem for feast days; and foreigners came to trade with her. She was under Roman rule, but she was still prominent among the nations. Jerusalem was rich (as indicated in her description, Rev.18:11-13) a big player in the scheme of things.

"Golden cup filled with abominable things, the filth of her adulteries." (NIV)

This is what she had to trade with the nations – her unfaithfulness and idolatry, her sacrifices for Caesar, and money changers to exchange currencies and goods with people all over the world.

Verse 5. Mystery Babylon The Great Mother Of Prostitutes

"This title was written on her forehead: Mystery Babylon the Great Mother of Prostitutes and of the abominations of the earth." (NIV)

"Title on her forehead." (NIV)

This symbolizes what is in the mind, the thoughts, Deut.6:8. It also symbolizes a name, a title, - describing the character, as here.

"Mystery Babylon the Great, the Mother of Prostitutes" (NIV)

Babylon (the tower of Babel) was the source, the beginning of idolatry. The tower of Babel had a temple at the top where priests would worship the gods of the stars, the sun and moon. That idolatry spread all over the world after men's languages were confused. Ziggurats (step pyramids) appeared all over the world with idolatrous temples at their tops. The pyramids were in Egypt, Mesopotamia, China, Peru, Mexico, the US. – all over. God had forbidden all such worship, Deut.4:15-19.

Jerusalem is here figuratively called Babylon. She had shared idolatry with the nations right up through the generation of Christ. Even though idolatry started in Babylon; Babylon was now long gone from history. The idolatrous Israel well fits the title of Babylon. The tribe of Dan we have already discussed (Rev.7:8). Remember, Dan was not listed with the 144,000 out of each tribe. Dan had taken Micah's idol north to Laish (renamed Dan), and there spread idolatry throughout Israel. It was also Jeroboam who set up idolatrous shrines in Bethel and Dan, 1 Kings 12:31. The nation of Israel had long practiced idolatry. She fits the name. Jerusalem, her capital, that represented the nation, well fits the name – "Babylon". Not only did Israel fit the name, she excelled even the nations around her in wickedness, Ezek.5:6-7.

We have already seen in Rev.11, that the city there was Jerusalem ("where our Lord was crucified") "the great city" which is figuratively called Sodom and Egypt, Rev. 11:6. The city so corrupt as to be called Sodom and Egypt; would it not also be called "Babylon"?

Peter was an elder at the home church, Jerusalem. When he writes salutations from there, he mentions, "She who is in Babylon, chosen together with you, sends you her greetings." 1 Pet.5:13, (NIV).

Verse 6. Drunk With The Blood Of The Saints

"I saw that the woman was drunk with the blood of the saints, the blood of those who bore testimony to Jesus. When I saw her, I was greatly astonished, (NIV)

"Drunk with the blood of the saints" (NIV)

This also identifies Jerusalem as the figurative – "Babylon." Jesus had told Jerusalem they she would be responsible for all the blood of the saints and his messengers - Mt.23:24-39.

It might be good here to remind us of what we see in the New Testament. There is an antagonism between spiritual Israel and unfaithful Israel. The promises were not made to physical, earthly, sinful, unbelieving Israel but to the One seed which is Christ and his offspring, Ga.3:16. The true Jew was circumcised of heart, not the flesh, Rom.2:29. The true Israel of God had the faith of Abraham, Rom.9:8. The earthly Jerusalem was under bondage to sin, but the Jerusalem above had the children of promise, Gal.4:25-26. Mount Zion, the heavenly Jerusalem God built, but the Jerusalem below man built, Heb.12. The two cities in the New Testament represent 1. sinful condemned man (earthly Jerusalem), and 2. righteous saved children of God (the heavenly Jerusalem). That same contrast is seen in the Revelation. There is the 1. woman, a prostitute, sitting on a beast; and there is the 2. woman clothed in the sun. They are antagonists. They are opposites.

Verse 7. The Mystery Of The Woman And THe Beast

"Then the angel said to me: 'Why are you astonished? I will explain to you the mystery of the woman and of the Beast she rides, which has the seven heads and ten horns. (NIV)

Verse 8. The Beast That Once Was, Now Is Not, And Will Come

'The Beast what you saw, once was, now it's not, and will come up out of the Abyss and go to his destruction. The inhabitants of the earth whose names have not been written in the Book of Life from the creation of the will be astonished when they see the Beast, because he once was, now is not, and yet will come. (NIV)

The Beast can refer to the whole Roman empire or the emperor of Rome at the time. Here, the beast refers to the emperor who once was (He had died. This was Nero). Now he was not. Not only so, under him Rome had been a terrible persecuting power. At his death, Rome temporarily stopped trying to put down uprisings of various groups, and struggled to survive an internal civil war of the empire. Josephus tells us that everyone wondered whether the empire would survive. (Josephus, "War of the Jews", Preface, Sect.2).

At Nero's death, John tells us he ("Nero") would come up out of the abyss (the place of the wicked dead for judgment) and go to his destruction (the lake of fire, verse 8).

"The beast -once was, now is not, yet will come."

Perhaps, if the Beast refers to the empire, it was a beast under Nero. During the civil war of Rome, the empire was not a beast or persecuting power because it was struggling to exist. The character of a beast came alive again under Vespasian, that is, the empire revived and again as a beast, resumed its persecution of the Jews, putting down their uprisings.

Verse 9. Seven Heads Are Seven Hills

"This calls for a mind with wisdom. The seven heads are seven hills on which the woman sits." (NIV)

The woman is idolatrous unfaithful Israel. Israel sat in the middle of the nations, Ezek.5:5. At the time of the Roman empire, Israel sat in the middle of the Roman empire (the conquered nations under Rome) and rode the beast (the Roman Empire). Rome sat on seven hills.

Verse 10. The Seven Heads Are Also Seven Kings

"They are also 7 Kings. Five have fallen, one is, the other has not yet come; but when he does come, he must remain for a little while." (NIV)

This is a key verse for understanding the date of the book. It gives us the key to where we are in history, parallel to this verse. Josephus, the first century Jewish historian, tells us information that we need to know to put it together. In Josephus, he tells us of a Roman civil war that occurred at the time of the death of Nero - June 9, 68A.D. (the 5th emperor of Rome). (Nero had 4 main generals: Galba, Otho, Vitellius, and Vespasian. The civil war occurred as a result of all 4 trying to assume the position of emperor.) Josephus tells us about it in summary form in (The Jewish War, book 4, chap.9, sect.2.)

It helps us to list the emperors:

5th emperor – <u>Nero</u>, reign 54 A.D. – Jun.7, 68 A.D.
/ 6th emperor – <u>Galba</u>, reign Jun.8, 68 A.D.- Jan.15,69 A.D,
Civil war 7th emperor – <u>Otho</u>, reign Jan.15, 69 A.D.- April 16, 69 A.D.
\ 8th emperor – <u>Vitellius</u>, reign April 19, 69 A.D.- Dec.20, 69 A.D.
9th emperor – <u>Vespasian</u>, reign Dec.69 A.D. – June 23, 79 A.D.

(Vespaian was declared to be emperor by his troops in July, 69 A.D. while away from Rome. He came back and defeated Vitellius in Rome, and was declared emperor by the senate in Dec. 69 A.D.)

10th emperor – <u>Titus</u> reign Jun.24,79A.D. – Sept.13,81 A.D.

11th emperor – <u>Domitian</u> reign Sept.14,81 A.D. -Sept.18,96A.D.

This verse mentions 5 emperors had fallen (died). The 5th was Nero. His death was June 7, 68 A.D. (This verse puts us definitely before the complete destruction of Jerusalem by Sept. 8, 70 A.D.) The book of Revelation had to have been written then sometime before 70 A.D. This verse put us sometime during 68 A.D. Because the book was not written in a day, there is no exact day of the authorship of the book. John wrote the book over a period of time as he received the various visions in the book. John was exiled during the reign of Domitius Nero to Patmos and there began writing the book.

What Jesus says to the church of Philadelphia: "I will keep you from the hour of trial that is going to (Greek – mellouses, about to) come on the whole world," (Rev.3:10) seems to put us before the start of the 3 ½ years period of "great distress" that came upon the Jews until their destruction with the city of Jerusalem. That seems to indicate John wrote the churches (including Philadelphia) sometime at least at or before early 67 A.D. Sometime during the Time Nero persecuted Christians (A.D. 64-68) John was exiled to Patmos. Most likely then, John started writing the book of Revelation between 65-66 A.D., when John was first exiled, and wrote until after the death of Nero. Then John was set free after Nero's death and probably still wrote the rest of Revelation thereafter and again prophesied to the people, Rev.10:11.

"Five have fallen" – right after the death of Nero, Jun.9, A.D. 68.

"One is" – would put us at the start of the Roman "civil war". I believe this can refer to no other time than the time of Galba. As some say - "One is" refers to Vespasian, but then it would not be just five had fallen, but rather eight had fallen. We are at the time of Galba, not Vespasian. However, because 3 died, "fell", in the civil war (or "three horns were broken off," Dan.7:8), after the three were broken off, that would make Vespasian a sixth king, and his son Titus the seventh.

[After the death of 3 – Galba, Otho, and Vitellius, then Vespasian became emperor, Dec. A.D.69. He stabilized the kingdom and reigned 10 years]

"The other has not yet come" – (I believe this was Titus. He was the son of Vespasian and followed his father as emperor.) In Dan.7:8 he is called a "little horn" because Titus was not yet a king, but rather a prince. He was powerful as a general under his father Vespasian who by that time was an older man. Vespasian was born in Nov., A.D. 9. He became emperor at 70, in Dec, A.D.69. It was his son Titus who wielded the power of his father as general.

"When he does come, he must remain for a little while". Titus only reigned from June 24, 79 A.D. to Sept.13, 81 A.D. (2 years and 3 months). This would fit a reign that would be for "a little while."

Verse 11 The Beast Is An Eighth King

"The Beast who once was, and now is not, is an 8th King. He belongs to the seven and is going to his destruction. (NIV)

"The beast who once was, and now is not" (NIV)

"Is an 8th king." (NIV)

Now, looking ahead (with the Roman civil war over) John, in the book of Revelation seems to not consider the "kings of the Roman civil war", (Galba, Otho, and Vitellius) when mentioning an eighth king. The three in the civil war had not really established themselves as emperors in the empire. They were "broken off". So, Vespasian becomes the sixth, Titus the seventh, and Domitian the eighth emperor in John's description. If we were including the three that were broken off, historically Domitian would be the eleventh. However, the three broken off were insignificant players in what John is emphasizing. The three did not act as "beasts" or persecuting powers of Rome during the civil war. Rather, the empire struggled to exist. The "beastliness" resumed with Vespasian when he resumed putting down the Jewish rebellion. The "eight kings" John groups together were all of the same character – They loved Caesar worship and all acted like beasts. After the rule of the last one, Domitian, the rulership of the empire went back to the rule of the senate, and the empires' character changed.

Domitian was the eighth king. He became the eighth (when excluding the three of the civil war.) There is the symbolism of eight representing a new beginning, like the eighth day being the beginning of a new week. Jesus is represented by the number 888 because he was the "first from the dead", a new beginning, "born from the dead". Domitian is represented as the eighth king because he was like the seven, and represented a new beginning of the persecution of Christians from A.D. 89-96. Some think Domitian resumed persecution where Nero had left off. Some thought Domitian was Nero come back from the dead.

[Note: Remember, during the time of Daniel, the Jews were considered "God's chosen people" and "your people", Dan.12:1. That the emperor would "oppress his saints" would refer to first God's people as Daniel knew them, the Jews. Christians were not called Christians until (in the first century) they first were called Christians at Antioch, Acts 11:26. Vespasian and Titus persecuted the Jews and destroyed their city.)

Under the eighth king, Domitian, the persecuting power of the Roman empire was again against Christians, as it had been under Nero.

Verse 12. Ten Horns Are Ten Kings

"The ten horns you saw are 10 kings who have not yet received a kingdom, but who for 1 hour will receive Authority as kings along with the Beast. NIV

Who were the ten horns?

Rev.17 says,

1. The Ten Horns are <u>ten kings</u>, verse 12.
2. The Ten horns are on the heads of the beast (lesser powers controlled by the heads).
3. The ten horns are <u>on the beast</u> (Roman empire).
4. The Ten horns are <u>on the beast the woman (prostitute) rides</u>.
5. "Who have <u>not yet received a kingdom</u>," verse 12.
6. "For <u>one hour</u> will receive authority as kings along with the beast," verse 12.
7. "They will <u>make war against the Lamb</u>," verse 14.
8. "The ten horns you saw will <u>hate the prostitute</u>" (unfaithful Jerusalem), verse 16.
9. "They will <u>bring her to ruin</u>," verse 16.
10. "They will <u>burn her with fire</u>," verse 16.
11. "<u>God has put it in their heart to accomplish his purpose</u> by agreeing to give the beast their power," verse 17.

Let's observe:

1. "The ten horns are 10 kings, verse 12. <u>Kings</u> are from the Greek, <u>basileus.</u> The word is often times used in scripture to mean ruler or governor.
2. The ten horns are on the heads of the beast. The emperors have power over them. The horns were subject to the emperors of Rome. (The high priests of the Jews were chosen by Rome and removed by Rome at will.) Rome governed the Jews.
3. The ten horns are on the beast on which the woman rides. They have a relationship with the woman (prostitute). (The ten horns were related to the woman because they were the Jewish leaders and high priests.)
4. "Who have not yet received a kingdom". (NIV) They received their authority "for ONE HOUR". (They had authority as high priests under Rome, but

when they received "authority for ONE HOUR" it was not from Rome, but from God – to accomplish God's purpose in the destruction of Jerusalem. The Jewish leaders opposed Rome in the Jewish- Roman war and especially in the destruction of Jerusalem, but both Rome and the Jewish leaders "agreed together by their actions" in accomplishing God's purpose to destroy Jerusalem.)

5. "For ONE HOUR will receive authority as kings along with the beast."

"ONE HOUR" – is used in Revelation in different places:

Rev.3:10 – "I will keep you from the "hour of trial" that is going to come upon the whole world." (NIV) The church of Philadelphia was to be kept from that hour of trial. (cf. Lk.21:35)

Rev.14:7 – "because the hour of his judgment has come…" (NIV

Rev.18:10 – "In one hour your doom has come…" (NIV)

Rev.18:17 – "In one hour such great wealth has been brought to ruin!" (NIV)

Rev.18:19 – "In one hour she has been brought to ruin." (NIV)

Except for Rev.3:10, the other passages could fit the period of the Jewish War, from July, 66 to Sept 8, 70 A.D. One thinks of the 3 1/2 year (42 months, 1260 day) period. But Philadelphia was already in that period. John had been exiled to Patmos in that period and was a companion with the churches in the "suffering and the kingdom," 1:9.

The "ONE HOUR" seems to refer to the "five months" of 9:5. This was the period of the terrible siege of Jerusalem by Titus. The 5 month "hour of trial" of the whole earth was the "Day of the Lord", Judgment Day. That was the "Day" that would close unexpectedly like a trap, Lk.21:34," (or as a "thief in the night"). Jesus was telling Philadelphia, he would deliver them from the judgment on earth.

Who had authority with Rome for that "ONE HOUR"? (During the siege of Titus, to destroy Jerusalem, and burn her with fire, bringing her to her ruin?) Who helped Rome destroy Jerusalem?

Answer – The Jews - The rebellious rebels against Rome; they also destroyed the Temple and Jerusalem and helped Rome to burn it down. Who gave them authority (permission) to do it? God did! God gave the rebel Jews power to rule ONE HOUR, (during the siege) along with (together with Rome) to accomplish His purpose.

Rev.17:17 – "God put it into their hearts to accomplish his purpose (both rebel Jews and Rome accomplished his purpose, to fulfill the prophecies of the destruction of Jerusalem, T.S.) by agreeing to give the beast their power to rule UNTIL God's words are fulfilled." (NIV)

Notice: The Ten kings did not "get their power from Rome. They agreed to "give the beast their power" - UNTIL "God's words were fulfilled," verse 17. They had not received a kingdom. They were not already "kings" but rather received authority "as kings" together with Rome for "ONE HOUR".

The interpretation hinges on two things here: 1. the "ONE HOUR" -what period does it refer to; and 2. When did their authority to rule as kings start?

We have tried to answer what time the ONE HOUR refers to. Some believe the ONE HOUR to the 3 ½ years of the "Jewish Roman War."

There is evidence to support this. Josephus tells us about the beginning of the Jewish – Roman War in ("the Jewish War", Book 2, Chapters 17-18.

It started with Eleazar, the son of the high priest Ananias, forbidding that any foreign offerings be made in the Temple, even for the emperor. He stopped the daily sacrifice for the Romans. Before it started in July, 66A.D., the Jews already expected the war to begin. It was because of incidents that had happened under Gessius Florus. Gessius Florus was the procurator (governor) over Judea in Syria. He ruled from 64-66A.D. He was so violent and unjust with the people of Judea; a reaction to Florus' rule was made by Jewish Zealots. That stirred up a bigger reaction by Rome.

(Josephus, "Jewish Antiquities," Book 20, Chapter 11).

The zealots, in reacting to the cruel rule of Florus went out and slaughtered a Roman garrison in Jerusalem. Others seized weapons at Masada. Cestius Gallus, the legate of Syria, was Florus' supervisor. He responded to the Zealots by taking the Syrian army and surrounding Jerusalem, and besieging it. Jews strongly resisted. Cestius withdrew from Jerusalem. Zealots pursued the army from the rear, and killed in pursuit over time, 5300 footmen and 380 horsemen ("The Jewish War." Book 2, chapter 19.) This was the reason the Jews expected Rome to go to war with them.

Now, in preparation for the war that the Jews felt was inevitable with Rome; they got organized. Great numbers of Jews gathered in the Temple of Jerusalem and they appointed 10 generals for the war. Several generals were high priests or from their families. Josephus names these ten:

1. Joseph, son of Gorion, governor in Jer.

6. Joseph, son of Simon -sent to Jericho.

2. Ananus, the high priest, gov. in Jer.

7. Manasseh – sent to Perea.

3. Jesus, son of Sapphias.

8. John, the Essene – sent to Thamna.

4. Eleazar, son of Ananus.

9. John, son of Matthias- made governor of Gophnitica.

5. Niger, governor of Idumea

10. Josephus, son of Matthias – both Galilees.

These Ten were not yet governors (rulers) when John wrote 17:12, "who for ONE HOUR will receive authority as kings." (NIV) Just before the war, they were chosen as governors. That would imply that John was writing the Revelation BEFORE the Jewish War broke out in July, 66A.D. Even though John could have been exiled, Rev.1:9, at the beginning of Nero's Persecution of Christians after Rome burned, July18 -23, 64 A.D.; it was before the Jewish War started in July, 66 A.D., Rev.17:12. These Ten, from their appointment onward to the destruction of Jerusalem, 70 A.D. could have helped Rome in leading them "In the Jewish War" to the end, the destruction of Jerusalem. This would make the ONE HOUR equal to the 3 ½ years of the "Jewish War." The Ten Jewish generals would be the Ten horns.

Did we solve the mystery of the Ten Horns? No, not quite. All the pieces of God's word ALWAYS fit perfectly – like putting a puzzle together. The Spirit is guiding us. We ask for understanding. Yes, we have the pieces that fit this part of the puzzle assembled. We have now - where the Ten Horns came from. But are we right about "ONE HOUR equals 3 ½ years," the period of the Jewish War?

Look at the statements the Spirit has used to describe the Ten Horns and "Babylon" (the prostitute.)

Rev.18:8 says, "In ONE DAY her plagues will overtake her." (NIV) Yes, judgment of the Jew began with the Jewish War and the resistance of the ten generals. But the Ten generals or Ten horns are given "power of kings for ONE HOUR" (NIV) to bring the prostitute (the city where Jesus was crucified) to ruin, The "power of kings" was given for ONE HOUR to destroy Jerusalem. Rev.18:10 says,

"Woe! Woe! O great city, O Babylon, city of power! In one hour your doom has come!"

The 3 ½ years fit the period of the Jewish War. But, remember- "In ONE DAY her plagues will overtake her." 18:8.(NIV)

The ONE HOUR fits the "five months" of 9:5, the focus of time when Jerusalem was closed on like a trap (Lk.21:34), the siege of Titus. Then, she was destroyed, much from within by the Jews and by the Romans from without and finally coming in.

Again and again, Josephus blames the Jews for bringing on the war with Rome by their actions. But even more so he blames the Jews for the destruction of their own Temple and city, Jerusalem. In the (Preface of "The Jewish War", sect 4) by Josephus, he says –

"For that it was a rebellious temper of our own that destroyed it, and they were among the tyrants of the Jews who brought the Roman power upon us, who unwillingly attacked us, and occasioned the burning of our temple."

Why does the Ten Horns not fit the vassal kings? Or why not the auxillary - neighboring kings? It is true that kings under Roman rule, and neighboring kings of other nations helped. Yes, they hated the Jews and joined in. Let's notice though:

1. They had a kingdom already. It would not fit – "not yet received a kingdom."
2. They had power before the Jewish War. – that does not fit "received authority or power for one hour". And, "they received power for one hour – for "one purpose" – to destroy the prostitute.
3. They do not fit well with – "They will make war with the Lamb," 17:14.(NIV) The Jewish generals, many of whom were high priests or of the families of high priests, knew Jesus' (the Lamb) prophecy that Jerusalem would be destroyed. They thought they could prevent that prophecy, Mt.24, of Jesus, from coming true. They tried to "save the Temple" and their precious power and money machine. They even thought they had; when they defeated Cestius Gallus who had besieged Jerusalem and then withdrew. Then in 70 A.D. On the Passover, they let James the apostle, brother of Jesus, speak from the wing of the Temple to recant that "Jesus was soon coming back". James did not, but confirmed Jesus was soon to come. The high priests Ananus and others said-

"We did wrong in affording such testimony to Jesus." Hegessipus, quoted by Eusebius. The high priests were still "making war with the Lamb." The high priests had crucified Jesus, persecuted the apostles in their ministry, and were still opposing Christ and his prophecies even in 70 A.D. when Jesus' prophecies came true. The high priests and their family made war with the Lamb for 40 years and vehemently opposed him. They were highly convinced they were right- that Jesus could not be the Messiah and that he was a blasphemer since he claimed to be the "Son of God."

Verse 13. They Have One Purpose

"They have one purpose and will give their power and authority to the Beast. (NIV)

This verse points to the resolve of the leaders of the Jews and high priests, the ten chosen to be governors, to oppose Christ. They had "one purpose" to defend the Temple and Jerusalem" and defeat Christ's prophecy in Mt.24 that the Temple would be destroyed. They therefore resisted the Romans to the very end, thus destroying the Temple and Jerusalem. "By their resistance, they with the Romans (though with opposite intents) accomplished the same end – the destruction of Jerusalem.

The testimony of the history of Josephus adds weight to our understanding when he tells us that John, representing one of the three Jewish rebel factions that were tearing up the city of Jerusalem –

"set on fire those houses that were full of grain, and of all other provisions. The same thing was done by Simon (representing another faction in the city, T.S.), when upon the other's retreat, he attacked the city also; as if they had on purpose, "DONE IT TO SERVE THE ROMANS," by destroying what the city had laid up against the siege. ...Accordingly, it so came to pass, that all the places that were about the temple were burned down... almost all that grain was burned, which would have been sufficient for a siege of many years. So they were taken by means of the famine... The city was engaged in a war on all sides." (Josephus, "The Jewish War," Book 5, Chap.1, Sect.4). And again Josephus writes:

"For it was a rebellious temper of our own that destroyed it (Jerusalem), and that they were the tyrants among the Jews who brought the Roman powers upon us, who unwillingly attacked us, and occasioned the burning of our temple." (Josephus, "The Jewish Wars," Preface, Sect.4).

Verse 14. War Against The Lamb

"They will make war against the lamb, but the lamb will overcome them because he is Lord of lords and King of Kings- and with him will be his called, chosen, and faithful followers" (NIV)

The Jews and Jewish leaders opposed Christ; but no one can stand against God and win. Of course - the Lamb defeated them because He is the Lord of lords and King of kings both of heaven and on earth. God's appointed events and times in prophecy were to be definitely fulfilled AS THEY WERE PROPHESIED.

Verse 15. The Waters You Saw

"Then the angel said to me, 'the waters you saw, where the prostitute sits are peoples, multitudes, nations and languages." (NIV)

The prostitute is Jerusalem (see beginning of Chapter 17). Here John tells you the "waters" are symbolic of "peoples, multitudes, nations, and languages." Jerusalem sat in the midst of the different nations conquered by the Roman empire and surrounding the Roman empire. She was prominent among all peoples and nations. Chapter 18:10-17 speak of her wealth and prominence among the nations.

Josephus tells us: Jerusalem had arrived at a higher degree of felicity than any other city under the Roman government." (Josephus, "The Jewish War," Preface, Section 4). Jerusalem was highly prominent among the nations.

Verse 16. The Beast And Ten Horns Hate The Prostitute

"The Beast and the ten horns you saw will hate the prostitute. they will bring her to ruin and leave her naked; they will eat her flesh and burn her with fire." (NIV)

Both the Beast (Roman empire) and the ten horns (Jewish leaders and factions) will hate (and by their actions destroyed) the prostitute (Jerusalem on earth) and will eat her flesh (killed citizens of the city) and burn her with fire (literally burned the Temple and Jerusalem to the ground).

Verse 17. God Has Put It In Their Hearts

"For God has put it into their hearts to accomplish his purpose by agreeing to give the Beast their power to rule until God's words are fulfilled." (NIV)

God works all things after the council of his own will. No one can resist him. He can use the good and the bad of us to weave events and make his purpose happen. He predicted Jerusalem and the Temple would be destroyed. All prophecies come to pass AT THEIR APPOINTED TIME. There is nothing man can do to prevent that. GOD's WORDS ARE FULFILLED, Isa.46:10-11.

Verse 18. The Great City That Rules Over The Kings Of The Earth

"The woman you saw is the great City that rules over the kings of the earth." (NIV)

The woman you saw is the great city. The woman represents a city, a great city. How did she rule over the kings of the earth? She played the prostitute. They were allured by her, taken in by her. She ruled over them by her seductions and corruptive influence. Ezekial 5:5-7 says,

"This is what the sovereign Lord says: This is 'Jerusalem which I have set in the center of the nations', with countries all around her. Yet in her wickedness she has rebelled against my laws and decrees more than the nations and countries around her. She has rejected my laws and has not followed my decrees. Therefore, this is what the sovereign Lord says: You have been more unruly than the nations around you and have not followed my decrees or kept my laws. You have not even conformed to the standards of the nations around you." (NIV)

That was said of the Jews in Ezekiel's time. How much more it was true of the Jews who had crucified the "son of God", and persecuted and killed apostles and saints in the first century.

CHAPTER EIGHTEEN

THE FALL OF BABYLON

Verse 1. The Earth Was Illuminated

"After this I saw another angel coming down from heaven. He had great Authority, and the Earth was illuminated by his splendor." (NIV)

Verse 2. Fallen! Fallen is Babylon The Great

"With a mighty voice he shouted: Fallen! Fallen is Babylon the Great! she has become a home for demons, and a haunt for every evil spirit, a haunt for every unclean and detestable bird." (NIV)

Who is Babylon the great? She is the "great city, which is figuratively called Sodom and Egypt (or "Babylon", T.S.), where also their Lord was crucified." Rev.11:9. (NIV)

She is called the "great city" -18:10,16, 19,21. She is the great prostitute sitting on a scarlet beast, 17:3; and is called Babylon the great, mother of prostitutes, 17:5. She is the great prostitute, 19:2, on whom God has avenged the blood of his servants (the prophets), 19:2. God judged her for the way she treated the saints, the apostles, and the prophets, 18:19-20.

"She has become a home for demons". (NIV)

This again reminds me of what Jesus predicted in Matt.12:43-45, where Jesus tells of seven demons who were even worse than the first, who filled the man's house that had been swept clean. There Jesus said, "The final condition of that man is worse than the first. That is how it will be with this wicked generation." (NIV). Jerusalem became a home for demons. Jerusalem went from bad, to worse, to totally sinful and corrupt. Jerusalem was the place where the Pharisees, the Sadducees, the Sanhedrin (the elders of Israel), the scribes, and the experts of the law, all condemned our savior to the cross. It was from the Jewish high priests and leaders of the Jews that letters were sent to drag men and women that were Christians back to Jerusalem for prison and death. It was from the Jewish leaders of different cities that riots and mobs were stirred up against the teachers of Jesus. It was still the high priest Ananias, his family and sons involved in the murder of James on the wing of the temple (according to Josephus). They were actively trying to change the appointed times of God to destroy Jerusalem for her wickedness. Their history testifies against them to the very end. They became a home for demons. In the first century, they had truly become demon-possessed; a people who belonged to their father the devil, Jn.8:44. They did the works of their father.

The phrase is repeated with three different expressions to emphasize what they were – of the devil. Such parallelism of equal ideas is called a Jewish Hebraism.

Verse 3. The Maddening Wine Of Her Adulteries

"For all the nations have drunk the maddening wine of her adulteries. The kings of the earth committed adultery with her, and the merchants of the earth grew rich from her excessive luxuries." (NIV)

Why was Jerusalem called a prostitute? Why is she said to have caused the nations to be drunk with the wines of her adulteries?

She was supposed to be the bride of God. She was never faithful. She went after other lovers. Look at Jer.3:1-2. Israel lived as a prostitute with many lovers. There he calls Israel "faithless Israel." God says, "I gave faithless Israel her certificate of divorce and sent her away because of her adulteries." Jer.3:8. "Yet I saw her unfaithful sister Judah had no fear; she also went out and committed adultery." (NIV) Both the Northern and southern kingdoms were unfaithful to God. God says in Ezek.5:5-7: that he had set Jerusalem "in the center of the nations", with countries all around her. "Yet in her wickedness she has rebelled against my laws and decrees MORE THAN the nations and countries around her." (NIV)

Jerusalem was more wicked than the nations she committed adultery with! In the first century, she was very dark with sin. She crucified our savior. Jesus repeatedly commented on how sinful and wicked she was. Look at these passages: Mt.12:39; and 16:4 – "A wicked and adulterous generation"; (NIV) Mt.17:17 and Lk.9:41– "unbelieving and perverse generation;" (NIV) Mk.8:38 – "adulterous and sinful generation;"(NIV) Lk 11:29 – "a wicked generation." (NIV) In Phil.2:15 she is called "a crooked and depraved generation." (NIV) Peter said on the day of Pentecost – "save yourselves from this corrupt generation." Acts 2:40 (NIV)

Verse 4. Come Out Of Her My People

"Then I heard another voice from Heaven say, 'come out of her my people so that you will not share in her sins, so that you will not receive any of her plagues;'" (NIV)

Jesus had warned his followers – "when you see standing in the holy place 'the abomination that causes desolation'… flee to the mountains." (NIV) Mt.24:15-16. He told them, "When you see Jerusalem being surrounded by armies, you will know that its desolation is near." Lk.21:20. (NIV) Here, God calls out to his people, the true people of God – "Come out of her my people." – Why? "so that you will not receive any of her plagues." (NIV)

Verse 5. Her Sins Are Piled Up To Heaven

"For her sins are piled up to heaven, and God has remembered her crimes." (NIV)

"For her sins are piled up to heaven." (NIV)

God does not come to judgment but after much long suffering and appealing. He is not willing that any should perish (without trying hard to get people to repent first). God states a principle in Gen 15:16: "In the fourth generation your descendants will come back here, for the sin of the Amorite has not yet reached its full measure." (NIV) When the sin of the Amorite was filled up, had become so sinful that it was time to bring judgment; then, God came in judgment on them.

Jerusalem's sins were piled up to heaven. They certainly had reached their "full measure." When God decides it is time for judgment, no pleading will change the judgment he has determined. In the prophets he told the prophets. In Jer.15:1 God tells the prophet: "Even if Moses and Samuel were to stand before me, my heart would not go out to these people. Send them away from my presence." (NIV) Ezek.14:14 says: "Even if these three men – Noah, Daniel and Job – were in it, they could save only themselves by their righteousness." (NIV) There comes a time when judgment is confirmed; judgment is determined; and we cannot affect the verdict.

"For her sins are piled up to heaven." (NIV)

Josephus testifies to the utter corruption of Jerusalem".

Verse 6. Pay Her Back Double

"Give back to her as she has given; pay her back double for what she has done. Mix her double portion from her own cup." (NIV)

"Give back to her as she has given." (NIV)

This principle is in the prophets throughout. In Jer.51:49 it says: "Babylon must fall because of Israel's slain. Just as the slain in all the earth have fallen because of Babylon." So too here, the figurative Babylon, Jerusalem must be paid back for what she had done. Jesus had said: "Because of this, God in his wisdom said, 'I will send them prophets and apostles, some of whom they will kill and others they will persecute. Therefore, this generation will be held responsible for the blood of all the prophets that has been shed from the beginning of the world, from the blood of Abel to the blood of Zechariah who was killed between the altar and the sanctuary. Yes, I tell you, this generation will be held responsible for all of it." Lk.11:49-51. (NIV)

"Pay her back double for what she has done." (NIV)

Again, the thought is repeated in a different way to emphasize what is said, "mix her double portion from her own cup."

The concept of repaying in double for what someone has done is not new with God. In the law, in Ex.22:4 a thief was to pay back double. The one to whom the judge declared guilty must pay double to his neighbor, Ex.22:9. When this principle is extended and applied, we can see that when you rob a neighbor of peace, of property, of honest judgment, of life, or anything else; he must pay back double. Isa.40:2 talks of Jerusalem and says, "her sin has been paid for, that she has received from the Lord's hand double for all her sins." (NIV) Jer. 16:18 says "I will repay them double for their wickedness and their sin, because they have defiled my land with the lifeless forms of their vile images and have filled my inheritance with their detestable idols." (NIV) Then, in Jer.17:18 he says, "Bring on them the day of disaster; <u>destroy them with double destruction</u>." (NIV)

<u>Did God destroy them here with double destruction?</u>

I think he did, just as the law he set up required. The Jews were shut up into the city of Jerusalem by the besieging army of Titus. Jesus warned them, "that day will close on you unexpectedly like a trap." Lk 21:34 (NIV) They could not get out. They could not escape that judgment. It was judgment on men executed by the Roman army. But more so, even by the Jewish factions that warred each other inside. Josephus describes them as Like men who had gone mad. It was a judgment that was by men upon men – horrible and ruthless. Yet, I cannot help but the judgment of the divine was also executed. I remember what Jesus said of "the seven demons who came back and inhabited the man, in Mt.12:43-45. There he said – so it would be with his generation. Rev.9 speaks of the demons who are let loose from the abyss and for five months (the siege of Titus lasted five months) are allowed to "torture them, but not kill them", Rev.9:5. (NIV) "During those days men will seek death, but will not find it, they will long to die, but death will elude them." (NIV) They suffered unimaginably. Jesus said, "For there will be great distress, unequaled from the beginning of the world until now- and never to be equaled again," Mt.24:21. (NIV).

But, there was a <u>second destruction</u>, the destruction in the heavens when they were judged. Lk. 19 tells of a son who went into a far country to have himself appointed as king and then to return. The subjects there hated him, and did not want him to be king over them. He was made king however. And returned home. The enemies of his, who did not want him to be king over them – "brought them before him and had them killed in front of him." Lk.19:27 (NIV) This reminds me of what he says in Rev.14:9-10 which says –

"If anyone worships the beast and his image and receives his mark on the forehead or on the hand, he too will drink of the wine of God's fury, which has been poured full strength into the cup of his wrath. He will be tormented with burning sulfur in the presence of the holy angels and of the Lamb."(NIV)

Verse 7. Give Her As Much Torture

"Give her as much torture and grief as the glory and luxury she gave herself. In her heart she boasts, 'I sit as Queen; I am not a widow, and I will never mourn.'" (NIV)

"I sit as Queen"

In Ezek.16:1-15, God uses an allegory to describe unfaithful Jerusalem. There she was dressed in a beautiful dress and ornaments. A beautiful crown was put on her head. She rose to be a queen, verse13. Her fame spread among the nations. She trusted in her beauty and used her fame to become a prostitute and lavished her favors on any one who passed by. She was really shameful and naked and destitute of true riches. In the first century she was even more shameful and sinful.

"I am not a widow." (NIV)

Being a widow was not a good thing in Jewish culture. The widow is often grouped with the orphan. They did not belong to anyone. They were often abandoned and on their own. Scriptures repeatedly command not to oppress or mistreat the widow and the fatherless. Jesus tells of the poor widow who gave less than a penny; and she had given all she had, Mk.12:42. 1 Tim.5:5 speaks of the widow in need. The picture was grim for the widow. Here in verse 7, Jerusalem says – I am not a widow (in society the widow was the lowliest, the most needy, and helpless). No – Jerusalem saw herself as a queen! She sat in the center of the nations and got the nations drunk with the wine of her adulteries.

"I will never mourn." (NIV)

Jerusalem saw herself as one who would go on and on, enjoying her selfish indulgence, reigning in luxury and power. She is called Babylon for a reason. One reason was she had the pompous spirit, the insolence of Babylon. The nation of Babylon thought like Jerusalem. Babylon thought – "I am the queen of kingdoms. I will continue forever – the eternal queen", Isa.47:5-7. (NIV) God brought Babylon to ruin. God brought Jerusalem to ruin. Jerusalem was the "daughter of Babylon". It was in Shinar (Babylon) that the Tower of Babel was built. At its top was a temple dedicated to the gods of the stars. After men's languages were confused, the influence of Babel spread all over the world, with ziggurats (step – pyramids) erected with temples at the top. Idolatry spread from Babylon. So too, Jerusalem followed suit. She indulged in idolatry and joined in with the nations; doing it more than even the nations. She was unfaithful to God. Jerusalem was the "mother of harlots." God destroyed her.

Verse 8. In One Day Her Plagues Will Overtake Her

"Therefore in one day her plagues will overtake her; death, mourning and famine. She will be consumed by fire, for mighty is the Lord God who judges her." (NIV)

"Therefore, in one day her plagues will overtake her." (NIV)

The <u>one day</u> suggests the quickness in which she was brought down. Jerusalem was brought down in a matter of days.

"<u>One day</u>" – prophetically seems to refer to the period of time in which she was judged and destroyed." Look at these verses that help us.

Lk.17:30-31 "It will be just like this on <u>the day that the Son of Man is revealed</u>. <u>On that day</u> no one who is on the roof of his house, with his goods inside, should go down to get them. Likewise, no one in the field should go back for anything. Remember Lot's wife! Whoever tries to keep his life will lose it." (NIV)

From this verse we learn that <u>the day of judgment began</u> – "when the son of man was revealed" that "<u>On that day</u>" the Christian Jews are warned not to hesitate by trying to gather anything – but to get out. "Remember Lot's wife" Jesus says. "Don't look back." The judgment is called "the Day of the Lord". It is not a single day, but it starts on a certain day. It is the day he begins to judge. He says in-

Lk.21:20-21 "When you see Jerusalem being surrounded by armies, you will know that its desolation is near. Then let those who are in Judea flee to the mountains, let those in the city get out, and let those in the country not enter the city. For this is the time of punishment in fulfillment of all that has been written." (NIV)

When did the "time of punishment" begin? When they saw the armies surround Jerusalem. This was the beginning of the "day of the Lord." This was the "time of punishment." This was the time of "judgment."

Lk.21:34-35 says "...that day will close on you unexpectedly like a trap. For it will come upon all those who live on the face of the earth. (In other words, it will come upon them like a thief.) Be always on the watch, and pray that you may be able to escape all that is about to happen, and that you may be able to stand before the Son of Man." (NIV)

The "day" refers to the "time of punishment," when the Romans surrounded Jerusalem and besieged it like a trap, Lk. 21:34. People were let in, but people were not let out. The Romans besieged Jerusalem from April 14 to Sept.8 when it had totally fallen. Their besiegement of Jerusalem was for five months. That was the "time of punishment"; the judgment upon the Jew and their nation.

Rev.18:8 "in one day her plagues will overtake her... death, mourning and famine. She will be consumed by fire." (NIV)

In Jn.11:24, Martha says, "I know he will rise again in the resurrection at the last day." That last day occurred when the armies surrounded Jerusalem. I believe the resurrection occurred just before the beginning of judgment. That is what we see in Rev.11 of the two witnesses. Verse 11-12 says, "But after the three and a half days a breath of life from God entered them and they stood on their feet, and terror struck those who saw them. Then I heard a loud voice (Jesus' voice) from heaven saying to them, 'Come up here'. And they went up to heaven in a cloud, while their enemies looked on." (NIV)

If that understanding is correct, the Lord came on Resurrection Day. Then, the judgment of the Jews in Jerusalem began.

The "day of the Lord" is coupled with the "hour". The "day of his judgment", or the "hour of his judgment", happens the same day. Mt.24:36 says, "No one know about the day or hour." Jesus had taught that when the gospel had been preached in all the world (Jewish world) …then the end would come," Mt.24:14. (NIV) In Rev. 14:6 you see an angel who "had the eternal gospel to preach – to those who live on the earth… He said in a loud voice 'Fear God and give him glory, because the hour of his judgment has come."(NIV) In this passage, it is called "the hour of his judgment."

In contrast to the "one day" is the "One Hour."

Rev.18:10 "in one hour your doom has come."

Rev.18: 17 "in one hour such great wealth has been brought to ruin."

Rev.18:19 "in one hour she has been brought to ruin."

I believe this "in one hour" expresses the quickness and unexpectedness the judgment comes upon them.

"She will be consumed by fire." (NIV)

Jerusalem was burned up. This is emphasized in Rev.18 several times: verses 8,9,18. Jesus had predicted this. Jesus tells the story of the king who invited his servants to come to his banquet. His servants paid no attention. Mt.22:7 gives the king's response.

"The king was enraged. He sent his army and destroyed those murderers and burned their city." (NIV)

Josephus speaks of the Temple being destroyed by fire:

"But as for that house (holy house), God had for certain long ago doomed it to the fire; and now that fatal day was come, according to the revolution of the ages; it was the tenth day of the month Lous [Ab] upon which it was formerly burned by the king of Babylon; although these flames took their rise from the Jews themselves, and were occasioned by them… (Josephus, "The Jewish Wars," Book 6; Chap.4; Sect.5). "The same month and day were now observed, as I said before, wherein the holy house was burned by the Babylonians." (Josephus, "The Jewish Wars," Book 6; Chap 4: Sect. 8).

Different parts of the city were burned as three Jewish factions fought each other in the city. They set fire to storehouses of grain. They set fire to people's houses; and to the house of the high priest and rulers' houses. Their barbarity was toward their own countrymen; putting the defenseless to the sword, piling up bodies, carrying on carnage without a conscience.

Peter talks about it in 2 Pet.2:7; in parallel with the judgment of Noah's world which was destroyed in verse 6:

"By the same word the present heavens and earth are <u>reserved for fire</u>, being kept for the <u>day of judgment and destruction of ungodly men</u>."

(Note: The physical heaven and earth were not burned up by fire. Rather, the ungodly of heaven and earth were destroyed by fire. Many Jewish cities were burned by fire during the Jewish – Roman war from 66-70 A.D. The main Jewish city, Jerusalem, was destroyed by fire in 70 A.D. In the heavens, where the wicked principalities and powers in the heavens come against Jesus (the Battle of Gog or Satan and Magog) – they were destroyed by fire. Ezek.39:6 says, "I will <u>send fire</u> on Magog (the land of Gog or Satan)." Heaven and earth were reserved for fire – a fiery judgment of the wicked. Notice that Jesus says – "Heaven and earth <u>will pass away</u>. But my words will never pass away." Mt.34-35. If we understand what is meant by "<u>heaven and earth</u>"; the <u>physical</u> heaven and earth did not "pass away, but rather its wicked inhabitants passed away in judgment." (See Appendix – "Heaven and earth."). The world of the first century "perished" and was judged (in A.D. 70), just as "the world that then was" of Noah's time "perished" and was judged.

Verse 9. The Kings Of The Earth - See The Smoke Of Her Burning

"When the kings of the Earth who committed adultery with her and shared her luxury see the smoke of her burning, they will weep and mourn over her." (NIV)

The nations around Judah and Jerusalem all had dealings with the Jews. Her trade with the world was extensive. The Gentile nations came to Jerusalem to the temple. Jews from all the nations where they had been scattered came to Jerusalem at least three times a year for the Festivals of Passover, Shavuot, and Sukkot. There were money exchangers for currency from all these nations. They preferred the currency of Tyre, likely because it was of good silver and true weight. There was trade and cargo there from all over the world.

The scripture here says they "shared her luxury." Many were very rich. Some had their own vineyards and wine presses, their own olive trees and presses; their own gardens and family cemeteries. Their houses were grandeur and they had many servants and slaves. Jerusalem was full of luxury and opulence. Jerusalem was corrupt and supplied them with much in indulging in the flesh.

They "see the smoke of her burning" (NIV)

Repeated and emphasized in the text. She was a total loss. She was erased, broken, and perished.

Verse 10. In One Hour Your Doom Has Come

"Terrified at her torment, they will stand far off and cry: "Woe! Woe! Oh, great City, Oh Babylon, city of power! In one hour, your doom has come!" (NIV)

"In one hour, your doom has come."

(See comment verse 8).

Verse 11. No One Buys Their Cargoes

"The merchants of the Earth will weep and mourn over her because no one buys their cargos anymore"- (NIV)

Evidently, as indicated in these verses, Jerusalem was heavily involved in trade of all kinds with nations all around her.

Verse 12. Cargoes Of

"Cargoes of gold, silver, precious stones and pearls; fine linen, purple, silk and Scarlet cloth; every sort of Citron wood, and articles of every kind made of ivory, costly wood, bronze, iron and marble;" (NIV)

Verse 13. Cargoes Of

"Cargoes of cinnamon and spice, of incense, myrrh, and frankincense, of wine and olive oil, a fine flour and wheat; cattle and sheep; horses and carriages; and bodies and Souls of men." (NIV)

Verse 14. The Fruit Is Gone From You

"They will say, 'the fruit you long for is gone from you. All your riches and splendor have vanished, never to be recovered." (NIV)

Verse 15. Terrified At Her Torment

"The merchants who sold these things and gained their wealth from her will stand far off, terrified at her torment. They will weep and mourn"- (NIV)

The money changers at the temple courts may be firstly indicated here. They were merchants who sold animals for sacrifice. It was easier for Jewish travelers who came from all the nations to which they had been scattered to buy animals from the temple merchants when they got to Jerusalem, than to bring the animals all the way with them. The Jewish travelers came to Jerusalem for the three main Jewish festivals.

The money changers also exchanged currency that was from all over the world for a fee. From the description here in Revelation, merchants from all over were trading with Jerusalem and it was a big business, very rich and lucrative. Josephus and Tacitus describe some of the houses of Jerusalem having their own gardens, and own private graveyards, groves of trees, and servant's quarters. They had grand halls and special buildings for their parties and lascivious affairs. Tacitus says the city of Jerusalem had over 600,000 in population in the first century. Josephus says there were about 1,100,000 who died in Jerusalem when it was destroyed. Because many Jews came to Jerusalem for the Passover, Josephus' large number who were killed makes sense. Many more would have been in Jerusalem at the time of the Passover.

Josephus records – "Now the number of those that were carried captive during this whole war was collected to be ninety-seven thousand; as was the number of those that perished during the whole siege eleven hundred thousand, the greater part of whom were indeed of the same nation [with the citizens of Jerusalem], but not belonging to the city itself; for they were come up from all the country to the Feast of Unleavened Bread, and were on a sudden shut up by an army." (Josephus, "The Jewish War", Chap.9, sect.3)

Verse 16. Woe! Woe! Oh Great City

"And cry out: Woe! Woe! Oh, great City, dressed in fine linen purple and scarlet, and glittering with gold and precious stones and pearls!" (NIV)

"Woe! Woe! Oh, great city." (NIV)

Josephus speaks of a man who four years before the Jewish war began pronounced "Woe, Woe, to Jerusalem" through the streets of Jerusalem. At that time the city was at peace and prosperity. The man cried out "A voice from the East, a voice from the West, a voice from the four winds, a voice against Jerusalem and the holy house…a voice against this whole people." Even though the man was chastised, flogged, and tortured; his message did not change. His voice was loud at the festivals. He continued for seven years and five months. He continued to cry out through the siege of Titus. Finally, one day he cried out – "Woe! Woe! To the city and Woe to myself also". A stone from one of the Roman engines stuck him and killed him. (Josephus, "The Jewish War," Book 6; Chap.5; Sect. 3).

Verse 17. Such Great Wealth Has Been Brought To Ruin

"In one hour such great wealth has been brought to ruin!' Every sea captain, and all who travel by ship, the sailors, and all who earned their living by the sea, will stand far off." (NIV)

"In one hour, such great wealth has been brought to ruin."

(See verse 8). Even John said, "Dear children, it is the last hour; and as you have heard that the antichrist is coming, even now, many antichrists have come. This is how we know it is the last hour." NIV I Jn. 2:18-19. One hour is not a literal one hour, but simply we are at the very end. Jerusalem fell in a very short time. Earlier in the New Testament, the scripture refers to things being the "last time" or the last days". By the time you get to I John, John says it was the "last hour". Time was progressively getting much shorter before the "end of all things" – meaning the culmination of the ages under the Mosaic period.

Verse 18. The Smoke Of Her Burning

"When do you see the smoke of her burning, exclaim, 'was there ever a city like this great City?'" (NIV)

"The smoke of her burning"

This is emphasized. In a very vivid mental picture, it emphasizes the finality of her destruction. It emphasizes the completeness of her judgment.

Verse 19. All The Ships Had Become Rich

"They will throw dust on their heads, and with weeping and mourning cry out: Woe! Woe! oh great city, where all who had ships on the sea became rich through her wealth! In one hour, she has been brought to ruin!" (NIV)

Again, this verse emphasizes how quickly Jerusalem was brought to ruin. This also seems to indicate the close trade between ships and what came through Jerusalem. That would tie the economies of Tyre (Marketplace of the nations, Isa. 23:3) closely with Jerusalem.,

Verse 20. Rejoice Saints, Apostles, and Prophets

"Rejoice over her, O heaven! rejoice, Saints and apostles and Prophets! God has judged her for the way she treated you." (NIV)

Here we see the response of God's people. They rejoice because it is victory. Wickedness has been repaid. Our savior was victorious. He has vindicated his people and his martyrs – saints, apostles, and prophets.

"God had judged her for the way she treated you". (NIV)

Jerusalem shed their blood. Jerusalem persecuted God's people. Mt.23:33-38. Jerusalem would be held responsible for all of the bloodshed of God's people, Lk.11:50-51.

Verse 21. A Boulder The Size Of A Large Millstone

"Then a mighty Angel picked up a boulder the size of a large Millstone and threw it into the sea, and said, 'With such violence the great city of Babylon will be thrown down never to be found again." (NIV)

"A large millstone". Here John helps us recall what Jesus said, "But is anyone causes one of these little ones who believe in me to sin, it would be better for him to have a large millstone hung around his neck and to be drowned in the depths of the sea, Mt.18:6: Lk 17:2. NIV. Here in this verse of Revelation, the whole city of Jerusalem is thrown into the sea with great violence. This is figurative of God's judgment of the wicked.

"Never be found again." (NIV)

The city of Jerusalem, the center of the world and the Mosaic law, the center of all priestly, sacrificial, and ceremonial functions, was destroyed. That world system would never be rebuilt again. That city (as she was) and Temple would never be rebuilt again.

Yes, the city was rebuilt by Emperor Hadrian in 130 A.D. and the city was renamed Aelia Capitolina at that time. But the city never has existed as it did in the first century. It has never been and will never be the center of the "world order" - which reigned under the Mosaic covenant, again. Christ's kingdom is eternal and He reigns forever. The Jews will never be the center of world rule again. Nor will that city and the temple ever be rebuilt to become as it was before in the first century.

Josephus said, "From King David, who was the first of the Jews who reigned therein, to the destruction under Titus were one thousand one hundred and seventy-nine years. But from its first building, until this last destruction were two thousand one hundred and seventy-seven years; yet has not its great antiquity, not its vast riches, nor the diffusion of its nation over all the habitable earth, nor the greatness of the veneration paid to it on a religious account, been sufficient to preserve it from being destroyed." (Josephus, "The Jewish Wars," Chap.10, sect.1).

Verse 22. Never Be Heard In You Again

"The music of harpists and musicians, flute players and trumpeters, will never be heard in you again. No workman of any trade will ever be found in you again. The sound of a millstone will never be heard in you again." (NIV)

Verse 23. By Your Magic Spell - Led Astray

"The light of a lamp will never shine in you again. The voice of a bridegroom and bride will never be heard in you again. Your merchants were the world's great men. By your magic spell all the nations were led astray." (NIV)

"The light of a lamp will never shine in you again. The voice of a bridegroom will never be heard in you again." Why? Because the judgment of earthly Jerusalem was final. She as the center for the worship of Jehovah would never happen again. She would never exist again as God's people. The Mosaic system that she represented was cancelled, abolished, done away with, and so was she. She was wicked and God destroyed her. HE WAS DONE WITH HER. In her place, God built the HEAVENLY JERUSALEM that will be for ever and ever.

Verse 24. In Her - The Blood Of Prophets And Saints

"In her was found the blood of prophets and of the saints, and of all who have been killed on the Earth." (NIV)

The city (earthly Jerusalem of the first century) that was responsible for the blood of the prophets, and the saints, will not exist again.

Israel today, was established on May 14, 1948, by David Ben-Gurion. The same day, president Harry S. Truman also recognized Israel as a new nation. However, God is not bringing back Israel. The people there are not descended from Abraham. They cannot trace their lineage. The records of genealogy were destroyed with the destruction of Jerusalem. Though some argue that they are Jews by genetics, no one today can trace his lineage to Abraham. The records are not there. Nor can any of them trace their ancestry to Aaron to show they are of the priestly tribe. Israel today has no priesthood. They have no temple. They have no true Jewish ancestry. They do not represent the God of the Jewish faith. There is no Jewish law given to them by God that still guides them. They are a modern creation. The earthly Jerusalem will not have part with the heavenly Jerusalem, Gal.4:30.

We do not even have prophets today. The office was fulfilled with the "completion of the age" (in the first century). They were "abolished"

(Greek – katargethesontai, "abolished, done away, canceled") along with the gift of knowledge in 1 Cor.13:8-10. They were abolished because they represented "part by part revelations" and when the "complete thing (Greek – telios) comes" (it did with our New Testament), the thing in part was done away. Daniel had prophesied of this time – "the completion of the age" when he told us it would "seal up vision and prophecy." Dan.9:24.

CHAPTER NINETEEN

HALLELUJAH!

Verse 1. The Roar Of A Great Multitude

"After this I heard what sounded like the roar of a great multitude in heaven shouting: 'Hallelujah! Salvation and Glory and power belong to our God," (NIV)

This is the saints of heaven celebrating the Fall of Babylon the Great (earthly Jerusalem). She was the harlot who betrayed her Lord. Once the earthly Jerusalem fell; the heavenly tabernacle of God could be "opened up", Heb.9:8, and all nations could flow into it, Isa.2.

"salvation" (NIV)

When Jesus returned ("at that time"- of the destruction of Jerusalem, Mt.24:30) He brought with him "salvation to those waiting for him," Heb.9:28. They were waiting eagerly for the "redemption of their bodies," Rom.8:23. Jesus brought "salvation" when he came.

"glory" (NIV)

Rom.8:18 says, "I consider that our present sufferings are not worthy to be compared with the glory that will be in us." When was that? That glory was when Christ came and resurrected his people. They received salvation and glory. 2 Thess.1:10 says, On the day he comes to be glorified in his holy people and to be marveled at among all those who have believed." (NIV)

"Salvation, glory, and power" (NIV)

All this comes from the Lord. Jesus accomplished all of this for his people. Here, heaven rejoices over what he has done.

Verse 2. True And Just Are His Judgments

"For true and just are his judgments. He has condemned the great prostitute who corrupted the Earth by her adulteries. He has Avenged on her the blood of his servants." (NIV)

"Vengeance is mine, saith the Lord", Rom.12:17-19. (NIV) God does bring justice. The saints witnessed God's vengeance upon their enemies. That normally is not seen in this life; but it definitely occurs in the spiritual world at judgment. In this context, wicked Jews (most of them in Jerusalem) had persecuted the prophets, and the saints, and had crucified the Lord of Glory, Mt.23:33-38. They had continued to persecute Christians after Christ was crucified for the next forty years. Jerusalem was the center and leadership of that persecution by the Jews. God ended it for that corrupt city in 70 A.D. God punished the enemies of God.

Verse 3. The Smoke Of Her Goes Up For Ever And Ever

"And again they shouted: 'Hallelujah!' The smoke from her goes up forever and ever." (NIV)

The saints here rejoice over the judgment of the wicked! "Hallelujah!" they shout. Is that Ok? What about Prov.17:5 that says, "He who mocks the poor shows contempt for their maker; whoever gloats over disaster will not go unpunished." (NIV) What is the difference between gloating over those hurt by life and natural disaster and the judgment that happens in this chapter? On earth, disasters and stations in life are circumstantial. Men have no control over what happens to them. They do have control over the choices they make. God is not mocked – the consequences of our choices are certain and just. That is judgment. Those who have done evil are punished, and we rejoice in God's judgment of the wicked. They had ample chances in life to turn from sin, as do we all.

Verse 4. The Twenty-four Elders And Four Living Creatures

"The twenty-four elders, and the four living creatures fell down and worship to God, who was Seated on the throne. and I cried: 'Amen, hallelujah!'" (NIV)

In the scene John sees, all are in agreement and rejoicing over God's justice.

Verse 5. Praise Our God All You His Servants

"Then a voice came from the throne saying: 'Praise our God all you his servants, you who fear Him, both small and great!'" (NIV)

"<u>A voice came from the throne</u>."(NIV)

God participates with us. He even commands us – "<u>Praise our God all you his servants</u>." (NIV) We Praise him for his justice. We praise him for his glory. We praise him for his salvation. We praise him for his power. We praise him for his wisdom. We praise him for his Love and forgiveness. WE PRAISE HIM – for ever and ever.

Verse 6. Our Lord God Almighty Reigns

"Then I heard what sounded like a great multitude, like the roar of rushing waters and like loud peals of thunder, shouting: 'Hallelujah! for our Lord God Almighty reigns." (NIV)

I believe this is at the time, Jesus has defeated his enemies, raised his people, judged the wicked, and glorified his saints. Now, he turns the kingdom back to the Father, 1 Cor.15:25-28. The response of those in heaven is – "Hallelujah! For our Lord God Almighty (the Father) reigns." That means then, that all has been accomplished by God's Son. God, the Father - his purpose in Christ has been fulfilled. Now, the wedding with Jesus' bride can take place.

Verse 7. The Wedding Of The Lamb Has Come

"Let us rejoice and be glad and give him glory! for the wedding of the Lamb has come, and his bride has made herself ready." (NIV)

Those words are words to celebrate and rejoice to. Following the understanding of Jewish customs (concerning espousal and weddings) we can see a beautiful picture of Christ and the church, his bride, revealed to us. The bride had been espoused to Jesus on earth. How? Jesus paid the dowry price. He purchased the church with his own blood. He died for her. That means, she became his property. The church belongs to Christ. We are not our own. Jesus also gave His chief gift to her – the Holy Spirit. The gifts of an espoused husband was given to the woman so she could properly adorn herself with beauty and graciousness, ready for his return. In this verse – "<u>his bride has made herself ready</u>." Spiritually speaking, the church makes herself ready for Christ by following His chief gift, the Spirit, and walking with the Spirit. The church by this grows in the fruit of the Spirit, and adorns herself with Christ, Rom.13:14. She is transformed, 2 Cor.3:18, and made ready, that she might present herself as a radiant church, without stain or wrinkle, holy and blameless, Eph.5:27. In the meantime, Jesus told his followers – "In my Fathers house are many rooms… I am going there to prepare a place for you. I will come back and take you to be with me." Jn.14:2-3 (NIV) Jesus went and cleansed the heavens. He defeated all the enemies in the heavenly realms, Eph.6:12 with Rom.16:20; Heb.2:14; 1 Cor.15:26,54; and many scriptures. He prepared the heavenly Jerusalem and made it ready for his bride. Then, Jesus came back to get his bride (his second coming in 70 A.D.) and resurrected her. Now, in this verse 7, "the wedding of the Lamb had come." The bride was to join with Jesus (God) as one. She would become one with him forever and dwell with her in the heavens. They are having spiritual children, as faith in Christ is embraced from generation to generation on earth. Eccl.1:4 says, "Generations come and generations go, but the earthy remains forever." (NIV) Isa.66:11 speaks of the heavenly Jerusalem and says, "For you will nurse and be satisfied at her comforting breasts; you will drink deeply and delight in her overflowing abundance." (NIV) Jesus has greatly honored his bride. We – are his bride.

Verse 8. Fine Linen, Bright And Clean

"Fine linen, bright and clean, was given to her to wear. (Fine linen stands for the righteous acts of the saints.) (NIV)

"<u>Fine linen, bright and clean</u>". (NIV)

John explains the symbolism – "<u>Fine linen stands for the righteous acts of the saints</u>." "The righteous acts of the saints." What are they? We should each search them out in our own lives. What things have I done to bring glory to God and not myself? What things have I done to help others; rather than further my own interests? What love have I shown in humility and care of others; and not in loving myself and protecting my own self-esteem? What status of myself have I protected, rather than lifting others up? What possessions have I freely given away that really was no sacrifice to me? Can I be honest with myself? God says man's righteousness is as filthy rags before him. Our righteousness is tainted, impure, fleshly motivated. How we need to be cleansed in our hearts and motives; our thoughts and intentions. Lord, make me see me as you see me. Make me see the impurities; the subtleties and deceptions of my flesh. May what I do, what I think, what I intend, be truly pleasing to you.

Verse 9. Blessed Are Those Who Are Invited

"Then the angel said to me, 'write, blessed are those who are invited to the wedding supper of the Lamb!' and he added, 'these are the true words of God.'" (NIV)

Yes! These are "the true words of God." All God's words are true. They are ALWAYS TRUE! But we are very much in agreement with what John here expresses: "Blessed are those who are invited to the wedding supper of the lamb." (NIV) Yes! Indeed! Praise God if those words are said to us! That's the most beautiful words we can hear – "come to the wedding supper of the Lamb." We are accepted! We are made whole! We are made ONE WITH GOD!

Verse 10. I Am A Fellow Servant

"At this I fell at his feet to worship Him. But he said to me, 'do not do it! I am a fellow servant with you and with your brothers hold to the testimony of Jesus. Worship God! For the testimony of Jesus is the Spirit of prophecy." (NIV)

Don't look down at John here. I think I would be ready to bow too. To be in the presence of an angel, seen in the heavens, awesome and powerful and even as a servant – "a flame of fire." I would be very scared, very overwhelmed, and probably very uncertain of what to expect; what to do; how to act. Isaiah was brought into the presence of God and Isaiah's response was – "Woe to me! I am ruined!" John also had this experience in the first century with the TRUE miraculous; yet here, in the presence of a fiery angel, he had conflict within himself knowing what to do. John after all, was just a man. He just needed help and direction. Jesus had hand-picked John for the Revelation. There was not a problem with John's faith or doctrine. There was just the limitation, when in human form he was raised in vision to see the unseen. How could he or we be prepared for such an experience?

"<u>The testimony of Jesus is the Spirit of prophecy.</u>" (NIV)

It is interesting - that the longer I study the word; the more I understand of the word; the more I come to realize that page after page, chapter after chapter and book after book God is telling us about Jesus in prophecy. Prophecies and hints are everywhere in the Old Testament about Jesus. It is all about him. God has been telling us all along – Jesus, Jesus, Jesus. God whispers it! He echoes it! He shouts it! Literally – the testimony of Jesus is the Spirit of prophecy.

THE RIDER ON THE WHITE HORSE

Verses 11-21 is a view of Christ and the armies of heaven, the forces to deliver judgment against evil, in the battle of God and Magog in the heavens.

Verse 11. Heaven Standing Open

"I saw heaven standing open and there before me was a white horse, whose Rider is called Faithful and True. With justice he judges and makes war." (NIV)

"<u>White horse</u>" (NIV)

I know from watching cowboy shows as a kid who this is. The good guy rides the white horse. He is full of virtue and is true. The rider on the black horse is the bad guy. He is sly and crafty. He is up to no good. WE KNOW THAT. And we know that here. The good guy wears a white hat too! Remember?

"<u>Whose rider is called Faithful and True.</u>" (NIV)

In Chap1:5, Jesus is called the <u>Faithful witness</u>. In 3:14, Jesus is called "<u>the faithful and true witness</u>." He is the only one who can judge justly.

"<u>With justice he judges and makes war.</u>" (NIV)

Jn.8:15-16 Jesus says, "You judge by human standards: I pass judgment on no one. But if I do judge, <u>my decisions are right</u>, because I am not alone. I stand with the Father who sent me. 2 Tim.4:1 says, In the presence of God and of Christ Jesus, the one <u>being about</u> (Greek - mellontos) to judge the living ones and the dead, both by the appearance of him and by the kingdom of him, (Marshall's Greek Interlinear). Now in the book of Revelation, the time had arrived for that judgment by Christ.

"And makes war."(NIV)

This is referring to the battle of Gog and Magog (the last battle between Satan and the enemies of Christ with Christ, the rider on the white horse and the armies of heaven following him.) (see explanation in Chap.20, verses 7-10). The verses here, 11- 21, we see the good guys – Jesus and his army. In chap. 20:7-10, we see the bad guys – Satan and his hordes, the wicked nations.

Verse 12. A Name No One Knows

"His eyes are like blazing fire, and on his head are many crowns. He has a name written on him that no one knows but he himself." (NIV)

"<u>His eyes are like blazing fire</u>." (NIV)

Jesus is described this way in Rev.1:14; 2:18. In 2:18 we have a positive identification – "These are the Words of <u>the Son of God</u>, whose <u>eyes are like blazing fire</u> and whose feet are like burnished bronze." The <u>rider on the white horse is the Son of God</u>. He does not have "kind eyes" here. He does not have "soft eyes" or "gentle eyes" here. His eyes are like blazing fire. It must make us think of God who is a "<u>consuming fire</u>", Heb.12:29, and Once more he would shake not only the earth but also the heavens. He would shake IN JUDGMENT!

"<u>On his head are many crowns</u>." (NIV)

Why are there many crowns? Because he is King of kings. He is above all nations, all powers, all principalities, ... EVERY name that can be named. Eph.1:20-21. All the crowns of his whole creation belong to him.

"<u>He has a name written on him that no one knows but he himself.</u>"(NIV)

Why can't anyone know it? That is not the thought. The name cannot BELONG to anyone else. ONLY Jesus knows that name. It belongs to him only. What is it? Well, it is written on him – so we can read it – verse 13, "His name is the Word of God." (NIV) We know that it is his name; but only he can wear that name.

There is a beautiful thought here. Just as Jesus wears a name unique to only him; a name only he can wear and know; so, he also gives us a unique name. Rev.2:17 says, "I will also give him a white stone with a new name written on it, known only to him that receives it." The idea here is the same as 19:12, that is – the name is unique and special ONLY to that individual. No one else can wear the name. Jesus WILL GIVE YOU A NEW NAME. It will not be the name from your father and mother. The King of kings, your savior, will name you, his name for you. Names are very important to God. Remember how he changed Abram's name? Sara's name? Peter's name? Paul's name? and so many others? You will have your special, unique, wonderful name from God. Cool isn't it?

Verse 13. A Robe Dipped In Blood

"He is dressed in a robe dipped in blood, and his name is the Word of God." (NIV)

"He is dressed in a robe dipped in blood" (NIV)

This does not mean he took the robe and dipped it in blood. Why would he do that? It is the Greek word "bebammenon". It is from the word "bapto" meaning "to immerse."

Jesus' robe was immersed, soaked completely, in blood. Why? He is executing judgment, everywhere, completely, fully, against the wicked. It is awful, horrible for them. (Cf. Isa. 63).

"His name is the Word of God." (NIV)

Does this not identify the rider on the white horse! We know who the "Word of God is! John.1:1ff tells us.

Verse 14. The Armies Of Heaven Were Following

"The armies of Heaven were following him, riding on white horses and dressed in fine linen, white and clean. (NIV)

"The armies of heaven were following him." (NIV)

I don't think the army of heaven was there to do anything – just to watch;

just to see His glory in righteous judgment. Historically, Jesus fights for his people. He wins the battle. He does not need our help. Perhaps Isa.63:5 attests to this: "There was no one to help, I was appalled that no one gave support; so my own arm worked salvation for me." Only God accomplishes the undoable; eternal things - in which only God alone can do.

"Riding on white horses and dressed in fine linen." (NIV) Of course - the white horses and being dressed in fine linen stand for the righteousness of the saints. It stands for virtue, purity, honesty, - the redeemed. Can you imagine the scene? Here is Jesus, the rider on the white horse - the King of Kings, with many crowns, with an iron rod, and a sharp two-edged sword coming out of his mouth. Following behind is his huge, numberless army, each one crowned with glory and honor; all on white horses and dressed in white linen. What a scene!

Verse 15. A Sharp Sword Out Of His Mouth

"Out of his mouth comes a sharp sword with which to strike the nations. 'He will rule them with an iron scepter.' *He Treads the winepress of the fury of the wrath of God almighty." (NIV)*

"A sharp sword." (NIV)

Of course, this is Jesus. He has the "sharp two-edged sword", Rev.2:12;1:16. The word used for the double-edged sword is interesting. It is the Greek – "rhomphaia". It was a weapon of large size and in chapter one and two, and here in verse 15, the word is used as a sword of judgment. In Hebrews 4:12, the word for sword is the Greek – "Machaira". It is a smaller sword, or dagger. In Hebrews 4:12, the short sword is used "to reveal the thoughts and intents of the heart." (NIV) In Ps.139:23-24, David says,

"Search me, O God, and know my heart; test me and know my anxious thoughts. See if there is any offensive way in me, and lead me in the way everlasting." (NIV)

In view of what David said, I think of what Heb.4:12 says as – laying on a surgical table and letting the Holy Spirit examine me, and reveal to me with his word (the sword), the thoughts and intents of my heart. Then, when he reveals it, with the Spirit's help and surgical skill, remove any offensive thing he finds. That is the process. That is "walking with the Spirit". That is "fellowship with the Spirit". If we do that – we as Christians will not be judged by the large sword of Jesus upon the enemies of God.

"Out of his mouth comes a sharp sword with which to strike the nations." (NIV)

All the nations, who were wicked, and did terrible things to God's people, Jesus raised from their places in waiting – Hades. Jesus raised them as a reluctant horde. He put hooks in their jaws, Ezek.38:4, and brought them out with their whole army. (It was a horde – many! Many! Many! Horde carries with it a meaning similar to our word "mob") Jesus brought them out, from all time since the world of Noah that perished. He brought the "dead" from their places. Jesus brought them out to come against Heavenly Jerusalem. Why? So, his people could see his vengeance upon their enemies. So, his people could see his justice. The build-up of the scene in Ezekiel 38-39 is dramatic. But then, you do not get to see a battle. Neither do you in Revelation. There is no contest. No struggle. No threat. No fear. None of that. Why should there be? The army of the wicked dead know they're beaten. It is THEIR judgment! It is their FINAL DOOM – FOR EVER AND EVER! They are going up against the Eternal One, the King of kings and Lord of Lords. He speaks and he can create the world. He speaks and they are reduced to heaps of bodies to be buried. And that is what the "armies of heaven do". Ezekiel tells us the wicked hordes are buried in the Valley of Hamon Gog (hordes of Gog). They are buried for seven months. That is seven (the number of completeness, as 7 days make a complete week). All of them are buried and meet their judgment. (For more comments, see Revelation, Chap.20:7-10.)

"He will rule them with an iron scepter."

This is not the staff of a gentle shepherd with his sheep. This is an iron rod with which to "strike (or smite) the nations." The context is clear. The rider on the white horse will smash the nations like breaking pottery.

"He treads the winepress of the fury of the wrath of God Almighty." (NIV)

This is vividly portrayed in Isaiah 63:1-6

"Who is this coming from Edom, from Bozrah, with his garments stained crimson? Who is this, robed in splendor, striding forward in the greatness of his strength? 'It is I', speaking in righteousness, mighty to save. Why are your garments red, like those of treading the winepress? I have trodden the winepress alone; from the nations no one was with me, I trampled them in my anger and trod them down in my wrath; their blood spattered my garments, and I stained all my clothing. For the Day of Vengeance was in my heart, and the year of my redemption has come. … I trampled the nations in my anger." (NIV)

Verse 16. Name - King Of Kings And Lord Of Lords

"On his robe and on his thigh, he has this name written: 'King of kings and Lord of lords.'" (See comments in verse 12). (NIV)

Verse 17. An Angel Standing In The Sun

"And I saw an angel standing in the Sun, Who Cried Out in a loud voice to all the birds flying in midair, 'come, gather together for the great supper of God.'" (NIV)

Since this is a figurative, scenic passage; the Sun could easily be the presence of the rider on the white horse, prophetically the Sun, and he is radiant and glorious.

You see the angel, almost as a dim shadow, because the glory of the Sun is behind him shining in such fullness around him, that you can barely see the angel. But you hear the angel's voice – "come gather together for the great supper of God."

"Come gather together for the great supper of God." (NIV)

Verse 18 reveals what the great supper is -

Verse 18. Eat The Flesh Of

"So that you may eat the Flesh of Kings, generals, and Mighty Men, horses and their Riders, In the Flesh of all people, free and slave small and great." (NIV)

Why does Jesus call this the "great supper of God"?

It seems repulsive. It does not seem like a feast at all. What could the thought be? I can only guess at the answer, and here it is. When

Jesus said "unless you eat my flesh and drink my blood you have no life in you." The thought is clear. It is a statement with a spiritual teaching – life is in participating in his body (his death for our life) and his blood (cleansing us from sin). We must have fellowship together with him to have life. So too here, we have fellowship with him in his victory over the wicked. It is a great supper, a celebration of victory over our enemies. But God has such a graphic and impactful way of saying something. It sticks immediately in our minds. We can't forget it. God's people will rejoice over the final judgment of the wicked. To do otherwise is to not believe that God is just in his judgments. His judgments are just. They are right.

Verse 19. The Beast And The Kings Of The Earth Gathered

"Then I saw the Beast and the kings of the earth and their armies gathered together to make war against the rider on the horse and his army." (NIV)

Many have tried to make this battle so figurative and vague, that somehow it speaks of what was happening on earth. I do not think that is the case at all. This is the armies of heaven following Jesus. This is showing us not what happens on earth, but the final doom, the final judgment of those who so persecuted and abused God's people on earth. All final reckoning will take place in the spirit world; the world of the unseen. The beast, the kings of the earth, and their armies will face the REAL, the REALITY. Reality is not on earth. On earth they look like they win; and on earth they did. Jerusalem was destroyed and Titus took captives triumphantly back to Rome. The arch of Titus in Rome still attests to his victory. But friend, that is never the end. The end is the final judgment which we all must face AFTER we die and leave this world. We are being shown the final end of the beast, the kings, their armies. Their final doom is represented here so we can KNOW – God is JUST. Ezekiel 39:17-21 tells us,

"Call out to every kind of bird and all the wild animals: assemble and come together from all around to the sacrifice on the mountains of Israel. There you will eat flesh and drink blood. You will eat the flesh of mighty men and drink the blood of princes of the earth as if they were rams and lambs and goats and bulls – all of them fattened animals from Bashan. At the sacrifice I am preparing for you, you will eat fat till you are glutted and drink blood till you are drunk. At my table you will eat your fill of horses and riders, mighty men and soldiers of every kind, declares the Sovereign Lord. I will display my glory among the nations, and all the nations will see the punishment I inflict and the hand I lay upon them." (NIV)

Verse 20. Thrown Alive Into The Fiery Lake

"But the Beast was captured, and with him the false prophet who had performed the miraculous signs on his behalf. With these signs she had deluded those who had received the mark of the beast and worshiped His image. The two of them were thrown alive into the fiery Lake of burning sulfur." (NIV)

"The beast...the false prophet" (NIV)

Their final end? The Lake of burning sulfur! Be assured – that is where ALL the wicked go. None escapes. There is not a single exception. God is not mocked. They WILL REAP what they sow. No one ever, ever, gets away with evil. Heb.4:13 says, "Nothing in all creation is hidden from God's sight. Everything is uncovered and laid bare before the eyes of him to whom we must give an account."

"...miraculous signs...these signs had deluded those who received the mark of the beast and worshipped his image." (NIV)

Were they real miracles? Well, I think no. They deluded; they deceived the people. That implies the miracles were not real. We would think only God can perform REAL miracles. We could challenge this reasoning. When Aaron threw his staff on the ground it became a snake. The wise men, sorcerers, and Egyptian magicians threw down their staffs and they became a snake. Then Aaron's staff swallowed up their staffs. Exodus 7:10-12. Did the wise men, sorcerers, and magicians perform miracles? It appears they did. God's power showed to be greater. Moses raised his staff and struck the waters of the Nile River, and the water turned to blood. (God attacked the false god Hopi, the god of the Nile.) The Egyptian magicians did the same things by their secret arts. Exodus 7:20-22. No, I do not understand what was going on here. I do know, God was showing his power was greater. Aaron stretched out his hand over the waters of the Nile and frogs came up and covered the land. The magicians did the same things with their secret arts. Exodus 8:6-7.

Yet, when Aaron stretched out his staff over the ground and the dust became gnats; the magicians tried to produce gnats and they could not. They told Pharaoh. "this is the finger of God." Yes, it was. And the magicians could no longer reproduce any magic. Rather, they and some of those of Pharaoh's officials told him after so many plagues, "How long will this man be a snare to us? Let the people go, so that they may worship the Lord their God. Do you not realize that Egypt is ruined?" Exodus 10:7. (NIV)

I do not know what God allowed or disallowed; nor the limits he placed upon these false prophets. Rev.13:13-14 does say,

"And he (the earth beast) performed great and miraculous signs, even causing fire to come down from heaven in full view of men. Because of the signs he was given power to do on behalf of the first beast, he deceived the inhabitants of the earth."

Were these real miracles? Well – "causing fire to come down from heaven" must have seemed pretty real. I do not understand. The details are not clear to me. Perhaps the Spirit will in the future cause me to understand what was happening and the lesson I was to learn from it. It does not matter to me. I trust him fully, even in the matters I still do not understand. Am I curious to understand? Oh, yes! But it does not make me anxious, nor doubtful. Worship ONLY God! That is certain.

Verse 21. The Rest Of Them Were Killed With The Sword

"The rest of them were killed with the sword they came out of the mouth of the rider on the horse. And all the birds gorged themselves on their Flesh." (NIV)

"The rest of them were killed with the sword that came out of the mouth of the rider." (NIV)

Jesus had said, "There is a judge for the one who rejects me and does not accept my words; that very word which I spoke will condemn him at the last day." Here that comes to pass. His word, from his mouth, overtakes them, judges them, and condemns them. They are punished and killed as he had said.

"And all the birds gorged themselves on their flesh." (NIV)

I think God has the last word here. He leaves the last word here in a way we do not forget. The ultimate ruin and disgrace he leaves us to think about is clear. The wicked will be food for the birds – the vultures, the birds that feast upon the dead.

CHAPTER TWENTY

THE THOUSAND YEARS

Verse 1. The Key To The Abyss

"And I saw an angel coming down out of heaven, having the key to the abyss and holding in his hand a great chain." (NIV)

"An angel…coming down… having the key to the abyss." (NIV)

Jesus told a parable in Lk.11:17-22. It is about the strong man and the one stronger that attacks and overpowers him. In the context of that passage we understand that the strong man is Satan and the one stronger is Jesus who overpowers him.

We should see it here. Who has the strength, the power to grab the dragon and chain him up? ONLY Jesus. Remember, Satan had the power over hell and death by reason of our sins. Jesus came along, died for our sins and took away Satan's power by bringing atonement for our sins that stood against us. Rev.1:18 says that the one "like the Son of Man" (Jesus) held the KEYS to death and hades. Here, an angel (Jesus) who has the KEY to the Abyss (death and hades), comes down, chains up the dragon (huge monster that he was) and throws him into the abyss.

"Holding in his hand a great chain." (NIV)

Have you ever seen the chains that are used for anchors of huge ships? I got to see the Queen Mary in Long Beach, and one link of the anchor chain was much larger than my foot. I took a photograph of it, being so impressed with the size of such a big chain. What a huge chain it would take to bind Satan, who is like Leviathan, the serpent of the sea. This was a huge task, but simple and easily managed for our savior.

Verse 2. He Bound Him For A Thousand Years

"He seized the Dragon, that ancient serpent, who is the devil, or Satan, and bound him for a thousand years." (NIV)

"He seized the Dragon, ancient serpent, devil, Satan, and bound him"

I love the impression those words leave with me. "He SEIZED him". Our savior grabbed a hold of Satan with such power and force that Satan was helpless before him. Who can resist God?

"For a thousand years". (NIV)

Psalms 50:10 God says, for every animal of the forest is mine, and the cattle on a thousand hills… verse12, "for the world is mine and all that is in it." (NIV) The cattle on a thousand hills is the same as saying "all"; every animal is mine, the world is mine

Deut. 7:9 says, "He is the faithful God, keeping his covenant of love to a thousand generations of those who love him and keep his commands." (NIV) Does he break his covenant of love with the 1001 generation, or the 1002? No. It is not used as a literal number. It is a number that symbolizes "all, every" generation. His love and faithfulness is inexhaustible. God loves "completely".

1 Chron.16:15 says, "He remembers his covenant forever, the word he commanded for a thousand years." (NIV) (also Ps.105:8). This is a Hebraism – two thoughts that are equal are put side by side for emphasis and clarification. By extending a thought you can clarify and define it. A "thousand" here in this verse is "forever", all the years.

In Ps.91:7-13 God makes a prophecy about Christ and says, "A thousand may fall at your side, ten thousand at your right hand. But it will not come near you. You will only observe with your eyes and see the punishment of the wicked" …, verse 10 "No harm will befall you; no disaster will come near your tent." (NIV) God uses a "thousand" here, and even "ten thousand" because the use of the very large number just emphasizes what he is saying.

2 Pet.3:8 says, "With the Lord a day is like a "thousand" years, and a "thousand" years are like a day." (NIV) A "thousand years" here

stands for "all' the years – a day is like "all" the years and "all years is like a day. In other words, God is timeless. God is not bound by time as we are.

Ps.90:4 "A thousand years in your sight are like a day that has just gone by." (NIV) God is not bound by time.

Note: There are those who try to make the verse in 2 Peter <u>a formula for interpreting prophecy</u> -that a <u>day =1000 years</u>. It is interesting that they never want to use the second part of the verse – that <u>1000 years = 1 day</u>. Hmmm? Why not interpret everywhere prophetic scripture mentions 1000 years - that it means a day? And, everywhere prophetic scripture mentions a day – it means a 1000 years? That is what the verse says if it is giving a formula for interpreting prophetic scripture. This would make prophecies hilarious and absurd!

Those who misinterpret or mishandle the Word of God like this forget that we have specific scripture that <u>does</u> give us an example where a <u>day = year</u> in prophetic language. Examine the context of Ezek.3:5: "I have assigned to you the same number of days as the years of their sin." (NIV) Ezekiel was to lay on his side for (390 days), the number of days to represent the years of Israel's sin. A day in prophetic language is equal to a year; NOT a 1000 years. A 1000 is symbolic of "all, every, completely".)

"<u>Is the number - '1000 years' - literal or symbolic in this chapter?</u>"

First, let's take the statement – "They came to life (saints) and <u>reigned with Christ a 1000 years</u>," verse 4. (NIV) Did the saints then quit reigning on the 1001 year? Or, the 1002 year?

In Rev.22:4-5, speaking of the saints in New Jerusalem it says, "They will not need the light of a lamp or the light of the sun. for the Lord God will give them light. And <u>they (saints) will reign for ever and ever</u>." (NIV) Could the saints reigning for a "<u>1000 years</u>" mean they reign for ever and ever? Do they reign for "<u>all</u>" the years?

That is the way scripture uses 1000 everywhere else – to mean "all, every, completely." Look at what Rev. says, chapter 7 and 14. The 144,000 (12 x12 x<u>1000</u>) is not an exact number but means "<u>all</u> Israel will be saved", Rom.11:26. "<u>All</u> the true Israel of God was saved. Does the 12,000 from each tribe mean exactly 12,000 in number were saved? The number 12,000 (12 x 1000) means "all" saved from that tribe. It is not a literal number; it is symbolic. So too, in chapter 20, the saints "reign for a 1000 years" is not a literal 1000 years. It is symbolic of "all the years". They reign for ever and ever!

An objector says, "Yes, but they will reign on the earth a 1000 years." It is a literal 1000 years.

"How do the saints "reign on the earth"? Paul tells us in Rom.5:17:

"For if by the trespass of one man, death reigned (in this life, our life while on the earth) death reigned through that one man, how much more will those who receive God's abundant provision of grace and of the gift of righteousness "reign in life" (this life, our life on earth) through the one man Jesus Christ." (NIV)

Rom. 5:21 says, "Just as sin reigned in death, so also grace might reign through righteousness to bring eternal life through Jesus Christ our Lord."

What is the "reign on the earth"? It is the reign of Christians who have been redeemed by the blood of Christ and given righteousness – our lives as Christians, bringing light to the world in jars of clay. We reign as kings and priests NOW on the earth, Rev. 5:10. Christians are not waiting to reign. We reign NOW through righteousness to bring people to salvation through the gospel. Remember, Jesus reigns in people's hearts through his Spirit. That kind of reign knows no boundaries, but affects every nation and all people. Jesus starts with the inner man to transform the inner man and change the world.

"What does Satan being "bound a 1000 years" mean? It emphasizes the thoroughness of his binding, the completeness, the totality of his binding. Look at the text. Satan was bound with a great chain, thrown into the abyss (prison for demons and the wicked). It was "locked and sealed," verse 3. Satan was totally defeated and his influence removed. He was bound for a "1000 years" – meaning completely, with utter thoroughness. Then he was thrown in the abyss. That is the holding place, waiting for the judgment. When was the judgment of both heaven and earth? In 70 A.D. Both heaven and earth were to be shaken (judged) Heb.12:26.

When did such a final judgment begin? I believe it was in the "hour of trial" that Rev.3:10 mentions. It was a TRIAL! It was the TRIAL and the courts were set. When did it begin? Jesus came back to get his own on Resurrection Day, 3 days after the Passover. Immediately after the resurrection took place, Titus besieged Jerusalem, April 14, 70 A.D. and the days of judgment began. Perhaps the judgment lasted 5 months, till Sept.8, 70 A.D. But the judgment in the heavens was taking place at the same time. During this time, Satan was chained and thrown into the abyss. He was only let out a short time to gather the wicked dead in the heavenly realms for the final battle of Gog and Magog – which ended in Satan's destruction and being thrown into the Lake of Fire.

Jesus had resurrected his people before the judgment started. They were taken to heaven to the city and villages without walls, bars, and gates, Zech.2:4-5. It was the heavenly Jerusalem. They were people who "were gathered from many nations to the mountains of Israel, who lived in peace and safety," Ezek.38:8. That is the context of the battle of Gog and Magog, that Satan fights, Rev.20:7-10 and is totally destroyed.

Verse 3. He threw Him Into The Abyss, Locked and Sealed It

"He threw him into the abyss, and locked and sealed it over him, to keep him from deceiving the nations anymore until the thousand years were ended. After that, he must be set free for a short time." (NIV)

"to keep him from deceiving the nations anymore." (NIV)

Satan was ultimately bound – to keep him from deceiving the nations anymore." Satan had deceived the nations when the Dragon gave his power to the sea beast (Rome), Rev. 13:2, and the earth beast. They deceived the inhabitants of the earth, Rev.13:14. Who was able to stop the Dragon working through Rome? The Angel was able. He bound Satan with the great chain and cast him into the Abyss. Who was the Angel? Michael (meaning – "who is like unto God"). He is the only one strong enough to bind the Dragon, like Leviathan the monster, and cast him into the abyss (Prison). Satan at that point and forever would have no more influence in the living world of men. He was utterly defeated and stopped, Rom. 16:20; Heb.2:14.

"Until the 1000 years were ended." (NIV)

One screams out, "See – the 1000 years ended; so, it was a literal 1000 years." Let's think. If the 1000 years symbolizes the thoroughness, completeness of Satan's binding, couldn't the angel "Loose him"? Look at the overall scene of what is happening:

1. Satan is deceiving the nations through Rome.

2. The angel binds Satan so he cannot deceive the nations anymore. (His earthly influence was stopped.)

3. Satan is thrown into the Abyss (prison). The abyss is the dungeons, prison, where the angels who sinned were kept, waiting for the judgment, 2 Pet.2:4. The beast, when he comes up out of the abyss goes to his destruction, Rev.17:8. When Satan was "set free for a short time," where was he going? He was going to his destruction! He was going to his Judgment. What was he free to do? He was free to gather the wicked in the heavens for the final battle, Gog and Magog. Gog (is Satan) and Magog (the land of Gog, the land of those condemned in the grave, those in Tartarus and the wicked of Hades). The battle was fought in the heavens and Satan and his wicked servants were absolutely defeated and thrown into Gehenna.

Note: Satan was the King over the abyss, Rev.9:11. The abyss was where the demons and the wicked were kept. The king's name there was Abaddon in Hebrew, or Apollyon in Greek. The name means "Destroyer." Satan is the destroyer, the king over destruction. But he himself was thrown into the abyss. He was "released for a short time" to muster a huge army (from the realm of the wicked dead) (from the nations -that were in the grave over the centuries, the lower earthly regions) to try again to defeat Jesus in the spiritual world. The battle that would be fought was in the heavens, Ezek. 38-39, the Battle of Gog and Magog. (Satan) Gog, in the land of Magog (the land of Gog) goes forth to battle Jesus and the New Jerusalem in the heavens. We shall explain what happens in detail a little later.

Verse 4. The Souls of Those Beheaded Came To Life

"I saw Thrones on which were seated those who had been given authority to judge. and I saw the souls of those who

had been beheaded because of their testimony for Jesus, and because of the word of God. they had not worshiped the Beast or his image and had not received his mark on their foreheads or their hands. They came to life and reigned with Christ for a thousand years." (NIV)

Verses 1-3 shows us Satan who is bound thoroughly, no longer to ever influence man on earth. He is put in the abyss (the prison in the spiritual world where all wicked go). Then he is released for a short time. (He is still totally bound where he cannot influence man). But Satan is released to go to his destruction. In the Battle of Gog and Magog, Satan goes to his destruction.

In verse 4, we see "the souls of those who were beheaded" (NIV) (In Rome, a form of execution. Remember the head of John the Baptist. (See Josephus, "Jewish Antiquities," Book18, Chap.5, note 1. And for the beheading of emperor Vitellius – see Josephus, "The Jewish War,' Book 4, chap.11, Sect.4). The souls were martyrs. They were the faithful who had not worshiped the Beast nor had his mark. These were the saints.

"They came to life." (NIV)

When did they come to life? At the resurrection. When the Two Witnesses were raised, all were raised. The resurrection took place then. When was that? During the Passover, 3 days after the Lamb was killed, Jesus rose from the dead. That is Resurrection Day. (The day varies for us because the Jewish calendar had 30 days for each month. The Gregorian calendar differs, so the days differ a little for us from year to year. In the year 2021, the Resurrection Day is Easter, April 4.) (In 70 A.D. the Passover was Apr.17. The Resurrection would have been April 20) The saints were raised on Resurrection Day! They were rescued from the judgment the Romans brought on the Jews.

"And reigned with Christ a 1000 years," (NIV) (Reigned with Christ forever and ever).

The martyrs were "seated on thrones in heaven and given authority to judge". (NIV)

Were not the saints told that they would "judge the world",1 Cor.6:2? (NIV) Satan and his hordes would be going to their judgment. Who would judge them? Yes, THE SAINTS! Woe to the enemies of God! They (the wicked) WOULD get their justice and nothing else. No mercy. They would be repaid by the Lamb.

Verse 5. The Rest Of The Dead Did Not Come To Life Until

"The rest of the Dead did not come to life until the thousand years had ended. This is the first resurrection." (NIV)

In verse 4 we saw the martyrs who reigned "for a thousand years", meaning "all the years".

What does it mean – "until the thousand years ended." (NIV) ("Ended" is the Greek word – telesthe. It could be translated, "was accomplished") (the completion for which something occurred). I believe the thought could be – when the establishment of their "forever reign" was accomplished or completed, (as a result of the First Resurrection), not until that finished, then the "rest of the dead", came to life.

(Perhaps the understanding is this: the resurrection that took place was for all those who had lived under the Mosaic covenant time. They would be the ones who were to judge the wicked of their time. When that judgment was completed, those saints would continue to reign, but then also those saints who began to now die, who lived under the new covenant time would begin to be raised.)

"The rest of the dead did not come to life until the thousand years was ended (NIV) ("were finished." Marshall's Interlinear Translation).

"The rest of the dead" (NIV) would refer to those who lived after the Mosaic period. The first group raised were the saints who lived under the Mosaic period. This was the first harvest. They took part in the "First resurrection" which occurred during the Passover feast.

1 Cor.15:23 tells us the order of the harvest: "But each in his own turn": 1. Christ, the first fruits; 2. then, when he comes, those who belong to him." Verse 24 says – "then the end will come when he hands over the kingdom to God the Father." (NIV) Notice, the ones raised comes before "the end comes", that is, the end of the Mosaic covenant period. The ones raised lived under the Mosaic period.

Luke 21 adds further to the time: verse 20-21 says, "When you see Jerusalem being surrounded by armies…flee to the mountains of Judea." (NIV). Verse 25 says - "there will be signs in the sun, moon and stars." Verse 26 - "men will faint from terror…for the heavenly bodies will be shaken. Verse 27 - "<u>At that time</u> they will see the Son of Man coming in a cloud with power and great glory". Verse 28 - "When these things begin to take place, <u>stand up and lift up your heads</u>, because your redemption is drawing near." Verse 34 - "Be careful…<u>that day will close on you unexpectedly like a trap</u>." (NIV) When the Roman army surrounded Jerusalem (besieged it) no one could get out. <u>That day</u> closed like a trap. Historically, the siege of the city began on April 14, 70 A.D., three days before the Passover. If Christians listened to Jesus, were watching and careful, they would flee the city to the mountains before the siege ("trap") closed. The signs would be there. Jesus would come on the Passover. They would be "passed over" (as in Egypt) by the death that followed. The Resurrection of the saints would follow 3 ½ days later, as in the case of the Two witnesses, Rev.11, who were killed on the Passover, and 3 ½ days later "came to life" and were resurrected.

Verse 6. The First Resurrection

"Blessed and holy are those who have part in the first resurrection. The second death has no power over them, but they will be Priests of God and of Christ and will reign with him for a thousand years." (NIV)

"<u>Blessed and holy are those who take part in the First Resurrection.</u>" (NIV)

Some interpret this as referring to the time when we are born again, John 3, in our earthly life. This does not fit the context. This is referring to the actual Resurrection Day, raised from the physical grave to life again at the second coming of Jesus in 70 A.D. John 5:25 refers to it as "the time has now come." (That time had come at the time Jesus was talking to people of his generation).

"<u>The Second Death has no power over them.</u>"(NIV)

The second death IS the Lake of Fire, Rev.20:14. It is destruction. (See discussion, verse 14).

SATAN'S DOOM – Ezekiel 38-39.

This is it! This is the biggest and last showdown between Christ and Satan. It's really no battle at all. After all, it's between God and a created angel, Satan. Satan will have his last go at it (but he is already whipped before he starts). Satan is a joke! Nevertheless, Satan took himself very seriously. He was desperate! This was his last "chance". This is the battle of Gog (Satan). He musters his army (hordes from the nations) in the land of Gog, called Magog. Then he descends upon Beulah land (promised land in heaven) and the heavenly Jerusalem.

It will help a lot to look at the prophecy in Ezekiel 38-39 and get oriented to the battle there –

Ezekiel 38-39:

Let us notice several keys to understanding the passage:

1.Who is Gog, Magog, Meshech and Tubal?

The Hebrew dictionaries don't seem to help answer that question. A good source to the answer is in a book called, "Noah's Three Sons", by Arthur C. Custance, C.1975, pub. By Zondervan. In pages 89-90, and 96, he discusses these sons of Japheth from a list in Genesis 10:2 and traces what we know about them from ancient history. His major theme is tracing the spread of nations in the Table of Nations of Genesis 10. This is a little lengthy but helpful. Custance says:

"Magog: Very little is known. It is not clear whether the name is the original form or compounded two elements, "ma" and "Gog". The prefix "ma" was often added in antiquity to a personal name, meaning "the place of". Magog would then mean the "place of Gog", i.e. the territory of Gog.

The ordinary word in Assyrian and Babylonian for "land" or "country" is "matu, often abbreviated to "mat." The country of "Gutu" according to Sayce, appears in Assyrian inscriptions as "Mat Gutu"."

"Magog" then would mean the "land of Gog."

Gog: "Bochart derived the word "Caucasus" from a compound form "Gog" and "Chasan" meaning the "stronghold of Gog". According to Josephus, the descendants of Gog were later known as Scythians, whom he says were otherwise known as Magogites. These people formed the greater part of the Russian stock. Mention is made of Gog in Ezekiel (38:2ff) as the 'chief prince' of Meshech and Tubal." It may be observed that "rosh", which in this passage is translated "chief prince" signified the inhabitants of Scythia. From it the Russians derive their name. Russia was known as Muskovi until the time of Ivan the Terrible, a name undoubtedly connected to Meshech."

Japhethites: "Now it has already been observed that before there arose a complete separation of the various nationalities – Medes, Persians, Greeks, Celts, etc. – the Japhethites were first divided into two major bodies. One of these comprised the ancestors of the Indians and Persians, whereas the second was the aggregate of those tribes which afterwards composed the nations of Europe. Thus the word "Indo-Euopean" well sums up our ethnological origins."

"Meshech and Tubal: These two names occur frequently as a couplet. (See, for example, Ezek. 32:26, 38:2-3). Meshech is found on the Assyrian monuments in the form of 'Muskaa', probably pronounced 'Muskai'. In the time of Ezekiel the position of these people is probably that described by Herodutus (III,94) i.e. in Armenia where a mountain chain connecting the Caucasus and the Anti – Taraus was named after them, the Moschici Montes.

In the Assyrian inscriptions the word Tubal occurs as Tubla, whereas it seems to have been known to classical geographers as Tibareni. According to Rawlinson, these two- the Mushki and Tabareni – dwelt in close proximity to each other on the northern coast of Asia Minor and were at one time among the most powerful people of that area."

What can we get from this? The Japhetites were people who lived north of Palestine. The raids of nations upon Palestine usually came from the North. In Gen.9:27 God says prophetically –

"May God extend the territory of Japheth. May Japheth live in the tents of Shem." What does that mean? The descendants of Japheth were conquerors, rulers. They extended their territory. The Medes, the Persians, the Greeks (world empires of the book of Daniel that dominated Israel) descended from Japheth. (Babylon came from Ham, Gen.10:6.) The Greeks descended from Javan. Connected with this is the development of the Greek and Roman gods. The Japhetite's began worshiping dead ancestors. Over time there became gods of clans and generations, families of gods – the Greek and Roman gods.

What can we safely assume? God would punish those (the Medes, the Persians, the Greeks, the Romans - Japhetites) whom God had used to punish His people, Israel. These people were conquerors, rulers, armies that in Israel's history had brought much suffering and death.

2. <u>Who is Gog?</u>

In Rev.20:7-8 it says, "When the thousand years is over, Satan will be released from his prison and will go out to deceive the nations in the four corners of the earth – Gog and Magog – to gather them for battle." Notice, <u>Satan</u> - here was going out "to deceive the nations in the four corners of the earth," (NIV) and this is set parenthetically with "<u>Gog and Magog</u>". John is reminding the reader of the battle prophecy of Ezekiel 38-39 by saying "Gog and Magog"; and John is letting you know it is now going to be fulfilled.

John is also using "Gog and Magog" parallel to "Satan going out to the nations in the four corners of the earth. <u>Satan is Gog</u>! It is "<u>Satan and the land of Satan</u>". "<u>Gog and Magog</u>" is "<u>Satan and those is the land of Satan</u>" were going out to battle with Christ and the heavenly Jerusalem. Now, where is the land of Satan? The wicked dead! Sin brought forth death. The unrepentant sinner lies in death. Death is Satan's Land. Those who lie in death (Not reborn by faith) are gathered up by Satan in the four corners of the earth (meaning all of them are gathered) to battle with Christ.

Now, let's get more information to understand what happens from Ezekiel 38-39.

3. <u>Ezekiel 38-39 is a prophecy about "future years"</u>- Ezek.38:8.

In 38:8 he says, that "in future years" the hordes would invade a land.

In 38:14 he says, "in that day, when my people Israel are living in safety." (NIV)

In 38:18 he says, "This is what will happen in that day: when Gog attacks the land of Israel." (NIV) (Spiritual Israel, the True Israel of God). This happens in Rev.20.

In 39:11 he says, "On that day I will give Gog a burial place in Israel." (NIV) In Rev.20:10 Gog (Satan) is thrown into the lake of burning sulphur.

4. The result of the battle: birds and animals are called to the great sacrifice prepared at God's table, 39:17-20. They will eat the flesh of mighty men and princes, and soldiers, 39:18,20.

Rev.19:17-18 says the birds are called to the great supper to eat the flesh of kings, generals, mighty men, horses, riders, the flesh of all people.

Then, Rev.19:19 says, "Then I saw the beast and the kings of the earth and their armies (the hordes of Ezek.38) gathered together to make war against the rider on the horse (Jesus, v.11 -"Faithful and True; v.13 his name is the Word of God) and his army." (NIV) Then in verses 20 the beast was captured and the false prophet … and the two of them were thrown alive into the lake of burning sulfur. This is not a battle on earth. This is a battle that takes place in the heavens and Jesus defeats the enemy of God's people and throws them in the Lake of fire. This was done in the view of God's people in heaven. They were aware and watching that they might see and witness their own vindication by God.

5. The purpose of the Battle is repeated in Ezekiel to emphasize God's purpose for the battle.

In Ezek.38:16, "In days to come, O Gog, I will bring you against my land, so that the nations may know me when I show myself holy through you before their eyes." (NIV) (Every knee will bow and confess that Jesus is Lord.)

In Ezek.38:23, "And so I will show my greatness and my holiness, and I will make myself known in the sight of many nations. Then they will know I am the Lord." (NIV) (All will know God is Lord in heaven).

(There will be no problem in believing in heaven).

6. How do I know the battle of "Gog and Magog" took place in heaven?

A key to knowing where the battle was - is in what he says about the land the hordes were to invade:

- The people were gathered from many nations to the "mountains of Israel" (God's home) 38:8.(NIV)
- The people (my people Israel, verse 14,16), "lived in safety", 38:8,14. (NIV

- The people lived in a land of unwalled villages,…all of them living "without walls, and without gates and bars." Zechariah prophesies of the heavenly Jerusalem- "Jerusalem will be a city without walls because of the great number of men and livestock in it. And I myself will be a wall of fire around it, declares the Lord and will be its glory within." Zech.2:4-5. (NIV)
- "I will bring you against my land", 38:16. (NIV) On earth, the hordes from the north (Romans) attacked Palestine and Jerusalem and burned many cities, put Jews to the sword, surrounded Jerusalem and the Temple and burned it down. The hordes won that battle and there is the Arch of Titus in Rome, still standing today to declare it. In Ezekiel, the battle is in the heavens, the hordes DO NOT WIN! They are slaughtered and buried everywhere if the birds didn't eat them. Jesus fights for the people who lived there in safety.

The hordes in the Ezekiel 38 army were "reluctant" to go. They were deceived and rallied by Satan. Speaking of the hordes, Ezekiel says:

- Of "Gog and Magog" Ezekiel says – "I will turn you around, put hooks in your jaws and bring you out (from the dead) with your whole army." Ezek.38:4 (NIV)
- On that day thoughts will come into your mind and you will devise a evil scheme." 38:10. (NIV)
- "I will execute judgment upon him…38:22. (NIV)
- "I am against you, O Gog, chief prince of Meshech and Tubal… I will turn you around, put hooks in your jaws and bring you out. (NIV) He would bring them from the far north and send them against the mountains of Israel", verse 8. [Notice, this army he would put hooks in their jaws (they were already captives) and turn them around (they were going the other way, or were at least facing the opposite direction). God turned them around as a horde,

an army - but certainly a disheveled, disorganized one. On that day, thoughts would come into their mind and they would devise an evil scheme, in 38:10. (not very good planning. More of a desperate last thought).

The battle of "Gog and Magog" (the battle of Satan and the people who live in his land, Death) are brought out and dragged along with hooks in their jaws, and God brings them from the north (the traditional place from which the attacking armies against Israel came from). They will invade "the mountains of Israel (God's promised land in heaven) where all the people live in safety without walls, gates or bars. The people there had been gathered from the nations and now lived in peace,38:11. [God gathered his people on Resurrection Day in 70 AD to heaven.]

God brings the hordes against his land in heaven "to show himself HOLY" before the nations", and to execute judgement on the hordes. The birds eat their flesh and their dead are everywhere. Then Revelation 19 tells us they are thrown into the lake of burning sulfur.

Verse 7. The Thousand Years Are Over

"When the thousand years are over, Satan will be released from his prison." (NIV)

"the thousand years are over" – not a literal thousand years, but Satan was "thoroughly chained, and bound" (see 20:2). When that thorough containment was over or completed, accomplished, Satan was released.

After being thoroughly chained, he is later released to ultimately be thrown in the lake of fire.

"is released from his Prison" (NIV) This is the abyss he came from, 20:3. It is a prison. 2 Peter 2:4 says, "For if God did not spare angels that sinned, but sent them to hell (Greek – tartarus), putting them into gloomy dungeons (some manuscripts say – "chains of darkness") to be held for judgment."

Verse 8. Gog And Magog

"And will go out to deceive the nations in the four corners of the Earth- Gog and Magog- to gather them for battle. In number they are like the sand on the seashore." (NIV)

"to deceive the nations" – Satan goes out to deceive again. He deceives over and over. This time Satan has to deceive the nations to get them gathered for battle. These nations were the nations already in the grave.

There is an interesting passage that may also fit into this context here, Isa.14:9-12 –

"The grave below is all astir to meet you at your coming; it rouses the spirits of the departed to greet you – all those who were leaders in the world; it makes them arise from their thrones- all those who were kings over the nations. They will all respond, they will all say to you- 'you also have become weak, as we are; you have become like us.' All your pomp has been brought down to the grave, along with the noise of your harps; maggots are spread out beneath you and worms cover you. How you have fallen from heaven, o morning star, son of the dawn. You have been cast down to the earth, you who once laid low the nations." (NIV) Verses 13-17 is a description that sounds like a description of Satan himself.

Satan had been cast to the earth. He knew his time was short. He went about as a roaring lion seeking whom he could devour. Then, Christ bound him, put him in the abyss. There he stayed until his final judgment. But before that judgment, Satan was brought out in the battle – "Gog and Magog – so that God could show his holiness before the nations in the heavens and vindicate his people by defeating the wicked dead. Then God throws them into the lake of burning sulfur.

"In the four corners of the earth" (NIV) meaning "in all the earth". (earth is Greek – ges, "land") This can mean all the land of the Roman empire, those under it. This would fit with "Gog, in the land of Magog, Meshech and Tubal which are basically the empires that came against the people of God in the book of Daniel, namely Medes, Persians, Greeks, and Romans. Now God is going to punish those empires that through the ages have harmed God's people. He uses Satan (Gog) to lead them.

"In number they are like the sand on the seashore" (NIV) - the hordes of Ezek.38-39.

Verse 9. Surrounded The Camp Of God's People

"They marched across the breadth of the Earth and surrounded the camp *of God's people, the city that he loves. but fire came down from heaven and devoured them." (NIV)*

"They ... surround the camp of God's people" (NIV)

Calling it the "camp of God's people" may call to mind the O.T. where the people camped on every side of the Tabernacle. It would include maybe all the people living outside of the city, the heavenly Jerusalem, as well as those within. There were those who lived in the "promised land", "a better country, a heavenly one", Heb. 11:16.

"The city that he loves" - the heavenly Jerusalem, the city of the living God", Heb.12:22. God destroyed earthly Jerusalem. (See Gal. 4:25-26.)

Verse 10. The Devil Was Thrown Into The Lake Of Burning Sulfur

"And the devil who deceived them, was thrown into the lake of burning sulfur, where the Beast and the false prophet had been thrown. They will be tormented day and night forever and ever." (NIV)

"And the devil... was thrown into the lake of burning sulfur." (NIV)

Yay! Yay! Yay! Man's greatest enemy – the devil is in the lake of fire! No more fearing him! No more worrying about what he could be doing!

No more imaginations about what havoc Satan is making all over the world! He is GONE! Jesus has defeated him totally, thoroughly, irreversibly! Jesus completed his purpose totally. He has put every enemy of the spirit world under his feet.

Remember in Eph.6:12 he says, "For our struggle is not against flesh and blood, but against the rulers, against the authorities, against the powers of this dark world (rulers on earth) and against the spiritual forces of evil in the heavenly (spirit world) realms." (NIV) Jesus has defeated all enemies in the heavens. Our future is secure – no wicked are in the heavens, the wicked cannot dwell with God, not the fallen angels, nor even Satan anymore. Satan is in the fire! As for the powers of this dark world (evil men -rulers, powerful men) – NO WORRY. Jesus is Lord of Heaven and earth! Jesus rules it all. He rules by faith in the hearts of men who have received him all over the world. Don't worry about evil men. Pray for them. Hey – we have already won! We know where we are going! Our savior is the King of Kings. He is our advocate. He is our brother! Wow – Oh – WoW!

"And the devil - was thrown into the lake of burning sulfur" (NIV)

When did this happen historically?

We know that this happened at the final judgment, right after Jerusalem had been destroyed in 70 A.D.

When was the judgment of the dead?

2Tim.4:1 says, (KJV) "I charge thee before God, and the Lord Jesus Christ, who shall judge the quick and the dead at his appearing and his kingdom." Some Christians believe Jesus will (sometime in the future). The translation leaves the idea in the text rather nebulous as to when. In the original Greek it is not nebulous. Marshall's Greek Interlinear Translation says – "I solemnly witness before God and Christ Jesus, the one "being about" to judge (Greek - mellontos – "being about"), (Greek – krinein – "to judge) living ones and dead." Jesus was "about" to judge the living and dead at His appearing.

1 Peter 4:5 says, (KJV) "Who shall give account to him that is ready to judge the quick and the dead." Again, Marshall's Greek Interlinear Translation says, "who will render account to the one who is ready having to judge living and dead." "Is ready having" is the translation of (Greek – etoimos exonti). Etomois is a "adjective adverb" and Exonti is "present participle active". He was "ready in the present time" to judge.

In 1 Peter 4:17-19 it says, "It is time for judgment to begin with the family of God." (NIV) IT IS TIME FOR JUDGMENT! When? When Peter wrote!

Acts 24:14-16 says, "that there shall be a resurrection of the dead, both of the just and the unjust." (NIV)

The Greek says – "a resurrection to be about (mellein) to be (esesthai) both of the just and of the unjust. Jn 5:29 tells us, "those who have done good will rise to live, and those who have done evil will rise to be condemned." (NIV) When John? Verse,25 – "a time is coming and has now come when the dead will hear the voice of the Son of God and those who hear will live." (NIV)

Acts 17:30-31 says, (NIV) "For he has set a day when he will judge the world with justice by the man he has appointed." (NIV) Marshalls says, "because he set a day which he is about (Greek – mellei) to judge (Greek – krinein) the inhabited earth." In the New Testament God was "about to" come in judgment! The judgment was SOON!

What about Satan's destruction?

We know that was SOON too in the New Testament. In Rom. 16:20 we read –

"The God of peace will soon crush Satan under you feet." (NIV) Satan's destruction would be SOON after Paul wrote the Roman letter. "Crush" is the Greek word – suntripsei. It means to grind to powder. God would destroy him. "Under your feet" is the phrase used in 1 Cor.15:25, "He must reign until he has put all his enemies under his feet. The last enemy to be destroyed is death." (NIV) Putting his enemies under his feet is destroying them. God would soon "crush (ground to powder) Satan under your feet" (NIV) (destroy him). This statement points to the fulfillment of the prophecy in Gen.3:15 where he (Jesus) was to crush your (Satan's) head. Soon that prophecy would be fulfilled. Jesus had said, "He who falls on this stone will be broken to pieces (humbled, made repentant) but he on whom it falls will be crushed (destroyed),(NIV) Mt.21:44. Lk.20:18 – "it will grind him to powder." Berean Literal Bible.

Heb. 2: 14 says, "so that by his death he might destroy HIM who holds the power of death – that is, the DEVIL." (NIV) That is what Jesus came to do – to destroy Satan. This is not 1 Jn.3:8. There it says, "The reason the Son of God appeared was to destroy the devil's WORK." (NIV) Jesus did come for that and he did destroy the devil's work. But Heb.2:14 says – by his death he might DESTROY HIM, ... that is, THE DEVIL. SATAN IS DEAD! He has been judged and thrown into the fire of brimstone.

"Where the beast and false prophet had been thrown." (NIV) That did not happen in this life. It did not happen on earth. "It is appointed for man once to die and after that to face judgment." Heb.9:27.

They were thrown in the lake of fire. Rev.19:20.

THE DEAD ARE JUDGED

THE Judgment Day for all men who had lived up to that time (under the Mosaic period - from Noah to then.) They had all lived under that "world order". In 1 Cor.7:31 "the world in its present form (schemati – order) was passing away." (NIV) The things of the Mosaic system was an "illustration for the present time", Heb.9:9, (NIV) (their time). They were "external regulations applying until the time of the new order." (NIV) Verse 10 – "Christ came as high priest of the good things already here." (paraphrase, T.S.) (Christ began the new world order, His kingdom. When God closed out the Mosaic System (the world order at that time), He opened up the heavenly Jerusalem, in the heavens, Rev.11:19. When Jesus accomplished everything he said, "He will wipe every tear from their eyes. There will be no more death or mourning or crying or pain, for the old order of things has passed away." (NIV) "He that was seated on the throne said, 'I am making everything new." (NIV)

What are we explaining this for? Because the "world order" of heaven and earth "passed away". A "New world order" came into being after the Mosaic system was destroyed with the destruction of the Temple and Jerusalem in 70 A.D. Then when the old order was destroyed, the New order (in its completion began), a kingdom never to be destroyed, "eternal in the heavens." Heb.12:28; 2 Cor. 5:1. The New Temple in the heavens could not be opened as long as the Old Temple on earth was still standing, Heb.9:8.

When God ended the Mosaic system, it's world order; he closed it out with a judgment. He did it just like – when he did with the world that perished by water in Noah's time, 2 Pet.3:5-6. The Old World Order was closed out with a Resurrection of the just and the unjust of that system; and a judgment of the peoples under that system.

Here, we are to the Judgment: the final act of God to end that world order and judge the people under it. Then he could open up the New World Order. The Events of 70 A.D. really changed the world! (See appendix: Restoration -"Changes made in the World Orders"). When Jesus came, the world changed! It takes the eye of faith to understand that.

Verse 11. A Great White Throne

"Then I saw a great white throne and him who was seated on it. Earth and Sky fled from his presence, and there was no place for them," (NIV)

"I saw a great white throne." (NIV) It was Judgment Day. First John lets you know - by it being the judgment – we are at the end. So next you see –

"Earth and sky fled from his presence." (NIV) In other words, heaven and earth (as they were then, their order) passed, or fled away. The old order of heaven and earth were no more. Remember, the world was already "Passing away" in 1 Cor. 7:31. Why? Because the New Order had already come at Jesus' death. His covenant was "of force after men are dead", Heb.9:17. (NIV) The place in the heavens that Jesus went to prepare was not complete yet even at his ascension. When he ascended it was in order to "fill all things," Eph.4:10 (KJV). He had work to do, as rule until he had put all enemies under his feet, 1 Cor.15. Yet, as it all came to completion, Jesus fulfilled everything God had purposed for him – then we come to the judgment, and that old world order was closed out.

"There was no place for them." (NIV) In other words, no use for them any longer. That Old World Order was obsolete, outdated, Heb.8:13, no longer useful – it was a ministry of death, 2 Cor.3:7.

Verse 12. The Dead Standing Before The Throne

"And I saw the Dead, Great and Small, standing Before the Throne, and books were opened. Another book was opened, which is The Book of Life. The dead were judged according to what they had done as recorded in the books." (NIV)

"Standing before the judge" (NIV)

What would that feel like? The judge on his throne – a figure of fire from the waist up and from his waist down, with eyes of fire. I would fall as a dead man, but no – He would give me the strength to stand (because the text says - they were standing). But their bodies went numb in fear and trembling. We overuse the word "Awesome" in our society, but – How "awesome" for Christians to be there, grinning ear to ear, thinking – "the judge is my savior!" Yet, for the wicked – they would be standing there with their minds in a whirl – passing thoughts like flashes over all the evil things they ever did in life, totally regretting, totally hopeless to escape PAYING for every evil deed they had ever done in the body. No argument would be strong enough: no excuse pitiful enough; No protest loud enough to ever change anything – the VERDICT, the SENTENCE, Depart ye into -.

"The books were opened" (NIV) – every detail, every bad thought, every angry word, every selfish moment, every prideful action, every stubborn refusal to do good; it's in there. Everything you have forgotten – now recalled, every painful experience brought to examination, every self – willed action revealed. "Gosh (they may think) I wish I had died in youth, or never been born at all. Why have I let myself come to this – "unprepared to meet God!".

"Another book was opened, the Book of Life"

The question comes: What is the name?

The answer comes: He is in the Book of Life!

Jesus loudly says: "He is mine. I know my sheep. And they do follow me." Jn.10:4.

Response of the person so judged: "Whoopie! No more to say. I belong to Jesus! There is no more need to be said!"

"If God is for us, who can be against us?" Rom.8:31. (NIV) Pass into the kingdom prepared for you by your savior. Thankfulness almost chokes us till we're almost breathless. But then our throats swell up with praise, unceasing, enthralled praise!

"He does not treat us as our sins deserve, or repay us according to our iniquities. For as high as the heavens are above the earth, so great is his love for those who fear him; as far as the east is from the west, so far has he removed our transgressions from us." Ps.103:10-12. (NIV)

"The dead were judged by what they had done, as recorded in the books." (NIV)

God's judgment is totally just.

Verse 13. The Sea, Death And Hades Gave Up Their Dead

"The sea gave up the dead that were in it, and death and Hades gave up the dead that were in them, and each person was judged according to what he had done." (NIV)

The sea, death, Hades – gave up their dead. (NIV)

Perhaps, the three are the same place, that is - the places of the dead, the realm of the dead, Isa.14:9f. The place of disembodied spirits (hades) was where the dead (realm of death) were kept in the lower regions of the earth or found in the depths of the sea or the abyss.

"…when I bring the ocean depths over you and its vast waters cover you, then I will bring you down with those who go down to the pit, to those of long ago. I will make you dwell in the earth below, as in ancient ruins, with those who go down to the pit, and you will not return or take your place in the land of the living." Ezekiel 26:19-20. (NIV)

Verse 14. The Lake Of Fire Is The Second Death

"Then death and Hades were thrown into the Lake of Fire. The Lake of Fire is the second death." (NIV)

"Death and Hades were thrown into the Lake of Fire." (NIV)

Jesus conquered death, destroyed it, 2 Tim.1:10; 1 Cor.15:54. Jesus conquered the realm of the dead where sinners were kept til judgment. He took over the power of them when he defeated Satan at the cross. Jesus then held the keys to death and hades, Rev.1:18. At the appointed time, when all was fulfilled that God purposed in Christ, Jesus destroyed death and hades (this verse).

"The second death IS the Lake of Fire. (gehenna)"

Christians do not fear the "second death." All are appointed to die physical death, Heb.9:27. Christians are told – "Fear not them which kill the body (physical death), but are not able to kill the soul; but rather fear him which is able to destroy both soul and body in hell (Greek – gehenna) Mt.10:28. The second death is the destruction of the soul. Jesus said, "He who overcomes will not be hurt at all by the second death," Rev.2:11. (NIV) There will be "no more death" for the faithful Christian, Rev.21:4.

There is more to understand about death.

There are 2 deaths: the first death and the second death.

First Death – physical death (separation of the physical body from the soul, Js.2:26). This is the death we experience in the physical world when we die. It is appointed for all men to experience this death, Heb.9:27.

For the righteous – we overcome the loss of the physical body when on resurrection day we are raised to inherit a spiritual body. "The whole creation groans – waiting for the redemption of the body", Rom.8:21-23. We are sown (the physical body) in corruption, we are raised in incorruption (the spiritual body, 1 Cor.15:42-44.) We overcome physical death, the first death.

Isa.26:19ff - "Your dead will live; their bodies will rise… the earth will give birth to her dead" (NIV) (the resurrection).

Ps.49:15 - "God will redeem my life (body) from the grave." (NIV)

Ps.103:4 - "…redeems your life from the pit." (NIV) Ps.112:6, "the righteous man will be remembered forever." (NIV)

Ps.112:4 "even in darkness (sleep of death) light dawns." (NIV)

Hos.13:14 "I will ransom them from the power of the grave; I will redeem them from death. Where O Death, are your plagues? Where o grave, is your destruction?" (NIV)

For the wicked – "Their tombs will remain their houses forever," Ps.49:11. (NIV)

The tomb, or grave, is the home of the physical body. The body is sown in the grave and the soul went to Hades, the place of disembodied spirits.

Ps.49:14, "their forms will decay in the graves, far from princely mansions." (NIV)

Isa.26:14 The wicked dead "live no more. Those departed spirits do not rise… You punished them and brought them to ruin; you wiped out all memory of them," (NIV)

Ps.37:38, "the future of the wicked will be cut off." (NIV)

Second Death - is the Lake of Fire Rev.20:14; or "gehenna", Mt.10:28.

For the Righteous – they "will not be hurt at all by the second death," Rev.2:11. (NIV).

They will "die no more," Rev.21:4. They will live forever with Jesus in heaven. "In righteousness they will see his face," Ps.17:15. (NIV) Of the throne of God and the Lamb, they "will see his face, and his name will be on their foreheads," Rev.22:4. (NIV) (On the earth, no one has ever seen God's face, Jn.1:18. But in heaven we will see his face.) "Their inheritance will endure forever," Ps.37:18 (NIV) The faithful Christian overcomes both the first and second death. He is victorious over death!

For the Wicked – "those who have done evil will rise (their souls, not their bodies), will rise. Their soul rise, not in the resurrection to life, but – "to be condemned" (in the judgment) Jn.5:29. (NIV)

"The future of the wicked will be cut off," Ps.37:38. (NIV) "The wicked will be no more," Ps.37:10. (NIV)

The wicked will be "forever destroyed," Ps.92:7 (NIV) The wicked will be "thrown into the fire… never to rise," Ps.140:10. (NIV)

They will be "remembered no more". "Their forms will decay in the grave, far from princely mansions," Ps.49:14. (NIV)

"Hades was thrown into the Lake of Fire"

Hades was the place of disembodied spirits. The grave was the place for dead bodies. Hades included the realms of both the righteous dead ("the bosom of Abraham," Lk.16:22) separated by a great gulf from the place for the wicked dead. Hades was located in the pit, the abyss, the bottomless pit, in the lower earthly regions. I understand that place to be at the farthest depths of the Sea, under the sea and in the earth. When Jesus died, he first descended into the "lower earthly regions" and brought (his) captives out, Eph.4:8. Jesus rescued his people from that region just as soon as he had died for their sins. I understand that he took the region of the righteous (Abraham's bosom) to heaven, the third heaven, paradise. He told the thief on the cross, "This day you will be with me in paradise", Lk.23:43. Saints were taken to Paradise at that time. However, they did not receive their resurrection bodies at that time. That is why Jesus brought back with him those who had died, on Resurrection Day at his second coming (to get those "waiting for him" Heb.9:28) 1 Thess. 4:14. The righteous dead and those still alive at his coming were all transformed with new spiritual bodies at that time and taken to heaven, in 70 A.D. The O.T. saints were "to inherit with us" (N.T. saints) Heb.11:39-40.

Hades was a holding place for the dead until Jesus came and died. He then changed all of that (what happens to the dead, after that point). Of the righteous he says,

"Blessed are the dead who die in the Lord from now (from that time it was written) on," Rev.14:13. (NIV)

But of the wicked, they were kept in the pit, the abyss, Hades, until the judgment of 70 A.D. At that time, at the judgment, they were transferred from the abyss (holding place of the dead) and went to their destruction (gehenna, Lake of Fire). The beast (the Roman Empire, but in the context specifically, the emperor Nero) would come up out of the abyss and go to his destruction, Rev. 17:8. The dead of hades were raised for judgment, Jn.5:21-29. Notice there in John, Jesus says – "the time was coming and has now come" – that the dead would be raised. The appointed time for it to happen had arrived in that generation.

What about the spiritual world? What happened to them?

Spirits, evil or good are not subject to the laws of our physical world. They do not have physical bodies. Our physical bodies age and die in the first death. They are not subject to physical death. They are already in the spiritual world. They have spiritual bodies. Their bodies are extremely more powerful and majestic than our physical bodies. But, the angels that sinned in the time of Noah, were put in chains in a special holding place just for them, Greek -"tartarus". They were held for judgment. Jesus came to reconcile everything to himself, whether on earth or in the heavens, Col.1:20. Jesus came to restore (put in order) everything, Acts 3:21. He was to rule in the heavens until he had done that. Then he would turn the kingdom back to the Father, 1 Cor. 15:25-28. The judgment of the angels that fell and of Satan took place in 70 A.D., just like judgment of men did. Jesus was completing his task to put everything in order both in heaven and on earth and even under the earth. Jesus put down all his enemies, including Satan and the fallen angels in 70 A.D. He judged them and threw them in the Lake of Fire. They suffered what is our Second Death – the Lake of Fire. Satan was thrown into the Lake of Fire, Rev. 20:10, after the battle of God and Magog that took place in the heavens. Satan and the fallen angels were part of the enemies in the heavens whom Jesus defeated to restore everything. When it was done, the scripture says, "the OLD ORDER of things has passed away… I am making everything new" Rev.21:4-5 (NIV) (Everything in the heavens and earth were new, renewed, restored -in the kingdom of God and Jesus in the heavens. Now that the Old Order had passed away, the heavenly kingdom opened up in the heavens. It could not open up in the heavens as long as the Old sanctuary on earth, the temple, and Jerusalem were still standing, Heb.9:8. The Old passed away. It was destroyed in 70 A.D. Then the New opened - the Kingdom in the heavens that Jesus went to prepare for us. Isn't that marvelous? It is so, so, very exciting. Jesus did EVERYTHING for us!

Verse 15. Thrown Into The Lake Of Fire

"If anyone's name was not found written in the Book of Life, he was thrown into the Lake of Fire." (NIV)

"written in the Book Of Life" (NIV)

We really want our name there, don't we? Please Lord, write our name there.

"Thrown into the Lake of fire." (NIV) This is the second death, the death of the soul. (Cf. Mt.10:28.)

CHAPTER TWENTY-ONE

The judgment had occurred in chapter 20. Now that Jesus had accomplished God's purpose through him; all things in prophesy were completed; and the age came to a close – we see the opening of the kingdom in heaven.

THE NEW JERUSALEM

Verse 1. A New Heaven And A New Earth

"Then I saw a new Heaven and a new Earth, for the first Heaven and the first Earth had passed away and there was no longer any sea." (NIV)

"New heaven and new earth."(NIV)

It's the NEW ORDER, the eternal Kingdom of God in the heavens and Jesus' reign over heaven and earth through his Spirit. It is now! If you do not "see" it, open your spiritual eyes to "understand" the greatness of what God has accomplished for us. Do not think after the flesh any longer! Desire to understand! Let his Spirit teach you. Quit trying to understand with just "human effort". This is a spiritual book. We are "in the Spirit, and the Spirit in us," if we are Christians. Let God's Spirit lead you in your understanding. The entire world changed when Jesus gave us the New Heaven and New Earth! Yay! Yay! Yay! Rejoice all heavens and earth.

"The first heaven and first earth had passed away" (NIV)

"The world in its present form" 1 Cor.7:31 (Greek - schemati) had been "passing away" even when Paul wrote to Corinth. Just like God did not "spare the ancient world when he brought the flood", 2 Pet.2:5, so too, he was going to end the world again that then existed. Of course, he does not mean the physical universe disappeared or was reduced to nothing. It was that the order (Greek - schemati) of the world was changed. That is what Heb.1:10-12 is talking about –

"In the beginning, O Lord, you laid the foundations of the earth and the heavens are the works of your hands. They will <u>perish</u> (like the world of Noah's time, 2 Pet.3:6, T.S.), but you remain; they will <u>wear out</u> like a garment (the world order of the Mosaic period got old, antiquated, obsolete, Heb.8:13, T.S.). You will roll them up like a robe; like a garment they will be <u>changed</u> (The priesthood changed. The law changed, Heb.7:12, T.S.) but you remain the same." (NIV) This is what Jesus was talking about, Matt.5:17 –

"Do not think that I have come to abolish the Law or the Prophets; I have not come to abolish them but to fulfill them. (Jesus was not against the Law and the Prophets. He came to fulfill all that was written, T.S.). I tell you the truth, <u>until heaven and earth disappear</u> (the order of the world at that time of both heaven and earth, T.S.), not the smallest letter, nor the least stroke of a pen, will by any means disappear from the Law <u>until everything is accomplished</u>." (NIV)

The statement – "<u>until heaven and earth disappear</u>" is parallel to the statement "<u>until everything is accomplished</u>." They are equal to each other. When <u>everything was accomplished, heaven and earth would disappear</u>. When <u>heaven and earth disappeared, everything would be accomplished</u>. Jesus came to accomplish everything. Then, that order of the world would disappear or pass away.

Notice what John says in verse four, after he mentions results of the "New order" – "for the old order of things has <u>passed away</u>." (NIV) That is what the first heaven and first earth did – they "<u>passed away</u>". It was the order that governed heaven and earth that passed away or changed; NOT the PHYSICAL UNIVERSE! The same language is used of the world of Noah's time. Why do some insist on an interpretation here that makes it the physical world?

Acts 3:21 says, "He (Jesus) must remain in heaven until the time comes for God to <u>restore</u> everything <u>as he promised long ago</u> through his holy prophets." (NIV) The word for <u>restore</u> in the Greek means – "<u>to set in order again</u>". Jesus was to rule in heaven UNTIL he had set in order again everything, to reconcile everything both in heaven and earth, to bring all things under his control. Then he was to turn the kingdom back to the Father, 1 Cor.15:23-28. This was <u>promised long ago</u>. Jesus fulfilled the Law and the Prophets! Did he not? What did he not fulfill? If he did not fulfill them as predicted, then Jesus would be a FALSE prophet, which he is CERTAINLY NOT.

"<u>There was no longer any sea</u>." (NIV)

Why? Why wasn't there any sea? What sea? Where? The oceans are still here in the world. We have seas. The scripture says – "There was no longer any sea". Then to what is he referring?

I believe he is talking about the sea, the sea of glass, before his throne.

We have looked at the "<u>sea of glass, clear as crystal</u>" in Rev.4:6. It was clear as crystal because it was pure, unmixed, unadulterated, - HOLY. It took passing through "clean water" to make you clean. You could not pass to the throne of God without first passing through that which would make you clean which was before his throne.

The same sea, is symbolized in Dan. 7:10 as a "<u>river of fire</u>" that came out from before his throne. Fire is a purifier of metal. It is figuratively that through which we must pass in order to be purified. Zech. 13:9 says,

"This third I will bring into the fire: I will refine them like silver and test them like gold. They will call on my name and I will answer them: I will say, 'They are my people,' and they will say, the Lord is our God." (NIV)

After they are refined by fire, then are they God's people. "<u>There was no longer any sea</u>" there before God. In heaven, ONLY those who have been PURIFIED by fire will be there. Rev.21:27 says – "Nothing impure will ever enter it." For those in heaven, purified by fire, there is <u>no need for the sea</u> before God's throne. His people will dwell in God and God in them.

Verse 2. The Holy City The New Jerusalem

"I saw the holy city the New Jerusalem coming down out of Heaven from God prepared as a bride beautifully dressed for her husband." (NIV)

"The holy city, the New Jerusalem"(NIV)

This is the heavenly Jerusalem:

The place that Jesus went to prepare for us, Jn.14:2-3.

This is the city above that is free, and our mother, Gal.4:26

The city of the living God, Heb.12:22.

A prepared city by God, Heb.11:16

The city whose architect and builder is God, Heb.11:10.

The city that God loves!

It is described in Rev.21-22.

"Coming down out of heaven." (NIV)

I believe this phrase is best understood as the city in heaven that extends into our world. As Christians, our citizenship is in heaven, Phil.3:20. Even while we live in this fallen world, Jesus dwells in us through his Spirit. We reign on earth "in righteousness" (Rom. 5:21) through His Spirit. We are part of the heavenly kingdom. That kingdom extends down into our world.

Verse 3. Now The Dwelling Of God Is With Men

"And I heard a loud voice from the throne saying, 'Now the dwelling of God is with men, and he will live with them. They will be his people, and God himself will be with them and be their God." (NIV)

This is in agreement with what we understand above. "The dwelling of God is with men." (NIV) It is a spiritual kingdom. God's Spirit DWELLS with our spirit. We are the temple (Greek – naos, "inner sanctuary, Holy of Holies") of God, 1 Cor.6:19.

Verse 4. The Old Order Of Things Has Passed

"He will wipe every tear from their eyes. There will be no more death or mourning or crying or pain, for the Old Order of Things has passed away." (NIV)

(For "death", see comments in 20:14.) (For "Old Order of things" see comments, see 21:1)

Verse 5. I Am Making Everything New

"He who was Seated on the throne said, 'I am making everything new!' Then he said, 'Write this down for these words are trustworthy and true." (NIV)

"I am making everything new"

What are the new things?

A. <u>In the world of the dead</u>:

1. Satan is not holding the keys to hades and death. They were taken away from him by Jesus, Rev.1:18.

2. There is no hades or second death for the Christian. Jesus threw them into the Lake of Fire, Rev.20:14. Therefore, there is no holding place. There is no place between dying and judgment. There is no waiting.

3. The realm of the dead – man is not waiting for the future judgment sometime in the future. The waiting place for the disembodied spirits does not exist anymore.

<u>The righteous</u> – are blessed from 70 A.D. onward. Rev.14:13.

They die and receive their inheritance. They immediately go to heaven and get to live in the presence of the Lord forever.

<u>The wicked</u> – die and immediately are judged and thrown into the Lake of Fire, Rev.20:15, to be remembered no more. They will never see the light of life, Ps.49:19. Compare Ps.87:11, (3-12).

Before Jesus came:

<u>The righteous</u> – waited, as in a sleep. They are talked about in scripture as if they had fallen to sleep, Jn.11:11-13. At his second coming, Jesus was to bring with him those who "had fallen asleep in him, 1 Thess.4:14. The righteous were as in a sleep, to awaken in <u>the morning</u>, Ps.49:14, that is, (at the resurrection).

"And I – in righteousness I will see your face" (Rev.22:4) (NIV); "when I awake, I will be satisfied with seeing your likeness," Ps.17:15. (NIV)

<u>The wicked</u> – waited in darkness. Like the rich man in Jesus' parable, Lk.16:23, he went to hades and "<u>he was in</u>

torment". (Now, the wicked skip the frying pan and go directly to the Lake of Fire.)

B. <u>Our physical world</u>:

<u>For the righteous</u>:

Satan is not the prince of our world any more. He was driven out, Jn.12:31.

Jesus is king of our world, both of heaven and earth.

Jesus rules in the hearts of men by faith all over the world.

Satan cannot do anything to us. He does not exist. Jesus threw him into the Lake of Fire, Rev.20:10

There is no demon possession. They have been destroyed.

The Spirit of Christ has come to indwell the Christian. He, the Spirit of God, is our helper, our partner in life.

Where we did not have the power to overcome sin; now we do have the power, Rom.8:4.

We can KNOW God. The mystery was fully proclaimed, and revealed for us.

We have tasted the heavenly gift and the powers of the Kingdom, Heb.6:5.

All things pertaining to life and godliness have been given to us, 2 Pet.1:3-4.

We are FREE in Christ and follow the law of love, godly love. We are not under any condemnation.

<u>For the wicked</u>:

They are still ruled by the flesh, the cravings of the flesh.

They are ignorant, and without God in the world.

They stand condemned, because they have not believed in the Son of God, Jn.3:18.

They go from bad to worse.

They have no spiritual life, 1 Jn. 5:11-12.

They walk in darkness and do not know what makes them stumble.

They have no hope in this world.

C. <u>The Heavens</u>.

The heavens have been cleansed of all uncleanness and wickedness, Ezek.39:16.

Our struggle is no longer against the spiritual hosts of wickedness in the heavenly realms, Eph.6:12. Jesus totally won the battle of Gog (Satan) and Magog (land of Satan) and destroyed them.

Satan can no longer go before God and accuse Christians, Rom.8:33-34. Satan is destroyed.

> The heavenly Jerusalem is finished, opened up, and receiving all the righteous.

> Heaven is totally the dwelling of God. He has made EVERYTHING NEW.

Verse 6. It Is Done

"He said to me: 'It is done. I am the Alpha and the Omega, the beginning and the end. To him who is thirsty I will give to drink without cost from the spring of the Water of Life." (NIV)

"<u>It is done</u>!" (NIV) Wow! Oh Wow! The eternal purpose of God was kept hidden for ages and ages, Col.1:25-26. History unfolded for generation after generation. Finally, hundreds of prophecies over hundreds and even thousands of years were fulfilled in the short span of Jesus' generation. Those prophecies and God's eternal purpose was fulfilled in three wonderful words- "<u>It is done</u>!" Wow!

Jesus – He is "the Alpha and the Omega, the beginning and the end!" Col.1:16 says,

"For by Him were all things created: things in heaven and on earth, visible or invisible, whether throne, or powers, or rulers, or authorities; all things were created <u>by</u> Him and <u>for</u> Him." (NIV) He is the beginning and the end.

"<u>Drink without cost from the water of life</u>." (NIV)

It costs us nothing. Salvation is a gift. Eternal life is a gift. It cost Jesus everything. Our life was given to us. His was taken away.

Verse 7. Overcome - Inherit All Of This

"He who overcomes will inherit all this, and I will be his God and he will be my son." (NIV)

"He who overcomes will inherit all of this." (NIV)

That is what Jesus kept telling the seven churches. Hang on, be steadfast, persevere, be watchful, be ready, keep your fervor… overcome.

That meant for them – repent of the various things they were doing wrong. They were not to let themselves be deceived. They were not to be forgetful of the things they knew and had been taught. They were not to grow cold toward the Lord by neglect. Overcome! Overcome! Finish the race!

Verse 8. Their Place Will Be

"But the Cowardly, the unbelieving, the vile, the murderers, the sexually immoral, those who practice magic Arts, the idolaters and all liars- their place will be in the fiery Lake of burning sulfur. This is the second death." (NIV)

This is so clear! It is stated so frankly and blunt. It is totally honest and forthright. Your choice is clear and simple!

"Do not be deceived: God cannot be mocked. A man reaps what he sows…" Gal.6:7-8 (NIV)

"The second death." (See comments, Rev.20:14).

Verse 9. Come, I Will Show you The Bride

"One of the Seven Angels who had the seven bowls full of the seven last plagues came and said to me, 'come I will show you the bride, the wife of the Lamb.'" (NIV)

Whew! I'm glad one of the seven angels, who had the seven bowls of the seven last plagues, wasn't bringing more bad news and judgment. Hurray – Good News! Great News. "Come follow me John, and I will show you the Bride, the wife of the Lamb," Eph. 5:32. But first, the angel has to set the stage, describe the scene, so he can present her.

Verse 10. He Showed Me The Holy City

"And he carried me away in the Spirit to a mountain great and high, and showed me the holy city, Jerusalem, coming down out of heaven from God." (NIV)

"The mountain great and high." (NIV)

This mountain represents the place for the heavenly city of Jerusalem. Isa. 2:1-2 says –

"This is what Isaiah son of Amoz saw concerning Judah and Jerusalem: In the <u>last days</u>, the <u>mountain of the Lord's temple</u> will be established as <u>chief among the mountains</u>; it will <u>be raised</u> above the hills, and all nations will flow into it." (NIV)

Just as the earthly Jerusalem was on a mountain side, Mount Zion, with three valleys on three of its sides; so, the mountain of the Lord's temple or house in the heavens would be established as chief among the mountains. Jerusalem was the center of all worship, sacrifices, priestly activity, festivals, culture for all the Jews scattered all over the world. So, the heavenly Jerusalem is the center of all activity in the New Kingdom of God. The mountain of God's house was prophesied to be lifted up above all other mountains, Micah 4:1, and would be chief among the mountains, Isa.2.

"<u>He showed me the holy city</u>, <u>Jerusalem</u>." (NIV)

The <u>holy city</u> Jerusalem (in the heavens) is contrasted with the earthly city Jerusalem, <u>a prostitute</u>, unfaithful city – in the book of revelation.

"<u>Coming down out of heaven from God</u>." (NIV)

This is explained earlier when in verse 2, he uses this phrase and then declares in verse 3, "Now the dwelling of God is with men." (NIV) Before, man only could worship God from a distance in their camps around the tabernacle. Only the high priest (who represented Jesus) could go into God's presence. The temple symbolized that God was still separated from man because of his sin. Once Jesus died for our sins and we were forgiven, Heb.10:19 says,

"Therefore brothers, since we have <u>confidence to enter the Most Holy Place</u> by the blood of Jesus, by a <u>new and living way</u> opened for us, through the curtain, that is, his body, and since we have a great high priest over the house of God, <u>let us draw near to God</u> with a sincere heart in full assurance of faith…" (NIV)

Now, our very bodies are the dwelling place for God's Spirit, 1 Cor. 6:19.

The heavenly holy city of God extends down to us on earth. God's dwelling place is with sanctified men.

Verse 11. It Shone With The Glory Of God

"It Shone with the glory of God, and its brilliance was like that of a very precious jewel, like a jasper, clear as crystal. (NIV)

"The city… shone with the glory of God." (NIV)

When we are born again, not of natural descent, but born of God, Jn.1:13; we are born of the water and the Spirit, Jn.3:5. We are given the Holy Spirit to indwell us. The Holy Spirit is the Spirit of Glory that rests upon us, 1 Pet.4:14. By walking with the Spirit, we are being changed, transformed into his (Jesus') likeness with ever- increasing glory, which comes from the Lord, who is the Spirit. We are not ashamed; nor are we embarrassed like Moses who covered his face because his glory was fading once he left the presence of God on Mt Sinai. No, God's Spirit, God's presence, dwells in us and so we with unveiled faces reflect the Lord's glory in ever-increasing measure. Someday, we will lay aside this dying tent, and receive the redemption of our bodies. We will get spiritual bodies from God himself. Then we will go to heaven and be one with the Father and the Son, sharing their Holy Spirit within us. We will share in their GLORY as brilliant, radiant Jewels in the crown of God.

Remember Jesus' prayer in Jn.17?

"I have given them the glory that you gave me, that they may be one as we are one: I in them and you in me." Jn.17:22-23. (NIV)

"Father, I want those you have given me to be with me where I am, (in heaven) and to see my glory, the glory you gave me because you loved me before the creation of the world." Jn.17:24, (NIV).

"and now, Father, glorify me in your presence with the glory I had with you before the world began." Jn.17:5, (NIV)

"The holy city was brilliant like that of a very precious jewel," (NIV)

The holy city that extends down out of heaven is PEOPLE, SAVED PEOPLE. They are living stones. It is a living building. We are built up as a habitation of God through his Spirit, Eph.2:20-21. When John describes the city here as made up of precious jewels and streets of gold – it sounds marvelous. But it is an illustration or symbol of us! Zech.9:16 says,

"The Lord their God will save them on that day as the flock of his people. They will sparkle in his land like jewels in a crown." (NIV)

We are to God like jewels in a jeweled city. To him we all sparkle and give him delight. We are highly precious to him.

The treasures of God are not gold and silver, but the sanctified lives of his saints. God owns the universe. All the hills are his. All the animals are his. All the rivers, lakes, streams, meadows, beaches are his. All the sea life, all the birds, all and every treasure is his. The stars, the planets, the constellations are his. But he views us, his people, as the jewels of his crown, the "apple of his eye."

"The holy city…is like a jasper, clear as crystal" (NIV)

Why "clear as crystal?" The city is pure - refined by fire, and made holy.

Verse 12. On The Gates Were Written The Names Of THe Twelve Tribes

"It had a great, high wall with twelve gates, and with twelve angels at the gates. On the gates were written the names of the 12 tribes of Israel." (NIV)

"It had a great high wall with twelve gates." (NIV)

Again, this is an allusion to the tabernacle that was surrounded by three tribes on the four sides, Num.2. There will be twelve (the number for "God's people") gates.

"There are twelve angels at the gates." (NIV)

Again, the number twelve, (the number of "God's people").

I cannot help but think about why are the angels at the gates? In the Holy of Holies, Ex.25:17-22, there were two cherubim facing each other overlooking the mercy seat. Why were they there? Angels were zealous for the holiness and righteousness of God. They guarded against all sin and wickedness, impurity and rebellion. They could swiftly bring God's wrath upon the wicked. What held them back from doing so and destroying all the wicked? They viewed continually God's sacrifice for sin on the mercy seat. James 2:13 tells us – "Mercy triumphs over judgment!" Mercy held the angels back from bringing judgment.

These angels at the gates are zealous for the "purity" of the city. The whole city is one huge "Holy of Holies". "Nothing impure will ever enter it," 21:27. The angels see to that.

The angels are there at each gate also to guard all "God's people" within. Ps.91:9-11 says,

"If you make the Most High your dwelling – even the Lord, who is my refuge – then no harm will befall you, no disaster will come near your tent. For he will command his angels concerning you to guard you in all your ways." (NIV)

"On the gates are the names of the twelve tribes of Israel." (NIV)

The names, according to the "pattern" of the tabernacle, can even tell you which three names are on the gates for the four sides – North, South, East and West, of the city.

Verse 13. Three Gates On The

"There were three gates on the east, three on the north, three on the south, and three on the west." (NIV)

The tabernacle had three tribes that camped around it on its four sides, Num.2. Three tribes times four sides equals the 12 tribes of Israel. This is an allusion to that idea.

Verse 14. Twelve Foundations

"The wall of the city had twelve foundations, and on them were the names of the twelve apostles of the Lamb." (NIV)

"The wall of the city had twelve foundations… with the names of the twelve apostles."

He names the twelve foundations, the names of the twelve apostles. It is not the men themselves, but the work they did. Paul says – "I laid a foundation as an expert builder, and someone else is building on it," 1 Cor.3:10. The apostles were commissioned to take the gospel to the world of their time, Mt.28:18-20. Through the gospel, they laid the foundation. The heavenly Jerusalem is the city that has foundations, whose designer and builder is God, Heb.11:10. The apostles were builders who laid the foundations and those foundations were named after them.

Verse 15. A Measuring Rod Of Gold

"The angel who talked with me had a measuring rod of gold to measure the city, it's gates and its walls." (NIV)

"a measuring rod." (NIV)

God measures what he would destroy, the earthly Jerusalem, Rev.11:1. He also measures that which he builds. The heavenly Jerusalem has God as its architect and builder, Heb.11:10.

"The rod of gold" (NIV)

The rod of gold suggests this is a very special task, a precious one. Because God uses "pure gold," gold refined in the fire – it may also suggest the angel is measuring everything for its purity. Nothing impure can be in the city.

In Rev.11:1, John was given a measuring rod, a reed. That reed was used to chastise or punish. It was a different tool in his hand than here.

Verse 16. The City Was Laid Out Like A Square

"The city was laid out like a square, as long as it was wide. He measured the city with the rod and found it to be 12,000 stadia in length, and as wide and high as it is long." (NIV)

"The city was laid out like a square." (NIV)

The city was 12,000 stadia in length, width and height. A stadia is a Greek measure of distance and is about 607 feet. 12,000 Stadia is about 1500 miles. That is huge! Well, if we understood it literally, the heavenly Jerusalem would be a huge place. I think God's offspring that was to be like the sand on the seashore and the stars in the heavens, (Gen.22:17-18) might have plenty of room. Notice, the whole city was laid out like a cube – the same in width, length and height.

However, as a symbolic number, we get 12 x 1000. Twelve is the number representing "God's people" whether we speak of the 12 tribes of Israel or the 12 apostles that laid the foundation of the church. "<u>1000</u>" means <u>all</u> of them. <u>All</u> of them who have the faith of Abraham are to be saved, Rom.11:26. The heavenly Jerusalem contains ALL the saved.

The city of Jerusalem on earth contained the temple area. The temple area was separate from the city, but was within it.

Neither the tabernacle nor the temple were laid out like a square. At that time, perhaps they were not viewed as perfected. But in heaven, those in the heavens have been perfected and so the city lies in a perfect cube.

The Tabernacle proper was 10 cubits (15 feet) wide, by 10 cubits high and 30 cubits (45 feet) long. The tabernacle proper contained the Holy place and the Holy of Holies. The size of the outside curtains that also contained the courtyard is found in Ex.26:15-25. The outside measured 60 cubits long and 20 cubits wide, 1 Kings 6:2. <u>The Holy of Holies was a perfect cube</u> – 10 x 10 x 10 cubits in the Tabernacle.

However, the dimensions of the <u>Holy of Holies</u>, was where God dwelt over the mercy seat of the ark of the covenant. In the temple, it was 20 cubits by 20 cubits by 20 cubits. The dimensions have great numeric symbolic significance.

First, because the <u>Holy of Holies where God dwelt was a cube</u>; it is telling us, here in verse 16, that <u>the whole city, the heavenly Jerusalem, is a Holy of Holies</u>. It is a perfect cube – as long as it is high, as it is wide. The <u>entire city is where God dwells</u>! Fantastic thought! That is what is also understood when he tells us in 21:22, "I did not see a temple there, because the Lord God Almighty and the Lamb are its temple." (NIV) Why did he not see a temple? Well first, the presence of a temple in the city would suggest that God still dwelt separate from his people. God would dwell in the temple and his people in the city. That is not the case in the heavenly Jerusalem. There is no temple. The whole city is the dwelling place of God, the Holy of Holies. The picture is one of complete unity of God's people with God and the Lamb. That is exactly what Jesus prayed for in Jn.17:20-23,

"My prayer is not for them alone. I pray for those who will believe in me through their message, (that's even us today) that all of them may be one, Father, just as you are in me and I am in you. May they also be in us so that the world may believe that you have sent me. I have given them the glory that you gave me, that they may be one as we are one: I in them and you in me. May they be brought to complete unity." (NIV)

How does that unity come about? It is a process. When we are born again, born from above, we begin to grow with the help of the Holy Spirit. Our minds are renewed. However, being on earth we are still in the flesh and our two natures are contrary one to the other. The flesh is contrary to the spirit and the spirit is contrary to the flesh. We can only overcome the flesh through the help of the Spirit. Our fleshly body is destroyed in death, but because we planted "live" spiritual seed we are raised with a spiritual body. That is the redemption of the body, Romans 8. We are raised to heaven. Now, we are spirits with spiritual bodies who have the Holy Spirit dwelling in us. Because God's Spirit dwells in us, we also dwell in him and in his Son. The Holy Spirit of God the Father is also the same Spirit as his Son Jesus. God is one person, made up of three existences: Father, Son, and Holy Spirit; just as on earth we are one person made in his image: body, soul and spirit. Once in heaven, our physical body has been replaced by a spiritual body and we are spirit, spiritual body and His Holy Spirit. We dwell God and God dwells in us! Fantastic. We are finally made complete in Him. The unity is wonderful. Of course, that does not mean we become God nor his Son; but we share eternal life with him through His life-giving Holy Spirit!

The city is a SQUARE (CUBE) of perfect unity!

(A note to consider: To understand who God is: He is one person in three parts. We know that the Holy Spirit is the same Spirit for the Father and the Son. Then what part does the Son represent? I believe he represents the eternal body (outward expression) of the Father. Col.2:9 says, "For in Christ all the fullness of Deity dwells in bodily form." (NIV) Some may object and say that just means while he was a man on earth that he had a body. No, I think not. Peter explains: "because you will not abandon me to the grave, nor will you let your HOLY ONE see decay, Acts 2:27. Jesus gave up his Spirit on earth – meaning the separation of his body from his spirit (the definition of death, Js.2:26). But death was not the end of existence. Death had no hold on him. Death could not keep him in the grave nor would his body see decay (destruction). No, Jesus took up his life again, Jn.10:18. Jesus is eternal. He is God! In prophecy – Jesus is viewed as God's (the Father's) body and God uses the son to do all that he does through him. Jesus is the "right arm" of God, Isa.53:1ff. If Jesus is God, how can he be subject to the Father? 1 Cor.15:28. The answer is simple. Isn't your body subject to your mind? Yet your body is you. You decide something in your mind but everything you do is through your body. Jesus is in a sense "God's body". But Jesus is eternal and "thinks, governs, etc." also. We are speaking perhaps of the functional relationship of the Father and Son, not their essence or being. In their being, can we comprehend? No. Being finite beings, we cannot grasp the infinite.)

Verse 17. A 144 Cubits Thick

"He measured its wall and it was 144 cubits thick, by man's measurement, which the angel was using." (NIV)

"The wall was 144 cubits thick."

Literally, 144 cubits is about 72 yards or 216 feet. That is as wide as ¾ a football field. That is a wide wall. Symbolically, the number is 12 x 12. That seems to tell us the city surrounded by this wall is the saints of the O.T. (represented by the 12 tribes) and the saints of the N.T. (represented by the 12 apostles).

The wall is symbolic of an idea in the context. In other contexts of scripture, we have other ideas. For example, in Zech. 2:4-5 it says, "Jerusalem will be a city without walls because of the great number of men and livestock in it. And I myself will be a wall of fire around it declares the Lord, and I will be its glory within." (NIV) Both passages are talking about the heavenly Jerusalem; but the ideas they are conveying with symbolic imagery is different. The two passages do NOT contradict each other, but rather, they both add two different ideas. In Zechariah, the idea is that God will be the city's protector as a wall of fire around it. They live in TOTAL security and peace by the power of God.

Verse 18. The Wall Was Made Of

"The wall was made of jasper, and the city of pure gold, as pure as glass." (NIV)

"The wall was made of jasper."(NIV)

Why? What does it represent? I do not know. Perhaps you can share with me an answer?

"The city of pure gold, as pure as glass."(NIV)

The city was made of pure gold. "Pure gold" is pure, refined in the fire, Zech.13:9. The city's purity is repeated for emphasis – "as pure as glass". It was crystal clear. You could see no impurities in it.

"The city was pure gold." In other words, the city was filled ONLY with those who were purified, refined in the fire. The purified are God's people.

Verse 19. The Foundations Were Decorated With Every Precious

"The foundations of the city walls were decorated with every kind of precious stone. The first foundation was jasper, the second sapphire, the third chalcedony, the fourth emerald," (NIV)

The foundations of the city were decorated with every kind of precious stone. That is us. We are the Jewels in God's handiwork. We are all precious stones. There is no wood hay or straw, it is burned up in the refiner's fire. God builds with gold, silver and costly stones, whose work we are, 1 Cor.3:12-13.

The high priest represented all of God's people before God. He was their "mediator" between sin - death and fellowship.

Ex.28:15-21 lists the twelve stones of the high priest's ephod, or breastplate. (The ephod and breastplate are discussed in Exodus, chapters 28 and 39.) Only the high priest could wear the breastplate. There were twelve stones for each of the names of the sons of Israel. Jesus is our high priest now. These twelve stones would decorate his breastplate. (Because he is also King of Kings and Lord of lords, many crowns are on his head, Rev.19:12.) The breastplate of stones is sometimes called the "breastplate of decision." Ex.28:29-30 says,

"Whenever Aaron entered the Holy Place, he would bear the names of the sons of Israel over his heart on the breastplate of decision as a continuing memorial before the Lord. ... Thus Aaron would always bear the means of making decisions for the Israelites over his heart before the Lord." (NIV)

Josephus says the names on the breastplate were in the birth order of the sons (Josephus, "Ant. of the Jews," Book 3, Chap.7, Sect.5). The Hebrew language is read from right to left, (the opposite for English). So, the names began from the right. The birth order of the twelve sons is: Reuben, Simeon, Levi, Judah, Dan (Manasseh replaced), Naphtali, Gad, Asher, Issachar, Zebulin, Joseph, and Benjamin. (Gen.49).

Because these stones decorate the foundations of the city walls of the heavenly Jerusalem; It first seems to suggest that the twelve tribes (represented by the stones) are part of the very foundation upon which the Holy of Holies city is built. Once, they were represented by Aaron before God. Now, they are accepted as part of the very foundation of the city of God.

"Jasper, sapphire, chalcedony, emerald" - Each of the stones represent each tribe. Each is special and individual with its own significance. I wish I knew the significance of each. Please, someone share.

Verse 20. The Stones

"The fifth sardonyx, the sixth carnelian, the seventh chrysolite, the eighth baryl, the ninth topaz, the tenth chrysoprase, the eleventh jacinth, and the 12th amethyst." NIV

Verse 21. Each Gate A Single Pearl

"The twelve gates were twelve pearls, each gate made of a single pearl. The great street of the city was of pure gold, like transparent glass." (NIV)

"The twelve gates were twelve pearls, each gate made of a single pearl."

Why gates of pearls? Mt.13:45-46 says,

"The kingdom of heaven is like a merchant looking for fine pearls. When he found one of great value, he went away and sold everything he had and bought it." (NIV) It seems to symbolize – that what is within the pearly gates, the kingdom of heaven, is worth everything we have, in order to enter in. It is the pearl of such great value! The pearl is the gospel, which leads us into the kingdom of our God.

"The great street of the city was of pure gold, like transparent glass." (NIV)

In many ways, we are reminded again – this is a PURE city, a HOLY city. It has a great street of pure gold, like transparent glass. (glass that you see perfectly through. There is no impurities that make it obscure, or mixed)

Notice the text says – "the great street of the city. There is one street. There is ONLY ONE way, one street, into the city.

Jesus said, "I am the way, the truth, and the life. No one comes to the Father except through me," Jn.14:6. (NIV) In the Book of Acts, those who are saved through Jesus, followers of Jesus, are called "the Way" many times, (I think 8 times). There were those "who belonged to the Way, Acts 9:2." There were those who "publicly maligned the Way," Acts 19:9. There was a "great disturbance about the Way," Acts 19:23. There were "followers of this Way unto their death," Acts 22:4 Jesus IS THE WAY, the ONLY WAY.

Even prophetically, Jesus provides "the highway to Heaven". Isa.40:3 says, "A voice of one calling: in the desert prepare a way for the Lord; make straight in the wilderness a highway for our God." This is fulfilled in Mt.3:3 and Jn.1:23. Isa.62:9-12 it says, "…in the courts of my sanctuary – 'as through, pass through the gates! Prepare the way for the people – Build up, Build up the Highway! Remove the stones. Raise a banner for the nations. The Lord has made a proclamation to the ends of the earth; say to the daughter of Zion, See, your savior comes! See, his reward is with him, and his recompense accompanies him. They will be called the Holy People, the Redeemed of the Lord; and you will be called Sought After, the city no longer deserted." (NIV) There is a Great Street of pure gold – the highway of our God leads there.

Verse 22. The Lord And Lamb Are Its Temple

"I did not see a temple in the city, because the Lord God Almighty and the Lamb are its temple." (NIV)

"I did not see a temple in the city,"(NIV)

Seeing a temple would imply that God is still separate from his people.

A temple implies God's dwelling place, and the people in the city would be their dwelling place.

There would be no temple there, because the temple was the place of the national worship of the Jews. Everything about the Mosaic covenant was given to the Jews. The Jews had an advantage in every way, Rom.3:1. They had the law, the prophets, the priests, the temple – all of it. But Jesus told the Samaritan woman at the well, "a time is coming when you will worship the Father neither in this mountain nor in Jerusalem … but true worshippers will worship the Father in spirit and in truth, Jn.4:21-24. (NIV) With the coming of Jesus – the good news was to the whole world. ALL who believed could have everlasting life, Jn 3:16. "Where two are gathered in my name, there I will be also," Mt.18:20. (NIV) The temple represented a "national religion" given to the Jews. In heaven, there would be no temple. God dwells in ALL of his people from all nations.

"Because the Lord God Almighty and the Lamb are its temple." (NIV)

We dwell in God and God dwells in us. (See comments – verse 16).

Verse 23. The City Did Not Need The Sun

"The city does not need the sun or the moon to shine on it, for the glory of God gives it light, and the Lamb is its lamp." (NIV)

"The city does not need the sun or the moon to shine on it," (NIV)

1 Tim.6:16 tells us - God "lives in unapproachable light." (NIV) For man on earth; it is unapproachable. No man on earth can bear to be in his presence. Prophetically, Jesus is represented as the "rising sun, Lk.1:78. God the Father's manifestation on earth was veiled by smoke and fire, like when he appeared on Mount Sinai. It was so awesome the people greatly feared it. Even when the high priest went into the Most Holy Place, the room was filled with smoke to protect him from the glory of God's presence. But in heaven, we can behold the glory of God in all his splendor. He will be our sun and light. We have no need of a sun or moon. "For the glory of God gives it light, and the Lamb is its lamp." (NIV)

Verse 24. The Kings Of The Earth Will Bring Their Splendor

"The nations will walk by its light, and the kings of the earth will bring their splendor into it." (NIV)

"The nations will walk by its light," (NIV)

The gospel call is to every nation, Mt. 28:18-20. The good news of the gospel is the light which leads the nations. 2 Cor.4:1-6. The gospel is the good news of Jesus – "the true light that gives light to every man," Jn.1:9. (NIV) Jesus is "the light of the world," Jn.8:12.

"The kings of the earth will bring their splendor into it." (NIV)

Whatever is glorious, whatever is honorable, whatever is pure will be brought into the kingdom.

Verse 25. There Will Be No Night There

"On no day will its gates ever be shut, for there will be no night there." (NIV)

"On no day will it's gates ever be shut, for there will be no night there." (NIV)

Jerusalem on earth was a fortified city. It had three walls around it in Jesus' time. The gates were shut at night to keep wild animals out and any oppressor. The gates were also shut on the sabbath to prevent any travel or work. In the heavenly Jerusalem – "There will be no more night," Rev.22:5 (NIV). There is no darkness there, for it does not belong there. 1Thess.5:4-5 says, "But you brothers, are not in darkness… You are all sons of the light and sons of the day. We do not belong to the night or to the darkness." (NIV)

There will be no more weekly sabbath days in heaven. Rather, Heb.4:1-6 speaks of there being a sabbath rest (continual rest) that remains for the people of God. In heaven, we are in that rest continually.

Verse 26. Glory Will Be Brought Into It

"The glory and honor of the nations will be brought into it." (NIV)

"The glory and honor of all nations will be brought into it."(NIV)

The best, the pure, the redeemed from all nations will flow into it, Isa. 2:1-2.

Verse 27. Nothing impure will enter it

"Nothing impure will ever enter it, nor will anyone who does what is shameful or deceitful, but only those whose names are written in the Lamb's Book of Life." (NIV)

"Nothing impure will ever enter it." (NIV)

We are told this in several ways. The description of heaven tells us – It is Holy, It is Holy! It is Holy! How? – IT IS PURE!

"Nor will anyone who does what is shameful or deceitful, (NIV) They are pure. They are truthful. They are faithful. They are His sons!

"But only those whose names are written in the Book of Life." (NIV) Each name in the Book of Life has been "set apart", cleansed, made holy, sanctified, glorified – made to sparkle as a jewel in the master's hand.

CHAPTER TWENTY-TWO

THE RIVER OF LIFE

Verse 1. The River Of The Water Of Life

"Then the angel showed me the river of the Water of Life, as clear as crystal, flowing from the throne of God and of the Lamb." (NIV)

The River of the Water of Life – is the Spirit, Jn7:37-38. Ezekiel 47 gives us a symbolic scene so beautiful, so filling, so magnificent – as we see the "River of the water of Life" poured out from heaven:

Ezekiel 47 is about the main event on Pentecost, Acts 2 – The pouring out of the Holy Spirit. In Ezekiel 47, water began to come out from the threshold of the temple on the East. The water was coming down from south of the altar. A man showed Ezekiel the water. As the water flowed the water got deeper and deeper – ankle deep, then knee deep, then waist deep, until now it was a river no one could cross. There was a great number of trees on each side of the river. "This water flows toward the eastern region (footnote - middle East) and goes down into the Arabah (footnote - the Jordan Valley) where it enters the sea" (footnote - the Dead Sea) Ezekiel 47:1-8. (NIV)

The Arabah was a "wilderness". The land was as a desert, desolate and impassable. Isa.35:1 says, "The land that was desolate and impassable shall be glad, and the wilderness (Arabah) shall rejoice." (NIV) In Ezek.47 what happens? As the river is poured out, the water becomes fresh. "Swarms of living creatures will live wherever the river flows. There will be large numbers of fish, because this water flows there and makes the salt water fresh; so where the river flows everything will live." Ezek.47:9, (NIV) "Fruit trees of all kinds will grow on both banks of the river. <u>Their leaves will not wither</u>, <u>nor will their fruit fail</u>. <u>Every month they will bear</u>, because the water from the sanctuary flows to them. Their fruit will serve for food and <u>their leaves for healing</u>." Ezek.47:12

I have often thought Ezekiel 47 would make a great symbolic scene of the "River of the Water of Life" being poured out from heaven, down – down – down to the desert regions and making everything it touches ALIVE and blossom with fruit. Then, show a parallel scene in the movie of Pentecost in which there is a whish like a tremendous flow of water, and then you see the Holy Spirit come down on the Apostles and the picture changes from black and white to being taken over with color and life.

"<u>As clear as crystal</u>" (NIV)

The water was totally pure, refreshing, life-giving, transforming!

"<u>From the throne of God</u>." (NIV)

The source of the water is from God. "Every good and Perfect gift is from above, coming down from the Father of heavenly lights." He gives us his life-giving Spirit as a drink, that wells up into everlasting life!

Verse 2. The Tree Of Life

"Down the middle of the great street of the city, on each side of the river, stood the tree of life, bearing 12 crops of fruit; yielding its fruit every month. And the leaves of the tree are for the healing of the nations." (NIV)

"<u>Down the middle of the great street of the city</u>." (NIV)

What? The river of the water of life is flowing down the great street? Of course, this is a figurative, symbolic scene. The river is flowing down the street. It is the one street in the city the figure speaks of. What does the river of water speak of? What does the tree of life speak of? But wait, the tree stands on either side of the river and the tree bears 12 crops every month.

"<u>The tree of life</u>" (NIV)

It is the tree that "gives life." It has healing in its leaves. Now what is the tree watered by? The River of the Water of Life. But what is the water of life? Jesus told the Samaritan woman – "whoever drinks the water I give him will never thirst. Indeed, the water I give him will become in him a spring of water welling up to eternal life," Jn.4:14. "If anyone is thirst, let him come to me and drink. Whoever believes in me, as the scripture has said, streams of living water will flow from within him. By this he meant the Spirit, whom those who believed in him were later to receive," Jn.7:37-38. (NIV) Now we can put together what is symbolized? The <u>River of the water of Life</u> (The life-giving Holy Spirit), flowing from the throne of God (the source of the Spirit), flows down the street and waters "the <u>Tree of Life</u>" (<u>is Christ and his spiritual kingdom, US</u>), that is on each side of the river (it flows to those before and after the river was poured out from heaven. Read Ezekiel 47 of the "river from the temple". The river (Holy Spirit) was poured out on the day of Pentecost. But for those who were and are saved, both Old Testament and New - in heaven, the Spirit supplies life to both sides of the river (when it was poured out). Just as we say that Jesus blood flowed both ways, for the saints of the Old Testament and for the saints of the New; so too, the river on Pentecost that was poured out, (the Spirit) flows for both ways, supplying life for both the "twelve tribes" and the "twelve apostles", -"God's people." <u>Why is the tree of life on both sides of the river</u>? It represents both the Old and New Testament saints. "God's people" ARE the "Tree of Life". Each individual is a branch and we bear fruit all year around. WE the branches abide in the tree, Jesus (who was prophetically the stump of Jesse, Isa.11:1.) The tree has grown up. It started with Jesus. We abide in him, Jn15:1-8. It is to the Father's glory that we bear much fruit! Jn.15:8

<u>"Leaves of the tree are for the healing of the nations.</u>" (NIV)

We, as part of the tree, have healing in our leaves. We bring healing to the nations through the gospel.

<u>Why twelve crops</u>? Because it supplies the twelve tribes and the 12 apostles, that is - the "people of God" that the number twelve represents. <u>ALL of God's people</u> produce fruit every month with the twelve crops.

<u>Why every month</u>? Because God's food supply is abundant. The food is produced as a crop year around. There is no winter season in heaven. There is no time that everything dies or goes dormant. It is always summer there.

Remember the story of Christ's triumphal entry into Jerusalem? That was "Passion Week." He had been in Jerusalem a day, then spent the night outside the city at Bethany. Early in the morning, as he was on his way back to the city (Jerusalem) he was hungry. He passed a fig tree that had no fruit, and <u>he cursed it</u>, Matt.21:18. Mark tells us that the tree had no fruit, only leaves – that it <u>"was not the season for figs</u>," Mark 11:12-13. Why would Jesus curse a fig tree when it was not the season for figs? He was teaching us – that we should bear fruit in season and out of season. In the kingdom, we are to bear fruit all the time. There is no winter. There is no time that we do not bear fruit. 2 Tim.4:2 says, "(Be attentive), be instant <u>in season</u>, <u>out of season</u>; reprove, rebuke, exhort with all long suffering and doctrine." In heaven, the tree of Life bears EVERY month, ALL the months. God's kingdom is a fruit-bearing kingdom!

Verse 3. No Longer Any Curse

"No longer will there be any curse. The Throne of God and of the Lamb will be in the city; and his servants will serve him." (NIV)

<u>"No longer will there be any curse</u>."(NIV)

What a statement. "NO MORE CURSE!" God had told Adam and Eve – literally, "in the day you eat thereof, <u>dying you shall die</u>." Death is not always instant. Death can be slow, lingering, painful, and even excruciating. It can drag on without relief for months and months; sometimes for years. Death can be a horrible death, a shameful death, a death that snuffs out the innocent child but then sucks out the life of those who are affected by it. It is a curse.

Death is not only death for people; the whole creation has been subjected to death. There is the death of animals, of trees and plants, of regions and deserts where nothing grows. Death is all around us. We experience it robbing us of life and beauty in the world around us. Everything and every loved one dies. As we get older, the people we knew in school begin to die. Then a parent dies. Then uncles and aunts. Then a brother or sister. As we near the end, relatives on all sides have died. My world, my loved ones, have been taken from me. I cannot talk to them. I cannot visit them. I cannot see them. They are permanently gone from this life. And so am I, losing life. My strength is half what it use to be. My stamina is not what it use to be. My mental sharpness is waning and I can't find words, thoughts, memories. I get tired much quicker. I ache more often. I keep discovering more and more deficits beginning to take root in my body. Death sucks the life out of you, until you are NO MORE on this earth. But THANK GOD – we as Christians have the hope of heaven where "THERE IS NO MORE CURSE."

Verse 4. They Will See His Face

"They will see his face, and his name will be on their foreheads." (NIV)

"They will see his face." (NIV)

Man has seen the face of Jesus. John says, we have heard him, seen him, touched him, 1 Jn.1:1. Philip said, "Lord, show us the Father." (NIV) Jesus said, "Don't you know me, Philip, even after I have been among you such a long time?" Jn14:8 (NIV) Jesus came to reveal the Father. "I am in the Father, and the Father is in me, Jn.14:10. (NIV). In Jesus "the fullness of the Deity lives in bodily form, Col.2:9. (NIV). Those in the first century had seen the Father in bodily form because they had seen Jesus. But we, as humans, cannot see the Father in our form as we exist here on earth. The Father lives in "unapproachable light." 1 Tim.6:16. (NIV) "No one has ever seen God," Jn.1:18. (NIV) Nor can they see him in this life. When we are changed and given transformed bodies, spiritual bodies, then we can go to be with him. Then, in heaven, we will see the Father. Rev.22:4 says - "They will see his face." (NIV) Wow Oh Wow! We will be ONE with the Father and with the Lamb.

"And his name will be on their foreheads." (NIV)

In Rev.14:1 says that the Lamb's name and the Father's name will be on their foreheads. Here it says "his name" will be on their foreheads. The texts are not contradictory but serve to help us understand the specific text in view. Since both the Father and the Son are two different expressions of the same person (There is ONE GOD), there is no concern whatever here.

"We will bear his name." (NIV)

We bear his name because we have been "purchased by the blood of Christ". We belong to him. Bearing his name is a sign of ownership.

"On our foreheads." (NIV)

Why on the forehead? Because that is where our thoughts are, our will, our emotions, our intentions. All of our spirit life is there, and he owns our life. Paul said,

"I have been crucified with Christ and I no longer live, but Christ lives in me. The life I live in the body I live by faith in the Son of God, who loved me and gave himself for me." Gal.2:20. (NIV)

Verse 5. They Will Not Need The Light Of

"There will be no more night. They will not need the light of a lamp or the light of the Sun, for the Lord God will give them light; and they will reign forever and ever." (NIV)

"There will be no more night." (NIV)

Again, we are reminded of what Paul wrote: "But you brothers, are not in darkness...You are all sons of the light and sons of the day. We do not belong to the night or to the darkness," 1Thess.5:4-5. The night, nor darkness belongs in heaven.

"They will not need the lamp of a light." (NIV)

In darkness, we use the light of a lamp to see. But if there is no darkness, no night; who will ever need a lamp or flashlight. In heaven they are totally obsolete. We will forget even what a flashlight was. Who will ever need it to see?

"or the light of the Sun" (NIV)

Not only do we not need a flashlight or lamp; we have something even better than the light of the Sun. How can that be? I have to think about it. Here on earth, my five senses are limited. There are animals that hear better than I do. There are animals that smell more keenly than I do. There are animals that can see better at night than I do. The cones in my eyes do not see everything out in the world. I was watching a nature show about birds. There were birds who attracted their mates with dances and with lovely display of feathers. But then the narrator explained to the listening audience that we could not see what the birds saw – feathers would change color into beautiful glowing colors, but the human eye could not see it. So, the camera man with a special lens, filmed what the bird saw. It was beautiful. Yet, without the special lens, our eyes cannot see it. Now, in heaven, our bodies will be transformed and our senses greatly sharpened. We will have heavenly bodies. We will be able to see the beauty we once could not see. We can even fly like birds, for we will be like the angels, Mk12:25.

"The Lord God will give them light." (NIV)

We know there are "waves" not even in the spectrum of the light of the sun. There exist things in the world of the unseen we haven't even dreamed of yet. Our sun was made to give light to the physical world. It is totally adequate for serving the physical world. But the spiritual world? The sun is only a "shadow", a "type" of what is in the heavens. It was a prophetic symbol for Christ, Lk1:78. The reality is in heaven.

"The Lord will give them light." (NIV)

The creator himself will give us light, heavenly, GODLY LIGHT! What will that be? Far more wonderful than even the Sun; far more revealing, far more beautiful, far more amazing beyond imagination! God will give us Spiritual Bodies, with new eyes that can see much, much, more, and it will be in light from God that "opens our eyes to see beyond our wildest imaginations and most incredible dreams.

"And they will reign for ever and ever." (NIV)

We are kings and priests unto God. We get to sit on his throne with him. We are crowned. We are Glorified with him. And we shall reign with him for ever and ever. Our AMAZING, LOVING God!

Verse 6. Things That Must Soon take Place

"The angel said to me, 'these words are trustworthy and true. The Lord, the God of the spirits of the prophets, sent his angel to show his servants the things that must soon take place." (NIV)

"<u>These words are trustworthy and true</u>." (NIV)

1 Sam.3:19 says, "And Samuel grew, and the Lord was with him, and let none of his words fall to the ground." (NIV) Neither should we! God's word is fully and absolutely reliable. I have never found a contradiction; a detail that was not true; a prophecy that has not been fulfilled!

God's Word is wholly God-breathed!

Please, if you have read this far, grant me the space here to say what is on my heart. The so-called "<u>Higher Criticism</u>" of the bible is absolutely false and destructive. Those who teach and believe it are the <u>enemies of Christ</u>. There are many doctorate theologians and scholars, preachers and pastors who embrace its destructive message. They attack the Scriptures and charge it with error. They claim they can point out many problems with it historically and culturally. They reduce its reliability and message to a mere story and charge it with sections of mythology. They attack the very words in which we draw from for our faith. May God hold them fully accountable for such insolence and for what they do, and their unbelief. GOD'S WORDS ARE TRUSTWORTHY AND TRUE! Believe it! Live for it! Die for it! Let <u>nothing</u> deceive you and rob you of your inheritance in heaven.

"The Lord, the God of the spirits of the prophets" (NIV)

"<u>Above all</u>, you must understand that <u>no prophecy of scripture</u> came about <u>by the prophet's own interpretation</u>. For prophecy <u>never had its origin in the will of man</u>, but men spoke from God <u>as they were carried along by the Holy Spirit</u>." 2 Pet.20-21. (NIV)

How more clearly could it be stated? Scripture is <u>from God</u>, PERIOD. It is not from men. Only unbelievers venture to charge God's Word with error. They are malicious, evil men, deceivers; wearing pastors' robes, bishops' robes; hiding before our eyes with false pretense. May they be exposed. May they be thrown out of our churches. May they be disgraced! They are devils in sheep's clothing.

"<u>Things that must soon take place</u>." (NIV)

Chapter 1, verse 1, said exactly the same words! From the beginning of the revelation to the end of the revelation; it is of "things that must soon take place." It was fulfilled soon after it was written. We must listen here to what the Spirit tells us. If we are to understand the revelation, we must hear the Spirit's instruction. The Revelation would occur SOON. Those who say the Revelation is not fulfilled yet; even after 2000 years, are blinded to the words of the Spirit. They do not follow the Spirit's lead. They follow their own spirit. They write the imaginations of their own mind. They keep us from seeing the fulfillment of all that Jesus has accomplished for us and the Blessing of it. We must not trust in the flesh; or our own efforts. Listen to the Spirit! Be corrected by the Spirit. May the Spirit guide you in all you do!

JESUS IS COMING

Verse 7. Behold, I Am Coming Soon

"Behold, I am coming soon! Blessed is he who keeps the words of the prophecy in this book." (NIV)

Behold, I am coming soon!"

How many times has Jesus told John he was coming soon? Let's see:

Rev.1:1 "what must soon take place."

Rev.1:3 "the time is near.""

Rev.1:7 "Look, he is coming with the clouds" (present tense)

Rev.2:5 "I will come to you."

Rev.2:16 "I will soon come to you."

Rev.2:25 "Only hold on to what you have until I come."

Rev.3:3 "I will come like a thief, and you will not know what time."

Rev.3:11 "I am coming soon."

Rev.3:20 "Here I am, I stand at the door and knock."

Rev.22:6 "things that must soon take place."

Rev.22:7 "Behold I am coming soon."

Rev.22:10 "Do not seal up the words of this prophecy...the time is near."

Rev.22:12 "Behold, I am coming soon."

Rev.22:20 "Yes, I am coming soon." "Amen. Come, Lord Jesus."

(All the quotations above in verse 7 are from the NIV)

Yes. He was coming SOON! Believe it. He came SOON – just like he said. Enough of this unbelief that the Lord has not come yet. Of course, he has. He fulfilled everything God had purposed for him to accomplish. He is the Beginning and the End. All things have been given to us by him who has loved us.

"<u>Blessed is he who keeps the words of the prophecy of this book</u>." (NIV)

A special blessing is given to the one who is listening and follows what is said in the book. Even though that blessing is especially for those to whom it was written because judgment was to be very soon; it blesses us today because we learn of all that our savior has accomplished for us and given to us. Our hope could never be more sure, our future never more secure and beautiful, our inheritance never more so amazing than what it is. God be praised forever and ever.

Verse 8. I Fell Down To Worship

"*I, John, am the one who heard and saw these things. And when I heard and saw them, I fell down to worship at the feet of the Angel who had been showing them to me.*" *(NIV)*

"<u>John</u>," is the author of the Book; but he is really only the scribe. It is the "<u>revelation of Jesus Christ</u>," Rev.1:1. (NIV)

Verse 16 tells us, "Jesus had sent his angel to give testimony to the churches." (NIV)

"I fell down at the feet of the angel who had been showing them to me." (NIV)

This angel, though awesome to man, is only "a servant, a flame of fire," Heb 1:7. We are not to worship angels. Col.2:18 says,

"Do not let anyone who delights in false humility and the worship of angels disqualify you for the prize." (NIV)

This was the angel Jesus had sent, verse 16, to give this testimony, Rev.1:1.

There is something I believe that I would share here. Jesus is the "fullness of Deity who lives in bodily form," Col.2:9. (NIV) Jesus became man. He showed us who the Father is by relating to us as a man. God gets on our level, becomes like us – in the flesh, and relates to us. That is how God is with his earthly creation. But how does he relate to his spiritual creation? He relates to them on their level. Jesus in the spiritual world is Michael the archangel. Michael is not a created angel. He is the manifestation of God in spiritual body form to relate to them on their level in their form. Jesus relates to us in "our likeness". Jesus relates to the angels in "their likeness." Jesus can take any form He likes because he is God; God relating to his creation, both physical and spiritual. God is so much more than his creation. We cannot "see him" as he is. He lives in "unapproachable light". He must through his Son, God's outward expression in bodily form, reveal himself to us.

In 1 Thess.4:16, Jesus comes the second time "with the voice of the archangel". (NIV) Several times in Revelation we see Jesus presented to us as an angel: Rev.1:12-20, he is the one walking among the seven golden candlesticks. In Rev. 10:1 1-6 he is the angel robed in a cloud. In Rev. 19:11-16, He is the rider on the white horse with the armies of heaven following him. In Rev.20:1-3, he is the mighty angel who binds Satan with a chain and throws him into the abyss.

Jesus in his bodily form is no stranger to the O.T. He appeared to Abraham as one of three men (angels) who came to him and the Lord stayed back with Abraham to tell him he would destroy Sodom and Gomorrah, Gen.18. Jesus appears to Moses at the burning bush and tells him to take his sandals off because he was on Holy ground, Ex.3. He met Moses in the tent of meeting, and talked with Moses face to face, as a man talks with his friend, Ex.33:11. We see him with Joshua as "the commander of the army of the Lord" and Joshua fell facedown to the ground in reverence," Josh 5:14. We see him with Manoah and his wife before the birth of Samuel. There he has them offer a sacrifice unto God, and ascends in the flame toward God. Their response was – "we have seen God," Judges 13:22. The visitor's name to Manoah and his wife was "wonderful" -meaning "beyond knowing", Jdgs.13:18. (Wonderful is the prophetic name of Christ, Isa.9:6). Jesus showed up all through the O.T. as a man, relating to man.

Jesus also shows up in the O.T. as Michael, the archangel, in the Book of Daniel. Michael is the "great prince who protects your people," Dan12:1. It was Michael who fought with Satan and his angels and Satan lost his place in heaven, Rev.12:7-9.

Michael (Micha – el – means "he who is like unto Jehovah.") Michael is NOT a created angel. His appearance is like the archangel. He is over all.

Here in this verse; we know this is NOT Michael. It is a created angel, a servant of God. John was not to bow to him nor worship him.

Verse 9. Do Not Do It

"But he said to me, 'do not do it! I am a fellow servant with you, and with your brothers the prophets; and of all who keep the words of this book. Worship God.!" (NIV)

The angel clearly tells John, I am a fellow servant. Worship God! Do Not Worship Angels.

Verse 10. Do Not Seal Up The Words Of The Prophecy

"Then he told me, 'do not seal up the words of the prophecy of this book because the time is near.'" (NIV)

"Do not seal up the words of the prophecy" … "because the time is near." (NIV)

Daniel lived during the time of the Babylonian captivity, 626 – 539 B.C. He was a young man when at the beginning of the captivity he and some friends were taken to Babylon under King Nebuchadnezzar's rule. The writing of the prophecy of his book would be about 600 years before the coming of Christ to the earth the first time. At the end of his book he is told: "close up and seal the words of the scroll until the time of the end, Dan. 12:4." (NIV) It would not be for many centuries before the prophecy of the end would be fulfilled. He is told again, in Dan.12:9, "the words are closed up and sealed until the time of the end." (NIV) He is told, "When the power of the holy people has been finally broken (the destruction of Jerusalem), all these things will be completed," Dan.12:7. (NIV) Jesus, in his prophecy of the destruction of Jerusalem, speaks of Daniel's prophecy and applies it to the time Jesus is speaking of when he says, "So when you see standing in the holy place the abomination that causes desolation, spoken of through Daniel the prophet -let the reader understand." (NIV) In applying Daniel's prophecy to the time of the destruction of Jerusalem in 70 A.D., we may clearly understand what is meant to "close up and seal the prophecy." Daniel's prophecy did not apply to his time; so - he closed it, sealed it, and so to speak - put it on the shelf for a generation some 600+ years later.

John is told, "do not seal up the book… because the time is near." (NIV) The prophecies' fulfillments were near. They would SOON take place, Rev.1:1 and Rev. 22:6. In other words he is telling John – the time for your prophecy to be fulfilled is upon us, very close. It will soon happen! Jesus said – "I am coming soon."

Verse 11. Let Him Who Does Wrong Continue To

"Let him who does wrong continue to do wrong; let him who is vile continue to be vile; let him who does right continue to do right; and let him who is Holy continue to be holy." (NIV)

The time for Jesus coming was so near; it was like there would be no more time for change or repentance. That time had passed. Whoever (by that time) was doing wrong would continue to do so till the day of judgment. Whoever was doing right would continue to do so till the judgment. The next verse reinforces this understanding – "Behold, I am coming soon! My reward is with me… according to what he has done," (NIV) (the judgment).

Verse 12. Behold, I Am Coming Soon

"Behold, I am coming soon! My reward is with me, and I will give to everyone according to what he has done." (NIV)

Verse 13. I Am THe Beginning And The End

"I am the Alpha and the Omega, the first and the last, the beginning and the end." (NIV)

Jesus is the beginning and the end. (See comments, Rev.1:8;1:17;2:8;21:6).

Verse 14. Blessed are Those Who Wash Their Robes

"Blessed are those who wash their robes, that they may have the right to the tree of life and may go through the gates into the city." (NIV)

"Blessed are those who have washed their robes" (been cleansed by the blood of Christ, the Lamb).

"And almost all things are by the law purged with blood: and without shedding of blood is no remission," Heb. 9:22. (NIV)

"Having therefore, brethren, boldness to enter the holiest by the blood of Jesus, by a new and living way, which he hath consecrated for us, through the veil, that is his flesh," Heb.10:19-20. (NIV)

"Wherefore Jesus also, that he might sanctify the people with his own blood, suffered without the gate…Jesus, that great shepherd of the sheep, through the blood of the covenant, make you perfect in every good work to do his will," Heb.13:12,20. (NIV)

"right to the tree of life" (NIV)

We are connected to Jesus, "the stump of Jesse" (the tree of life) that grew into a great spiritual tree over heaven and earth.

I often try to correct people who say "I have a right to do it!" They mean, "I have a right to drink and get drunk." "I have a right to go to parties and get sexually involved." "I have a right to do what I want". They do not have "the right" to do evil and wrong. They have the "choice" to do what they want; but they will REAP THE CONSEQUENCES OF WHAT THEY CHOOSE! But, if we choose to be faithful to Jesus, He gives us "the right" to the tree of life. Jesus is faithful! He always fulfills his promises.

"May go through the gates into the city." (NIV)

We (faithful Christians) may go through the pearly gates. Remember, no impure thing will enter. We must be cleansed by Christ and his Spirit.

Verse 15. Outside Are The Dogs

"Outside are the dogs, those who practice magic arts, the sexually immoral, the murderers, the idolaters, and everyone who loves and practices falsehood." (NIV)

"Outside are the dogs." (NIV)

Peter says a "dog returns to its vomit, and a sow that is washed goes back to her wallowing in the mire," 2 Pet.2:22. Of whom is Peter speaking? He is speaking of those who once escaped the corruption of the world and then got entangled with the world again. Their latter end is worse than the first. Oh, dear believer, be diligent. Be not deceived by this world neither be drawn back into it. If you have escaped – do not look back! Hang on to the treasure of Jesus with all your heart. Let nothing crepe into your life and gain a foothold that can rob you of eternity with him. Keep your eye on Him. Insist on it. Outside heaven are the "dogs" – those who have known Christ and left him.

"Those who practice magic arts." (NIV)

Marshall's Interlinear translation says, "and the sorcerers (Greek – pharmacoi, "sorcerers"). It is a word from which we get our word pharmacy. I believe those who practiced the magic arts used plants, a "witches' brew". Some had very powerful effects on the mind and caused hallucinations, feelings of euphoria, mental visions and trips. They who practiced magic arts were dangerous and deceivers. Such are not in heaven.

"The sexually immoral." (NIV)

God has told us that "marriage is honorable in all, the marriage bed is undefiled: but God will judge the adulterer and all of the sexually immoral," Heb.13:4. (NIV) God says, "Nevertheless, to avoid fornication, let every man have his own wife, and let every woman have her own husband," 1 Cor.7:2. (NIV) God has allowed for the attraction of the sexes in marriage. This is the proper place to experience "oneness." Outside of the parameters that God has set - is sin, and it leads to death. Do not participate in sex outside of marriage. It is a fire in the lap – you will be burned and it will consume you, Prov.26-27. It leads "straight to the grave," Prov.5:5.

"Murderers." (NIV)

Yes, there are murderers who have taken an innocent's life. Yet, Jesus puts murder in the context of what is in the heart, and malice and ill will toward another. Jesus said, "But I tell you that anyone who is angry with his brother is subject to the judgment. Anyone who says to his brother, Raca (Aramaic term for contempt) is answerable to the Sanhedrin (Jewish council at the time). But anyone who says 'you fool' will be in danger of the fire of hell.' Mt.5:21-22. (NIV)

"Idolaters." (NIV)

Yes, we understand that "anything" can become your "idol" if it "rules over you" in your desire for it. It is best to answer the question here – what is very important to me? Getting rich? Being highly thought of as a scholar, an authority? Having power over others? Sex? Drugs? Food? Gambling? What "rules your life?" What defines you? What do you seek to happen, to achieve? Do you focus on earthly goals? Or, do you no longer live, but Christ lives in you? He is your focus! He is your desire!

"Everyone who loves and practices falsehood." (NIV)

There is much of this even in the churches. New Christians are not taught how to "spiritually" follow the Spirit and be taught by him,1 Jn2:27. They follow men who teach their own human ideas and themselves do not know how to follow the Spirit. These teachers have knowledge. They have thought out and created all kinds of different understandings about God's word. But, it is not FROM God's word. It is from their own imaginations and vanity. Arrogance, pride God resists, Js.4:6. The Holy Spirit resists pride. That is why not many scholars, and doctorate degree theologians ever understand the Bible. It is a "spiritual" book and it is necessary that the Spirit of God gives his people "enlightenment" (understanding) of the things that have been revealed. Make no mistake. The "miraculous" is NOT "spiritual". The miraculous is the Greek word "charismati". Spiritual is the Greek word "pneumatikos." The two are very different. The Corinthians were behind in no gift ("charismati"), 1 Cor.1:7. Yet Paul told them he could not speak unto them as unto spiritual ("pneumatikos"), but as unto carnal, mere babes in Christ. He pointed to the evidence of what he said to all the divisions the church had. Therefore, if you claim to "speak in tongues" or have the gift of "healing" – that DOES NOT make you "spiritual". Being "spiritual" is of the heart, not an outward show. Being "spiritual" is recognized in exemplifying the fruit of the Spirit in Gal. 5. – love, joy, peace, patience, kindness, gentleness, self-control... Pretense and outward show does not belong in God's church. Yet, such is what we see in many of the churches.

Verse 16. I Am The Bright Morning Star

"I, Jesus, have sent my angel to give you this testimony for the churches. I am the root and the offspring of David, and the bright Morning Star. (NIV)

Verse 17. The Spirit And The Bride Say Come

"The Spirit and the bride say, 'come!' And let him who hears say, 'come!' Whoever is thirsty, let him come; and whoever wishes, let him take the free gift of the Water of Life." (NIV)

"The Spirit and the bride say, 'come!'" (NIV) The invitation is always there. The Spirit and the bride (church) say 'come!' The Spirit through his work in the world invites all to come to Jesus. The bride, the church, invites all to come in the world and drink of the water of life freely.

"Let him who hears say, 'come!'" (NIV) If we truly hear and respond, we will say come also.

Verse 18. A Warning

"I warn everyone who hears the words of the prophecy of this book: if anyone adds anything to them, God will add to him the plagues described in this book." (NIV)

"I warn everyone who hears the prophecy of this book: If anyone adds…"

Prov.30:6 "Do not add to his words, or he will rebuke you and prove you a liar." (NIV) A rebuke can be harsh. Being proved a liar can be humiliating. Here, in verse 18, he says if you add to his word – "God will add to him the plagues described in this book." Adding to God's word is very serious and consequential. Yet, people add to God's word all the time. People repeat what they have heard frequently. They repeat what is a popular theory or belief. They like being viewed by others as "in the know", or "that they fit in". There are countless claims that something is in the Bible – and it is not. "Well, it's in the Bible", they say. "Cleanliness is next to godliness" – "it's in the Bible." "Where?" "Well, I don't know, but I know it's in there." People use phrases as if the phrase illustrates a Biblical principle – "I don't care what you know until I know I much you care!" That is supposed to stop us from talking. If a person doesn't like what you know, you are challenged with - (if we interpret what they are saying), "you have to show how much you care, how much you love people, before I care to listen to you." Is that Biblical? How long do I have to "prove myself to you" before you will listen?

What other phrases are not really in scripture? "Spare the rod, spoil the child". "Once saved, always saved". "To your own self be true." "God helps those who help themselves." "God is three persons in one." These are statements not in scripture. Some statements may be true or restate a biblical principle, but they are not in the Bible. Other statements may not be true and are not in the Bible. Yet people claim those statements are in the Bible because they believe them. People quote these statements with authority, as if they are in the Bible.

There are MANY such sayings and beliefs that are popular in Christendom that are counter to the word of God. Yet, these sayings and beliefs have become so popular by the teaching of popular "scholars, theologians, preachers, pastors" that they are championed by MANY of their denomination and serve to "justify" our divisions into denominations as the body of Christ. People add to the word all the time without so much as a hesitation of caution. BEWARE dear friend. Stay only with the <u>words of scripture</u>. Make sure your understanding or explanation fits the entire teaching of the Bible. Do not ignore scriptures you cannot explain clearly. Those scriptures may be trying to correct you or enhance your understanding and clarify it. Do not be hasty with the word of God. Do not assume what you believe is correct; no matter how long you have believed it or heard it from others. Be willing to be totally open to the Spirit's teaching and think upon all He shows you. It may not make sense with what you believe or fit "your" framework of understanding at the time. Be patient. Let the scripture teach you. Use the words of the scripture.

Verse 19. If Anyone Takes Words Away

"And if anyone takes words away from this book of prophecy, God will take away from him his share in the tree of life and in the holy city, which are described in this book." (NIV)

"<u>If anyone takes words away from this book</u>..."

The same thoughts in verse 18 apply here in verse 19. We cannot change what is written in God's word. It is the authority. We cannot alter it. Those who are careless in using God's Word, and do not follow the Spirit will pay a horrible price. Those who use religion to serve their own interests and fleshly pursuits will inherit condemnation. Tampering with the Word of God is inescapably foolish and condemning. We must not be pretentious. We must not be careless.

Verse 20. I Am Coming Soon

"He Who testifies to these things says, 'Yes, I am coming soon.' Amen, Come Lord Jesus." (NIV)

Jesus testifies (at the time the book is written), "Yes, I am coming SOON."

Jesus testifies against you if you contradict his statement – "Yes, I am coming SOON."

Let NO ONE contradict him. Let NO ONE say, "He did not come soon." Let no one say – "Jesus has not come yet" and make our savior out to be a liar. If you do not understand what Jesus was talking about – don't teach anything that would add to his words or take away from them. Be very careful what you say. We are held accountable for every idle word that comes from our mouth. Do not contradict what Jesus said here! The warning of verse 18-19 is attached to Jesus' words in 20. I know a lot of people who contradict his words here. Please beware.

Verse 21. Grace Be With God's People

"The grace of the Lord Jesus be with God's people, amen." (NIV)

God bless you in the reading of his Word. May it fill your heart and your understanding. May it inspire you to greater faithfulness to him.

CPSIA information can be obtained
at www.ICGtesting.com
Printed in the USA
BVHW092022080722
641664BV00003B/306